PACEMAKER®

Basic
Mathematics

Third Edition

GLOBE FEARON

Pearson Learning Group

REVIEWERS

We thank the following educators, who provided valuable comments
and suggestions during the development of this book:

Rosemarie Estok, Woodbridge Public Schools, Woodbridge, New Jersey
Audris Griffith, Glen Bard West High School, Glen, Illinois
Dorie Knaub, Downey Unified School District, Downey, California
Christine Sweat, Highland Middle School, Jacksonville, Florida

Subject Area Consultant: Kay McClain, Department of Teaching and Learning,
Vanderbilt University, Nashville, Tennessee
Pacemaker Curriculum Advisor: Stephen C. Larsen, formerly of The University of Texas at Austin

Supervising Editor: Stephanie Petron Cahill
Senior Editor: Phyllis Dunsay
Editor: Dena Pollak
Production Editors: Laura Benford-Sullivan, Andrew Roney
Designers: Evelyn Bauer, Jennifer Visco
Photo Coordinator: Jennifer Hixson
Editorial Assistants: Kathy Bentzen, Wanda Rockwell
Market Manager: Donna Frasco
Research Director: Angela Darchi
Cover Design: Evelyn Bauer
Electronic Composition: Burmar Technical Corp., Linda Bierniak, Mimi Raihl, Phyllis Rosinsky

About the Cover: Mathematics is a way to help people understand and deal with their environment.
The images on the cover of this book show how an understanding of basic mathematics is relevant in
everyday life. Runners need to calculate their speed over distances. Architects use geometric structures
and formulas to build cities. Newspapers and magazines display data visually in graphs. Mechanics
use gearing ratios to repair machines such as cars and airplanes. How do you use mathematics in your
everyday life?

ISBN 0-835-93583-3

Printed in the United States of America
5 6 7 8 9 10   03 02 01

Globe
Fearon

Pearson Learning Group

1-800-321-3106
www.pearsonlearning.com

Contents

A Note to the Student

Today, students often wonder why they *still* have to study math. After all, calculators and computers are everywhere. These wonderful machines can answer the most complex problems in seconds.

Certainly there is some truth to that. But a calculator or a computer can only do what you tell it to do. You have to ask the right question to get the right answer. If you don't know whether to multiply or divide to solve a problem, a calculator can't help you. A calculator can't tell you whether or not an answer makes sense. To make these decisions, you must know something about basic mathematics.

You already use some form of mathematics in your life every day. You tell time. You measure. You spend money and count your change. You figure out how long it will take to get from one place to another. In fact, you couldn't survive in our fast-paced world without using basic math skills.

The purpose of this book is to help you develop the math skills you need to succeed in today's world. You will learn about whole numbers and how to add, subtract, multiply, and divide them. You will also learn about fractions, decimals, percents, different systems of measurement, and other basics of mathematics. Some of this information may not seem very useful right now. But a solid understanding of basic math will help you make good decisions all your life—at school, at home, and on the job.

For example, perhaps you want to figure out the discount on a sale item in your favorite store. Perhaps you want to know what skills you need to work as a computer programmer or a physical therapist. *Basic Mathematics* can help you find the answers to your questions. In every chapter, there are special features that show you how math relates to your life. The **Math in Your Life** and **On-the-Job Math** features take math out of the classroom and into the real world.

You probably hear a lot about problem solving in your math class. Do you wonder what it has to do with you? As an adult, you'll need to solve problems often. This is true both on the job and in the home. *Basic Mathematics* has many activities that allow you to practice problem solving in real-world situations. You'll also find lessons just on problem solving to help you succeed at this skill.

What about those calculators that seem so helpful until you try to use one? The **Using Your Calculator** features take the mystery out of calculators. You'll learn how to use a calculator to solve math problems using whole numbers, fractions, decimals, and integers.

Throughout the book you'll find notes in the margins of the pages. These friendly **margin notes** are there to remind you of something you already know.

You will also find several study aids in the book. At the beginning of every chapter, you'll find **Learning Objectives.** They will help you focus on the important points covered in the chapter. You'll also find **Words to Know,** a look ahead at the vocabulary you may find difficult. The colorful photos, graphs, and drawings in the book bring math concepts to life. **Test Tips** in the Chapter Review will help you prepare for—and succeed on—tests.

Everyone who put this book together worked hard to make it useful, interesting, and enjoyable. The rest is up to you. We wish you well in your studies. Our success is in your accomplishment.

Unit 1 ▷ Whole Numbers

Every year, U.S. car dealers import, or bring in, millions of cars from other countries.

The chart shows about how many cars are imported into the United States in one year.

1. From which country does the United States import the greatest number of cars?

2. From which country does the United States import the fewest number of cars?

3. How did you find your answer for **Questions 1** and **2**?

Imported Cars in a Year	
Country	**Number of Cars**
Japan	1,114,000
Germany	204,000
South Korea	132,000
Mexico	463,000
Canada	1,552,000

1

Nonprofit organizations often raise money at large concert events. They sold 8,000 tickets for this concert. Tickets cost $10 each. They raised $80,000. A second concert raised $150,000. Why might the second concert have raised more money?

Chapter 1

Understanding Whole Numbers

Words to Know

whole numbers	0, 1, 2, 3, 4, 5, 6, 7, and so on
number line	numbers in order shown as points on a line
even numbers	numbers that end in 0, 2, 4, 6, or 8
odd numbers	numbers that end in 1, 3, 5, 7, or 9
digits	the symbols used to write numbers: 0, 1, 2, 3, 4, 5, 6, 7, 8, and 9
rename	to show a number another way; to show place value, 28 can be renamed as 2 *tens* + 8 *ones*
rounding	changing a number to the nearest ten, hundred, thousand, or so on

Number Journal Project

Keep a daily journal of whole numbers you see. Look for them in different places. Read containers, signs, newspapers, and magazines. Write what each number is about and where you found it.

2001	year	newspaper
110	calories	milk carton
$1,000	money	"For Sale" sign

Learning Objectives

- Identify whole numbers.
- Identify odd and even numbers.
- Recognize place value.
- Read and write whole numbers.
- Compare and order whole numbers.
- Round whole numbers.
- Solve problems by reading a table.
- Apply whole numbers to computer memory.

1-1   What Is a Whole Number?

The numbers 0, 1, 2, 3, 4, 5, and so on, are called **whole numbers.** Whole numbers are used to count. They tell how many or how much.

Look at the **number line** below. It shows numbers in order on a line. This number line shows the whole numbers from 0 to 16. A number line can begin or end with any number.

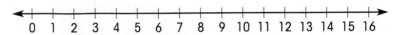

EXAMPLE

Find the missing numbers on the number line below.

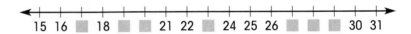

STEP 1   Copy the number line above.

STEP 2   Begin with 15 and count each point.
Fill in the blanks as you count.

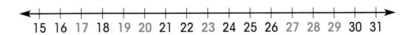

Practice

Find the missing numbers on each number line. Be sure to copy each number line onto your paper first.

1.

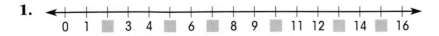

2.

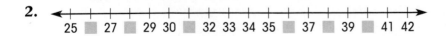

1·2 Odd and Even Numbers

Look at the number line below. The numbers in blue are called **even numbers.** The numbers in black are called **odd numbers.** There is a pattern. Every even number is followed by an odd number.

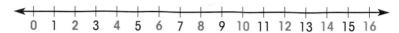

Notice that even numbers end in 0, 2, 4, 6, or 8. Odd numbers end in 1, 3, 5, 7, or 9. You can look at the last digit on the right in a number. This digit tells you if the number is even or odd.

▶ **EXAMPLE**

Write only the odd numbers from this set of numbers:

11	12	13	14	15	16	17	18	19	20
21	22	23	24	25	26	27	28	29	30

STEP 1 Look at the last digit in each number.

11   12   and so on…

STEP 2 Write the numbers that end in 1, 3, 5, 7, or 9.

11, 13, 15, 17, 19, 21, 23, 25, 27, 29

The odd numbers in the set above are:
11, 13, 15, 17, 19, 21, 23, 25, 27, and 29.

Practice

1. Write only the odd numbers from this set of numbers:

51	52	53	54	55	56	57	58	59	60
61	62	63	64	65	66	67	68	69	70

2. Write only the even numbers from this set of numbers:

91	92	93	94	95	96	97	98	99	100
101	102	103	104	105	106	107	108	109	110

Place Value to Thousands

You can use the **digits** 0, 1, 2, 3, 4, 5, 6, 7, 8, and 9 to write any number. It is important to put each digit in the correct place.

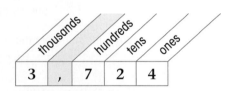

24 means 2 *tens* and 4 *ones*.

42 means 4 *tens* and 2 *ones*.

The numbers 24 and 42 are different numbers.

You can **rename** a number to show the place value of each digit.

► **EXAMPLE**

Rename 3,724 to show the place value of each digit.

STEP 1 Look at the place value of each digit.

3 means 3 thousands.
7 means 7 hundreds.
2 means 2 tens.
4 means 4 ones.

STEP 2 Write the number this way:

3,724 = 3 *thousands* + 7 *hundreds* + 2 *tens* + 4 *ones*

To show the place value of each digit, rename 3,724 as 3 *thousands* + 7 *hundreds* + 2 *tens* + 4 *ones*.

Practice A

Rename each number to show the place value of each digit.

1. 17   **2.** 69   **3.** 46   **4.** 81   **5.** 55

6. 2,473   **7.** 7,502   **8.** 5,439   **9.** 8,037   **10.** 4,800

Practice B

The place value of each digit in a number is shown below.
Write the number.

11. 3 tens + 2 ones   **12.** 9 tens + 5 ones   **13.** 7 tens + 4 ones

14. 6 tens + 6 ones   **15.** 8 tens   **16.** 8 ones

17. 3 thousands + 4 tens + 6 ones   **18.** 7 thousands + 5 hundreds

19. 4 hundreds + 3 tens   **20.** 5 thousands + 6 hundreds + 2 tens

Everyday Problem Solving

Ms. Polk's class is collecting soda can tabs for a charity. They want to collect 5,000. They group the tabs by thousands, hundreds, tens, and ones.

1. How many hundreds are in 1,000?

2. The class has 3,421 tabs. How many thousands are there?

3. Eileen has 999 tabs. How many more tabs does she need to make 1,000?

4. Is 3,421 an even number or an odd number? How do you know?

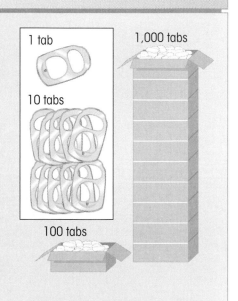

1 tab

10 tabs

100 tabs

1,000 tabs

1·4 ▶ Place Value to Millions

A place-value chart can help you to understand large numbers.

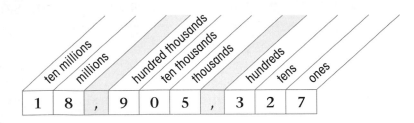

ten millions | millions | hundred thousands | ten thousands | thousands | hundreds | tens | ones
1 | 8 , | 9 | 0 | 5 , | 3 | 2 | 7

▶ **EXAMPLE**

Find the value of the underlined digit in 18,<u>9</u>05,327.

STEP 1 Identify the place of the underlined digit. Look at the place-value chart above.

hundred thousands
↓
18,<u>9</u>05,327

STEP 2 Write the underlined digit. Then write the name of the place.

9 hundred thousands

The value of the digit 9 in the number 18,905,327 is 9 *hundred thousands*.

Practice

Find the value of the underlined digit in each number.

1. 7,<u>8</u>32

2. 56,<u>5</u>29,100

3. 1<u>4</u>,635,123

4. 4<u>6</u>,718

5. 90,<u>7</u>16

6. 6<u>2</u>9,350

7. 90,3<u>1</u>5

8. 1,678,94<u>3</u>

9. <u>9</u>7,510

10. 3,4<u>56</u>,789

11. 78,<u>8</u>600

12. 1<u>7</u>9,360,121

13. 1,<u>5</u>78,469

14. 563,<u>3</u>99

15. <u>6</u>7,013,269

16. 2<u>0</u>0,856

USING YOUR CALCULATOR
A Place-Value Game

You can use the calculator to play a game about place value. You will use the keys shown on the picture.

Player 1   Key a number into the calculator. Choose a digit in that number.

PRESS   [3] [4] [7] [2] | 3472.

CHOOSE   four

Player 2   Tell the place value of the digit.

SAY   4 *hundreds*

Key in one or more digits.

PRESS   [9] [1] | 347291.

Player 3   Tell the place value of the same digit in the new number.

SAY   4 *ten thousands*

All   Change roles and play again.

PRESS   [C] | 0.

DISPLAY   Shows the number you enter.

3472.

CLEAR   Use to erase.   [C]

NUMBER KEYS   Use to enter numbers.

[7] [8] [9] [÷]
[4] [5] [6] [×]
[1] [2] [3] [−]
[0] [.] [=] [+]

FUNCTION KEYS   You will use these in later chapters.

Play the place-value game. Player 1 begins with each number below.

1. 237   **2.** 46   **3.** 2,428   **4.** 63,821

5. 125,325   **6.** 7,013,825   **7.** 10,025,362   **8.** 367,420

9. 9,863,254   **10.** Now player 1 begins with any number.

1·5 Reading and Writing Whole Numbers

A place-value chart can help you to read and write numbers. Numbers are read from left to right.

ten millions	millions		hundred thousands	ten thousands	thousands		hundreds	tens	ones
4	9	,	1	0	8	,	5	0	0
2	8	,	0	0	0	,	1	3	2

Commas group every three places starting from the right. They can help you read and write numbers.

▶ **EXAMPLE 1**

Read the number 49,108,500 in the place-value chart above. Write it in words.

STEP 1 Find the place name to the left of each comma.

49 million 108 thousand 500 hundred

STEP 2 Read the number before each comma and then the place name.

forty-nine million, one hundred eight thousand, five hundred

The number 49,108,500 is read: forty-nine million, one hundred eight thousand, five hundred.

▶ **EXAMPLE 2**

Use digits to write twenty-eight million, one hundred thirty-two. Write zeros for missing places.

STEP 1 Write the number for each group named.

28 million 132

STEP 2 Write a comma every three places from the right. Write zeros for any missing places.

28,000,132

Twenty-eight million, one hundred thirty-two can be written as 28,000,132.

Practice A

Read each number. Write each number in words.

1. 32,584

2. 74,800,000

3. 6,002,070

4. 175,081

5. 837,000,495

6. 463,000

Practice B

Use digits to write each number.

7. three million, six hundred thousand, forty-nine

8. nine hundred fifty-eight thousand, six hundred three

9. one hundred fifty-two million, seven hundred three

10. sixteen million, five hundred thousand

11. seven hundred million, twelve

12. six hundred sixteen thousand, ninety-five

13. twenty million, three thousand, sixty

14. forty-one million, forty-one thousand, forty-one

Everyday Problem Solving

A newspaper headline can have a whole number in it.

1. Write the number in Headline A in words.

2. Write the number in Headline B using digits.

3. Create your own headline involving at least one whole number. Write that number in words.

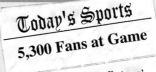

Ⓐ **Today's Sports**
5,300 Fans at Game

Ⓑ **Local News**
One Million People Will Vote

1·6 ▸ Comparing Whole Numbers

You can use symbols to show if a number is larger than, or smaller than, or the same as another number.

$$10 > 4 \qquad\qquad 2 < 13 \qquad\qquad 5 = 5$$
10 is greater than 4   2 is less than 13   5 is equal to 5

The symbol > means *is greater than*. The symbol < means *is less than*. The symbol = means *is equal to*.

▸ **EXAMPLE 1**

Compare. 6,325 and 978

STEP 1	Line up the digits by place and count the number of digits.	6,325 ← 4 digits 978 ← 3 digits
STEP 2	Compare the number of digits.	6,325 has more digits.
STEP 3	Use a symbol to show how the numbers compare.	6,325 > 978

The number 6,325 is greater than 978.

You can compare numbers with the same number of digits. You will need to compare each digit.

▸ **EXAMPLE 2**

Compare. 8,536 and 8,701

STEP 1	Line up the digits by place and count the number of digits.	8,536 ← 4 digits 8,701 ← 4 digits
STEP 2	Compare the number of digits.	They have the same number of digits.
STEP 3	Compare the value of each digit, starting at the left. Skip digits that are the same.	8,536 8,701 └5 is less than 7
STEP 4	Use a symbol to show how the numbers compare.	8,536 < 8,701

The number 8,536 is less than 8,701.

▶ **EXAMPLE 3**　　　　Compare. 52,743 and 52,743

STEP 1	Line up the digits by place and count the number of digits.	52,743 ← 5 digits 52,743 ← 5 digits
STEP 2	Compare the number of digits.	They have the same number of digits.
STEP 3	Compare the value of each digit, starting at the left. Skip digits that are the same.	52,743 52,743 All digits are the same.
STEP 4	Use a symbol to show how the numbers compare.	52,743 = 52,743

Practice A

Choose the greater number in each pair.

1. 2　　10

2. 152　　99

3. 5,628　　10,000

4. 1,002　　1,003

5. 25,000　　2,500

6. 700　　800

7. 68,431　　68,331

8. 69,000　　70,000

9. 12,158　　12,185

10. 11,000　　9,999

11. 4,195　　4,099

12. 349,999　　350,000

Practice B

Compare each pair of numbers from left to right. Use the symbol >, <, or =.

13. 2,007 ▤ 2,676

14. 567 ▤ 89

15. 312 ▤ 321

16. 5,876 ▤ 5,303

17. 709 ▤ 1,100

18. 4,567 ▤ 4,567

19. 5,601 ▤ 7,601

20. 62,514 ▤ 63,412

21. 50,982 ▤ 50,820

22. 72,999 ▤ 72,999

23. 31,008 ▤ 29,999

24. 17,230 ▤ 17,320

Ordering Whole Numbers

You can use what you know about comparing numbers to order numbers. You can order numbers from least to greatest.

EXAMPLE

Order the numbers from least to greatest.

3,208   569   3,502

STEP 1 Find the smallest number by counting the digits. Circle the smallest number.

3,208 ← 4 digits
569 ← 3 digits
3,502 ← 4 digits

STEP 2 Compare the other two numbers.

3,208
3,502
└ 2 is less than 5.

STEP 3 Write the numbers in order from least to greatest.

569   3,208   3,502

The numbers from least to greatest are:
569   3,208   3,502

You can also order numbers from greatest to least. Begin by looking for the largest number.

Practice A

Order the numbers from least to greatest.

1. 25	**2.** 573	**3.** 1,003	**4.** 8,060
52	564	985	860
9	580	958	80,006

5. 32,153	**6.** 9,100	**7.** 25,525	**8.** 97
33,000	9,090	6,825	968
31,978	9,091	26,125	978

Practice B

Order the numbers from least to greatest.

9. 46   87   3   **10.** 789   505   690

11. 712   478   203   **12.** 888   349   901

13. 2,309   1,781   890   **14.** 305   2,020   2,041

15. 23,560   19,709   24,001   **16.** 54,800   60,723   51,244

Practice C

Order the numbers from greatest to least.

17. 15   35   20   **18.** 23,152   32,182   33,132

19. 1,287   7,002   1,087   **20.** 62,961   69,001   65,452

Everyday Problem Solving

Sam found information on the U.S. population for his history report. He used the chart below to answer these questions.

1. Which state had the greatest population?

2. Which state had the least population?

3. Did New York have fewer people than Connecticut? Explain.

4. If 1,000 more people settle in Rhode Island, what would be the population?

5. Make a new chart. List the states by population from least to greatest.

Year 1790	
State	Population
Connecticut	238,000
Massachusetts	379,000
New York	340,000
Rhode Island	69,000

1·8 Problem Solving: Reading Tables

Some word problems can be solved by using numbers from a table.

EXAMPLE

Hector and Lucy both play the same video game. They both are on the high scores list. Who is the best player on the list?

Game High Scores	
Name	**Points Scored**
Hector	285,800,000
Lucy	357,100,000
Nori	260,000,000
Marcel	306,200,000
Jewel	399,800,000
Cliff	322,700,000

STEP 1   READ   What do you need to find out?
You need to find the best player.
Which player scored the most points?

STEP 2   PLAN   What do you need to do?
Compare each number.
Find the greatest number.

STEP 3   DO   Follow the plan.
399,800,000   Jewel
322,700,000   Cliff
357,100,000   Lucy
399,800,000 > 357,100,000

STEP 4   CHECK   Does the answer make sense?
Look at the other numbers in the table. Are all the other numbers less than 399,800,000? ✓

The best player is Jewel.

Problem Solving

READ the problem. Use the table on page 16 to follow the steps under PLAN. DO the plan to solve each problem.

1. How many points did Marcel score?

PLAN
Find Marcel in the table.
Write the number next to him under "Points Scored."

2. Who scored 357,100,000?

PLAN
Find 357,100,000 in the table.
Write the name of the person next to it in the first column.

3. Which player scored more, Cliff or Hector?

PLAN
Compare the numbers next to Cliff and Hector.
Choose the person with the greater number of points.

4. Which player scored the least number of points?

PLAN
Compare each number in the table.
Choose the person with the least number of points.

Problem Solving Strategy

Often, problems can be solved by making a table.

Dan and his friends scored the following on their favorite video game: Dan, 35,354; Bill, 34,352; Dave, 33,534; Marie, 34,354; and Jill, 35,254. Who scored the highest? Who scored the lowest?

Copy the table shown. Use it to solve the problem. The first row is done for you.

Video Game Scores	
Person	Score
Dan	35,354

1-9   Rounding Whole Numbers

Look at the numbers below. These are the hundreds numbers.

100, 200, 300, 400, 500, 600, 700, 800, 900

Changing numbers to the nearest ten, hundred, or thousand is called **rounding.**

► EXAMPLE 1

Round 352 to the nearest hundred.

STEP 1	Underline the digit in the rounding place. Look at the digit to the right.	3<u>5</u>2
STEP 2	Compare this digit to 5.	5 is equal to 5.
STEP 3	If this digit is 5 or more, add 1 to the rounding place.	3<u>5</u>2 ↓ Add 1. 4
STEP 4	Change the digits to the right to 0.	400

352 rounded to the nearest hundred is 400.

If the digit in the rounding place is a 9, you may need to round up to the next-higher place.

► EXAMPLE 2

Round 42,971 to the nearest hundred.

1 hundred + 9 hundreds
= 1 thousand

STEP 1	Underline the digit in the rounding place. Look at the digit to the right.	42,<u>9</u>71
STEP 2	Compare this digit to 5.	7 is greater than 5.
STEP 3	Since the digit in the rounding place is 9, change it to 0 and add 1 to the place to the left.	42,<u>9</u>71 ↓ Add 1. 43,0
STEP 4	Change the digits to the right to 0.	43,000

42,971 rounded to the nearest hundred is 43,000.

Do not change the digit in the rounding place, if the digit to the right is less than 5.

▶ **EXAMPLE 3**

Round 542,489 to the nearest thousand.

STEP 1	Underline the digit in the rounding place. Look at the digit to the right.	542,489
STEP 2	Compare this digit to 5.	4 is less than 5.
STEP 3	Since this digit is less than 5, do not change the digit in the rounding place.	542,489 ↓ Do not change. 542,
STEP 4	Change the digits to the right to 0.	542,000

542,489 rounded to the nearest thousand is 542,000.

Practice A

Round each number to the nearest ten.

1. 213 **2.** 467 **3.** 843 **4.** 961

5. 2,458 **6.** 1,661 **7.** 4,228 **8.** 32,702

Practice B

Round each number to the nearest hundred.

9. 88,027 **10.** 53,595 **11.** 50,514 **12.** 105,336

13. 29,947 **14.** 20,682 **15.** 69,817 **16.** 245,568

Practice C

Round each number to the nearest thousand.

17. 77,223 **18.** 43,567 **19.** 20,501 **20.** 109,736

21. 49,933 **22.** 20,682 **23.** 99,817 **24.** 425,508

Practice D

Round each number to the nearest ten, to the nearest hundred, and to the nearest thousand. The first one is done.

		Tens	Hundreds	Thousands
25.	3,256	3,260	3,300	3,000
26.	4,641	?	?	?
27.	9,897	?	?	?
28.	12,560	?	?	?
29.	29,705	?	?	?
30.	129,999	?	?	?
31.	934,650	?	?	?
32.	350,549	?	?	?
33.	744,375	?	?	?

Everyday Problem Solving

Mr. Barnes is the manager of a sneaker store. Use the table to answer the following questions.

1. Which size is sold most often? Write the number of sneakers sold in this size in words.

2. Mr. Barnes needs to order more sneakers. Orders are rounded to the nearest hundred. How many will he order in size 7? In size 9?

3. Make a new chart of **Sneakers Sold**. List the **Number of Pairs** in order from least to greatest. Then write the correct sizes.

4. Which chart is easier to use, the chart on the right or the chart you made for **question 3**? Explain.

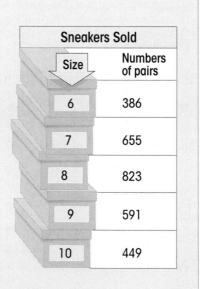

Sneakers Sold	
Size	Numbers of pairs
6	386
7	655
8	823
9	591
10	449

digit
even number
number line
odd number
rename
round
whole numbers

Vocabulary Review
Complete each sentence with a word from the list.

1. Because 156 ends in a 6, it is a(n) __?__ but 157 is a(n) __?__.
2. The value of the __?__ 3 in 360 is 3 hundreds.
3. __?__ are the numbers we use to count.
4. You can __?__ a number to the nearest ten.
5. You can show numbers as points on a __?__.
6. You can __?__ 32 as 3 tens + 2 ones.
7. **Writing** Write an example to explain each word.

Chapter Quiz

LESSONS 1·1 and 1·2

Test Tip
To decide if a number is odd or even, just look at the last digit.

Identifying Whole, Odd, and Even Numbers
Copy the number line and answer the questions.

1. Find the missing numbers.
2. List only the even numbers shown above.

LESSONS 1·3 and 1·4

Test Tip
To find a place in a number, always start with the ones place.

Recognizing Place Value
Write the value of each underlined digit.

3. <u>3</u>,607,800   4. 1<u>5</u>,987   5. 2,0<u>1</u>3,000

6. 30,7<u>4</u>1   7. 56,90<u>3</u>   8. 2,805,<u>7</u>04

LESSON 1·5

Test Tip
Commas help you group parts of a number.

Reading and Writing Whole Numbers
Write each number using digits or in words.

9. fifty-two thousand, nine hundred eleven
10. two hundred sixteen thousand, forty-five
11. 105,000,089   12. 34,320   13. 5,023

MATH IN YOUR LIFE
Understanding Computer Memory

Did you ever try to play a computer game but found out your computer did not have enough memory? To play games and use software, you need to know about memory.

Memory is the space something takes up on a computer or disk. Memory is measured in bytes. A *byte* is a unit of information. A *megabyte* is the same as 1,000,000 bytes. Megabyte is abbreviated as MB.

You can change megabytes to bytes by writing six zeros to the right. Then you can compare sizes of memory.

1 MB	is the same as	1,000,000 bytes
10 MB	is the same as	10,000,000 bytes
64 MB	is the same as	64,000,000 bytes

This tiny chip stores computer memory.

Look at the computers below. Decide if each computer has enough memory to fit the software.

1.
Memory: 68MB

 Software:
63,000,000 bytes

2.
Memory: 13MB

Software:
30,000 bytes

3.
Memory: 7MB

Software:
7,400,000 bytes

Critical Thinking

If you are going to buy a computer, what do you need to know about memory size? What do you need to know about software size?

Do not change the digit in the rounding place, if the digit to the right is less than 5.

<table>
<tr><td>► **EXAMPLE 3**</td><td colspan="2">Round 542,489 to the nearest thousand.</td></tr>
</table>

STEP 1	Underline the digit in the rounding place. Look at the digit to the right.	54<u>2</u>,489
STEP 2	Compare this digit to 5.	4 is less than 5.
STEP 3	Since this digit is less than 5, do not change the digit in the rounding place.	54<u>2</u>,489 ↓ Do not change. 54<u>2</u>,
STEP 4	Change the digits to the right to 0.	54<u>2</u>,000

542,489 rounded to the nearest thousand is 542,000.

Practice A

Round each number to the nearest ten.

1. 213	**2.** 467	**3.** 843	**4.** 961
5. 2,458	**6.** 1,661	**7.** 4,228	**8.** 32,702

Practice B

Round each number to the nearest hundred.

9. 88,027	**10.** 53,595	**11.** 50,514	**12.** 105,336
13. 29,947	**14.** 20,682	**15.** 69,817	**16.** 245,568

Practice C

Round each number to the nearest thousand.

17. 77,223	**18.** 43,567	**19.** 20,501	**20.** 109,736
21. 49,933	**22.** 20,682	**23.** 99,817	**24.** 425,508

Practice D

Round each number to the nearest ten, to the nearest hundred, and to the nearest thousand. The first one is done.

		Tens	Hundreds	Thousands
25.	3,256	3,260	3,300	3,000
26.	4,641	?	?	?
27.	9,897	?	?	?
28.	12,560	?	?	?
29.	29,705	?	?	?
30.	129,999	?	?	?
31.	934,650	?	?	?
32.	350,549	?	?	?
33.	744,375	?	?	?

Everyday Problem Solving

Mr. Barnes is the manager of a sneaker store. Use the table to answer the following questions.

1. Which size is sold most often? Write the number of sneakers sold in this size in words.

2. Mr. Barnes needs to order more sneakers. Orders are rounded to the nearest hundred. How many will he order in size 7? In size 9?

3. Make a new chart of **Sneakers Sold.** List the **Number of Pairs** in order from least to greatest. Then write the correct sizes.

4. Which chart is easier to use, the chart on the right or the chart you made for **question** 3? Explain.

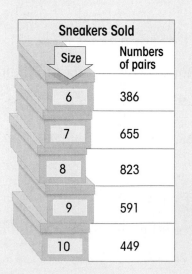

Sneakers Sold	
Size	Numbers of pairs
6	386
7	655
8	823
9	591
10	449

Comparing and Ordering Whole Numbers

Compare the numbers. Use the symbol >, < , or =.

14. 2,398 2,399   **15.** 18,007 ■ 17,999

16. 1,607,800 ■ 1,607,800   **17.** 7,611 ■ 7,630

Order the numbers from least to greatest.

18.	19.	20.
5,609	12,386	45,700
6,905	13,682	7,213
9,605	12,655	38,924

LESSON 1·8

Solving Problems By Reading a Table

Use the table to solve the problem.

Test Tip
Compare each number in the chart.

21. A hardware store sells types of nails in bins. Julie needs to refill bins that contain fewer than 1,500. Which nail types should she refill?

Nail Bins	
Type	Amount
finishing	1,543
roofing	570
tacking	1,055

LESSON 1·9

Rounding Whole Numbers

Round each number to the nearest hundred.

Test Tip
Underline the rounding place, then circle the digit to the right of the rounding place.

22. 456   **23.** 1,231   **24.** 703,862

Round each number to the nearest thousand.

25. 456   **26.** 1,231   **27.** 703,862

Group Activity

With your group, find five numbers in three different sections of a newspaper. Write the numbers and sections in a chart. How many numbers are less than 1,000? How many are greater than 1,000,000? Compare the sizes of the numbers in the different sections of the paper.

Some people fly thousands of miles each year. One Frequent Flier's club rewards you with a free ticket after flying 30,000 miles. How many miles do you need to fly to get two free tickets?

Chapter 2 ▶ Adding Whole Numbers

Words to Know

add	put numbers together; find the total amount
sum	the amount obtained by adding; the total
plus	the symbol or word that means to add
horizontal	written across the page from left to right
vertical	written as one thing under the other
column	numbers placed one below the other
solve	to find the answer to a problem
regroup	to rename and then carry a tens digit to the place on the left when adding
estimate	to quickly find an answer that is close to an exact answer; to make a good guess

Logging Minutes Project

Keep a daily log of the minutes you spend doing two activities, such as homework and watching TV. One hour equals 60 minutes. Add the minutes for each activity.

DAY	HOMEWORK	TV
Monday	15	60
	20	+ 30
	+ 45	90
	80	

Learning Objectives

- Add whole numbers.
- Add larger numbers.
- Add with regrouping.
- Estimate sums.
- Solve problems using addition.
- Apply addition to counting calories.

2·1 What Is Addition?

Addition is putting numbers together to get a total. When you **add**, the answer is called the **sum**.

$$5 + 3 = 8 \leftarrow \text{Sum}$$

Five   plus   three   equals   eight

Addition problems may be written across, or in **horizontal** form. Addition problems may also be written with one number under the other, or in **vertical** form.

EXAMPLE

Write three plus four equals seven, using numbers.

STEP 1 Write numbers and symbols in horizontal form. $3 + 4 = 7$

STEP 2 Write numbers and symbols in vertical form.

$$\begin{array}{r} 3 \\ + 4 \\ \hline 7 \end{array}$$

Practice A

Write each addition problem in horizontal form using numbers.

1. Four plus two equals six.

2. Eight plus three equals eleven.

3. Four plus five equals nine.

4. Six plus seven equals thirteen.

5. Two plus ten equals twelve.

6. Seven plus eight equals fifteen.

Practice B

Write each problem in words and in vertical form using numbers.

7. $6 + 4 = 10$

8. $5 + 8 = 13$

9. $6 + 2 = 8$

10. $1 + 5 = 6$

11. $7 + 8 = 15$

12. $9 + 9 = 18$

13. $8 + 4 = 12$

14. $1 + 9 = 10$

15. $8 + 1 = 9$

Basic Addition

A number line can help you add.

EXAMPLE

Add. $5 + 3$

STEP 1 Find the first number on the number line. Circle the number.

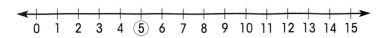

STEP 2 Move to the *right* as many spaces as the second number. Where you stop is the sum.

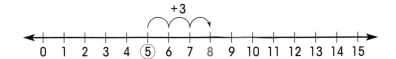

The number line shows that $5 + 3 = 8$.

Practice A

Use a number line to add.

1. $9 + 1$ **2.** $6 + 7$ **3.** $4 + 9$ **4.** $0 + 7$

5. $8 + 6$ **6.** $7 + 9$ **7.** $9 + 8$ **8.** $7 + 8$

9. $7 + 5$ **10.** $9 + 7$ **11.** $3 + 0$ **12.** $8 + 5$

Practice B

Use a number line to add.

13. $\begin{array}{r} 6 \\ + 9 \\ \hline \end{array}$ **14.** $\begin{array}{r} 9 \\ + 3 \\ \hline \end{array}$ **15.** $\begin{array}{r} 7 \\ + 6 \\ \hline \end{array}$ **16.** $\begin{array}{r} 5 \\ + 0 \\ \hline \end{array}$ **17.** $\begin{array}{r} 4 \\ + 8 \\ \hline \end{array}$

18. $\begin{array}{r} 6 \\ + 5 \\ \hline \end{array}$ **19.** $\begin{array}{r} 6 \\ + 8 \\ \hline \end{array}$ **20.** $\begin{array}{r} 8 \\ + 8 \\ \hline \end{array}$ **21.** $\begin{array}{r} 9 \\ + 5 \\ \hline \end{array}$ **22.** $\begin{array}{r} 7 \\ + 9 \\ \hline \end{array}$

USING YOUR CALCULATOR
Beat the Calculator

You can use a calculator to add. If you know your basic addition facts, you may be faster than a calculator.

Write one number from 0 to 9 on two sets of index cards.

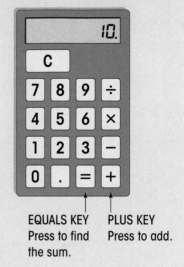

EQUALS KEY
Press to find the sum.

PLUS KEY
Press to add.

Caller Choose two index cards and call out the numbers as an addition problem.
SAY seven plus three

Player 1 Use a calculator to find the sum.
PRESS 7 + 3 = [10.]

Player 2 Use basic facts to find the sum.
THINK 7 + 3 = 10

Players 1 and 2 Call out the sum when you know it. The faster player gets one point.
SCORE 1 point

All Change places and play again. When someone scores 8 points, he or she wins.

Play the Beat the Calculator game. The "caller" can choose any of these different versions of the game.

1. Choose and call out three numbers to add.

2. Write the addition problem instead of saying it aloud.

3. Give a sum and ask players to write an addition problem. Check to make sure it is correct.

Column Addition

Sometimes, you need to add more than two numbers. You can use **column** addition. Group the numbers two at a time. Then, find each sum.

▶ **EXAMPLE**

Add. $2 + 3 + 4 + 6$

STEP 1		STEP 2		
Write the numbers in a column.	2 3 4 + 6	Group the numbers two at a time. Find each sum.	2 3 4 + 6 15	5 10 ┐ 15

The sum of 2, 3, 4, and 6 is 15.

Practice

Add.

1. 3
+ 1

2. 7
+ 4

3. 5
+ 3

4. 2
+ 7

5. 8
+ 7

6. 5
+ 4

7. 4
+ 3

8. 9
+ 7

9. 6
+ 6

10. 3
+ 9

11. 3
1
+ 2

12. 6
3
+ 9

13. 5
3
+ 7

14. 2
7
+ 6

15. 4
2
+ 3

16. 2
5
2
+ 8

17. 5
1
2
+ 3

18. 4
2
3
+ 2

19. 5
3
0
+ 1

20. 7
1
9
+ 0

2·4 Adding Larger Numbers

You can use basic facts to add larger numbers. The digits in each number need to be lined up by place value. Then, you can add the digits in each column.

► **EXAMPLE 1**

Add.   5,304 + 675

thousands		hundreds	tens	ones
5	,	3	0	4
		6	7	5

STEP 1 Line up the digits in each number by place value.

STEP 2 Add the digits in each column starting with the ones place.

```
  5,304
+   675
  5,979
```

The sum of 5,304 and 675 is 5,979.

► **EXAMPLE 2**

Add.   5,302 + 11 + 675

STEP 1
Line up the digits in each number by place value.

```
  5,302
     11
+   675
```

STEP 2
Add the digits in each column, starting with the ones place.

```
  5,302
     11
+   675
  5,988
```

The sum of 5,302, 11, and 675 is 5,988.

Practice A

Add.

1.
```
  37
+ 41
```

2.
```
  95
+  3
```

3.
```
  47
+ 42
```

4.
```
  64
+ 23
```

5.
```
  73
+ 15
```

6.
```
  67
+ 32
```

7.
```
  83
+ 12
```

8.
```
  120
   32
+  35
```

9.
```
   26
  102
+  51
```

10.
```
   13
   43
+ 102
```

Practice B

Add.

11. 200 + 705	**12.** 711 + 234	**13.** 403 + 222	**14.** 514 + 123	**15.** 3,562 + 5,420
16. 4,275 + 1,022	**17.** 2,318 + 3,641	**18.** 1,708 + 7,191	**19.** 1,502 213 + 13	**20.** 7,134 12 + 233

Practice C

Add. Remember to line up the digits in each number
by place value.

21. 245 + 53 **22.** 506 + 132 **23.** 173 + 22

24. 1,204 + 555 **25.** 2,381 + 5,213 **26.** 514 + 6,144

27. 2,053 + 123 + 321 **28.** 303 + 1,002 + 4,102

Everyday Problem Solving

Football is a popular sport. Receivers run down the field to
catch passes from the quarterback. As they run down the field
they gain yards.

1. How many yards did Cris Carter gain?

2. Which receiver gained 13,177 yards?

3. How many total yards did Art Monk and
Henry Ellard gain?

4. Which receiver gained 3,200 more yards
than Henry Ellard? How do you know?

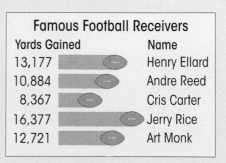

Famous Football Receivers

Yards Gained	Name
13,177	Henry Ellard
10,884	Andre Reed
8,367	Cris Carter
16,377	Jerry Rice
12,721	Art Monk

Problem Solving: Clue Words for Addition

To find the answer to a word problem, you need to **solve** it. Clue words can help you find the answer to a word problem.

CLUE WORDS FOR ADDITION
in all   *together*   *altogether*   *total*   *both*

▶ **EXAMPLE**

Jerry drove 322 miles on Monday. He drove 204 miles on Tuesday. On Wednesday, he drove 173 miles. How many miles did he drive in all?

STEP 1   READ   What do you need to find out?
You need to find the number of miles Jerry drove in all.

STEP 2   PLAN   What do you need to do?
The clue words in all tell you to add the miles.

STEP 3   DO   Follow the plan.
Start adding with the number of miles Jerry drove on Monday.

Remember to line up the numbers by place value.

$$
\begin{array}{r}
322 \text{ miles on Monday} \\
204 \text{ miles on Tuesday} \\
+\ 173 \text{ miles on Wednesday} \\
\hline
699 \text{ miles in all}
\end{array}
$$

STEP 4   CHECK   Does the answer make sense?
Use a different order to add.

$$
\begin{array}{r}
173 \text{ miles} \\
204 \text{ miles} \\
+\ 322 \text{ miles} \\
\hline
699 \text{ miles } ✓
\end{array}
$$

Jerry drove 699 miles in all. Remember to write "miles" as part of your answer.

Problem Solving

READ the problem. Answer the questions under PLAN.
DO the plan to solve the problem.

1. Nick made 15 sales calls in the morning. Then he made 12 sales calls in the afternoon. How many sales calls did he make in all?

   PLAN
   What are the clue words?
   What do the clue words tell you to do?

2. Dan typed 6 letters. Maria typed 12 letters. Together, how many letters did they type?

   PLAN
   What are the clue words?
   What do the clue words tell you to do?

3. The first bus carried 40 students. The second bus carried 24 students. The third bus carried 33 students. How many students were carried altogether on all three buses?

   PLAN
   What are the clue words?
   What do the clue words tell you to do?

Problem Solving Strategy

Often, problems can be solved by working backward.

Sean read 10 books during the summer. His sister Meg read some books. They read 28 books altogether. How many books did Meg read?

Fill in the blank to find how many books Meg read.

$$\begin{array}{r} 10 \\ + \ \blacksquare \\ \hline 28 \text{ books} \end{array}$$

2·6 Adding with One Regrouping

Sometimes when you add the digits in a column, the sum is 10 or greater than 10. You need to rename the number and **regroup**.

EXAMPLE

Add.   24 + 548

STEP 1

Start in the ones place and add the digits.
Regroup 12 by writing a 1 over the tens place.

$$\begin{array}{r} \overset{1}{} \\ 24 \\ +\ 548 \\ \hline 2 \end{array}$$

STEP 2

Add all the digits in the tens place.
Add the other columns.

$$\begin{array}{r} \overset{1}{} \\ 24 \\ +\ 548 \\ \hline 572 \end{array}$$

The sum of 24 and 548 is 572.

Practice A

Add.

1.   28
      + 3

2.   35
      + 57

3.   67
      + 23

4.   48
      + 23

5.   64
      + 19

6.   101
      + 359

7.   19
      + 813

8.   231
      + 174

9.   3,814
      +   251

10.   7,528
      +   412

11.   3,027
      + 3,882

12.   2,318
      + 4,931

13.   7,902
      +   505

14.   6,331
      + 2,559

15.   5,448
      + 2,951

16.   16
      + 70

Practice B

Add. In some problems, you will not need to regroup.

17. 48
 + 47

18. 2,617
 +   782

19. 302
 + 59

20. 548
 + 245

21. 237
 + 411

22. 6,293
 + 2,704

23. 567
 + 1,352

24. 86
 + 1,422

Practice C

Add. Remember to line up the digits in each number by place value.

25. 9,177 + 619

26. 345 + 1,723

27. 75 + 182 + 301

28. 536 + 202 + 141

29. 4,123 + 4,329

30. 11 + 362 + 215

31. 86 + 3,712

32. 3,413 + 124 + 852

33. 95 + 672 + 501

Everyday Problem Solving

The school held elections for student government. The school newspaper printed the election results in a table.

1. How many students altogether voted in the election? Add the number of votes in the table. Tell how many *students* voted.

2. Suppose Marla had received 56 more votes. Would she win the election instead of Chris? How do you know?

SCHOOL NEWS

Election Results

Candidate Names	Number of Votes
Ben James	252
Marla Carne	324
Chris Yencheck	381

Adding with More Than One Regrouping

Sometimes when you add two numbers, you need to regroup more than once.

▶ EXAMPLE 1

Add.   9,548 + 837

STEP 1   Write the numbers in vertical form.
STEP 2   Add. Regroup if needed.

```
  1 1
  9,548
+   837
 10,385
```

The sum of 9,548 and 837 is 10,385.

Sometimes, you need to regroup in every place.

▶ EXAMPLE 2

Add.   9,736 + 5,489

STEP 1   Write the numbers in vertical form.
STEP 2   Add. Regroup if needed.

```
  1 1 1
  9,736
+ 5,489
 15,225
```

The sum of 9,736 and 5,489 is 15,225.

Practice A

Find each sum. Do not forget to regroup.

1. 347 + 173	**2.** 618 + 798	**3.** 739 + 167	**4.** 389 + 582	**5.** 761 + 839
6. 1,243 + 4,069	**7.** 9,595 + 2,512	**8.** 5,744 + 2,856	**9.** 389 + 3,752	**10.** 4,507 + 1,696
11. 135 1,529 + 791	**12.** 7,392 412 + 1,295	**13.** 5,327 1,062 + 587	**14.** 821 3,506 + 181	**15.** 290 2,271 + 1,846

Practice B

Add. Remember to line up the digits in each number by place value.

16. $312 + 408 + 596$

17. $155 + 723 + 86 + 412$

18. $96 + 816 + 540$

19. $1,372 + 868 + 45$

20. $92 + 107 + 253 + 34$

21. $1,633 + 48 + 905 + 18$

Practice C

Each sum below is wrong. Find the error and the correct sum.

22.
```
  5,628
+   392
  5,910
```

23.
```
  7,675
+ 1,238
  8,803
```

24.
```
    561
+   899
  1,350
```

25.
```
  2,789
+ 3,119
  5,898
```

26.
```
  3,866
+   342
  3,108
```

Everyday Problem Solving

Victor lives in Denver, Colorado. He plans to fly to several cities to visit relatives during the year. Use the chart to answer the questions.

1. Victor plans to travel from Denver to Indianapolis and then back home. How many miles will he travel?

2. In May, Victor will travel from Denver to Dallas and back home. How many miles will he travel?

3. Victor travels from Denver to San Francisco and then back home in October. He makes the same trip again in December. How many miles does he travel during those two trips?

Travel Miles	
Denver to:	**Distance in Miles**
New York, NY	1,771
Dallas, TX	781
San Francisco, CA	1,235
Indianapolis, IN	1,058

2·8 Estimating Sums

You can **estimate** to quickly find an answer that is close to but not an exact answer to a problem.

EXAMPLE

Use rounding to estimate $572 + 347 + 55$.

STEP 1 Round each number to the nearest hundred.

$$5\underline{7}2 \rightarrow 600$$
$$3\underline{4}7 \rightarrow 300$$
$$\underline{0}55 \rightarrow 100$$

STEP 2 Add the rounded numbers.

$$\begin{array}{r} 600 \\ 300 \\ +\ 100 \\ \hline 1{,}000 \end{array}$$

The estimated sum is 1,000.

You can use estimation to check an exact sum.
The *exact* sum of $572 + 347 + 55$ is 974.
The *estimated* sum of $572 + 347 + 55$ is 1,000.

974 is close to 1,000. The exact sum makes sense.

Practice A

Estimate each sum to the nearest hundred.

1.	**2.**	**3.**	**4.**	**5.**
126	588	291	374	835
+ 452	+ 234	+ 763	+ 588	+ 656

Practice B

Use estimation to check each exact sum. If an answer does not make sense, find the correct sum.

6.	**7.**	**8.**	**9.**	**10.**
238	405	782	381	629
93	372	822	92	315
+ 179	+ 267	+ 58	+ 75	+ 447
310	1,044	1,962	448	1,391

ON-THE-JOB MATH
Dietician

Selene Yang is a dietician. She works in a large health center in a city. Selene helps patients choose foods to meet requirements that their doctors have prescribed.

Selene likes her job because she enjoys talking with people and helping them develop good eating habits.

1. Selene planned the following diet for Ann. Estimate to the nearest hundred the number of calories she ate. Then, find the exact number.

BREAKFAST	calories	LUNCH	calories	DINNER	calories
scrambled egg	116	hot dog	160	chicken breast	155
muffin	139	apple	76	corn	164
oatmeal	130	tomato juice	38	skim milk	90
skim milk	90	cake	136	baked potato	93
				tomato salad	50

2. Ann's doctor now feels that Ann should be eating between 1,100 and 1,400 calories a day. How might Selene change the diet to meet the doctor's new requirements? Explain your thinking.

Critical Thinking
What do you think Selene should do when a patient does not like the foods she has selected? Work with a partner to decide what she should do. Share your answer with the class.

adding
column
estimate
horizontal
plus
regroup
solve
sum
vertical

Vocabulary Review

Complete each sentence with a word from the list.

1. When the sum of the digits in a column is 10 or more, you can __?__ to add.

2. You can __?__ to find an answer that is close to the exact answer.

3. An answer to an addition problem is the __?__.

4. Putting numbers together to get a total is called __?__.

5. You can __?__ a problem by finding the answer.

6. Forming a __?__ is when you place numbers below one another to make a __?__ problem.

7. Symbols or words that tell you to add are called __?__ signs.

8. You can write a __?__ problem across the page.

9. **Writing** Create a crossword puzzle using the words in the list above. Be sure to give ACROSS and DOWN clues for the words.

Chapter Quiz

LESSONS 2·1 and 2·2

Test Tip
Check that the sum is greater than each addend.

Adding Whole Numbers

Use a number line to add.

1.	6	**2.**	8	**3.**	3
	+ 7		+ 2		+ 4

4.	7	**5.**	9	**6.**	5
	+ 7		+ 6		+ 4

7. $9 + 8$ **8.** $6 + 5$ **9.** $3 + 9$

LESSONS 2·3 and 2·4

Test Tip
Remember to line up the digits in each number by place value.

Adding Larger Numbers
Add.

10.		**11.**		**12.**		**13.**	
	7		8		34		78
	8		5		12		10
	+ 1		+ 2		+ 13		+ 11

LESSON 2·5

Test Tip
Look for clue words to help you solve problems.

Solving Problems by Using Addition
Solve each problem.

14. One computer file uses 12,460 bytes. Another file uses 34,500 bytes. How many bytes do they use altogether?

LESSONS 2·6 and 2·7

Test Tip
Line up the place values when adding whole numbers. Be sure to regroup if needed.

Adding with Regrouping
Add.

15.		**16.**		**17.**	
	67		109		2,405
	153		357		6,893
	+ 8		+ 1,084		+ 562

18. 1,834 + 755   **19.** 176 + 439 + 921

LESSON 2·8

Test Tip
Compare the estimated sum with the exact sum to check your work.

Estimating Sums
Estimate each sum to the nearest hundred. Then, find the exact sum.

20.		**21.**		**22.**	
	467		567		1,378
	+ 344		+ 827		+ 2,482

Group Activity

With your group, make a vacation plan. Your budget includes $650 for travel, $850 for lodging, and $450 spending money. Look in brochures to decide where to go and how to manage your money. Explain.

Musical artists need to sell 500,000 copies of their album to call it a Gold Album. If your favorite tape or CD had sold 450,000 copies, how many more would need to be sold for it to reach Gold?

Words to Know

subtract	to take away one number from another; to find the amount that remains
difference	the amount obtained by subtracting; the amount by which one number is larger or smaller than another
minus	the symbol or word that means to subtract
regroup	to rename and then carry a tens digit to the place on the right when subtracting

Years Ago Timeline Project

Research events that interest you. Include events in history, art, music, or science. Include events that are important to you and your family. Find out the date on which each event occurred. Make a timeline. Then find out how many "years ago" each event occurred. Subtract the year of the event from *this* year.

Learning Objectives

- Subtract whole numbers.
- Subtract larger numbers.
- Subtract with regrouping.
- Subtract from zeros.
- Solve word problems using subtraction.
- Apply subtraction to monthly expenses.

U.S. independence
224 years ago

My birth
15 years ago

This year
0 years ago

| 1776 | 1955 | 1985 | 1990 | 2000 |

Mom was born
45 years ago

Won first place
10 years ago

What Is Subtraction?

Subtraction is taking one number away from another number. When you **subtract**, you **minus** one number from another. The answer is called the **difference**.

8   –   3   =   5 ◄—Difference

Eight minus three equals five

Horizontal means written across. Vertical means written one under the other.

Subtraction problems may be written in horizontal or vertical form, using numbers.

► **EXAMPLE**

Write seven minus four equals three, using numbers.

STEP 1 Write numbers and symbols in horizontal form. $7 - 4 = 3$

STEP 2 Write numbers and symbols in vertical form.
$$\begin{array}{r} 7 \\ -\ 4 \\ \hline 3 \end{array}$$

Practice A

Write each subtraction problem in horizontal form using numbers.

1. Nine minus three equals six.

2. Twelve minus four equals eight.

3. Fifteen minus six equals nine.

4. Fourteen minus nine equals five.

5. Eleven minus seven equals four.

6. Twelve minus zero equals twelve.

Practice B

Write each problem in words and in vertical form using numbers.

7. $9 - 4 = 5$

8. $12 - 6 = 6$

9. $17 - 8 = 9$

10. $13 - 9 = 4$

11. $11 - 11 = 0$

12. $18 - 9 = 9$

13. $10 - 9 = 1$

14. $7 - 4 = 3$

15. $16 - 7 = 9$

3·2 ▸ Basic Subtraction

A number line can help you subtract.

▸ **EXAMPLE**

Subtract.   9 − 3

STEP 1 Find the first number on the number line.
Circle the number.

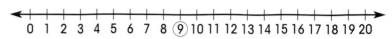

STEP 2 Move to the *left* as many spaces as the second number.
Where you stop is the difference.

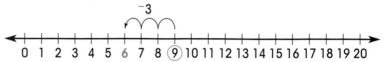

The number line shows that 9 − 3 = 6.

Practice A

Use a number line to subtract.

1. 8 − 2	**2.** 12 − 3	**3.** 15 − 7	**4.** 9 − 9
5. 14 − 9	**6.** 11 − 5	**7.** 13 − 6	**8.** 17 − 9
9. 7 − 4	**10.** 15 − 15	**11.** 12 − 8	**12.** 16 − 7

Practice B

Use a number line to subtract.

13. 7 − 3	**14.** 14 − 5	**15.** 12 − 12	**16.** 14 − 8	**17.** 11 − 6
18. 15 − 8	**19.** 13 − 4	**20.** 16 − 0	**21.** 18 − 9	**22.** 17 − 8

USING YOUR CALCULATOR
Beat the Calculator

You can use a calculator to subtract.
If you know your basic subtraction facts,
you may be faster than a calculator.

Write one number from 0 to 9 on one set
of index cards and 0 to 18 on another set
of index cards.

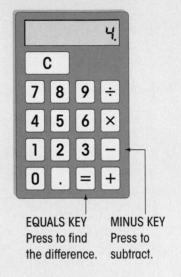

EQUALS KEY
Press to find
the difference.

MINUS KEY
Press to
subtract.

Caller   Choose two index cards. Put the
             larger number first. Call out the
             numbers as a subtraction problem.
             SAY   seven minus three

Player 1 Use a calculator to find the difference.
             PRESS   7 − 3 = [4]

Player 2 Use basic facts to find the difference.
             THINK   7 − 3 = 4

Players   Call out the difference when you know
1 and 2   it. The faster player gets 1 point.
             SCORE   1 point

All   Change roles and play again. When
             someone scores 8 points, he or she wins.

**Play the Beat the Calculator game. The "caller"
can choose any of these different versions of the game.**

1. Choose and call out two numbers to subtract. Then choose
   and call a third number to add.

2. Write the subtraction problem instead of saying it aloud.

3. Give a difference and ask players to write a subtraction problem.
   Check to make sure it is correct.

Subtracting Larger Numbers

You can use basic facts to subtract larger numbers. Line up the digits in each number by place value.

▶ EXAMPLE

Subtract. 968 − 625

hundreds tens ones

	9	6	8
−	6	2	5

STEP 1 Line up the digits in each number by place value.

STEP 2 Subtract the numbers in each column. Always start with the ones.

$$\begin{array}{r} 968 \\ -\ 625 \\ \hline 343 \end{array}$$

The difference between 968 and 625 is 343.

Practice A

Subtract.

1. $\begin{array}{r} 67 \\ -\ 41 \end{array}$ **2.** $\begin{array}{r} 98 \\ -\ 5 \end{array}$ **3.** $\begin{array}{r} 47 \\ -\ 12 \end{array}$ **4.** $\begin{array}{r} 69 \\ -\ 24 \end{array}$ **5.** $\begin{array}{r} 73 \\ -\ 52 \end{array}$

6. $\begin{array}{r} 819 \\ -\ 705 \end{array}$ **7.** $\begin{array}{r} 689 \\ -\ 78 \end{array}$ **8.** $\begin{array}{r} 9,568 \\ -\ 5,420 \end{array}$ **9.** $\begin{array}{r} 7,868 \\ -\ 3,641 \end{array}$ **10.** $\begin{array}{r} 5,376 \\ -\ 26 \end{array}$

11. $\begin{array}{r} 597 \\ -\ 44 \end{array}$ **12.** $\begin{array}{r} 957 \\ -\ 56 \end{array}$ **13.** $\begin{array}{r} 8,469 \\ -\ 7,128 \end{array}$ **14.** $\begin{array}{r} 6,998 \\ -\ 547 \end{array}$ **15.** $\begin{array}{r} 9,557 \\ -\ 3,446 \end{array}$

Practice B

Subtract. Remember to line up each digit by place value.

16. 588 − 65   **17.** 609 − 106   **18.** 673 − 51

19. 9,762 − 550   **20.** 5,394 − 344   **21.** 6,739 − 28

Problem Solving:
Clue Words for Subtraction

There are words in a word problem that mean subtraction.

CLUE WORDS		
how much more	*how much less*	*how many more*
left	*remain*	*difference*

EXAMPLE

Remember:
Not all problems have clue words.

Kim and Paul hiked 9 miles on Tuesday. They hiked 12 miles on Wednesday. How many more miles did they hike on Wednesday than on Tuesday?

STEP 1   READ   What do you need to find out?
You need to find how many more miles Kim and Paul hiked on Wednesday than on Tuesday.

STEP 2   PLAN   What do you need to do?
The clue words how many more tell you to subtract. Begin with the 12 miles hiked on Wednesday.

STEP 3   DO   Follow the plan.
Subtract.

$$
\begin{array}{r}
12 \text{ miles} \leftarrow \text{Wednesday} \\
- \ \ 9 \text{ miles} \leftarrow \text{Tuesday} \\
\hline
3 \text{ miles} \quad \textit{more}
\end{array}
$$

STEP 4   CHECK   Does the answer make sense?
Add to check.

$$
\begin{array}{r}
9 \\
+ \ 3 \\
\hline
12 \ \checkmark
\end{array}
$$

Kim and Paul hiked 3 more miles on Wednesday than on Tuesday.

Problem Solving

READ the problem. Answer the questions under PLAN. Do the plan to solve the problem.

1. Nat's new car cost $8,769. Lori's car cost $6,152. How much more did Nat's car cost than Lori's?

   PLAN
   What are the clue words?
   What do the clue words tell you to do?

2. Kay saved $287. Meg saved $155. How much less did Meg save than Kay?

   PLAN
   What are the clue words?
   What do the clue words tell you to do?

3. The monthly rent for Apartment 1B is $575. The monthly rent for Apartment 1A is $561. What is the difference between the rents in Apartment 1A and 1B?

   PLAN
   What are the clue words?
   What do the clue words tell you to do?

Problem Solving Strategy

You can solve a problem by working backward.

> Jim had some videotapes. He sold 15 at a garage sale. He had 20 left. How many videotapes did he start with?

Add the given numbers to fill in the blank and find how many videotapes he had to start with.

$$\begin{array}{r} \blacksquare \\ -\ 15 \\ \hline 20 \text{ videotapes} \end{array}$$

Sometimes you need to **regroup** before you can subtract the digits in a column. Look at the problem below.

$$\begin{array}{r} 34 \\ -\ 19 \\ \end{array}$$

You cannot subtract the digits in the ones column. You need to regroup a ten for more ones.

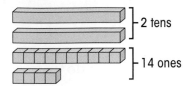

-2 tens

-14 ones

$$34 = 2 \ tens + 14 \ ones = 20 + 14$$

Follow the steps below to do the subtraction.

▶ **EXAMPLE 1**

Subtract. $34 - 19$

STEP 1
Regroup to show
more ones.

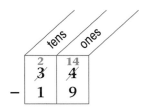

STEP 2
Subtract the digits in
each place.

$$\begin{array}{r} {\scriptstyle 2\ 14} \\ 3\!\!\!/4\!\!\!/ \\ -\ 19 \\ \hline 15 \\ \end{array}$$

The difference between 34 and 19 is 15.

You can regroup in any place. Subtract the digits in each column. If you cannot subtract in a column, then regroup.

▶ **EXAMPLE 2**

Remember to lineup the digits vertically by place value.

Subtract.   8,574 − 6,831

STEP 1
Subtract the digits in the ones and tens places.

$$\begin{array}{r} 8,574 \\ -\ 6,831 \\ \hline 43 \end{array}$$

STEP 2
Regroup for more hundreds. Subtract the hundreds and thousands.

$$\begin{array}{r} {\scriptstyle 7\ 15} \\ 8,\!\cancel{5}74 \\ -\ 6,831 \\ \hline 1,743 \end{array}$$

The difference between 8,574 and 6,831 is 1,743.

The answer to a subtraction problem can be checked by addition. The top number in the subtraction should be the same as the sum.

$$\begin{array}{r} 8,574 \\ -\ 6,831 \\ \hline 1,743 \end{array} \qquad \begin{array}{r} 6,831 \\ +\ 1,743 \\ \hline 8,574\ \checkmark \end{array}$$

Practice A

Subtract. Remember to regroup for more ones.

1. $\begin{array}{r}83\\-16\end{array}$	**2.** $\begin{array}{r}92\\-37\end{array}$	**3.** $\begin{array}{r}61\\-39\end{array}$	**4.** $\begin{array}{r}87\\-19\end{array}$	**5.** $\begin{array}{r}32\\-23\end{array}$
6. $\begin{array}{r}74\\-45\end{array}$	**7.** $\begin{array}{r}51\\-32\end{array}$	**8.** $\begin{array}{r}95\\-\ 7\end{array}$	**9.** $\begin{array}{r}57\\-18\end{array}$	**10.** $\begin{array}{r}93\\-57\end{array}$

Practice B

Subtract. Remember to regroup for more ones or more tens.

11. $\begin{array}{r}315\\-192\end{array}$	**12.** $\begin{array}{r}325\\-134\end{array}$	**13.** $\begin{array}{r}634\\-551\end{array}$	**14.** $\begin{array}{r}611\\-409\end{array}$	**15.** $\begin{array}{r}823\\-715\end{array}$
16. $\begin{array}{r}531\\-161\end{array}$	**17.** $\begin{array}{r}655\\-417\end{array}$	**18.** $\begin{array}{r}438\\-293\end{array}$	**19.** $\begin{array}{r}492\\-137\end{array}$	**20.** $\begin{array}{r}856\\-475\end{array}$

Practice C

Subtract. Remember to regroup whenever you need.

| 21. | 419
− 295 | 22. | 836
− 545 | 23. | 5,724
− 2,800 | 24. | 867
− 359 |

| 25. | 518
− 247 | 26. | 8,362
− 5,450 | 27. | 9,856
− 3,009 | 28. | 3,622
− 1,715 |

| 29. | 622
− 371 | 30. | 8,458
− 7,195 | 31. | 685
− 392 | 32. | 8,533
− 6,604 |

Practice D

Subtract. Remember to line up digits by place value.

33. 45,899 − 12,985   **34.** 7,538 − 4,216   **35.** 41,745 − 22,624

36. 35,729 − 13,563   **37.** 29,472 − 14,391   **38.** 5,529 − 2,317

Everyday Problem Solving

The Manasquan High School took a survey to find out the heights of their students. The table shows the survey results.

Manasquan High School Survey		
Heights	Number of Female Students	Number of Male Students
5 ft 1 in. to 5 ft 3 in.	165	80
5 ft 4 in. to 5 ft 6 in.	152	130
5 ft 7 in. and taller	56	180

1. How many more females than males are there between 5 ft 1 in. and 5 ft 3 in.? Subtract 165 and 80.

2. How many more males than females are 5 ft 7 in. or taller?

3. How many fewer females than males were part of the entire survey? First add all the females. Then add all the males and subtract.

MATH IN YOUR LIFE
Monthly Expenses

Donna earns $1,100 a month at her job. Each month, she needs to pay rent, the phone bill, and the gas and electric bill and to buy groceries. After paying her expenses, how much will Donna have left for spending money?

For Donna to find out how much she has left, she needs to follow two steps. Step 1: Add all her expenses. Step 2: Subtract the total from her monthly earnings.

JANUARY EXPENSES:			
Rent	$600	Monthly earning	$1,100
Phone	$43	Total expenses	− $880
Gas and electric	$52	Spending money	$220
Groceries	+ $185		
Total	$880		

Donna has $220 left over for spending money after her expenses are paid.

Donna earns the same amount every month. Find out Donna's spending money after her expenses are paid for each month below. Follow the steps above.

	1. February Bills:	2. March Bills:	3. April Bills:	4. May Bills:
Rent	$600	$600	$600	$600
Phone	$40	$58	$45	$40
Gas and electric	$50	$50	$47	$45
Groceries	$180	$193	$175	$183

Critical Thinking

What other items would you include in your monthly expenses?

Subtracting with More Than One Regrouping

Sometimes, you will need to regroup more than once, so you can subtract.

EXAMPLE 1

Subtract.   721 − 298

STEP 1
Regroup for more ones.
Subtract.

$$\begin{array}{r} \overset{1\ 11}{72\cancel{1}} \\ -\ 298 \\ \hline 3 \end{array}$$

STEP 2
Regroup for more tens.
Subtract.

$$\begin{array}{r} \overset{6\ 11}{\cancel{7}\cancel{2}\cancel{1}} \\ -\ 298 \\ \hline 423 \end{array}$$

The difference between 731 and 298 is 423.

In some problems, you do not need to regroup in every place.

EXAMPLE 2

Subtract.   34,681 − 9,253

STEP 1
Regroup for
more ones.
Subtract.

$$\begin{array}{r} \overset{7\ 11}{34,68\cancel{1}} \\ -\ 9,253 \\ \hline 428 \end{array}$$

STEP 2
Regroup for
more thousands.
Subtract.

$$\begin{array}{r} \overset{2\ 14\ \ \ 7\ 11}{3\cancel{4},68\cancel{1}} \\ -\ 9,253 \\ \hline 25,428 \end{array}$$

The difference between 34,681 and 9,253 is 25,428.

The answer to a subtraction problem can be checked by addition. The top number in the subtraction problem should be the same as the sum.

$$\begin{array}{r} 34,681 \\ -\ 9,253 \\ \hline 25,428 \end{array} \qquad \begin{array}{r} 9,253 \\ +\ 25,428 \\ \hline 34,681 \checkmark \end{array}$$

Practice

Subtract. Regroup when you need to. Show all your work.

1. 523 − 165	**2.** 714 − 358	**3.** 395 − 207	**4.** 821 − 473	**5.** 871 − 281
6. 927 − 247	**7.** 652 − 462	**8.** 739 − 545	**9.** 9,532 − 5,860	**10.** 6,423 − 3,186
11. 4,726 − 2,853	**12.** 8,614 − 6,796	**13.** 5,239 − 3,655	**14.** 9,268 − 1,749	**15.** 8,451 − 5,953
16. 7,378 − 4,889	**17.** 7,753 − 4,846	**18.** 7,582 − 5,619	**19.** 6,492 − 1,657	**20.** 9,673 − 5,794
21. 23,858 − 11,299	**22.** 11,723 − 10,446	**23.** 39,535 − 28,287	**24.** 36,225 − 24,877	**25.** 73,325 − 47,717

Everyday Problem Solving

Aaron keeps track of his savings account in a *passbook* from the bank. The *balance* is the amount of money in the account on that date. A *withdrawal* means that money has been taken out of the account. A *deposit* means that money has been added to it. Some of the amounts are missing in his passbook.

1. What was Aaron's balance on October 20?
Subtract $40 from $632.

2. What was Aaron's balance on October 21?

3. Aaron withdrew money on October 25. He forgot the amount withdrawn. He knows that the balance is $400. How much did he take out?

Savings Account Passbook

DATE	WITHDRAWAL	DEPOSIT	BALANCE
10/11		$ 682	$ 682
10/15	$ 50		$ 632
10/20	$ 40		?
10/21	$ 128		?
10/25	?		$ 400

3·7 Regrouping with Zeros

When you subtract from zeros, regroup more than once.

▶ EXAMPLE 1

Subtract.   8,000 − 5,624

    STEP 1 Regroup for more hundreds.

$$\begin{array}{r} {}^{7\ 10}\\ 8,\!\cancel{0}00 \\ -\ 5,\!624 \\ \hline \end{array}$$

    STEP 2 Regroup for more tens.

$$\begin{array}{r} {}^{9}\\ {}^{7\ \cancel{10}10}\\ 8,\!\cancel{0}\cancel{0}0 \\ -\ 5,\!624 \\ \hline \end{array}$$

Remember:
1 thousand = 10 hundreds
1 hundred = 10 tens
1 ten = 10 ones

    STEP 3 Regroup for more ones. Subtract beginning with the ones place.

$$\begin{array}{r} {}^{9\ 9}\\ {}^{7\ \cancel{10}\cancel{10}10}\\ 8,\!\cancel{0}\cancel{0}\cancel{0} \\ -\ 5,\!624 \\ \hline 2,\!376 \end{array}$$

The difference between 8,000 and 5,624 is 2,376.

▶ EXAMPLE 2

Subtract.   200 − 109

    STEP 1 Regroup in every place.

    STEP 2 Subtract, beginning with the ones place.

$$\begin{array}{r} {}^{9}\\ {}^{1\ \cancel{10}10}\\ \cancel{2}\cancel{0}\cancel{0} \\ -\ 109 \\ \hline 91 \end{array}$$

The difference between 200 and 109 is 91.

Practice A

Subtract. Remember to regroup for more ones, tens, and hundreds as needed.

1. 600 − 276	**2.** 800 − 629	**3.** 400 − 103	**4.** 9,000 − 5,920	**5.** 7,000 − 2,045
6. 5,000 − 2,974	**7.** 6,000 − 3,621	**8.** 50,000 − 39,764	**9.** 40,000 − 31,769	**10.** 20,000 − 12,584

Practice B

Subtract. Remember to regroup whenever you need to.

11. 7,040 -67	**12.** 8,100 $-5,089$	**13.** 32,007 -635	**14.** 20,020 $-4,883$	**15.** 31,005 $-10,648$
16. 3,002 $-1,229$	**17.** 17,006 $-5,845$	**18.** 54,080 $-32,320$	**19.** 20,060 $-8,397$	**20.** 80,800 -937
21. 8,090 $-6,797$	**22.** 5,000 -234	**23.** 36,700 $-14,855$	**24.** 47,020 $-9,263$	**25.** 30,500 $-26,456$

Practice C

Subtract. Remember to line up the digits by place value.

26. $580 - 354$

27. $7,000 - 4,892$

28. $1,500 - 783$

29. $43,030 - 21,724$

30. $34,008 - 567$

31. $2,001 - 38$

32. $47,900 - 5,963$

33. $7,000 - 5,555$

34. $2,700 - 1,584$

Everyday Problem Solving

The number of seats at baseball stadiums are not the same. Use the table to answer the questions.

1. How many fewer seats are available in Wrigley Field than in the Astrodome?

2. How many more seats are available in 3 Com Park than in Shea Stadium?

3. Suppose that an extra 20,000 seats were added to Wrigley Field. Would the stadium then have more seats than 3 Com Park?

National League Baseball Stadiums	
Stadium	**Seating Capacity**
Wrigley Field	38,765
The Astrodome	53,821
Dodger Stadium	56,000
3 Com Park	63,000
Shea Stadium	55,601

Problem Solving: Add or Subtract?

Sometimes, you must decide whether to add or subtract in order to solve a word problem. The clue words can help you to decide.

EXAMPLE

Marla drives to work. Driving costs her $532 a year. Joel takes the bus to work. Bus fare costs Joel $366 a year. How much less does Joel spend than Marla?

STEP 1   READ   What do you need to find?
You need to find how much less Joel spends.

STEP 2   PLAN   What do you need to do?
The clue words how much less tell you to subtract. Begin with $532.

STEP 3   DO   Follow the Plan.
Subtract.

$$\begin{array}{r} \overset{\scriptscriptstyle 12}{\overset{\scriptscriptstyle 4\ \cancel{2}\ \cancel{12}}{\$\cancel{5}\cancel{3}\cancel{2}}} \\ -\ \ 366 \\ \hline \$166 \end{array}$$

STEP 4   CHECK   Does your answer make sense?
Add to check.

$$\begin{array}{r} \overset{\scriptscriptstyle 1\ 1}{\$366} \\ +\ \ 166 \\ \hline \$532\ \checkmark \end{array}$$

Joel spends $166 less than Marla.

Problem Solving

READ each problem. Answer the questions under PLAN.
DO the plan to solve the problem.

1. Diane spent $320 last week. She spent $247 this week.
   How much less did she spend this week than last week?

   PLAN
   What are the clue words?
   What do they mean?

2. Ramon bought 600 boxes of cards. He sold
   439 boxes. How many does he have left to sell?

   PLAN
   What is the clue word?
   What do the clue words tell you to do?

3. Barbara bought a new computer for $1,500.
   She also bought a printer for $479. How much
   did she pay in all?

   PLAN
   What are the clue words?
   What do they mean?

Problem Solving Strategy

Drawing a diagram can help you solve a problem.

Anna and Sam work at different places. They drive together.
Anna drives 35 miles to Sam's office. Then she drives on to
her office. Anna drives a total of 60 miles. How much
farther does Anna drive to get to her office?

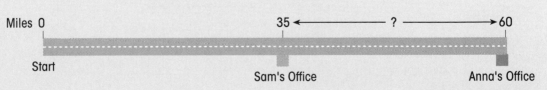

Look at the diagram. What operation should you use?

Chapter

3 ▷ Review

difference

minus

regroup

subtract

Vocabulary Review

True or false? If the statement is false, change the underlined word to make the statement true.

1. When you <u>subtract</u>, you take one number away from another number.

2. The answer in a subtraction problem is called the <u>sum</u>.

3. Naming 1 thousand as 10 hundreds or 1 hundred as 10 tens is called <u>regrouping</u>.

4. This is a subtraction problem: Five <u>plus</u> two equals three.

5. **Writing** Create flash cards for these words: subtraction, difference, regrouping, and minus. Write the word on one side and its definition and an example on the back.

Chapter Quiz

LESSONS 3·1 and 3·2

Test Tip
Practicing your basic facts will help you to remember them.

Subtracting Whole Numbers
Subtract.

1. $12 - 4$	**2.** $9 - 5$	**3.** $16 - 9$
4. $15 - 7$	**5.** $13 - 6$	**6.** $13 - 7$
7. $11 - 8$	**8.** $17 - 8$	**9.** $17 - 9$
10. $12 - 7$	**11.** $13 - 5$	**12.** $15 - 9$

LESSON 3·3

Test Tip
Be sure to subtract the bottom number from the top number.

Subtracting Larger Numbers
Subtract.

13. $\begin{array}{r} 56 \\ -33 \\ \hline \end{array}$ **14.** $\begin{array}{r} 778 \\ -251 \\ \hline \end{array}$ **15.** $\begin{array}{r} 160 \\ -140 \\ \hline \end{array}$

16. $\begin{array}{r} 3,457 \\ -1,442 \\ \hline \end{array}$ **17.** $\begin{array}{r} 8,705 \\ -3,402 \\ \hline \end{array}$ **18.** $\begin{array}{r} 8,584 \\ -4,122 \\ \hline \end{array}$

Test Tip
Look for clue words to help you
to solve word problems.

Solving Problems Using Subtraction

Solve each problem. Write the clue words. Show your work.

19. The history book has 1,759 pages. Cory read 632 pages. How many pages are left to be read?

20. Jan bought a used car. He drove the car 925 miles the first year. He drove the car 1,200 miles the second year. How many more miles did he drive the second year than the first year?

21. The school bought 452 reams of paper last month. This month, 296 reams were bought. How many reams were bought in all?

Test Tip
Line up the digits in vertical
form by place value. Then
subtract.

Subtracting with Regrouping

Subtract. Show your work in vertical form.

22.
$$859 - 74$$

23.
$$856 - 177$$

24.
$$600 - 361$$

25. $5,000 - 205$ 26. $7,006 - 3,674$

27. $695 - 547$ 28. $25,080 - 6,757$

29. $8,706 - 983$ 30. $20,000 - 18,394$

Group Activity

With your group, use the newspaper to find the price of the same model car from different places. Compare the price of each car. Then compare the options that come with each car. Discuss with your group which car you would buy and why. Record your decision and reasons on paper.

A flash of lightning is often followed by a rumble of thunder. Suppose the time between the lightning and the thunder is 2 seconds. How far away did the lightning strike? Multiply the time by the speed of sound, 1,100 feet per second.

Chapter 4

Multiplying Whole Numbers

Words to Know

multiplication	a quick way to add; repeated addition
multiply	to add a number to itself one or more times; $2 + 2 + 2 + 2 = 8$ or $4 \times 2 = 8$
factors	the numbers that are multiplied to obtain a product
product	the final answer to a multiplication problem
partial product	number obtained by multiplying a number by only one digit of a two or more digit number

Nutrition Label Project

Collect nutrition labels from your favorite foods. These labels give the number of servings per package. They also give nutritional information for one serving. Find out how many Calories there are in an entire package. Multiply the number of servings by the Calories. Share your information with the class.

Learning Objectives

- Multiply whole numbers.
- Multiply larger numbers.
- Multiply with regrouping.
- Multiply numbers by 10, 100, 1,000.
- Multiply by numbers that contain zero.
- Solve word problems using multiplication.
- Solve two-part word problems.
- Apply multiplication to counting items for inventory.

4·1   What Is Multiplication?

Multiplication is the process of adding the same number one or more times.

EXAMPLE 1

For whole numbers, the product is greater than either factor unless 1 is a factor. Use this fact to check your product.

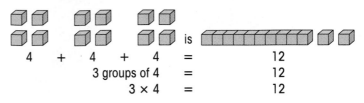

$$4 \quad + \quad 4 \quad + \quad 4 \quad = \quad 12$$
$$\text{3 groups of 4} \quad = \quad 12$$
$$3 \times 4 \quad = \quad 12$$

The numbers you **multiply** are called **factors**. The answer is called the **product**.

EXAMPLE 2

Horizontal	Vertical

$$3 \quad \times \quad 4 \quad = \quad 12 \qquad \text{or}$$

Factor $\times$ Factor $=$ Product

$$3 \leftarrow \text{Factor}$$
$$\times \;\; 4 \leftarrow \text{Factor}$$
$$\overline{12} \leftarrow \text{Product}$$

The order in multiplication does not matter.

$$3 \times 4 = 4 \times 3 = 12$$

Practice A

Write each addition problem as a multiplication problem.

1. $8 + 8 = 16$

2. $9 + 9 + 9 = 27$

3. $3 + 3 + 3 + 3 + 3 = 15$

4. $6 + 6 + 6 + 6 = 24$

5. $8 + 8 + 8 + 8 + 8 + 8 + 8 = 56$

6. $3 + 3 + 3 + 3 = 12$

Practice B

Write each problem in vertical form using numbers.

7. $6 \times 7 = 42$ **8.** $9 \times 2 = 18$ **9.** $8 \times 3 = 24$ **10.** $4 \times 5 = 20$

Basic Multiplication

You can use the multiplication table below to learn the basic multiplication facts.

► **EXAMPLE**

Use the table to multiply. 5×6

STEP 1   Find the row that begins with the number **5**.

STEP 2   Find the column that begins with the number **6**.

STEP 3   The product is where the row meets the column.

x	0	1	2	3	4	5	6	7	8	9
0	0	0	0	0	0	0	0	0	0	0
1	0	1	2	3	4	5	6	7	8	9
2	0	2	4	6	8	10	12	14	16	18
3	0	3	6	9	12	15	18	21	24	27
4	0	4	8	12	16	20	24	28	32	36
5	0	5	10	15	20	25	**30**	35	40	45
6	0	6	12	18	24	30	36	42	48	54
7	0	7	14	21	28	35	42	49	56	63
8	0	8	16	24	32	40	48	56	64	72
9	0	9	18	27	36	45	54	63	72	81

Factor

Factor →

Product

The multiplication table shows that $5 \times 6 = 30$.

Practice

Use the multiplication table to multiply.

1. 6×5 **2.** 8×7 **3.** 3×9 **4.** 6×7

5. 4×3 **6.** 7×7 **7.** 8×9 **8.** 5×4

9. 7×3 **10.** 4×7 **11.** 2×9 **12.** 8×8

13. 4×5 **14.** 3×6 **15.** 7×8 **16.** 9×4

4-3 ► Multiplying Larger Numbers

You will use basic multiplication facts to multiply larger numbers. When you multiply larger numbers, multiply each place.

► **EXAMPLE 1**

Remember: $3 \times 2 = 6$
$3 \times 7 = 21$

Multiply. 3×72

STEP 1 Multiply the digit in the *ones* place by 3.

$$
\begin{array}{r}
72 \\
\times\ \ 3 \\
\hline
6\ (3 \times 2)
\end{array}
$$

STEP 2 Multiply the digit in the *tens* place by 3.

$$
\begin{array}{r}
72 \\
\times\ \ \ 3 \\
\hline
216\ (3 \times 7)
\end{array}
$$

The product of 3 and 72 is 216.

When you multiply by a two-digit number, there will be two **partial products**. Add the partial products to get the product.

► **EXAMPLE 2**

Remember: $3 \times 2 = 6$
$3 \times 7 = 21$
$2 \times 2 = 4$
$2 \times 7 = 14$

Multiply. 72×23

STEP 1 Multiply 72 by the *ones* place in the bottom number.

$$
\begin{array}{r}
72 \\
\times\ \ 23 \\
\hline
216\ \text{First partial product}
\end{array}
$$

STEP 2 Multiply 72 by the *tens* place in the bottom number. Write a zero in the *ones* place. Write the second partial product to the left of the zero.

$$
\begin{array}{r}
72 \\
\times\ \ 23 \\
\hline
216 \\
1\,440\ \text{Second partial product}
\end{array}
$$

STEP 3 Add the partial products.

$$
\begin{array}{r}
72 \\
\times\ \ 23 \\
\hline
216 \\
+\ 1\,440 \\
\hline
1{,}656\ \text{Product}
\end{array}
$$

The product of 72 and 23 is 1,656.

You can use the same steps to multiply by larger numbers.

▶ **EXAMPLE 3**

Multiply. 512×431

STEP 1 Multiply 512 by the *ones* place in the bottom number.

```
    512
  × 431
    512  First partial product
```

STEP 2 Multiply 512 by the *tens* place in the bottom number. Write a zero in the *ones* place. Write the second partial product to the left of the zero.

```
     512
   × 431
     512
  15 360  Second partial product
```

STEP 3 Multiply 512 by the *hundreds* place in the bottom number. Write zeros in the *tens* and *ones* places. Write the third partial product to the left of the zeros.

```
      512
    × 431
      512
   15 360
  204 800  Third partial product
```

STEP 4 Add the partial products.

```
        512
      × 431
        512
     15 360
  +  204 800
    220,672  Product
```

The product of 512 and 431 is 220,672.

Practice A

Multiply.

1.   43
       × 3

2.   81
       × 8

3.   52
       × 4

4.   64
       × 2

5.   93
       × 3

6.   124
       × 2

7.   532
       × 3

8.   312
       × 4

9.   644
       × 2

10.   421
       × 4

Practice B

Multiply.

11. $\begin{array}{r} 63 \\ \times\ 23 \\ \hline \end{array}$ **12.** $\begin{array}{r} 87 \\ \times\ 11 \\ \hline \end{array}$ **13.** $\begin{array}{r} 71 \\ \times\ 24 \\ \hline \end{array}$ **14.** $\begin{array}{r} 52 \\ \times\ 42 \\ \hline \end{array}$ **15.** $\begin{array}{r} 93 \\ \times\ 31 \\ \hline \end{array}$

16. $\begin{array}{r} 811 \\ \times\ 22 \\ \hline \end{array}$ **17.** $\begin{array}{r} 812 \\ \times\ 34 \\ \hline \end{array}$ **18.** $\begin{array}{r} 623 \\ \times\ 31 \\ \hline \end{array}$ **19.** $\begin{array}{r} 833 \\ \times\ 32 \\ \hline \end{array}$ **20.** $\begin{array}{r} 231 \\ \times\ 12 \\ \hline \end{array}$

21. $\begin{array}{r} 943 \\ \times\ 121 \\ \hline \end{array}$ **22.** $\begin{array}{r} 731 \\ \times\ 332 \\ \hline \end{array}$ **23.** $\begin{array}{r} 711 \\ \times\ 421 \\ \hline \end{array}$ **24.** $\begin{array}{r} 523 \\ \times\ 123 \\ \hline \end{array}$ **25.** $\begin{array}{r} 431 \\ \times\ 213 \\ \hline \end{array}$

Practice C

Multiply. Remember to line up the digits in each number by place value.

26. 82×4 **27.** 63×3 **28.** 73×23

29. 97×11 **30.** 413×22 **31.** 623×313

32. 523×32 **33.** 712×431 **34.** 432×123

Everyday Problem Solving

This sign shows the ticket prices at Wild Rides park.

1. How much does it cost for 5 rides on the Corkscrew? Multiply 5 by the cost of the Corkscrew.

2. How much does it cost for 3 rides on the Starclimber?

3. Ayanna plans to take 5 rides on the Corkscrew. She plans to take 3 rides on the Water Slide. Why should Ayanna buy an all-day pass?

Wild Rides Ticket Prices	
All Day Pass (unlimited rides)	$21
Corkscrew (each ride)	$ 4
Starclimber (each ride)	$ 3
Water Slide (each ride)	$ 2

You can use a calculator to check your multiplication.

Ann wrote this multiplication on the board. Is it correct?

$$
\begin{array}{r}
321 \\
\times\ \ 34 \\
\hline
1\,284 \leftarrow \text{Partial product} \\
9\,530 \leftarrow \text{Partial product} \\
\hline
10{,}814 \leftarrow \text{Product}
\end{array}
$$

To find an error, first check the partial products.

PRESS [3] [2] [1] [×] [4] [=] | 1284.

PRESS [3] [2] [1] [×] [3] [0] [=] | 9630.

> **Calculator Tip**
> Remember that the 3 in 34 means 3 tens. Multiply 321 by 30 for the second partial product.

Ann made a mistake in the second partial product. Now, add the correct partial products found on the calculator.

PRESS [1] [2] [8] [4] [+] [9] [6] [3] [0] [=] | 10914.

Is 10,914 the correct product? Multiply 321 × 34 on the calculator to check.

PRESS [3] [2] [1] [×] [3] [4] [=] | 10914.

10,914 is the correct product!

Use your calculator to check each problem. If there is an error, write the problem correctly. There may be an error in the addition.

1.	2.	3.	4.
502	423	1312	611
× 41	× 32	× 33	× 78
502	846	3 936	4 888
+ 2 008	+ 12 590	+ 39 360	+ 42 770
2,510	13,036	43,296	46,558

4·4   Multiplying with One Regrouping

Sometimes, a multiplication fact has a product greater than 9. For example,

$$6 \times 8 = 48$$

You can rename 48 as 4 tens + 8 ones.

▶ **EXAMPLE**

Remember:
$8 \times 6 = 48$
$8 \times 7 = 56$
$8 \times 5 = 40$

Multiply. 576×8

STEP 1   Multiply the digit in the *ones* place by 8. Rename 48: 4 *tens* + 8 *ones*. Regroup. Put the 8 in the *ones* place. Put the 4 above the *tens* place.

$$\begin{array}{r} {\scriptstyle 4} \\ 576 \\ \times \quad 8 \\ \hline 8 \end{array}$$

STEP 2   Multiply the digit in the *tens* place by 8. Add 56 + 4. Put the 0 in the *tens* place. Put a 6 above the *hundreds* place.

$$\begin{array}{r} {\scriptstyle 6\ 4} \\ 576 \\ \times \quad 8 \\ \hline 08 \end{array}$$

STEP 3   Multiply the digit in the *hundreds* place by 8. Add 40 + 6. Put the sum in the *hundreds* and *thousands* places.

$$\begin{array}{r} {\scriptstyle 6\ 4} \\ 576 \\ \times \quad 8 \\ \hline 4,608 \end{array}$$

The product of 576 and 8 is 4,608.

Practice A

Multiply. Be sure to show your work as done above.

1. 79 × 4	**2.** 83 × 6	**3.** 16 × 9	**4.** 283 × 2	**5.** 154 × 8
6. 673 × 5	**7.** 88 × 6	**8.** 538 × 4	**9.** 47 × 7	**10.** 148 × 9

Practice B

Multiply. Regroup if you need to.

11.	**12.**	**13.**	**14.**	**15.**
794	521	681	345	411
× 6	× 4	× 7	× 5	× 8

16.	**17.**	**18.**	**19.**	**20.**
26	38	73	42	63
× 15	× 41	× 12	× 28	× 53

21.	**22.**	**23.**	**24.**	**25.**
531	812	189	926	423
× 24	× 42	× 17	× 51	× 232

Practice C

Multiply. Remember to line up the digits in each number
by place value.

26. 56×8 **27.** 538×4 **28.** $4,508 \times 4$

29. 681×17 **30.** 862×81 **31.** $7,641 \times 9$

32. 775×11 **33.** 321×34 **34.** 423×215

Everyday Problem Solving

Joe has $500 to spend on a camping vacation.
He saw this ad in a magazine.

1. How much will 4 days of
   fishing cost?

2. How much will 4 nights at a
   cabin cost?

3. How much spending money will
   Joe have left over if he chooses the
   package deal?

Camping and Fishing
Adventures

1-Day Fishing	$25
1-Night Cabin Stay	$65

4-Day Package Deal
includes
Fishing and
Cabin Stay $299

Multiplying with More Than One Regrouping

4·5

Sometimes, there will be regrouping in more than one partial product. Then, there will be more than one row of regrouping digits.

▶ **EXAMPLE**

Multiply. 536×96

STEP 1 Multiply 536 by the ones digit in the bottom number. Regroup as needed.

$$\begin{array}{r} {}^{2\ 3} \\ 536 \\ \times\ \ \ 96 \\ \hline 3216 \end{array} \text{(536} \times \text{6 ones)}$$

STEP 2 Cross out the regrouping digits 23. Then, multiply 536 by the *tens* digit in the bottom number. Regroup as needed.

$$\begin{array}{r} {}^{3\ 5} \\ {}^{\cancel{2}\cancel{3}} \\ 536 \\ \times\ \ \ 96 \\ \hline 3216 \\ 48240 \end{array} \text{(536} \times \text{9 tens)}$$

STEP 3 Add the partial products.

$$\begin{array}{r} {}^{3\ 5} \\ {}^{\cancel{2}\cancel{3}} \\ 536 \\ \times\ \ \ 96 \\ \hline 3\ 216 \\ +\ 48\ 240 \\ \hline 51{,}456 \end{array}$$

The product of 536 and 96 is 51,456.

Practice A

Multiply. Remember to show the regrouping digits.

1.	**2.**	**3.**	**4.**
374	598	676	485
$\times\ 42$	$\times\ 63$	$\times\ 28$	$\times\ 56$

Practice B

Multiply. Regroup if you need to.

5. 38
  × 41

6. 74
  × 36

7. 87
  × 54

8. 45
  × 28

9. 412
  × 39

10. 943
  × 12

11. 593
  × 76

12. 925
  × 88

Practice C

Multiply. Remember to line up the digits in each number by place value.

13. $6,934 \times 46$

14. $67 \times 1,345$

15. $2,985 \times 72$

16. 196×519

17. 397×436

18. $3,278 \times 125$

Everyday Problem Solving

This table shows last month's driving records for four of Ace Trucking's drivers.

1. Complete the table by finding the distance each driver traveled. To find the distance, multiply speed by hours driven. (distance = speed × hours)

2. Which driver traveled the greatest distance?

3. Which driver traveled the least distance?

4. What is the total number of miles the drivers traveled altogether?

Ace Trucking			
Driver	Average Speed	Hours Driven	Total Distance
Ann	58 mph	75 hrs	?
Don	61 mph	58 hrs	?
Carlos	65 mph	97 hrs	?
Bianco	55 mph	83 hrs	?

Problem Solving: Clue Words for Multiplication

Clue words can help you find the answer to a word problem.

CLUE WORDS FOR MULTIPLICATION			
of	*for 6 hours*	*in 5 months*	*at $13 each*

▶ **EXAMPLE**

Norm packs 16 boxes in 1 hour. How many boxes does Norm pack in 7 hours?

STEP 1   READ   What do you need to find out?
You need to find how many boxes Norm can pack in 7 hours.

STEP 2   PLAN   What do you need to do?
The clue words **in 7 hours** tell you to multiply the number of boxes by the number of hours.

STEP 3   DO   Follow the plan.
Multiply 16 boxes by 7 hours.

$$\begin{array}{r} 16 \\ \times\ \ 7 \\ \hline 112 \text{ boxes} \end{array}$$

STEP 4   CHECK   Does your answer make sense?
Draw a picture.

16 boxes	*16 boxes*	*16 boxes*	*16 boxes*
1st hour	2nd hour	3rd hour	4th hour

16 boxes	*16 boxes*	*16 boxes*
5th hour	6th hour	7th hour

Add to find the total number of boxes.

$$16 + 16 + 16 + 16 + 16 + 16 + 16 = 112 ✓$$

Norm packs 112 boxes in 7 hours.

Problem Solving

READ the problem. Answer the questions under PLAN.
DO the plan to solve the problem.

1. Mr. Ryan ordered 23 computers at $1,295 each. How much did he spend for computers?

   PLAN
   What are the clue words?
   What do the clue words tell you to do?

2. The drama club put on a play. A total of 1,246 tickets were sold. Tickets were sold for $8. How much money did the drama club make from ticket sales?

   PLAN
   What are the clue words?
   What do the clue words tell you to do?

3. A program was on sale at the play. The program cost $2. They sold 987 programs. How much money was made from selling programs?

   PLAN
   There are no clue words. Each program costs the same, so you can multiply the cost of the program by the number of programs sold.

Problem Solving Strategy

Often, problems can be solved by working backward.

Diane packs 9 boxes in 1 hour. She packs 63 boxes. How many hours does she work?

Fill in the blank to find the number of hours.

$$\begin{array}{r} 9 \\ \times\ \blacksquare \\ \hline 63 \end{array}$$

4·7 Multiplying Whole Numbers by 10, 100, 1,000

You can use what you know to learn a shortcut for multiplying whole numbers by 10, by 100, or by 1,000.

$$45 \times 10 = 450$$
1 zero   1 zero

$$45 \times 100 = 4,500$$
2 zeros   2 zeros

$$45 \times 1,000 = 45,000$$
3 zeros   3 zeros

To multiply by 10, by 100, or by 1,000, place as many zeros as you need to the right of the number.

▶ EXAMPLE

Multiply. 617×100

2 zeros

STEP 1 Count the zeros in 100. 617×100

STEP 2 Write 617. Then place two $617 \times 100 = 61,700$
zeros to the right of the number.

The product of 617 and 100 is 61,700.

Practice A

Multiply.

1. 37×10

2. 86×100

3. $59 \times 1,000$

4. 29×100

5. $5,279 \times 100$

6. 305×10

7. 596×100

8. $421 \times 1,000$

9. $1,401 \times 1,000$

10. $152 \times 1,000$

11. $3,715 \times 1,000$

12. $700 \times 1,000$

ON-THE-JOB MATH
Inventory Clerk

Inventory is the number of goods a store has on the shelves and in the warehouse. Bob is an inventory clerk. He counts the items in a store.

Bob travels to different stores everyday. He likes his job, because he meets new people and travels.

Bob uses multiplication to make his job easier.

Bob has to fill in the table below. To begin, he has to find out how many Tasty Oats boxes there are in the store. He counts 16 cartons on the shelves. He knows there are 12 boxes in each carton. So, Bob multiplies.

Bob takes inventory on all kinds of food. Here, Bob is taking an inventory of avocados.

$$
\begin{array}{r}
16 \text{ cartons} \\
\times\ 12 \text{ boxes per carton} \\
\hline
32 \\
+\ 160 \\
\hline
192 \text{ total boxes of cereal}
\end{array}
$$

Copy the table below. Multiply to find the total number of boxes of each cereal. The first is done for you.

Name of Cereal	Number of Cartons	Boxes per Carton	Total Boxes of Cereal
Tasty Oats	16	12	192
Sweet Puffs	72	24	?
Healthy Grains	126	16	?
Berry Bran	35	48	?

Critical Thinking

While taking inventory of pasta, Bob found 5 cartons of spaghetti. They do not say how many boxes are in one carton. What should he do to finish the inventory?

Multiplying by Numbers That Contain Zero

When you multiply any number by zero, the product is zero.

$$3 \times 0 = 0 \quad 978 \times 0 = 0 \quad 1{,}349{,}576 \times 0 = 0$$

You can multiply by a number that contains a zero. The partial product for the zero digit is zero.

▶ **EXAMPLE**

Multiply. 927×305

STEP 1 Multiply by the digit in the *ones* place.

$$
\begin{array}{r}
{\scriptstyle 1\ 3} \\
927 \\
\times\ 305 \\
\hline
4635
\end{array}
$$

STEP 2 Multiply by the digit in the *tens* place. Place a zero in the *ones* place as a placeholder. Then, write a zero for each digit in 927.

$$
\begin{array}{r}
{\scriptstyle 1\ 3} \\
927 \\
\times\ 305 \\
\hline
4635 \\
0000
\end{array}
$$

STEP 3 Multiply by digit in the *hundreds* place. Add the partial products.

$$
\begin{array}{r}
{\scriptstyle \cancel{\times}\ \overset{2}{\cancel{3}}} \\
927 \\
\times\quad 305 \\
\hline
4\ 635 \\
0\ 000 \\
+\ 278\ 100 \\
\hline
282{,}735
\end{array}
$$

The product of 927 and 305 is 282,735.

Practice A

Multiply. Remember to write all the partial products.

1.	498 × 70	**2.**	926 × 306	**3.**	793 × 50	**4.**	387 × 942	**5.**	580 × 409
6.	635 × 804	**7.**	829 × 470	**8.**	625 × 709	**9.**	360 × 549	**10.**	290 × 378
11.	537 × 420	**12.**	805 × 609	**13.**	970 × 260	**14.**	761 × 801	**15.**	807 × 903

Practice B

Multiply. Remember to line up the digits in each number by place value.

16. 623×506

17. 535×402

18. 645×204

19. 29×609

20. 753×250

21. 850×503

Everyday Problem Solving

Jon wants to buy a car. He compares the distance each car can travel on a full tank of gas.

1. Find the distance Car A can travel on a full tank of gas. Multiply 35 mpg by 20 gallons.

2. Which car can travel 616 miles on a full tank of gas?

3. Which car can travel the farthest on a full tank of gas?

Car	Miles per Gallon	Size of Tank
Car A	35 mpg	20 gallons
Car B	23 mpg	25 gallons
Car C	28 mpg	22 gallons

Problem Solving: Two-Part Problems

Some problems have a hidden question. You need to answer this question before you can solve the problem.

EXAMPLE

Matt bought 6 basketballs for his team. Each basketball costs $15. He bought a basketball hoop for $32. How much did Matt spend altogether?

STEP 1   **READ** **What do you need to find out?**
You need to find how much Matt spent altogether. But first, you need to find how much 6 basketballs cost.

STEP 2   **PLAN** **What do you need to do?**
How much do 6 basketballs cost?
Multiply to find out.
How much did Matt spend altogether?
Add to find out.

STEP 3   **DO** **Follow the plan.**

Multiply   Add

$$\begin{array}{r} \overset{3}{\$15} \\ \times\ 6 \\ \hline \$90 \text{ for basketballs} \end{array}$$

$$\begin{array}{r} \$90 \text{ basketballs} \\ +\ \$32 \text{ basketball hoop} \\ \hline \$122 \text{ altogether} \end{array}$$

STEP 4   **CHECK** **Does your answer make sense?**
Use a calculator to check.

PRESS [1] [5] [×] [6] [=] | ⎸ 90. ⎹

Do not clear the display.

PRESS [+] [3] [2] [=] | ⎸ 122. ⎹ ✓

Matt spent $122 for the 6 basketballs and a basketball hoop.

Problem Solving

READ the problem. Answer the questions under PLAN.
DO the plan to solve the problem.

1. Zachary saves $25 a week. There are 52 weeks in a year. How much will he save in 5 years?

   PLAN
   How much will Zachary save in 1 year?
   How much will he save in 5 years?

2. A round-trip plane ticket to Jamaica costs $529. Four people can stay for 1 week in a hotel room for $1,248. How much will a Jamaican vacation for 4 people cost?

   PLAN
   What is the cost of 4 plane tickets?
   What is the cost for 4 people to stay in a hotel for a week?
   What is the cost of the whole trip?

3. A new theater opened in town. The first night it sold 1,245 season tickets at $125 each. It also sold $2,452 worth of snacks. How much money did the theater make its first night?

   PLAN
   How much money was made from ticket sales?
   How much was made from snack sales?
   How much money was made altogether?

Problem Solving Strategy

Sometimes, you need to make a table to solve a word problem.

Al counts the money in a cash register. There are 56 ten-dollar bills, 78 five-dollar bills, and 123 one-dollar bills. How much money is there altogether?

Cashier Name __AL__

BILLS		COUNT		AMOUNT
$10	x	56	=	____
$ 5	x	78	=	____
$ 1	x	123	=	____

| factor |
| multiplication |
| multiply |
| partial product |
| product |

Vocabulary Review

Tell whether *true* or *false*. If it is false, replace the underlined word to make it true.

1. Two numbers that are multiplied together are called <u>factors</u>.

2. Multiplication is a faster way to do repeated <u>addition</u>.

3. The answer to a multiplication problem is called the <u>product</u>.

4. Some <u>addition</u> problems have a partial product.

5. **Writing** Explain partial products to a classmate. Draw a sample problem and label it.

Chapter Quiz

LESSONS 4·1 to 4·3

Test Tip
When multiplying larger numbers, remember to move the second partial product over one place value to the left.

Multiplying Numbers
Multiply.

1. 6×7 2. 9×2 3. 8×5

4. 3×5 5. 3×8 6. 7×8

7. 4×9 8. 9×8 9. 6×4

10. $\begin{array}{r} 22 \\ \times\ 13 \\ \hline \end{array}$ 11. $\begin{array}{r} 35 \\ \times\ 11 \\ \hline \end{array}$ 12. $\begin{array}{r} 31 \\ \times\ 15 \\ \hline \end{array}$

13. $\begin{array}{r} 423 \\ \times\ \ 22 \\ \hline \end{array}$ 14. $\begin{array}{r} 123 \\ \times\ \ 12 \\ \hline \end{array}$ 15. $\begin{array}{r} 3,112 \\ \times\ \ \ \ 21 \\ \hline \end{array}$

LESSONS 4·4 and 4·5

Multiplying with Regrouping
Multiply.

Test Tip
When the product of digits in a column is 10 or more, you must regroup.

16. 65	**17.** 78	**18.** 87
$\underline{\times3}$	$\underline{\times5}$	$\underline{\times32}$

19. 87	**20.** 345	**21.** $3,463$
$\underline{\times64}$	$\underline{\times21}$	$\underline{\times164}$

LESSONS 4·6 and 4·9

Solving Problems Using Multiplication
Solve each problem.

Test Tip
Read problems carefully and look for clue words that tell you what to do.

22. Suni bought 4 pairs of shoes on sale for $28 each. How much did Suni spend on shoes?

23. Chester earned $345 dollars a month for 3 months during the summer delivering papers. During the rest of the year, he earns $1,350 on his paper route. How much does he earn in 1 year delivering newspapers?

LESSONS 4·7 and 4·8

Multiplying with Zeros

24. 40	**25.** 102	**26.** 307
$\underline{\times3}$	$\underline{\times6}$	$\underline{\times46}$

Test Tip
When multiplying by multiples of 10, add the number of zeros in the multiple of 10 factor to the other factor to find the product.

27. 231×10 **28.** $4,060 \times 100$

29. $6,023 \times 1,000$ **30.** 500×20

Group Activity
Work with your group to plan a four-city concert tour for a musical group. You must decide how much to charge for tickets. Use an almanac to find the number of seats in four stadiums. Estimate how much money will be made if all the tickets are sold for each performance.

The rain forest is a place where many types of trees and plants grow. People are cutting trees down without replanting so animals are losing their homes. Right now, 20 acres of trees are being cut down every 5 minutes. How many acres are being cut every 1 minute? Divide.

Chapter 5 Dividing Whole Numbers

Words to Know

division	the process of finding out how many times one number contains another
dividend	the number to be divided
divisor	the number to divide by
quotient	the number obtained by dividing one number into another; the answer in a division problem
remainder	the number left over in a division problem

Life Journal Project

In your journal, list all the ways you think that you use division in your life. Check the list each day and see if you can add more ideas. For each idea, write a word problem that shows how division is used in your life. Go through the chapter for ideas.

Learning Objectives

- Divide whole numbers.
- Divide larger numbers.
- Divide and get remainders.
- Check division problems.
- Use estimating to choose the best answer.
- Solve word problems using division.
- Solve word problems using any operation
- Apply division to find miles per gallon.

5·1 What Is Division?

Division is the process of finding how many times one number contains another.

> **EXAMPLE 1**

What is 12 divided by 3?

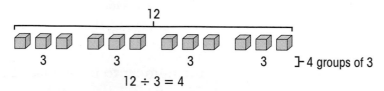

$$12 \div 3 = 4$$

The number to be divided is the **dividend**. The number to divide by is the **divisor**. The answer is the **quotient**. Division problems can be written in two different forms.

> **EXAMPLE 2**

$$\underset{\text{Dividend}}{12} \div \underset{\text{Divisor}}{3} = \underset{\text{Quotient}}{4} \quad \text{or} \quad 3\overset{4}{\overline{)12}}$$

Quotient

Divisor   Dividend

Practice A

Use numbers to write each division problem in both forms.

1. Eight divided by two equals four.

2. Sixteen divided by eight equals two.

3. Six divided by three equals two.

4. Thirty-two divided by four equals eight.

Practice B

Use numbers to write each problem in the other form.

5. $8 \div 2 = 4$

6. $28 \div 4 = 7$

7. $18 \div 6 = 3$

8. $48 \div 6 = 8$

5·2 Basic Division

You can use the multiplication table below to learn the basic division facts.

▶ **EXAMPLE**

What is $12 \div 3$?

STEP 1 Find the row that begins with the number 3.

STEP 2 Move across that row until you find the number 12.

STEP 3 Move up that column until you come to the top. The number in that box is the quotient.

$$12 \div 3 = 4$$

x	0	1	2	3	4	5	6	7	8	9
0	0	0	0	0	0	0	0	0	0	0
1	0	1	2	3	4	5	6	7	8	9
2	0	2	4	6	8	10	12	14	16	18
3	0	3	6	9	**12**	15	18	21	24	27
4	0	4	8	12	16	20	24	28	32	36
5	0	5	10	15	20	25	30	35	40	45
6	0	6	12	18	24	30	36	42	48	54
7	0	7	14	21	28	35	42	49	56	63
8	0	8	16	24	32	40	48	56	64	72
9	0	9	18	27	36	45	54	63	72	81

The multiplication table shows that $12 \div 3 = 4$.

Practice

Use the multiplication table to find the quotient.

1. $6 \div 2$ **2.** $9 \div 3$ **3.** $15 \div 5$ **4.** $32 \div 4$ **5.** $49 \div 7$

6. $3\overline{)6}$ **7.** $9\overline{)18}$ **8.** $7\overline{)21}$ **9.** $6\overline{)30}$ **10.** $8\overline{)40}$

11. $27 \div 3$ **12.** $36 \div 9$ **13.** $9\overline{)81}$ **14.** $7\overline{)63}$ **15.** $4\overline{)16}$

5·3 ▶ Dividing with Remainders

The **remainder** is the number left over in division. What happens when you divide 7 by 2?

3 groups of 2 —[2   2   2   1 ←— Remainder 1

$7 \div 2 = 3 \text{ R}1$

There are 3 equal groups with 1 left over.
The remainder is 1. You can write:

$7 \div 2 = 3 \text{ R } 1$

Remainder 1

You can do division in another way.

▶ **EXAMPLE**

dividend ÷ divisor

↓

divisor $\overline{)\text{dividend}}$

What is $17 \div 3$?

STEP 1 Rewrite the division problem. $3\overline{)17}$

STEP 2 Think:
"What times 3 is closest to 17 without going over?"
$$3 \times 4 = 12$$
$$3 \times 5 = 15$$
$$3 \times 6 = 18$$

Write **5** above the *ones* place. $\dfrac{5}{3\overline{)17}}$ ←— Five 3s in 17

STEP 3 Multiply **5 × 3.** Write the product underneath 17.
$$\begin{array}{r} 5 \\ 3\overline{)17} \\ 15 \end{array}$$

STEP 4 Subtract.
The remainder is 2.
Check that the remainder is less than the divisor. $2 < 3$ ✓
Stop dividing.
$$\begin{array}{r} 5 \\ 3\overline{)17} \\ -15 \\ \hline 2 \end{array}$$ ←— Remainder

STEP 5 Write the quotient with the remainder in the answer.
$$\begin{array}{r} 5 \text{ R2} \\ 3\overline{)17} \end{array}$$

17 divided by 3 is 5 R 2.

Practice A

Divide. If the remainder is 0, do not write it.

1. $7 \div 3$ **2.** $6\overline{)9}$ **3.** $5 \div 2$ **4.** $3\overline{)9}$

5. $9 \div 4$ **6.** $5\overline{)8}$ **7.** $5\overline{)7}$ **8.** $4\overline{)5}$

9. $8 \div 3$ **10.** $2\overline{)9}$ **11.** $5 \div 3$ **12.** $5\overline{)9}$

13. $7 \div 4$ **14.** $5\overline{)6}$ **15.** $9 \div 8$ **16.** $8 \div 2$

Practice B

Divide. Remember to write the quotient above the ones place.

17. $11 \div 5$ **18.** $3\overline{)10}$ **19.** $20 \div 4$ **20.** $6\overline{)25}$

21. $27 \div 8$ **22.** $8\overline{)50}$ **23.** $51 \div 6$ **24.** $4\overline{)36}$

25. $37 \div 5$ **26.** $9\overline{)30}$ **27.** $3\overline{)25}$ **28.** $8\overline{)20}$

29. $42 \div 8$ **30.** $5\overline{)18}$ **31.** $8\overline{)18}$ **32.** $7\overline{)57}$

33. $48 \div 9$ **34.** $7\overline{)55}$ **35.** $4\overline{)39}$ **36.** $6\overline{)52}$

Everyday Problem Solving

Grant School has a small lunchroom. Six students can sit at each table. Find out how many tables you need for each group of students.

1. There are 30 students. How many tables do they need? Divide 30 by 6.

2. There are 28 students. Will they need 4 tables or 5 tables. Why?

3. There are 38 students. How many tables do they need?

4. Are 9 tables enough for 53 students? Why?

5·4 Dividing Larger Numbers

You can divide larger numbers one step at a time.
To begin, you need to decide where to place the first
digit in the quotient.

EXAMPLE

Remember:
$4 \times 1 = 4$
$4 \times 2 = 8$
$4 \times 3 = 12$
$4 \times 4 = 16$

Divide. $137 \div 4$

STEP 1 Rewrite the division problem.

$$4\overline{)137}$$

STEP 2 Does 4 divide into 1? No.
Does 4 divide into 13? Yes.
Think: "What times 4 is
closest to 13 without
going over?" $3 \times 4 = 12$

$$\begin{array}{r} 3 \\ 4\overline{)137} \end{array}$$

Write 3 above the *tens* place.

STEP 3 Multiply 3×4. Write the product
underneath 13. Then, subtract.

Bring down the next digit.

$$\begin{array}{r} 3 \\ 4\overline{)137} \\ -12\downarrow \\ \hline 17 \end{array}$$

STEP 4 Does 4 divide into 17? Yes.
Think: "What times 4 is
closest to 17 without going
over?" $4 \times 4 = 16$

$$\begin{array}{r} 34 \\ 4\overline{)137} \\ -12\downarrow \\ \hline 17 \end{array}$$

Write 4 above the *ones* place.

STEP 5 Multiply 4×4.
Write the product underneath 17.
Then, subtract.

Check that the remainder is less
than the divisor. $1 < 4$ ✓
Stop dividing.

$$\begin{array}{r} 34 \\ 4\overline{)137} \\ -12\downarrow \\ \hline 17 \\ -16 \\ \hline 1 \end{array} \leftarrow \text{Remainder}$$

STEP 6 Write the quotient with the
remainder in the answer.

$$\begin{array}{r} 34 \text{ R1} \\ 4\overline{)137} \end{array}$$

The quotient of $137 \div 4$ is 34 R1.

Practice A

Divide.

1. $4\overline{)84}$ 2. $2\overline{)86}$ 3. $3\overline{)39}$ 4. $2\overline{)27}$

5. $3\overline{)68}$ 6. $4\overline{)96}$ 7. $8\overline{)96}$ 8. $3\overline{)84}$

9. $6\overline{)89}$ 10. $5\overline{)90}$ 11. $7\overline{)84}$ 12. $6\overline{)96}$

Practice B

Divide.

13. $4\overline{)848}$ 14. $5\overline{)560}$ 15. $4\overline{)328}$ 16. $3\overline{)278}$

17. $3\overline{)282}$ 18. $3\overline{)298}$ 19. $3\overline{)685}$ 20. $6\overline{)869}$

21. $7\overline{)364}$ 22. $6\overline{)438}$ 23. $5\overline{)675}$ 24. $8\overline{)369}$

Everyday Problem Solving

The Food Co-op helps people in need. Henry is dividing the available food among 9 families. Each family will receive the same amount of food.

1. How many cans of tomato soup will each family receive? Divide 46 by 9. How many cans are left over?

2. How many muffins will each family receive? How many are left over?

3. Can Henry give 4 boxes of pasta to each family? Why or why not?

4. Henry wants to give each family 3 jars of spaghetti sauce. How many more jars of sauce does he need?

Available Food
46 cans of tomato soup
100 eggs
60 muffins
34 boxes of pasta
18 jars of spaghetti sauce

Checking Division

You can check the answer to a division problem. Multiply the quotient by the divisor. If this product equals the dividend, your answer is correct.

▶ **EXAMPLE 1**

143 ← Quotient
2)286 ← Dividend
↑
Divisor

Check the division problem.

$$\begin{array}{r} 143 \\ 2\overline{)286} \end{array}$$

STEP 1 Multiply the quotient by the divisor.

STEP 2 Does the product equal the dividend?

$$\begin{array}{r} 143 \leftarrow \text{Quotient} \\ \times\ \ 2 \leftarrow \text{Divisor} \\ \hline 286 \leftarrow \text{Product } \checkmark \end{array}$$

The division is correct.

You can also check a division problem that has a remainder.

▶ **EXAMPLE 2**

Remainder
↓
143 R1
2)287 ← Dividend

Check the division problem.

$$\begin{array}{r} 143 \text{ R1} \\ 2\overline{)287} \end{array}$$

STEP 1 Multiply the quotient by the divisor.

STEP 2 Add the remainder.

STEP 3 Does the sum equal the dividend?

$$\begin{array}{r} 143 \leftarrow \text{Quotient} \\ \times\ \ 2 \leftarrow \text{Divisor} \\ \hline 286 \\ +\ \ 1 \leftarrow \text{Remainder} \\ \hline 287 \leftarrow \text{Sum } \checkmark \end{array}$$

The division is correct.

Practice

Check each answer. If the answer is incorrect, show the correct division.

1. $\begin{array}{r} 104 \\ 5\overline{)520} \end{array}$
2. $\begin{array}{r} 430 \\ 2\overline{)862} \end{array}$
3. $\begin{array}{r} 112 \text{ R3} \\ 4\overline{)450} \end{array}$
4. $\begin{array}{r} 21 \text{ R4} \\ 6\overline{)130} \end{array}$

5. $\begin{array}{r} 53 \text{ R5} \\ 7\overline{)376} \end{array}$
6. $\begin{array}{r} 127 \\ 3\overline{)372} \end{array}$
7. $\begin{array}{r} 241 \\ 4\overline{)964} \end{array}$
8. $\begin{array}{r} 32 \text{ R1} \\ 7\overline{)225} \end{array}$

USING YOUR CALCULATOR
Checking Division

Remember the two ways to write division problems.

$$\begin{array}{r} 12 \leftarrow \text{Quotient} \\ 3\overline{)36} \end{array}$$

↑ ↑

Divisor Dividend

$$36 \div 3 = 12$$

↑   ↑   ↑

Dividend Divisor Quotient

You can use a calculator to check your division. It does not matter the way the division is written.

Enter the dividend into the calculator.

PRESS | 3 | 6 | ÷ | *36.*

Enter the divisor into the calculator.

PRESS | 3 | *3.*

Press the equal sign to get the quotient.
See if the quotient on the calculator is the same as the one that was given to you.

PRESS | = | *12.*

The quotients are the same. So your division is correct.

Calculator Tip

Remember to enter the dividend into the calculator first.

Use a calculator to check each quotient. Tell if the quotient is correct or incorrect.

$$\begin{array}{r} 10 \\ \textbf{1.}\ 7\overline{)77} \end{array} \qquad \begin{array}{r} 13 \\ \textbf{2.}\ 6\overline{)78} \end{array} \qquad \begin{array}{r} 899 \\ \textbf{3.}\ 11\overline{)8,899} \end{array} \qquad \begin{array}{r} 208 \\ \textbf{4.}\ 31\overline{)6,448} \end{array}$$

$$\begin{array}{r} 501 \\ \textbf{5.}\ 50\overline{)25,050} \end{array} \qquad \begin{array}{r} 12 \\ \textbf{6.}\ 50\overline{)550} \end{array} \qquad \begin{array}{r} 28 \\ \textbf{7.}\ 15\overline{)430} \end{array} \qquad \begin{array}{r} 18 \\ \textbf{8.}\ 20\overline{)375} \end{array}$$

9. $612 \div 18 = 34$ **10.** $200 \div 12 = 17$ **11.** $165 \div 11 = 15$

Problem Solving: Clue Words for Division

Clue words can help you find the answer to a word problem.

CLUE WORDS FOR DIVISION
how much did each
how many times
into how many

▶ **EXAMPLE**

Marilyn sold 8 identical sets of dishes. Her sales totaled $192. How much did each set of dishes cost?

STEP 1   READ   What do you need to find out?
You need to find how much each set cost.

STEP 2   PLAN   What do you need to do?
The clue words, how much did each, tell you to divide. Divide the total sales by the number of sets Marilyn sold.

STEP 3   DO   Follow the plan.
Divide the total sales of $192 by the 8 sets.

$$\begin{array}{r} \$24 \\ 8\overline{)\$192} \\ -16\downarrow \\ \hline 32 \\ -32 \\ \hline 0 \end{array}$$

STEP 4   CHECK   Does the answer make sense?
Multiply to check the division.

$$\begin{array}{r} \$24 \\ \times8 \\ \hline \$192\ \checkmark \end{array}$$

Each set of dishes costs $24.

Practice

READ the problem. Answer the questions under PLAN.
DO the plan to solve the problem.

1. Juanita ran 1,600 yards. This was 4 laps around the track. How many yards is each lap?

   PLAN
   What are the clue words?
   What do the clue words tell you to do?

2. On Stan's last sales trip, he drove 2,464 miles. The trip lasted 14 days. How many miles did Stan drive each day?

   PLAN
   What are the clue words?
   What do the clue words tell you to do?

3. Kim paid $153 for 9 books. Each book costs the same amount. How much did each book cost?

   PLAN
   What are the clue words?
   What do the clue words tell you to do?

Problem Solving Strategy

Sometimes, a formula can help you solve a problem. These formulas tell you to divide to find time or rate.

1. Bruce drove 165 miles at 55 miles per hour. How long did the trip take? Divide the 165-mile distance by the rate of 55 miles per hour.

2. Cathy drove 96 miles in 2 hours. How fast was she driving? Divide the distance by the time.

$$Time = \frac{Distance}{Rate}$$

$$Rate = \frac{Distance}{Time}$$

Dividing by Numbers with More Than One Digit

You can use what you know about dividing by a small number to divide by a larger number. Use the steps below to divide by a two-digit number.

▶ **EXAMPLE**

Divide. $26\overline{)598}$

STEP 1 Does 26 divide into 5? No.
Does 26 divide into 59? Yes.
Estimate: "About how many times does 25 go into 60?"
2×25 is close to 60.

Write **2** over the *tens* place.

$$\begin{array}{r} 2 \\ 26\overline{)598} \end{array}$$

STEP 2 Multiply 2×26.
Check that the product is not larger than the number above.
$52 < 59$ ✓

$$\begin{array}{r} 2 \\ 26\overline{)598} \\ 52 \end{array}$$

STEP 3 Subtract.
Bring down the next digit.

$$\begin{array}{r} 2 \\ 26\overline{)598} \\ -52\downarrow \\ \hline 78 \end{array}$$

STEP 4 Does 26 divide into 78? Yes.
Estimate: "About how many times does 25 go into 78?"
3×25 is close to 78.

Write **3** over the *ones* place.

$$\begin{array}{r} 23 \\ 26\overline{)598} \\ -52\downarrow \\ \hline 78 \end{array}$$

STEP 5 Multiply 3×26.
Then, subtract.

Check that the remainder is less than the divisor.
Stop dividing.

$$\begin{array}{r} 23 \\ 26\overline{)598} \\ -52\downarrow \\ \hline 78 \\ -78 \\ \hline 0 \checkmark \end{array}$$

The quotient of $598 \div 26$ is 23.

Practice

Divide.

1. 22)594 **2.** 17)829 **3.** 32)992 **4.** 40)487

5. 52)578 **6.** 32)585 **7.** 15)960 **8.** 41)697

9. 92)828 **10.** 37)899 **11.** 55)605 **12.** 64)870

13. 67)938 **14.** 42)882 **15.** 23)851 **16.** 25)355

17. 70)840 **18.** 35)705 **19.** 11)475 **20.** 19)589

21. 42)890 **22.** 28)589 **23.** 51)919 **24.** 15)497

Everyday Problem Solving

As a salesperson, Mr. Roberts travels each week to visit clients. His last four trips are shown on the map to the right.

1. Mr. Roberts averaged a speed of 48 miles per hour from Handertown to Greenville. How many hours did the trip take? Divide the distance by the average speed.

2. The trip from Greenville to Camden took 11 hours. What was Mr. Roberts' average speed? Divide the distance by the number of hours.

3. Mr. Roberts averaged 55 miles per hour for the trips from Camden to Branchburg and from Branchburg to Handertown. Without dividing, tell which trip took more time. Explain your answer.

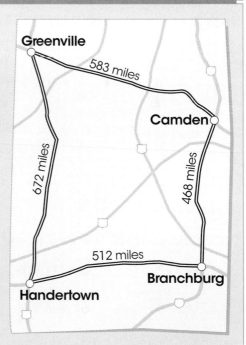

Greenville

583 miles

Camden

672 miles

468 miles

512 miles

Branchburg

Handertown

Zeros in the Quotient

Sometimes, you will need to place a zero in the quotient.

▶ **EXAMPLE**

Divide. $6\overline{)4,836}$

STEP 1 Does 6 divide into 4? No.
Does 6 divide into 48? Yes.
Think: ? × 6 = 48. Write 8
above the *hundreds* place.

$$\begin{array}{r} 8 \\ 6\overline{)4,836} \\ -\,4\,8\downarrow \\ \hline 03 \end{array}$$

Multiply 6 × 8.
Then subtract. Bring down the 3.

STEP 2 Does 6 divide into 3? No.
Write 0 above the *tens* place.
Bring down the 6.

$$\begin{array}{r} 80 \\ 6\overline{)4,836} \\ -\,4\,8\downarrow\downarrow \\ \hline 036 \end{array}$$

Do not stop dividing until each
digit in the dividend has been
brought down.

STEP 3 Does 6 divide into 36? Yes.
Think: ? × 6 = 36.
Write 6 above the ones place.

$$\begin{array}{r} 806 \\ 6\overline{)4,836} \\ -\,4\,8\downarrow\downarrow \\ \hline 036 \\ -\,36 \\ \hline 0\,\checkmark \end{array}$$

Multiply 6 × 6.
Then, subtract.

Check that the remainder
is less than the divisor.
Stop dividing.

The quotient of 4,836 ÷ 6 is 806.

Practice A

Divide. Sometimes, the zero in the quotient is in the ones place.

1. $8\overline{)6,472}$ **2.** $2\overline{)1,808}$ **3.** $5\overline{)3,025}$ **4.** $4\overline{)1,800}$

5. $7\overline{)4,830}$ **6.** $8\overline{)6,720}$ **7.** $11\overline{)6,644}$ **8.** $27\overline{)8,316}$

9. $32\overline{)7,680}$ **10.** $25\overline{)7,700}$ **11.** $19\overline{)9,538}$ **12.** $43\overline{)8,901}$

Practice B

Divide. Be sure to write the remainder as part of your answer.

13. $35\overline{)7,080}$ **14.** $26\overline{)2,357}$ **15.** $50\overline{)5,032}$ **16.** $14\overline{)4,225}$

17. $5\overline{)3,029}$ **18.** $7\overline{)3,540}$ **19.** $9\overline{)8,015}$ **20.** $8\overline{)7,217}$

21. $10\overline{)4,907}$ **22.** $26\overline{)2,800}$ **23.** $34\overline{)2,901}$ **24.** $17\overline{)5,108}$

Practice C

Divide.

25. $9\overline{)8,640}$ **26.** $19\overline{)1,059}$ **27.** $6\overline{)2,004}$

28. $25\overline{)10,200}$ **29.** $7\overline{)3,740}$ **30.** $9\overline{)8,902}$

Everyday Problem Solving

You can buy some items on an installment plan. You give the store a down payment. Then, you pay the remaining amount in equal payments.

CONSUMER FURNITURE
Installment plan

ITEM	COST	DOWN PAYMENT	NUMBER OF PAYMENTS
Television	$460	$100	6
Living room set	$2,708	$200	12

1. Neal bought a television set on the installment plan. How much was the down payment?

2. Neal paid the down payment for the television set. How much does he now owe? Subtract the down payment from the cost.

3. How much will each payment be for the television set? Divide the remaining amount of $360 by the 6 equal payments.

4. Pat bought a living room set on the installment plan. How much is each payment?

Problem Solving: Choose the Operation

Clue words help you decide how to solve a problem. You can add, subtract, multiply, or divide.

CLUE WORDS			
Add	**Subtract**	**Multiply**	**Divide**
in all	*how many more*	*total*	*how many times*
total	*difference*	*of*	*into how many*
altogether	*how many fewer*	*at*	*how much did each*
		for	
		in each	

EXAMPLE

The florist ordered 18 flats of plants. There were 24 plants in each flat. How many plants were ordered?

STEP 1 READ What do you need to find out?
You need to find the number of plants.

STEP 2 PLAN What do you need to do?
The clue words in each tell you to multiply. Multiply the number of flats by the number of plants in each flat.

STEP 3 DO Follow the plan.
Multiply 18 flats by the 24 plants in each flat.

$$\begin{array}{r} 18 \text{ flats} \\ \times\ 24 \text{ plants} \\ \hline 72 \\ +\ 360 \\ \hline 432 \text{ total plants} \end{array}$$

STEP 4 CHECK Does the answer make sense?
Divide to check the multiplication.
$432 \div 18 = 24$ plants in each flat. ✓

The florist ordered 432 plants.

Problem Solving Practice

READ the problem. Decide what operation to use for the PLAN. Then, DO the plan to solve the problem.

1. Sara sold 36 begonias, 11 geraniums, and 25 lilies. How many plants did she sell in all?

PLAN
What are the clue words?
What do the clue words tell you to do?

2. Walter displayed 8 rows of roses. Each row had 19 roses. How many roses were on display?

PLAN
What are the clue words?
What do the clue words tell you to do?

3. Mike fills each empty flowerpot with 2 pounds of potting soil. How many pots can he fill with 150 pounds of potting soil?

PLAN
What are the clue words?
What do the clue words tell you to do?

4. The florist arranged a shipment of 600 mums into 20 groups. How many mums were in each group?

PLAN
What are the clue words?
What do the clue words tell you to do?

5. Six flower arrangements were delivered. Each arrangement cost $35. What was the total cost?

PLAN
What are the clue words?
What do the clue words tell you to do?

MATH IN YOUR LIFE
Determining Miles per Gallon (mpg)

Armando drove his car 352 miles. He used
16 gallons of gas. He wants to find the number of
miles he can drive on 1 gallon of gas. This is the
number of miles his car gets per gallon of gas. It is
the miles per gallon or mpg for his car.

Armando can find the mpg. He divides the total
miles driven by the number of gallons of gas used.

```
                        22   ← Number of miles per gallon
Gallons of gas →  16)352     ← Miles driven
                   − 32
                     32
                   − 32
                      0
```

Armando's car gets 22 mpg.

Find the mpg for each vehicle.

1. Compact car
377 miles
13 gallons

2. Luxury car
238 miles
17 gallons

3. Small truck
360 miles
20 gallons

4. Van
680 miles
34 gallons

Solve.

5. The new car sticker for Marsha's car shows that her car should
get about 26 mpg. Marsha drove 784 miles on 28 gallons of gas.
How did her car compare with its sticker information?

Critical Thinking
Cars will get more miles per gallon of gasoline
on the highway than on city streets. Why do you
think this is true?

5·10 Estimating and Thinking

Estimating an answer allows you to choose an answer that seems sensible. An answer that "makes sense" is neither too big nor too small to be possible.

► **EXAMPLE**

Shelly drove a total of 354 miles. She used 20 gallons of gas. Estimate how many miles she traveled on each gallon.   (a) 50   (b) 6   (c)18

Look at each answer to see if it makes sense.

(a) 50   This answer is too big. She would have traveled more miles if she could travel 50 miles per gallon.

(b) 6   This answer is too small. She would have traveled fewer miles if she could only travel 6 miles per gallon.

(c) 18   This answer makes sense and is close to the exact answer.

Shelly travels about 18 miles per gallon of gas.

Practice

Choose the estimate that is close to the exact answer.

1. Shelly made 7 trips between Union City and Jefferson last month. She traveled a total of 476 miles. Estimate how many miles each trip was.

   (a) 9   **(b)** 100   **(c)** 70

2. For her job, Shelly visited 396 clients in her state. She saw these clients in 12 months. Estimate how many clients she visited each month.

   (a) 30   **(b)** 300   **(c)** 3,000

3. From her records, Shelly found that she spent $308 for gas during the last 14 weeks. Estimate how much money she spent on gas each week.

   (a) $50   **(b)** $100   **(c)** $20

Chapter

5 ▷ Review

Vocabulary Review

dividend

division

divisor

quotient

remainder

Fill in the blanks.

Complete each sentence with a word from the list.

1. __?__ is the process of finding how many times one number contains another.

2. In $42 \div 6 = 7$, the 6 is called the __?__.

3. The problem $7 \div 3$ has a __?__ of 1.

4. The __?__ of $42 \div 6 = 7$ is 42.

5. In $42 \div 6 = 7$, the 7 is called the __?__.

6. **Writing** A division problem has a divisor of 8 and a quotient of 10 R 7. Find the dividend and write the problem in two ways.

Chapter Quiz

LESSONS 5·1 and 5·2

Test Tip
You can use a multiplication table to find quotients.

Dividing Whole Numbers

Find each quotient.

1. $49 \div 7$

2. $56 \div 7$

3. $7\overline{)28}$

4. $5\overline{)45}$

5. $48 \div 8$

6. $27 \div 3$

7. What is eighteen divided by nine?

8. What is fifty-four divided by six?

LESSONS 5·3 and 5·4

Test Tip
Be sure to locate the correct place for the first digit of the quotient.

Dividing with Remainders

Divide.

9. $8\overline{)50}$

10. $14 \div 3$

11. $7\overline{)21}$

12. $30 \div 8$

13. $5\overline{)70}$

14. $600 \div 7$

LESSON 5·5

Test Tip
Check: multiply the divisor by the quotient. Add the remainder.

Checking Division

Check each answer.

15.
$$\begin{array}{r} 7\text{ R1} \\ 9\overline{)64} \end{array}$$

16.
$$\begin{array}{r} 31\text{ R1} \\ 7\overline{)220} \end{array}$$

LESSONS 5·6 and 5·9

Test Tip
Use clue words to help you decide which operation to use.

Problem Solving

Solve.

17. There are 12 boxes. Each box has 50 notebooks. How many notebooks are there in all?

18. There are 32 stamps on each roll. Mark has 288 stamps. How many rolls does he have?

LESSONS 5·7 and 5·8

Test Tip
When dividing, be sure the remainder is less than the divisor.

Dividing Larger Numbers

Divide.

19. $345 \div 12$

20. $191 \div 18$

21. $815 \div 4$

22. $546 \div 27$

23. $2,175 \div 7$

24. $1,985 \div 38$

LESSON 5·10

Test Tip
Try each estimate to see which one makes sense.

Estimating Answers

Choose the best estimate.

25. Marta is rolling nickels for the bank. Each roll holds 40 nickels. How many rolls are needed for 760 nickels?
(a) 20   (b) 200   (c) 2,000

Group Activity

In your group, research the term *unit price*. Write down its meaning. Visit a supermarket and record 10 examples of how unit pricing is used in the store. Then, create a word problem, with the answer, that asks the reader to find the unit price of an item.

This sports photographer takes photographs of other mountain climbers. He always tries to get the best photographs. To be sure, he always takes three photos of the same scene. Rolls of film come in sizes that make 24 or 36 photos. How many "different" scenes will he photograph from a roll of 24? from a roll of 36?

Chapter 6

More About Numbers

Words to Know

divisible	can be divided without a remainder
factors	numbers multiplied to get a product
greatest common factor (GCF)	the largest factor that two or more numbers share
multiples	possible products of a given number
least common multiple (LCM)	the smallest multiple that two or more numbers share
prime number	number with only itself and 1 as factors
composite number	number with more than two factors
exponent	tells how many times to use a number as a factor
square	product of multiplying a number by itself
square root	number that was squared

Class Team Project

Find out how many students are in each of your classes. Your teachers want to divide each class into equal-sized teams. List all the different-sized teams that could be made for each class. The smallest team can be one person. The largest team can be the entire class. How many different teams can you make?

Learning Objectives

- Use divisibility tests.
- Find the factors of a number.
- Find the multiples of a number.
- Write prime factorizations.
- Find squares and square roots.
- Solve problems with extra information.
- Apply number sense to reading electrical meters.

6-1 Divisibility Tests for 2, 5, and 10

Sometimes, when you divide one number by another number, the remainder is zero. When this happens, the first number is **divisible** by the second number.

$18 \div 3 = 6$ R0 $18 \div 4 = 4$ R2
18 is divisible by 3.   18 is not divisible by 4.

You can use divisibility tests to quickly see if numbers are divisible by 2, 5, or 10.

Remember:
A number is even if it ends in 0, 2, 4, 6, or 8.

Divisible by 2   A number is divisible by 2 if it is an even number.
$126 \div 2 = 63$ R0

Divisible by 5   A number is divisible by 5 if the last digit is 0 or 5.
$6{,}840 \div 5 = 1{,}368$ R0

Divisible by 10   A number is divisible by 10 if the last digit is 0.
$80 \div 10 = 8$ R0

▶ **EXAMPLE**

Tell if the number 5,235 is divisible by 2, 5, or 10.

STEP 1   Write the number. Look at the last digit.   **5,235**

STEP 2   Is the number even?   No.   It is not divisible by 2.

STEP 3   Is the last digit a 0 or 5?   Yes.   It is divisible by 5.

STEP 4   Is the last digit a 0?   No.   It is not divisible by 10.

The number 5,235 is only divisible by 5.

Practice A

Tell if each number is divisible by 2. Write *Yes* or *No*.

1. 875 **2.** 634 **3.** 7,301 **4.** 37,598 **5.** 268,180

Practice B

Tell if each number is divisible only by 5 or by both 5 and 10.

6. 67,475 **7.** 390,740 **8.** 89,370 **9.** 456,785 **10.** 700,005

Practice C

Tell if each number is divisible by 2, 5, or 10.

11. 48,296 **12.** 9,990 **13.** 16,005 **14.** 55,558 **15.** 800,000

16. 2,615 **17.** 3,180 **18.** 1,274 **19.** 2,695 **20.** 7,312

Everyday Problem Solving

Mika is a camp director. She uses the floor plans to assign campers to cabins. She does not want any empty beds in a cabin she assigns.

1. There will be 45 campers in June. Mika wants to assign them all to the same type of cabin. Is 45 divisible by 2, 5, or 10? Which type of cabin could she use?

2. In August, there will be 70 campers. Which type of cabin could she use if all the campers were in the same type of cabin?

3. There are 8 camp counselors. Which cabins could they use? How many cabins of that type would they need?

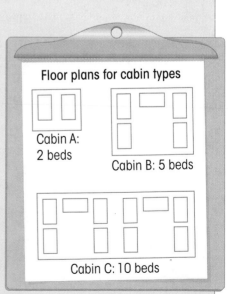

Floor plans for cabin types

Cabin A: 2 beds

Cabin B: 5 beds

Cabin C: 10 beds

6·2 ▶ Divisibility Tests for 3, 6, and 9

You can use divisibility tests to quickly see if numbers are divisible by 3, 6, or 9.

Divisible by 3 A number is divisible by 3 if the sum of the digits is also divisible by 3. Try 471.

$4 + 7 + 1 = 12$ $12 \div 3 = 4$ R0
So, 471 is divisible by 3.

You can apply the divisibility tests for 2 and 3 to test for 6.

Divisible by 6 A number is divisible by 6 if it is divisible by both 2 and 3. Try 108.

$108 \div 2 = 54$ R0 $108 \div 3 = 36$ R0
So, 108 is divisible by 6.

Divisible by 9 A number is divisible by 9 if the sum of the digits is also divisible by 9. Try 513.

$5 + 1 + 3 = 9$ $9 \div 9 = 1$ R0
So, 513 is divisible by 9.

▶ **EXAMPLE 1**

Is 255 divisible by 6?

STEP 1 Find the sum of the digits.		$2 + 5 + 5 = 12$
STEP 2 Is 12 divisible by 3?	Yes.	$12 \div 3 = 4$ R0
STEP 3 Is 255 divisible by 2?	No.	It is not even.

The number 255 is not divisible by 6.

▶ **EXAMPLE 2**

Is 7,431 divisible by 3 or 9?

STEP 1 Find the sum of the digits.		$7 + 4 + 3 + 1 = 15$
STEP 2 Is 15 divisible by 3?	Yes.	$15 \div 3 = 5$ R0
STEP 3 Is 15 divisible by 9?	No.	$15 \div 9 = 1$ R6

The number 7,431 is divisible by 3 but not by 9.

Practice A

Tell if each number is divisible by 6. Write *Yes* or *No*.

1. 243   **2.** 66   **3.** 3,783   **4.** 5,940   **5.** 7,602

6. 7,458   **7.** 15,555   **8.** 9,720   **9.** 578,564   **10.** 21,864

Practice B

Tell if each number is divisible by 3, 9, or both.
Write *3, 9,* or *Both 3 and 9.*

11. 1,524   **12.** 7,470   **13.** 3,141   **14.** 2,568   **15.** 6,246

16. 333   **17.** 5,109   **18.** 8,883   **19.** 78,777   **20.** 4,953

21. 498   **22.** 52,668   **23** 101,904   **24.** 525,000   **25.** 258,129

Everyday Problem Solving

Alyse makes jewelry for craft fairs. She uses the chart
for the beads she needs. When she orders, she does
not want to have any beads left over.

1. Alyse needs 183 dozen black beads.
What size boxes could she order?

2. Alyse needs 249 dozen yellow beads.
What size boxes could she order?
How many boxes could she order?

3. Alyse needs 756 dozen green beads.
What size boxes could she order?

4. Alyse needs 162 dozen red beads. She can order
any size box. She wants the least number of boxes.
Which size boxes should she order?

Beads by the Dozens	
Size of Box (any color)	Number of Dozens
Small	3
Medium	6
Large	9

Divisibility Test for 4

If a number can be divided by 4 with a remainder of 0, it is divisible by 4. You can use a divisibility test to quickly see if numbers are divisible by 4.

Divisible by 4 A number is divisible by 4 if the number formed by the last two digits is divisible by 4.

▶ **EXAMPLE**

Tell if 845,628 is divisible by 4.

STEP 1 Write the number. 845,628

STEP 2 Look at the last two digits. 845,628

STEP 3 Is this number divisible by 4? Yes. $28 \div 4 = 7$ R0

The number 845,628 is divisible by 4.

Practice

Tell if each number is divisible by 4. Write *Yes* or *No*.

1. 5,890

2. 784

3. 45,032

4. 349,821

5. 20

6. 6,000

7. 128,530

8. 1,245,904

9. 540

10. 6,981

11. 7,504

12. 1,980

13. 87,664

14. 210,971

15. 923,456

16. 79,894

17. 4,440,413

18. 678,004

19. 4

20. 42

21. 444,500

22. 78,992

23. 64,992,824

24. 4,956

USING YOUR CALCULATOR
Test for Divisibility

You can use a calculator to quickly test for divisibility.

Is 8,679 divisible by 6?

Divide 8,679 by 6.

PRESS 8 6 7 9 ÷ 6 | 1446.5 |

↑
This dot means that
the number is not
a whole number

> **Calculator Tip**
> On a calculator, an R for remainder is not shown on the display. If you do not see a whole number on the display, your answer has a remainder other than zero.

The quotient 1,446.5 is not a whole number. This means that 8,679 is not divisible by 6.

Is 12,468 divisible by 3?

Divide 12,468 by 3.

PRESS 1 2 4 6 8 ÷ 3 | 4156. |

The quotient 4,156 is a whole number. This means that 12,468 is divisible by 3.

Use a calculator to tell if each number is divisible by 2, 3, 4, 5, 6, 9, or 10. Copy the table and write *Yes* or *No*. The first one has been done for you.

		Divisible by					
	2	3	4	5	6	9	10
1. 132	Yes	Yes	Yes	No	Yes	No	No
2. 1,756							
3. 18,921							
4. 27,150							
5. 540							

Factors and Greatest Common Factor

The two numbers you multiply are **factors** of the product. When you divide, the divisor and the quotient are the factors.

$$3 \times 4 = 12$$
Factor × Factor = Product

$$\text{Factor} \rightarrow 3\overline{)12} \quad \begin{array}{l} 4 \leftarrow \text{Factor} \end{array}$$

Product

You can divide to find all the factors of a number. The remainder must be 0. Divide by 1, 2, 3, and so on. Stop dividing when the factors repeat.

$$\begin{array}{cccc} 12 & 6 & 4 & 3 \\ 1\overline{)12} & 2\overline{)12} & 3\overline{)12} & 4\overline{)12} \ \text{STOP!} \end{array}$$

The symbol F_{12} means the factors of 12.

You can list the factors of 12 from least to greatest.

$$F_{12} = \{1, 2, 3, 4, 6, 12\}$$

▶ **EXAMPLE 1**

Find the factors of 20.

STEP 1 Divide starting with the whole number 1.

$$\begin{array}{ccccc} 20 & 10 & 6\ \text{R2} & 5 & 4 \\ 1\overline{)20} & 2\overline{)20} & 3\overline{)20} & 4\overline{)20} & 5\overline{)20} \ \text{STOP!} \end{array}$$

STEP 2 List the factors from least to greatest without repeating any numbers.

$$F_{20} = \{1, 2, 4, 5, 10, 20\}$$

The factors of 20 are 1, 2, 4, 5, 10, and 20.

If you list the factors for each of two numbers, you may find that some of their factors are the same. They are called common factors. The **greatest common factor (GCF)** is the largest of the common factors.

▶ **EXAMPLE 2**   Find the greatest common factor of 18 and 24.

STEP 1 Find the factors $F_{18} = \{1, 2, 3, 6, 9, 18\}$
            of each number. $F_{24} = \{1, 2, 3, 4, 6, 8, 12, 24\}$

STEP 2 List the common factors.   1, 2, 3, 6

STEP 3 Find the greatest   6
            common factor.

The greatest common factor of 18 and 24 is 6.

Practice A

Find the factors of each number.

1. 10   **2.** 21   **3.** 64   **4.** 48   **5.** 51

6. 81   **7.** 32   **8.** 5   **9.** 50   **10.** 75

Practice B

Find the greatest common factor of each pair of numbers.

11. 10   8   **12.** 15   45   **13.** 20   10   **14.** 17   51   **15.** 13   4

16. 50   75   **17.** 22   66   **18.** 36   54   **19.** 16   30   **20.** 12   28

Everyday Problem Solving

Jena is planning a party for 120 people. She needs to rent chairs and tables. She wants to use only one size table. She does not want any empty chairs at a table.

1. If she uses 4-person tables, how many tables will she need?

2. If she uses 5-person tables, how many tables will she need? What will it cost for the tables?

3. What will it cost to rent 6-person tables? What is the total cost with chairs?

Seating for Party	
Table Sizes	Cost
4-person table	$13.00 each
5-person table	$15.00 each
6-person table	$20.00 each
8-person table	$25.00 each
Chairs	$2.00 each

Multiples and Least Common Multiple

The **multiples** of a number are the products you get when you multiply that number by whole numbers. The numbers in blue are some multiples of 12.

$$12 \times 1 = 12 \qquad 12 \times 2 = 24 \qquad 12 \times 3 = 36$$
$$12 \times 4 = 48 \qquad 12 \times 5 = 60 \qquad 12 \times 6 = 72$$

You can list some multiples of 12.

$$M_{12} = \{12, 24, 36, 48, 60, 72 \ldots\}$$

The three dots show that the multiples go on.

The symbol M_{12} means the multiples of 12.

To find the multiples of a number, multiply that number by the whole numbers. Begin with 1.

EXAMPLE 1

Find the first five multiples of 9.

STEP 1 Multiply the given number by 1, 2, 3, 4, and 5.

$$9 \times 1 = 9 \qquad 9 \times 2 = 18$$
$$9 \times 3 = 27 \qquad 9 \times 4 = 36$$
$$9 \times 5 = 45$$

STEP 2 List these multiples from least to greatest.

$$M_9 = \{9, 18, 27, 36, 45\ldots\}$$

The first five multiples of 9 are 9, 18, 27, 36, and 45.

For two different numbers, you may find that some multiples are the same. These are called common multiples. The **least common multiple (LCM)** is the smallest of the common multiples.

EXAMPLE 2

Find the least common multiple of 5 and 15.

STEP 1 List some multiples of each number.

$$M_5 = \{5, 10, 15, 20, 25, 30\ldots\}$$
$$M_{15} = \{15, 30, 45, 60\ldots\}$$

STEP 2 List the common multiples.   15, 30

STEP 3 Find the least common multiple.   15

The least common multiple of 5 and 15 is 15.

Practice A

Find the first five multiples of each number. List them from least to greatest.

1. 7 **2.** 10 **3.** 6 **4.** 25 **5.** 50

6. 22 **7.** 40 **8.** 16 **9.** 18 **10.** 1

Practice B

Find the least common multiple of each pair of numbers.

11. 8 12 **12.** 10 18 **13.** 13 3 **14.** 15 25

15. 10 25 **16.** 6 15 **17.** 14 21 **18.** 40 50

19. 9 15 **20.** 16 40 **21.** 21 6 **22.** 60 80

23. 12 40 **24.** 72 32 **25.** 4 42 **26.** 16 24

Everyday Problem Solving

Alfonso and Adena want to go to the beach together. Alfonso has every fifth day off from work, and Adena has every third day off.

1. They both began work on June 1. What is the first day they will have off together?

2. What is the LCM of 3 and 5?

Jen has every sixth day off. Bob has every eighth day off.

3. They both began work on June 1. What is the first day they will have off together?

4. What is the LCM of 6 and 8?

•JUNE•						
SUN	MON	TUES	WED	THURS	FRI	SAT
		1 START WORK	2	3	4	5
6	7	8	9	10	11	12
13	14	15	16	17	18	19
20	21	22	23	24	25	26
27	28	29	30 finish work			

Prime Numbers

A **prime number** has only two factors. The two factors are the number itself and 1. A **composite number** has more than two factors.

$$17 = 1 \times 17 \qquad\qquad 15 = 1 \times 15 \text{ and } 15 = 3 \times 5$$
$$F_{17} = \{1, 17\} \qquad\qquad F_{15} = \{1, 3, 5, 15\}$$

Prime   Composite

Every composite number can be shown as the product of prime numbers. This is called *prime factorization*. You can make a factor tree.

▶ **EXAMPLE**

Write the prime factorization of 60.

STEP 1 Write the number.

60

STEP 2 Choose two factors. These factors do not have to be prime numbers.

60
6 × 10

STEP 3 Factor each number again until all the factors are prime numbers. If a factor is a prime, bring it down to the next line.

60
6 × 10
2 × 3 × 2 × 5

STEP 4 Write the prime factors in order from least to greatest.

2 × 2 × 3 × 5

The prime factorization of 60 is $2 \times 2 \times 3 \times 5$.

Practice A

Tell if each number is *prime* or *composite*. Test by factoring each number.

1. 13   **2.** 15   **3.** 99   **4.** 41   **5.** 57

Practice B

Write the prime factorization of each number. Use a factor tree.

6. 8   **7.** 18   **8.** 24   **9.** 75   **10.** 28

6·7 Exponents

Some expressions ask you to multiply a number by itself one or more times. An **exponent** tells you how many times the number is used as a factor.

2^3 ← Exponent

You can find the value of expressions that contain exponents.

$$2^3 = 2 \times 2 \times 2 = 8$$
2^3 is read, *two to the third power.*

▶ **EXAMPLE**

Find the value of the expression 4^3.

STEP 1 Rewrite the expression as a product of the number without exponents.

$4 \times 4 \times 4$

STEP 2 Multiply.

$4 \times 4 \times 4 = 64$

The value of 4^3 is 64.

An expression that has a zero as the exponent has a value of 1. The expression 8^0 equals 1.

$$5,432^0 = 1$$

Practice

Find the value of each expression.

1. 5^3 **2.** 2^5 **3.** 100^2

4. 8^2 **5.** 11^1 **6.** 10^3

7. 1^0 **8.** 3^3 **9.** 0^4

10. 9^1 **11.** 1^{22} **12.** 20^2

13. 400^0 **14.** 15^2 **15.** 12^2

Squares and Square Roots

When you multiply a number by itself, the product is called the **square** of the number.

The square of 4 is 16. $4 \times 4 = 4^2 = 16$.

The symbol for square is the exponent ^{2}. The number that was squared is called the **square root**.

The square root of 16 is 4, because 4^2 equals 16.

The symbol for square root is $\sqrt{}$.

▶ **EXAMPLE**

Find $\sqrt{49}$.

STEP 1 Think:"What number squared   Try 6.
equals 49?" $6^2 = 6 \times 6 = 36$

STEP 2 Decide if the product is too big or   36 is too small.
too small.

STEP 3 If the product is too small, try the   Try 7.
next largest whole number. $7^2 = 7 \times 7 = 49$
If the product is too large, try the
next smallest whole number.

The correct answer is 7. So, $\sqrt{49} = 7$.

Practice A

Find the square of each number.

1. 6^2 **2.** 8^2 **3.** 9^2 **4.** 3^2 **5.** 13^2

Practice B

Find the square root of each number.

6. $\sqrt{4}$ **7.** $\sqrt{25}$ **8.** $\sqrt{10,000}$ **9.** $\sqrt{16}$

10. $\sqrt{121}$ **11.** $\sqrt{49}$ **12.** $\sqrt{900}$ **13.** $\sqrt{196}$

ON-THE-JOB MATH
Electric Meter Reader

Sharon reads meters for a power company. Your electric meter shows how many kilowatt-hours of electricity you use. An electric meter has five dials. The dials are read from left to right.

|2|3|5|4|8|

The meter above shows 23,548 kilowatt-hours. If you know the reading for the month before, you can tell how much electricity you used that month.

Read the numbers on the meter to solve the first word problem.

1. The meter below is an August 1 reading. On July 1, the same meter showed 10,455. How many kilowatt-hours were used during the month? Subtract to find out.

2. Electricity costs 8¢ a kilowatt-hour. This is $8 for 100 kilowatt-hours. How much does 1,000 kilowatt-hours cost?

Critical Thinking

Mr. Miller is away. Sharon cannot read the meter. The electric company wants to send Mr. Miller a bill for the month. Sharon needs to estimate how much electricity he used. How can she do this?

Problem Solving: Extra Information

Some word problems give you more information than you need. To solve a problem with extra information, first decide what facts are needed.

▶ **EXAMPLE**

Ms. Cohen spent 8 hours shopping for party supplies. She bought 5 packages of white paper plates for $3 each. What was the total cost for the paper plates?

STEP 1 **READ** **What do you need to find out?**
You need to find the total cost of the paper plates.

STEP 2 **PLAN** **What do you need to do?**
What information do you need?
The number of packages.
The cost of each package.
Multiply to find the total cost.

STEP 3 **DO** **Follow the plan.**
Multiply.

$$
\begin{array}{rl}
5 & \text{packages} \\
\times\ \$3 & \text{each} \\
\hline
\$15 & \text{for paper plates}
\end{array}
$$

STEP 4 **CHECK** **Does your answer make sense?**
Check to see that you used only the numbers you needed.
5 packages × $3 ✓

What information was not needed?
8 hours spent shopping

The total cost of the paper plates was $15.

Problem Solving

READ the problem. Answer the questions under PLAN.
DO the plan to solve the problem. Remember to use
only the information you need.

1. Danielle bought 3 CDs for $15 each. She bought a CD
   case for $20. How much did the CDs cost altogether?

   PLAN
   What information do you need to solve the problem?
   What operation will you use?

2. Cal had 59 boxes to pack and 10 pieces of furniture
   to move. By noon, he had packed 43 boxes. How
   many boxes does he still have to pack?

   PLAN
   What information do you need to solve the problem?
   What operation will you use?

3. Ms. Kelly earns $630 a week. She travels 12 miles to
   work each day. She works 35 hours each week. How
   much does Mrs. Kelly earn an hour?

   PLAN
   What information do you need to solve the problem?
   What operation will you use?

Problem Solving Strategy

You can have different problems for the same situation.

> Mrs. Lee is having a New Year's Eve party for
> 73 guests. She bought 8 packages of noisemakers
> for $5 each. There are 10 noisemakers in a package.

1. How much did all the packages of noisemakers cost?

2. How many noisemakers did she buy?

3. Each guest got 1 noisemaker. How many noisemakers were left over?

composite number

divisible

exponent

factors

greatest common factor

least common multiple

multiples

prime number

square

square root

Vocabulary Review

True or false? If the statement is false, change the underlined word to make the statement true.

1. 21 is <u>divisible</u> by 7

2. 2 and 4 are <u>factors</u> of 16.

3. The <u>greatest</u> common multiple of 12 and 24 is 24.

4. 81 is a <u>multiple</u> of 9.

5. 22 is a <u>prime number</u>.

6. In the expression 4^5, 5 is the <u>exponent</u>.

7. 18 is a <u>composite</u> number.

8. The <u>least</u> common factor of 12 and 18 is 6.

9. The <u>square</u> of 6 is 6×6, or 36.

10. The <u>square root</u> of 36 is 6.

11. Writing Choose one word from the vocabulary list. Explain the meaning of the word to a classmate.

LESSONS 6·1 to 6·3

Test Tip
Use long division to check for divisibility. If the remainder is 0, the number is divisible by the divisor.

Chapter Quiz

Using Divisibility Tests

Use a divisibility test to answer each question.

1. Is 3,258 divisible by 6?

2. Is 59,848 divisible by 4?

3. Is 10,319 divisible by 9?

4. Is 4,235 divisible by 5?

Finding Greatest Common Factors

Find the greatest common factor of each pair of numbers.

5. 18   24   **6.** 12   15   **7.** 4   12

Finding Least Common Multiples

Find the least common multiple of each pair of numbers.

8. 6   7   **9.** 9   12   **10.** 6   8

Writing Prime Factorizations

Find the prime factorization of each number.

11. 12   **12.** 50   **13.** 30

Finding Exponents, Squares, and Square Roots

Find the value of each expression.

14. 3^3 **15.** 2^4 **16.** 4^3

17. $\sqrt{64}$ **18.** $\sqrt{81}$ **19.** $\sqrt{16}$

Solving Problems with Extra Information

Solve.

20. Jon drove 12 miles to the shore. He then drove 25 miles to the Cape. He had 12 gallons of gas. How far did he drive in all?

Group Activity

Work with your group to solve the following problem. The school marching band is marching in a parade. There are 135 band members. Arrange the marchers so that there are an equal number of students in each row. How many different ways can the marchers be arranged? Explain.

Unit 1 **Review**

Choose the letter for the correct answer.

Use the table to answer Questions 1–3.

Favorite Books	
Book	**Pages**
Mystery	576
Adventure	804
Drama	813
Biography	528

1. Which book has an odd number of pages?
   - **A.** Mystery
   - **B.** Adventure
   - **C.** Drama
   - **D.** Biography

2. How many more pages does the drama book have than the mystery book?
   - **A.** 237
   - **B.** 347
   - **C.** 363
   - **D.** None of the above

3. Which list is in order from the least to the greatest number of pages?
   - **A.** Mystery, Biography, Adventure
   - **B.** Biography, Mystery, Adventure
   - **C.** Adventure, Drama, Biography
   - **D.** Drama, Adventure, Mystery

4. Bryan drove 348 miles in 4 days. He drove the same number of miles each day. How many miles did Bryan drive each day?
   - **A.** 87 miles
   - **B.** 344 miles
   - **C.** 352 miles
   - **D.** None of the above

5. Neil ate 1,212 calories for breakfast, 1,057 calories for lunch, and 1,172 calories for dinner. How many calories did he eat in the 3 meals?
   - **A.** 2,229 calories
   - **B.** 2,269 calories
   - **C.** 3,331 calories
   - **D.** 3,441 calories

6. Each of 8 shipments weighs 73 pounds. What is the total weight?
   - **A.** About 9 pounds
   - **B.** 81 pounds
   - **C.** 584 pounds
   - **D.** None of the above

Critical Thinking

Use the Favorite Books chart above. Which two books have a total of 1,104 pages?

CHALLENGE You want to read at least 1,500 pages. Which books can you read? Why?

Unit 2 ▶ Fractions

Type of Fruit	Amount of Juice Produced
1 medium orange	$\frac{1}{3}$ cup
1 medium lemon	$\frac{1}{6}$ cup
1 medium grapefruit	$\frac{2}{3}$ cup
1 medium tangerine	$\frac{1}{4}$ cup

Number of Fruit Needed to Produce 1 Cup of Juice	
Orange	🍊🍊🍊
Lemon	🍋🍋🍋🍋🍋🍋
Grapefruit	🍊◖
Tangerine	🍊🍊🍊🍊

Key: 🍊 =1 whole fruit ◖ = $\frac{1}{2}$ fruit

After being picked, about 900 pounds of oranges have been sent to a packaging plant. Here the oranges will wait to be cleaned, checked, packaged, and sent to food stores and juice plants.

The graph and table above give information about four types of fruit and the amount of juice that each one can produce.

1. How many grapefruit are needed for 1 cup of juice?

2. How much juice can you get from one medium lemon?

3. Which fruit needs the largest number to make 1 cup of juice?

127

The people in the picture are working at the Pacific Stock Exchange. They buy, sell, and trade stocks. They use mixed numbers and fractions in their work. A mixed number is a whole number together with a fraction. The last stock today went up two and a half points. What would this mixed number look like?

Chapter 7

Fractions and Mixed Numbers

Words to Know

fraction	a form of a number that shows part of a whole
numerator	the top number in a fraction
denominator	the bottom number in a fraction
equivalent fractions	fractions with different numbers but equal values
lowest terms	when only 1 divides evenly into both the numerator and denominator of a fraction
like fractions	fractions with the same denominator
unlike fractions	fractions with different denominators
mixed number	a number made up of a whole number and a fraction

Fraction and Mixed Number Journal Project

Keep a daily journal of every fraction and mixed number you see. Look for them in different places. Read containers, signs, newspapers, and magazines. Write what each one is about and where you found it.

$\frac{1}{2}$	discount	store sign
$2\frac{1}{2}$	stock points	newspaper

Learning Objectives

- Identify fractions and their parts.
- Recognize equivalent fractions.
- Write fractions in lowest terms and in higher terms.
- Find common denominators.
- Compare and order fractions and other numbers.
- Change mixed numbers and fractions.
- Solve problems using patterns.
- Apply fractions to cooking.

A **fraction** is part of a whole or part of a set. Every fraction has a numerator and a denominator.

$$\frac{3}{4}$$ ← Numerator
← Denominator

The **numerator** is the top number. It tells how many parts of the whole are being used.

The **denominator** is the bottom number. It tells how many parts there are in the whole.

> **EXAMPLE 1**

Write a fraction to tell what part of the square is blue.

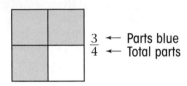

$$\frac{3}{4}$$ ← Parts blue
← Total parts

Three-fourths of the square is blue.

> **EXAMPLE 2**

Write a fraction for the situation.

There are **four students in the Math Club. Three of the students are girls.** Write a fraction to tell what part of the Math Club is girls.

$$\frac{3}{4}$$ ← Girls in Math Club
← Total students in Math Club

Three-fourths of the club is girls.

Practice

Write a fraction to tell what part of the whole is blue.

1.

2.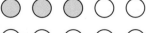

3. There are 24 hours in a day. What fraction of the day is 8 hours?

Equivalent fractions have the same value. Three equivalent fractions are pictured below.

► **EXAMPLE**

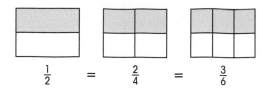

$$\frac{1}{2} \quad = \quad \frac{2}{4} \quad = \quad \frac{3}{6}$$

Each shape is equivalent. The shaded area in each shape is the same. This means that each fraction has the same value. $\frac{1}{2}$, $\frac{2}{4}$, and $\frac{3}{6}$ are equivalent fractions.

Practice

Tell if each pair of fractions is equivalent. Write *Equivalent* or *Not equivalent*.

1.
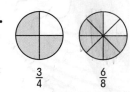
$$\frac{3}{6} \qquad \frac{4}{8}$$

2.
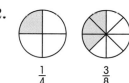
$$\frac{1}{4} \qquad \frac{3}{8}$$

3.
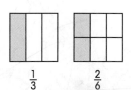
$$\frac{1}{3} \qquad \frac{2}{6}$$

4.
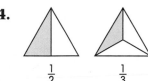
$$\frac{1}{2} \qquad \frac{1}{3}$$

5.
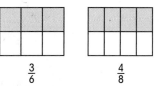
$$\frac{3}{4} \qquad \frac{6}{8}$$

6.
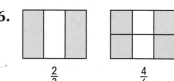
$$\frac{2}{3} \qquad \frac{4}{6}$$

7.
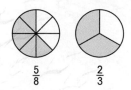
$$\frac{5}{8} \qquad \frac{2}{3}$$

8.
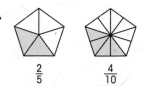
$$\frac{2}{5} \qquad \frac{4}{10}$$

7·3 Reducing Fractions to Lowest Terms

To reduce a fraction, you divide the numerator and denominator by the same factor. A fraction is in **lowest terms** if you cannot divide any further.

$$\frac{6}{9} = \frac{6 \div 3}{9 \div 3} = \frac{2}{3} \longleftarrow \text{Lowest terms}$$

You can reduce a fraction to lowest terms. Divide both numerator and denominator by their GCF.

▶ **EXAMPLE**

Reduce $\frac{15}{20}$ to lowest terms.

The Greatest Common Factor, or GCF, is the largest of the common factors of two or more numbers.

STEP 1 List the factors of numerator and denominator.

$F_{15} = \{1, 3, 5, 15\}$
$F_{20} = \{1, 2, 4, 5, 10, 20\}$

STEP 2 Find the greatest common factor.

$GCF = 5$

STEP 3 Divide numerator and denominator by the GCF.

$\frac{15 \div 5}{20 \div 5} = \frac{3}{4}$

The fraction $\frac{15}{20}$ in lowest terms is $\frac{3}{4}$.

Practice A

Decide if each fraction is reduced to lowest terms. Write *Yes* or *No*.

1. $\frac{1}{3}$ 2. $\frac{3}{9}$ 3. $\frac{2}{3}$ 4. $\frac{3}{3}$ 5. $\frac{1}{4}$

6. $\frac{3}{5}$ 7. $\frac{4}{8}$ 8. $\frac{6}{9}$ 9. $\frac{3}{4}$ 10. $\frac{2}{10}$

Practice B

Reduce each fraction to lowest terms.

11. $\frac{4}{8}$ **12.** $\frac{5}{35}$ **13.** $\frac{9}{24}$ **14.** $\frac{8}{32}$ **15.** $\frac{3}{9}$

16. $\frac{12}{27}$ **17.** $\frac{6}{15}$ **18.** $\frac{6}{8}$ **19.** $\frac{5}{10}$ **20.** $\frac{7}{49}$

21. $\frac{13}{39}$ **22.** $\frac{4}{16}$ **23.** $\frac{8}{12}$ **24.** $\frac{49}{56}$ **25.** $\frac{6}{10}$

26. $\frac{10}{80}$ **27.** $\frac{6}{9}$ **28.** $\frac{9}{12}$ **29.** $\frac{8}{24}$ **30.** $\frac{7}{63}$

31. $\frac{15}{18}$ **32.** $\frac{6}{18}$ **33.** $\frac{12}{24}$ **34.** $\frac{7}{21}$ **35.** $\frac{3}{12}$

36. $\frac{4}{10}$ **37.** $\frac{8}{16}$ **38.** $\frac{12}{18}$ **39.** $\frac{15}{20}$ **40.** $\frac{4}{24}$

Everyday Problem Solving

At Rita's Pizza Place, the same sized pizza pie can be sliced in eighths or sixths.

1. A pizza pie was sliced into 8 equal pieces. Sam ate 2 pieces. What fraction of the pie did he eat? Write the fraction in lowest terms.

2. A pizza pie was sliced into 6 equal pieces. Irene ate 2 pieces. What fraction of the pie did she eat? Write the fraction in lowest terms.

3. Bill ate $\frac{4}{8}$ of one pie. Bonnie ate $\frac{3}{6}$ of another pie. Did both Bill and Bonnie eat $\frac{1}{2}$ a pie? How do you know?

Changing Fractions to Higher Terms

Sometimes, you need to write a fraction in higher terms. This will change the numbers, but keep the value the same.

$$\frac{4}{5} = \frac{4 \times 2}{5 \times 2} = \frac{8}{10} \leftarrow \text{Higher terms}$$

The fractions $\frac{4}{5}$ and $\frac{8}{10}$ are equivalent fractions.

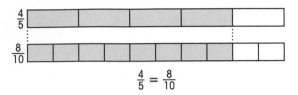

$$\frac{4}{5} = \frac{8}{10}$$

Sometimes, you know the denominator you want to use for the higher-term fraction.

EXAMPLE

Write $\frac{3}{4}$ in higher terms.

Use the denominator 12.　　$\frac{3}{4} = \frac{?}{12}$

STEP 1 Divide the new higher denominator by the given denominator.　　$12 \div 4 = 3$

STEP 2 Multiply the numerator and denominator of the given fraction by the quotient from step 1.　　$\frac{3 \times 3}{4 \times 3} = \frac{9}{12}$

The fraction $\frac{3}{4}$ can be written as $\frac{9}{12}$.

Practice

Change each fraction to higher terms. Use the higher denominator shown.

1. $\frac{1}{2} = \frac{?}{8}$

2. $\frac{5}{9} = \frac{?}{18}$

3. $\frac{6}{10} = \frac{?}{30}$

4. $\frac{2}{9} = \frac{?}{27}$

5. $\frac{2}{7} = \frac{?}{35}$

6. $\frac{1}{3} = \frac{?}{21}$

7. $\frac{1}{12} = \frac{?}{60}$

8. $\frac{4}{9} = \frac{?}{36}$

9. $\frac{3}{7} = \frac{?}{42}$

10. $\frac{7}{9} = \frac{?}{45}$

11. $\frac{1}{5} = \frac{?}{25}$

12. $\frac{5}{7} = \frac{?}{49}$

13. $\frac{1}{4} = \frac{?}{20}$

14. $\frac{2}{8} = \frac{?}{24}$

15. $\frac{2}{3} = \frac{?}{15}$

16. $\frac{4}{6} = \frac{?}{36}$

17. $\frac{2}{5} = \frac{?}{50}$

18. $\frac{3}{15} = \frac{?}{45}$

19. $\frac{3}{8} = \frac{?}{32}$

20. $\frac{1}{6} = \frac{?}{54}$

21. $\frac{7}{9} = \frac{?}{63}$

22. $\frac{1}{2} = \frac{?}{18}$

23. $\frac{3}{11} = \frac{?}{22}$

24. $\frac{3}{4} = \frac{?}{24}$

Everyday Problem Solving

The cooking class made sheet cakes.

1. Mary sliced her cake into 4 equal pieces. She put chocolate frosting on 3 of the pieces. What part of the cake has chocolate frosting?

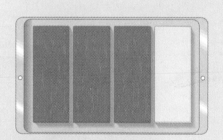

2. Mary then sliced the same cake into 3 equal parts the other way. Now how many parts are there? What part of the cake has chocolate frosting?

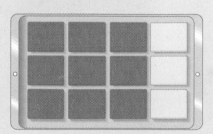

7·5 Finding Common Denominators

Like fractions have the same denominators.
Unlike fractions have different denominators.

Like fractions				Unlike fractions			
$\frac{1}{15}$	$\frac{4}{15}$	$\frac{6}{15}$	$\frac{7}{15}$	$\frac{3}{2}$	$\frac{5}{4}$	$\frac{9}{11}$	$\frac{8}{15}$

You can change unlike fractions to like fractions.

Change $\frac{5}{6}$ and $\frac{3}{8}$ to like fractions.

▶ **EXAMPLE**

The Least Common Multiple, or LCM, is the smallest multiple that two or more numbers have in common.

STEP 1 Find the least common multiple of the given denominators.

$M_6 = \{6, 12, 18, 24, ...\}$
$M_8 = \{8, 16, 24, ...\}$
LCM = 24

STEP 2 Use the least common multiple as the new denominator.

$\frac{5}{6} = \frac{?}{24} \qquad \frac{3}{8} = \frac{?}{24}$

STEP 3 Divide the LCM by the given denominators.

$24 \div 6 = 4$
$24 \div 8 = 3$

STEP 4 Multiply the numerator and denominator of each fraction by the quotients from Step 3.

$\frac{5 \times 4}{6 \times 4} = \frac{20}{24} \qquad \frac{3 \times 3}{8 \times 3} = \frac{9}{24}$

You can write $\frac{5}{6}$ and $\frac{3}{8}$ as $\frac{20}{24}$ and $\frac{9}{24}$. The new fractions have the same denominator. They are like fractions.

Write the like fractions from each exercise.

1. $\frac{2}{5}$ $\frac{2}{15}$ $\frac{3}{5}$ 2. $\frac{5}{12}$ $\frac{7}{12}$ $\frac{3}{11}$ 3. $\frac{3}{10}$ $\frac{2}{20}$ $\frac{6}{10}$

4. $\frac{3}{4}$ $\frac{6}{7}$ $\frac{1}{7}$ 5. $\frac{7}{8}$ $\frac{2}{9}$ $\frac{4}{9}$ 6. $\frac{3}{8}$ $\frac{3}{5}$ $\frac{1}{8}$

Practice B

Change each pair of fractions to like fractions.

7. $\frac{2}{3}$ $\frac{3}{4}$ 8. $\frac{4}{5}$ $\frac{5}{6}$ 9. $\frac{3}{8}$ $\frac{7}{10}$ 10. $\frac{1}{7}$ $\frac{4}{5}$

11. $\frac{3}{9}$ $\frac{3}{4}$ 12. $\frac{5}{8}$ $\frac{7}{12}$ 13. $\frac{1}{2}$ $\frac{1}{11}$ 14. $\frac{1}{3}$ $\frac{5}{9}$

15. $\frac{2}{3}$ $\frac{4}{7}$ 16. $\frac{1}{2}$ $\frac{1}{9}$ 17. $\frac{1}{5}$ $\frac{2}{7}$ 18. $\frac{3}{4}$ $\frac{1}{10}$

19. $\frac{2}{5}$ $\frac{1}{3}$ 20. $\frac{1}{6}$ $\frac{4}{9}$ 21. $\frac{7}{10}$ $\frac{1}{5}$ 22. $\frac{8}{9}$ $\frac{2}{3}$

23. $\frac{3}{4}$ $\frac{2}{7}$ 24. $\frac{1}{4}$ $\frac{5}{6}$ 25. $\frac{2}{3}$ $\frac{3}{8}$ 26. $\frac{7}{15}$ $\frac{3}{10}$

27. $\frac{1}{2}$ $\frac{3}{4}$ 28. $\frac{5}{6}$ $\frac{5}{9}$ 29. $\frac{2}{5}$ $\frac{3}{4}$ 30. $\frac{3}{5}$ $\frac{2}{3}$

Everyday Problem Solving

At the supermarket, Carmine bought $\frac{1}{2}$ pound of cherries, $\frac{7}{8}$ pound of pears, and $\frac{5}{8}$ pound of apples.

1. Name the like fractions.

2. Change all three fractions to like fractions.

You can compare like and unlike fractions.

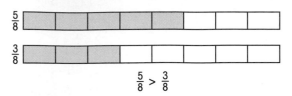

$$\frac{5}{8} > \frac{3}{8}$$

If the fractions are like fractions, compare the numerators.

▶ **EXAMPLE 1**

Review the symbols below.
  < means *less than*
  > means *greater than*

Compare $\frac{5}{8}$ and $\frac{3}{8}$. Use <, >, or =.

STEP 1 Are the fractions like fractions? **Yes.**

$$\frac{5}{8} \qquad \frac{3}{8}$$
Like fractions

STEP 2 Compare the numerators.

5   >   3
is greater than

STEP 3 Write the fractions in the same order.

$$\frac{5}{8} \quad > \quad \frac{3}{8}$$

The fraction $\frac{5}{8}$ is greater than the fraction $\frac{3}{8}$.

To compare unlike fractions, you first need to change the fractions to like fractions.

▶ **EXAMPLE 2**

Compare $\frac{5}{8}$ and $\frac{5}{6}$. Use <, >, or =.

STEP 1 Are the fractions like fractions? **No.**

$$\frac{5}{8} \qquad\qquad \frac{5}{6}$$
Unlike fractions

STEP 2 Change the fractions to like fractions. Use the common denominator of 24.

$$\frac{5 \times 3}{8 \times 3} = \frac{15}{24} \qquad \frac{5 \times 4}{6 \times 4} = \frac{20}{24}$$

STEP 3 Compare the like fractions.

$$\frac{15}{24} \quad < \quad \frac{20}{24}$$
is less than

When you compare fractions, order is important.
$$\frac{5}{8} < \frac{5}{6}$$
$$\frac{5}{6} > \frac{5}{8}$$

STEP 4 Rewrite using the given fractions.

$$\frac{5}{8} \quad < \quad \frac{5}{6}$$

The fraction $\frac{5}{8}$ is less than the fraction $\frac{5}{6}$.

Practice A

Compare each pair of fractions. Use >, <, or =.

1. $\frac{3}{8}$ < $\frac{7}{8}$

2. $\frac{5}{12}$ $\frac{5}{12}$

3. $\frac{7}{9}$ $\frac{5}{9}$

4. $\frac{5}{5}$ > $\frac{4}{5}$

5. $\frac{9}{10}$ > $\frac{9}{10}$

6. $\frac{2}{7}$ $\frac{3}{7}$

7. $\frac{11}{12}$ > $\frac{7}{12}$

8. $\frac{1}{3}$ $\frac{1}{3}$

9. $\frac{1}{4}$ $\frac{3}{4}$

Practice B

Change the fractions to like fractions. Then, compare each pair of fractions. Use >, <, or =.

10. $\frac{2}{8}$ $\frac{1}{4}$

11. $\frac{5}{8}$ $\frac{4}{5}$

12. $\frac{1}{3}$ $\frac{4}{15}$

13. $\frac{5}{6}$ $\frac{3}{4}$

14. $\frac{2}{9}$ $\frac{1}{8}$

15. $\frac{1}{6}$ $\frac{5}{9}$

16. $\frac{9}{10}$ $\frac{5}{6}$

17. $\frac{5}{15}$ $\frac{1}{3}$

18. $\frac{3}{10}$ $\frac{1}{15}$

19. $\frac{3}{8}$ $\frac{2}{7}$

20. $\frac{3}{4}$ $\frac{7}{8}$

21. $\frac{2}{3}$ $\frac{3}{4}$

Everyday Problem Solving

Sometimes you compare fractions in everyday situations.

1. Mora hiked $\frac{3}{4}$ mile. Jan hiked $\frac{3}{8}$ mile. Who hiked further?

2. Sam used $\frac{3}{4}$ cup of flour for baking. Brian used $\frac{2}{3}$ cup of flour. Who used less flour?

3. Joe drew a line that was $\frac{6}{16}$ inch long. Ling drew a line that was $\frac{3}{8}$ inch long. Who drew the longer line?

Ordering Fractions

You can place fractions in order from least to greatest. Use what you know about comparing fractions.

► EXAMPLE

Write these fractions in order from least to greatest.

$\frac{3}{5}, \frac{1}{2}, \frac{7}{10}$

STEP 1 Change the fractions to like fractions. Use the least common denominator.

$\frac{3 \times 2}{5 \times 2} = \frac{6}{10}$

$\frac{1 \times 5}{2 \times 5} = \frac{5}{10}$

STEP 2 Look at the numerators. Write the like fractions in order from least to greatest.

$\frac{5}{10}$ $\frac{6}{10}$ $\frac{7}{10}$

STEP 3 Write the given fractions in order from least to greatest.

$\frac{1}{2}$ $\frac{3}{5}$ $\frac{7}{10}$

The fractions in order are $\frac{1}{2}, \frac{3}{5}, \frac{7}{10}$.

Practice

Write the fractions in order from least to greatest.

1. $\frac{1}{2}$ $\frac{3}{8}$ $\frac{3}{4}$

2. $\frac{7}{10}$ $\frac{3}{5}$ $\frac{8}{15}$

3. $\frac{2}{3}$ $\frac{3}{4}$ $\frac{5}{8}$

4. $\frac{1}{3}$ $\frac{3}{10}$ $\frac{2}{5}$

5. $\frac{2}{9}$ $\frac{1}{6}$ $\frac{2}{15}$

6. $\frac{4}{5}$ $\frac{1}{2}$ $\frac{3}{4}$

7. $\frac{3}{7}$ $\frac{1}{3}$ $\frac{2}{21}$

8. $\frac{3}{8}$ $\frac{3}{4}$ $\frac{3}{11}$

9. $\frac{2}{3}$ $\frac{5}{8}$ $\frac{7}{9}$

10. $\frac{4}{9}$ $\frac{2}{3}$ $\frac{1}{2}$

11. $\frac{5}{7}$ $\frac{3}{4}$ $\frac{5}{14}$

12. $\frac{3}{5}$ $\frac{7}{20}$ $\frac{1}{4}$

13. $\frac{7}{10}$ $\frac{2}{5}$ $\frac{1}{3}$

14. $\frac{5}{7}$ $\frac{5}{9}$ $\frac{5}{6}$

15. $\frac{3}{4}$ $\frac{11}{20}$ $\frac{1}{5}$

16. $\frac{2}{9}$ $\frac{2}{3}$ $\frac{2}{5}$

17. $\frac{3}{7}$ $\frac{1}{4}$ $\frac{5}{14}$

18. $\frac{2}{5}$ $\frac{3}{8}$ $\frac{1}{2}$

USING YOUR CALCULATOR
Comparing Fractions

Here is another way to compare fractions.

Compare $\frac{7}{8}$ and $\frac{5}{6}$.

Multiply the numerator of one fraction by the denominator of the other fraction. Start with the first numerator.

PRESS [7] [×] [6] [=] [42.]

PRESS [5] [×] [8] [=] [40.]

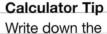

> **Calculator Tip**
> Write down the products from the calculator after you multiply. Press CLEAR between products.

Compare the products. Compare the fractions.

42 > 40

Replace the products with the given fractions.

$\frac{7}{8}$ > $\frac{5}{6}$

Compare $\frac{2}{7}$ and $\frac{6}{21}$.

PRESS [2] [×] [2] [1] [=] [42.]

PRESS [6] [×] [7] [=] [42.]

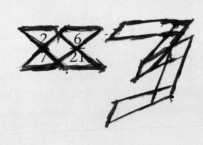

42 = 42

$\frac{2}{7}$ = $\frac{6}{21}$

Use a calculator to compare the fractions. Use >, <, or =.

1. $\frac{5}{9}$ $\frac{7}{8}$

2. $\frac{16}{20}$ $\frac{28}{35}$

3. $\frac{2}{11}$ $\frac{2}{7}$

4. $\frac{9}{10}$ $\frac{3}{4}$

5. $\frac{3}{17}$ $\frac{2}{15}$

6. $\frac{8}{9}$ $\frac{15}{19}$

7. $\frac{9}{11}$ $\frac{11}{13}$

8. $\frac{11}{12}$ $\frac{15}{19}$

9. $\frac{9}{19}$ $\frac{7}{17}$

Changing Fractions to Mixed Numbers

A proper fraction is a fraction whose numerator is smaller than its denominator.

$\frac{1}{2}$ is a proper fraction.

An improper fraction is a fraction whose numerator is larger than or equal to its denominator.

$\frac{8}{3}$ is an improper fraction.

A **mixed number** is a whole number and a fraction.

$2\frac{2}{3}$ is a mixed number.

You can change an improper fraction to a mixed number.

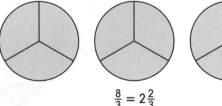

$$\frac{8}{3} = 2\frac{2}{3}$$

To change an improper fraction to a mixed number, divide the numerator by the denominator.

EXAMPLE 1

Change $\frac{8}{3}$ to a mixed number.

STEP 1 Divide the numerator by the denominator.

$$\begin{array}{r} 2 \\ 3\overline{)8} \\ -6 \\ \hline 2 \text{ out of 3 parts} \end{array}$$

STEP 2 Write the remainder as a fraction.

$$\begin{array}{r} 2\frac{2}{3} \\ 3\overline{)8} \\ -6 \\ \hline 2 \end{array}$$

The fraction $\frac{8}{3}$ is the mixed number $2\frac{2}{3}$.

Sometimes, the fraction part of the mixed number needs to be reduced to lowest terms.

► **EXAMPLE 2**

Change $\frac{28}{8}$ to a mixed number.

STEP 1 Divide the numerator by the denominator.

$$\begin{array}{r} 3 \\ 8\overline{)28} \\ -24 \\ \hline \end{array}$$
4 out of 8 parts

STEP 2 Write the remainder as a fraction.

$$\begin{array}{r} 3\frac{4}{8} \\ 8\overline{)28} \\ -24 \\ \hline 4 \end{array}$$

STEP 3 Reduce the fraction part to lowest terms.

$$3\frac{4}{8} = 3\frac{1}{2}$$

The fraction $\frac{28}{8}$ is the mixed number $3\frac{1}{2}$.

Sometimes an improper fraction can be written as a whole number.

$$\frac{15}{3} \longrightarrow 3\overline{)15}^{\,5} \longrightarrow \frac{15}{3} = 5$$

Practice

Change each fraction to a mixed number or a whole number.

1. $\frac{17}{9}$	**2.** $\frac{8}{5}$	**3.** $\frac{10}{3}$	**4.** $\frac{16}{8}$	**5.** $\frac{18}{3}$
6. $\frac{22}{7}$	**7.** $\frac{54}{8}$	**8.** $\frac{29}{3}$	**9.** $\frac{42}{6}$	**10.** $\frac{20}{4}$
11. $\frac{80}{9}$	**12.** $\frac{65}{3}$	**13.** $\frac{14}{11}$	**14.** $\frac{70}{12}$	**15.** $\frac{35}{5}$
16. $\frac{9}{4}$	**17.** $\frac{25}{3}$	**18.** $\frac{82}{9}$	**19.** $\frac{63}{7}$	**20.** $\frac{56}{6}$

7·9 ▷ Changing Mixed Numbers to Fractions

Mixed numbers can be changed to improper fractions. Change the whole number part to a fraction. Then, add the fraction part.

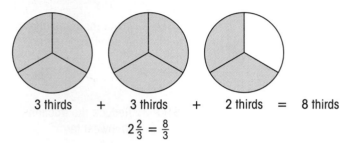

3 thirds + 3 thirds + 2 thirds = 8 thirds

$$2\frac{2}{3} = \frac{8}{3}$$

▶ **EXAMPLE**

Change $5\frac{2}{3}$ to a fraction.

STEP 1 Multiply the whole number by the denominator of the fraction.

$5\frac{2}{3}$
$5 \times 3 = 15$

STEP 2 Add the numerator to the product from Step 1.

$15 + 2 = 17$

STEP 3 Write the sum as the numerator of the fraction. The denominator is the same.

$\frac{17}{3}$

The mixed number $5\frac{2}{3}$ is the improper fraction $\frac{17}{3}$.

You can write a whole number as a fraction. $3 = \frac{3}{1}$

Practice

Change each mixed number or whole number to an improper fraction.

1. $4\frac{3}{4}$ **2.** 4 **3.** $5\frac{2}{5}$ **4.** $3\frac{6}{7}$

5. $9\frac{4}{5}$ **6.** $7\frac{3}{4}$ **7.** 9 **8.** $8\frac{5}{9}$

9. $5\frac{8}{9}$ **10.** $6\frac{7}{12}$ **11.** $12\frac{1}{3}$ **12.** 6

MATH IN YOUR LIFE
Cooking

In a few minutes, Nina's guests will be arriving for her party. She still needs to prepare the spinach dip. Nina can only find her measuring cup marked $\frac{1}{8}$ cup. She uses equivalent fractions to help her.

$\frac{1}{2}$ cup = $\frac{4}{8}$ cup soft cream cheese

This means that Nina will fill the measuring cup 4 times to measure the cream cheese.

4 times

> ### Spinach Dip
> $\frac{1}{2}$ cup soft cream cheese
> $\frac{1}{8}$ cup half-and-half
> 1 cup shredded cheese
> $\frac{1}{4}$ cup chopped onion
> $\frac{3}{4}$ cup chopped spinach
> Option: 3 Tbsp chopped olives

1. How many times must she fill the measuring cup to measure each of the other ingredients?

2. A recipe option calls for 3 tablespoons of chopped olives. Nina remembers that this is about $\frac{1}{16}$ of a cup. How can she measure the olives using the $\frac{1}{8}$ cup?

3. Nina plans to serve the dip with tortilla chips. She wants $\frac{1}{4}$ bag of chips for each guest. How many guests can be served with 2 bags of chips?

Critical Thinking

The next day Nina's $\frac{1}{8}$-cup cracked. She found her $\frac{1}{4}$-cup measuring cup. If she used this cup to make more spinach dip, what will she need to do differently?

7-10 ▸ Ordering Numbers You Know

Sometimes, you will need to order numbers in different forms from least to greatest. Order mixed numbers and fractions as you would whole numbers.

▶ **EXAMPLE**

Like mixed numbers have like fractional parts.

Write the numbers in order from least to greatest.

$$2\frac{1}{2} \qquad \frac{9}{4} \qquad 3$$

STEP 1 Change the improper fraction to a mixed number.

$$\begin{array}{r} 2\frac{1}{4} \\ 4\overline{)9} \\ -8 \\ \hline 1 \end{array}$$

STEP 2 Change the mixed numbers to like mixed numbers.

$$2\frac{1}{2} = 2\frac{2}{4}$$
$$2\frac{1}{4} = 2\frac{1}{4}$$

STEP 3 List the numbers vertically. Find the least and the greatest numbers.

$$2\frac{2}{4}$$
$$2\frac{1}{4} \leftarrow \text{least}$$
$$3 \leftarrow \text{greatest}$$

STEP 4 Write the numbers in order from least to greatest.

$$2\frac{1}{4}, 2\frac{2}{4}, 3$$

STEP 5 Rewrite the numbers in the given form.

$$\frac{9}{4}, 2\frac{1}{2}, 3$$

The numbers from least to greatest are: $\frac{9}{4}$, $2\frac{1}{2}$, 3

Practice A

Write each group of numbers in order from least to greatest.

1. $3\frac{1}{2}$	2. 4	3. $2\frac{3}{4}$	4. $\frac{7}{3}$
3	$\frac{5}{2}$	$2\frac{1}{2}$	$1\frac{2}{3}$
$\frac{3}{2}$	$3\frac{1}{2}$	$2\frac{1}{4}$	2

Practice B

Write each group of numbers in order from least to greatest.

5. $3, 2\frac{2}{3}, \frac{10}{3}$

6. $1\frac{5}{6}, 1\frac{1}{2}, \frac{5}{3}$

7. $4\frac{1}{4}, \frac{9}{2}, 4$

8. $3\frac{2}{3}, \frac{7}{2}, 3\frac{5}{6}$

9. $2\frac{3}{4}, 2\frac{1}{2}, 2\frac{3}{8}$

10. $1\frac{1}{3}, 1\frac{1}{4}, 1\frac{1}{2}$

11. $5\frac{3}{5}, 5\frac{1}{2}, 5\frac{3}{10}$

12. $\frac{6}{2}, 2\frac{1}{2}, \frac{11}{4}$

13. $10, \frac{10}{3}, 3\frac{1}{2}$

14. $8\frac{3}{4}, \frac{24}{4}, 8\frac{3}{8}$

Everyday Problem Solving

Hiking trails were built in a local park. Use the chart to answer the questions.

1. Which trail is the longest?

2. Which trail is the shortest?

3. List the distances in order from least to greatest.

4. List the names of the trails in order from shortest to longest.

5. Cindy walked the entire distance of one of the trails. She walked $3\frac{9}{12}$ miles. Which trail did she walk?

Trail	Distance
Vista	$3\frac{1}{2}$
Pleasant	$3\frac{3}{8}$
Field	$3\frac{3}{4}$
Stream	$3\frac{5}{8}$

Sometimes, you need to solve problems that are not word problems. You may need to find and complete a pattern. You can use the same problem-solving steps.

EXAMPLE

Copy and complete the sequence. Write each fraction in lowest terms.

$$\frac{1}{8}, \frac{1}{4}, \frac{3}{8}, \frac{1}{2}, \underline{\quad?\quad}, \underline{\quad?\quad}, \underline{\quad?\quad}, 1$$

STEP 1   **READ**   What do you need to find out?
Find the three missing fractions.

STEP 2   **PLAN**   What do you need to do?
Write each fraction with a **common denominator**. Then, look for the **pattern** and complete it. Reduce to lowest terms where needed.

Change the fractions to like fractions

$$\frac{1}{4} = \frac{1 \times 2}{4 \times 2} = \frac{2}{8}$$

$$\frac{1}{2} = \frac{1 \times 4}{2 \times 4} = \frac{4}{8}$$

$$1 = \frac{1 \times 8}{1 \times 8} = \frac{8}{8}$$

STEP 3   **DO**   Follow the plan.
Write each fraction with a **common denominator of 8.**

$$\frac{1}{8}, \frac{1}{4}, \frac{3}{8}, \frac{1}{2}, \underline{\quad?\quad}, \underline{\quad?\quad}, \underline{\quad?\quad}, 1$$

$$\frac{1}{8}, \frac{2}{8}, \frac{3}{8}, \frac{4}{8}, \underline{\quad?\quad}, \underline{\quad?\quad}, \underline{\quad?\quad}, \frac{8}{8}$$

Look for a **pattern** and complete it.

$$\frac{1}{8}, \frac{2}{8}, \frac{3}{8}, \frac{4}{8}, \frac{5}{8}, \frac{6}{8}, \frac{7}{8}, \frac{8}{8}$$

Reduce to the lowest terms, where needed.

$$\frac{6}{8} = \frac{3}{4}$$

STEP 4   **CHECK**   Does your answer make sense?
The fractions $\frac{5}{8}, \frac{6}{8}, \frac{7}{8}$ complete a pattern. ✓

The complete sequence is: $\frac{1}{8}, \frac{1}{4}, \frac{3}{8}, \frac{1}{2}, \frac{5}{8}, \frac{3}{4}, \frac{7}{8}, 1$

Problem Solving

READ each problem. Answer the questions under PLAN. DO the plan to solve the problem.

1. $\frac{1}{6}, \frac{1}{3}, \frac{1}{2},$ ___?___, ___?___, ___?___, $1\frac{1}{6}$

PLAN
What is the least common denominator?
What is the pattern?
What are the fractions in lowest terms?

2. $1, \frac{7}{8}, \frac{3}{4},$ ___?___, $\frac{1}{2},$ ___?___, $\frac{1}{4},$ ___?___

PLAN
What is the least common denominator?
What is the pattern?
What are the fractions in lowest terms?

3. $1\frac{1}{2}, 1\frac{3}{4}, 2,$ ___?___, $2\frac{1}{2},$ ___?___, ___?___

PLAN
What is the least common denominator?
What is the pattern?
What are the fractions in lowest terms?

Problem Solving Strategy

Sometimes, you need to find one number in a pattern.

Find the 10th number in this pattern.

$\frac{1}{3}, \frac{2}{3}, 1, 1\frac{1}{3}, 1\frac{2}{3}, 2, ...$

Count the numbers. Continue the pattern. Stop at the 10th number.

$$\frac{1}{3}, \frac{2}{3}, 1, 1\frac{1}{3}, 1\frac{2}{3}, 2, 2\frac{1}{3}, 2\frac{2}{3}, 3, 3\frac{1}{3}$$

$$1 \quad 2 \quad 3 \quad 4 \quad 5 \quad 6 \quad 7 \quad 8 \quad 9 \quad 10$$

denominator
equivalent fraction
fraction
like fractions
lowest terms
improper fraction
mixed number
numerator
unlike fractions

Vocabulary Review

Choose a word from the list to complete each sentence.

1. The __?__ of $\frac{3}{4}$ is 3.
2. The fraction $\frac{20}{40}$ in __?__ is $\frac{1}{2}$.
3. A(n) __?__ for $\frac{6}{8}$ is $\frac{3}{4}$.
4. The __?__ of $\frac{7}{8}$ is 8.
5. If 3 circles out of 5 are shaded, then the __?__ of shaded circles is $\frac{3}{5}$.
6. $\frac{5}{6}$ and $\frac{1}{6}$ are __?__.
7. $\frac{3}{7}$ and $\frac{1}{2}$ are __?__.
8. $7\frac{1}{2}$ is the __?__ for $\frac{15}{2}$.
9. $\frac{19}{3}$ is an __?__.
10. **Writing** Explain why an improper fraction is always greater than or equal to 1.

Chapter Quiz

LESSONS 7·1 and 7·2

Test Tip
The top number of a fraction tells the part. The bottom number tells the whole.

Identifying Fractions

Write a fraction to tell what part of each whole is blue. Is each fraction pair equivalent?

1.

2.
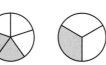

LESSONS 7·3 and 7·4

Test Tip
Multiply or divide the numerator and denominator by the same number.

Writing in Lowest Terms and Higher Terms

Write each fraction in lowest terms.

3. $\frac{16}{18}$ 4. $\frac{9}{27}$ 5. $\frac{6}{10}$

Write each fraction in higher terms.

6. $\frac{1}{6} = \frac{?}{18}$ 7. $\frac{2}{3} = \frac{?}{30}$

LESSON 7·5

Test Tip
Like fractions have the same denominators.

LESSONS 7·6 and 7·7

Test Tip
You can compare and order like fractions

LESSONS 7·8 and 7·10

Test Tip
To change an improper fraction to a mixed number, divide. To change a mixed number to an improper fraction, multiply and then add.

LESSON 7·11

Test Tip
Like fractions can help you to find a pattern.

Finding Common Denominators
Change the fractions to like fractions.

8. $\frac{4}{5}$ $\frac{7}{10}$ **9.** $\frac{5}{6}$ $\frac{1}{4}$ **10.** $\frac{1}{3}$ $\frac{4}{9}$

Comparing and Ordering
Compare. Use >, <, or =.

11. $\frac{6}{7}$ $\frac{5}{7}$ **12.** $\frac{2}{3}$ $\frac{5}{6}$

13. $\frac{1}{3}$ $\frac{1}{4}$ **14.** $\frac{3}{4}$ $\frac{6}{8}$

Write the fractions in order from least to greatest.

15. $\frac{1}{2}$ $\frac{3}{8}$ $\frac{3}{4}$ **16.** $\frac{5}{6}$ $\frac{2}{3}$ $\frac{1}{2}$

Changing Mixed Numbers and Fractions
Change to a mixed number or a whole number.

17. $\frac{34}{5}$ **18.** $\frac{18}{4}$ **19.** $\frac{15}{3}$

Change to an improper fraction.

20. $2\frac{1}{3}$ **21.** $5\frac{1}{2}$ **22.** $3\frac{3}{4}$

Write the numbers in order from least to greatest.

23. $\frac{7}{4}$ 2 $1\frac{1}{2}$ **24.** $\frac{7}{3}$ 2 $2\frac{1}{2}$

Finding Patterns
Complete the pattern.

25. $\frac{1}{4}$, ___, $\frac{3}{4}$, 1, ___, $1\frac{1}{2}$, $1\frac{3}{4}$, ___

Group Activity
With your group, look at the Business section of a newspaper. See how fractions and mixed numbers are used on the stock exchange. Pick three stocks. List the closing price for each stock. List the stock prices in order from least to greatest.

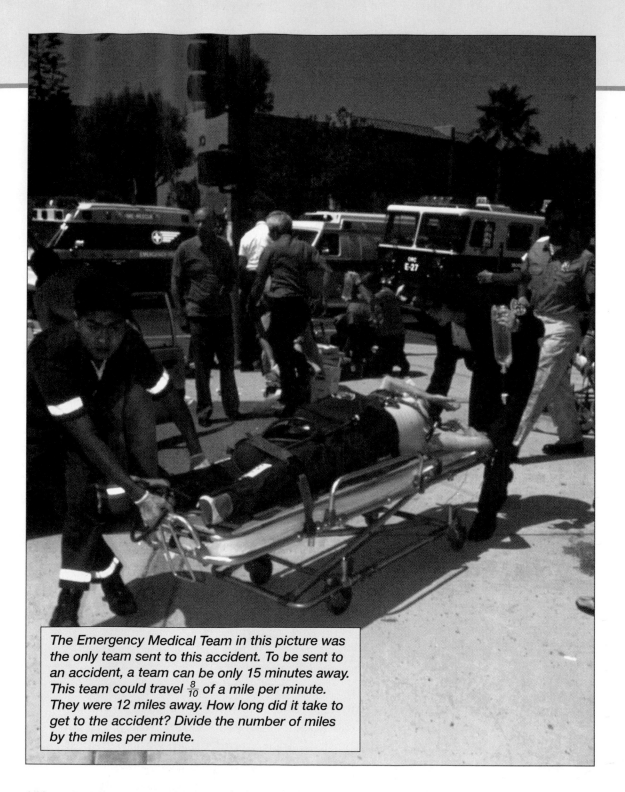

The Emergency Medical Team in this picture was the only team sent to this accident. To be sent to an accident, a team can be only 15 minutes away. This team could travel $\frac{8}{10}$ of a mile per minute. They were 12 miles away. How long did it take to get to the accident? Divide the number of miles by the miles per minute.

Chapter 8 ▶ Multiplying and Dividing Fractions

Words to Know

canceling	dividing a numerator and a denominator by the same number
invert	to reverse the positions of the numerator and denominator of a fraction

Recipe Project

Look through several magazines or cookbooks for recipes that have fractions and mixed numbers. Choose 3 of your favorite recipes. Find out how many servings the recipe makes when it is completed. Now, cut the ingredients to serve only one person.

Learning Objectives

- Multiply fractions.
- Multiply fractions using canceling.
- Multiply fractions, whole numbers, and mixed numbers.
- Divide fractions by fractions.
- Divide whole numbers, mixed numbers, and fractions.
- Apply multiplying fractions to finding gallons of gasoline.
- Solve word problems by multiplying and dividing fractions.

Multiplying Fractions

What is one-half of one-third? This means $\frac{1}{2} \times \frac{1}{3}$.

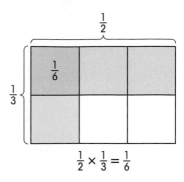

$$\frac{1}{2} \times \frac{1}{3} = \frac{1}{6}$$

One-half of one-third is one-sixth.

Knowing the basic multiplication facts will help you to multiply fractions.

▶ **EXAMPLE 1**

Multiply. $\frac{1}{2} \times \frac{1}{3}$

STEP 1 Multiply the numerators. $\frac{1}{2} \times \frac{1}{3} = \frac{1}{}$

STEP 2 Multiply the denominators. $\frac{1}{2} \times \frac{1}{3} = \frac{1}{6}$

STEP 3 Reduce to lowest terms. $\frac{1}{6}$ is in lowest terms.

The product of $\frac{1}{2}$ and $\frac{1}{3}$ is $\frac{1}{6}$.

▶ **EXAMPLE 2**

Multiply. $\frac{3}{4} \times \frac{2}{5}$

The Greatest Common Factor of 6 and 20 is 2. Divide 6 and 20 by 2 to reduce $\frac{6}{20}$ to lowest terms.

STEP 1 Multiply the numerators. $\frac{3}{4} \times \frac{2}{5} = \frac{6}{}$

STEP 2 Multiply the denominators. $\frac{3}{4} \times \frac{2}{5} = \frac{6}{20}$

STEP 3 Reduce to lowest terms. $\frac{6 \div 2}{20 \div 2} = \frac{3}{10}$

The product of $\frac{3}{4}$ and $\frac{2}{5}$ is $\frac{3}{10}$.

Practice

Multiply. Write each product in lowest terms.

1. $\frac{1}{3} \times \frac{3}{4}$

2. $\frac{5}{6} \times \frac{1}{2}$

3. $\frac{2}{3} \times \frac{2}{3}$

4. $\frac{3}{5} \times \frac{2}{3}$

5. $\frac{3}{4} \times \frac{1}{2}$

6. $\frac{2}{5} \times \frac{3}{5}$

7. $\frac{3}{5} \times \frac{3}{4}$

8. $\frac{2}{3} \times \frac{5}{6}$

9. $\frac{4}{7} \times \frac{3}{4}$

10. $\frac{5}{8} \times \frac{1}{5}$

11. $\frac{2}{3} \times \frac{3}{4}$

12. $\frac{3}{4} \times \frac{3}{4}$

13. $\frac{2}{3} \times \frac{2}{5}$

14. $\frac{1}{2} \times \frac{2}{3}$

15. $\frac{4}{5} \times \frac{1}{2}$

16. $\frac{2}{5} \times \frac{5}{6}$

17. $\frac{3}{4} \times \frac{4}{5}$

18. $\frac{2}{3} \times \frac{4}{5}$

19. $\frac{3}{5} \times \frac{5}{6}$

20. $\frac{5}{6} \times \frac{3}{4}$

21. $\frac{2}{3} \times \frac{3}{8}$

22. $\frac{3}{4} \times \frac{4}{9}$

23. $\frac{3}{5} \times \frac{5}{12}$

24. $\frac{7}{8} \times \frac{4}{7}$

Everyday Problem Solving

This is a drawing of Lee's garden.

1. What fraction of the garden is planted in corn?

2. What fraction of the corn is white corn?

3. What fraction of the garden is white corn? Multiply $\frac{1}{2} \times \frac{3}{4}$.

4. What fraction of the garden is yellow corn?

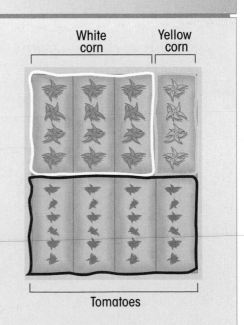

White corn   Yellow corn

Tomatoes

Canceling

Canceling is dividing the numerator of one fraction and the denominator of another fraction by the same number. Cancel fractions whenever you can before multiplying. Look for common factors.

► **EXAMPLE**

Multiply. $\frac{2}{3} \times \frac{3}{4}$

STEP 1 Divide the numerator 2 and the
denominator 4 by 2.
$2 \div 2 = 1$ Cross out 2 and write 1.
$4 \div 2 = 2$ Cross out 4 and write 2.

$\frac{\overset{1}{\cancel{2}}}{3} \times \frac{3}{\underset{2}{\cancel{4}}}$

STEP 2 Divide the numerator 3 and the
denominator 3 by 3.
$3 \div 3 = 1$ Cross out each 3 and write 1.

$\frac{\overset{1}{\cancel{2}}}{\underset{1}{\cancel{3}}} \times \frac{\overset{1}{\cancel{3}}}{\underset{2}{\cancel{4}}}$

STEP 3 Multiply the new fractions.

$\frac{1}{1} \times \frac{1}{2} = \frac{1}{2}$

The product of $\frac{2}{3}$ and $\frac{3}{4}$ is $\frac{1}{2}$.

Without canceling, you would have to reduce $\frac{6}{12}$ to lowest terms, $\frac{6}{12} = \frac{1}{2}$.

Practice A

Multiply. Remember to cancel before you multiply.

1. $\frac{2}{3} \times \frac{6}{7}$

2. $\frac{2}{5} \times \frac{9}{10}$

3. $\frac{3}{4} \times \frac{2}{9}$

4. $\frac{3}{7} \times \frac{14}{15}$

5. $\frac{5}{6} \times \frac{12}{25}$

6. $\frac{4}{7} \times \frac{7}{8}$

7. $\frac{1}{3} \times \frac{9}{10}$

8. $\frac{4}{5} \times \frac{5}{18}$

9. $\frac{3}{5} \times \frac{5}{9}$

10. $\frac{5}{8} \times \frac{2}{5}$

11. $\frac{8}{15} \times \frac{5}{12}$

12. $\frac{3}{4} \times \frac{8}{9}$

Practice B

Multiply. You will not need to cancel in every problem.

13. $\frac{3}{10} \times \frac{8}{21}$

14. $\frac{7}{8} \times \frac{16}{49}$

15. $\frac{5}{9} \times \frac{9}{10}$

16. $\frac{3}{8} \times \frac{6}{7}$

17. $\frac{7}{9} \times \frac{18}{19}$

18. $\frac{1}{5} \times \frac{1}{4}$

19. $\frac{4}{9} \times \frac{3}{28}$

20. $\frac{1}{4} \times \frac{8}{9}$

21. $\frac{4}{5} \times \frac{1}{3}$

22. $\frac{3}{8} \times \frac{16}{17}$

23. $\frac{5}{12} \times \frac{4}{5}$

24. $\frac{8}{9} \times \frac{3}{10}$

25. $\frac{2}{5} \times \frac{1}{2}$

26. $\frac{3}{13} \times \frac{1}{2}$

27. $\frac{7}{18} \times \frac{6}{7}$

28. $\frac{7}{15} \times \frac{12}{21}$

29. $\frac{7}{8} \times \frac{1}{4}$

30. $\frac{9}{10} \times \frac{15}{24}$

Everyday Problem Solving

Gina has a recipe for Power Cereal. She wants to make $\frac{3}{4}$ of the recipe. Remember that *of* means to multiply.

1. How much wheat germ will she need? Multiply $\frac{2}{3}$ by $\frac{3}{4}$.

2. How many cups of raisins will she need?

3. How many cups of sunflower seeds will she need?

4. Will she need more or less than 2 cups of quick oatmeal? Why?

Power Cereal

2 Cups Quick Oatmeal

$\frac{2}{3}$ Cup Wheat Germ

$\frac{3}{4}$ Cup Raisins

$\frac{1}{3}$ Cup Sunflower Seeds

1 Tablespoon Brown Sugar

Serves 2 people

Multiplying Fractions and Whole Numbers

To multiply a fraction and a whole number, first change the whole number to a fraction.

You can change any whole number to a fraction. Make the whole number the numerator. Make the denominator 1.

$$2 = \frac{2}{1} \qquad 16 = \frac{16}{1} \qquad 39 = \frac{39}{1}$$

▶ **EXAMPLE**

Multiply. $8 \times \frac{2}{3}$

To change $\frac{16}{3}$ to a mixed number, divide the numerator by the denominator:

$$\begin{array}{r} 5\frac{1}{3} \\ 3)\overline{16} \\ -15 \\ \hline 1 \end{array}$$

STEP 1   Change the whole number to a fraction.

$$8 = \frac{8}{1}$$

STEP 2   Multiply numerators and denominators.

$$\frac{8}{1} \times \frac{2}{3} = \frac{16}{3}$$

STEP 3   Change the product to a mixed number in lowest terms.

$$\frac{16}{3} = 5\frac{1}{3}$$

The product of 8 and $\frac{2}{3}$ is $5\frac{1}{3}$.

Practice

Multiply. Cancel, if possible.

1. $5 \times \frac{3}{4}$

2. $\frac{7}{8} \times 5$

3. $\frac{3}{4} \times 7$

4. $\frac{4}{5} \times 7$

5. $\frac{3}{10} \times 7$

6. $15 \times \frac{2}{7}$

7. $\frac{8}{9} \times 5$

8. $7 \times \frac{3}{4}$

9. $\frac{2}{3} \times 9$

10. $12 \times \frac{5}{6}$

11. $81 \times \frac{5}{9}$

12. $22 \times \frac{3}{8}$

13. $36 \times \frac{5}{12}$

14. $\frac{1}{8} \times 20$

15. $\frac{5}{6} \times 11$

16. $32 \times \frac{7}{16}$

17. $15 \times \frac{1}{3}$

18. $\frac{2}{5} \times 10$

19. $\frac{5}{12} \times 8$

20. $6 \times \frac{3}{8}$

USING YOUR CALCULATOR
Multiplying Fractions and Whole Numbers

You can use your calculator to find the product of
a whole number and a fraction.

Multiply. $\frac{3}{8} \times 24$

First, multiply the whole number and the numerator.

PRESS $\boxed{2}\ \boxed{4}\ \boxed{\times}\ \boxed{3}\ \boxed{=}$ | 72. |

> **Calculator Tip**
> Do not press
> clear between
> steps.

Do not press CLEAR. Leave the product on the screen.
Divide it by the denominator of the fraction.

PRESS $\boxed{\div}\ \boxed{8}\ \boxed{=}$ | 9. |

The product of $\frac{3}{8}$ and 24 is 9.

**Copy each problem on paper. Then, use your calculator
to multiply.**

1. $500 \times \frac{4}{5}$

2. $\frac{5}{8} \times 6,400$

3. $\frac{2}{3} \times 1,500$

4. $312 \times \frac{5}{8}$

5. $\frac{5}{6} \times 84$

6. $\frac{27}{4} \times 4$

7. $\frac{3}{5} \times 600$

8. $1,400 \times \frac{4}{7}$

9. $\frac{5}{9} \times 270$

10. $330 \times \frac{2}{3}$

11. $\frac{1}{2} \times 900$

12. $\frac{2}{3} \times 9$

13. $\frac{3}{4} \times 1,600$

14. $1,800 \times \frac{5}{6}$

15. $\frac{7}{10} \times 1,200$

Multiplying Mixed Numbers

Before you can multiply mixed numbers, you have to change each mixed number to an improper fraction.

Here is how you can change $5\frac{1}{3}$ and $2\frac{1}{2}$ to improper fractions:

$$5\frac{1}{3} = \frac{3 \times 5 + 1}{3} = \frac{16}{3} \qquad 2\frac{1}{2} = \frac{2 \times 2 + 1}{2} = \frac{5}{2}$$

▶ **EXAMPLE**

Multiply. $5\frac{1}{3} \times 2\frac{1}{2}$

In an improper fraction, the numerator is larger than the denominator.

STEP 1 Change each mixed number to an improper fraction.
$5\frac{1}{3} = \frac{16}{3}$ $2\frac{1}{2} = \frac{5}{2}$

$5\frac{1}{3} \times 2\frac{1}{2}$

$\frac{16}{3} \times \frac{5}{2}$

STEP 2 Cancel if you can. Then, multiply.

$\frac{\overset{8}{\cancel{16}}}{3} \times \frac{5}{\underset{1}{\cancel{2}}} = \frac{40}{3}$

STEP 3 Change the product to a mixed number.

$\frac{40}{3} = 13\frac{1}{3}$

The product of $5\frac{1}{3}$ and $2\frac{1}{2}$ is $13\frac{1}{3}$.

Before you can multiply a mixed number and a whole number, you have to change each number to an improper fraction.

Practice A

Multiply. Be sure to change mixed numbers.

1. $6\frac{2}{3} \times 1\frac{1}{8}$

2. $3\frac{1}{7} \times 2\frac{1}{10}$

3. $1\frac{2}{3} \times 4\frac{1}{5}$

4. $3\frac{1}{3} \times 3\frac{1}{2}$

5. $2\frac{3}{4} \times 3\frac{1}{9}$

6. $4\frac{1}{2} \times 7\frac{1}{3}$

Practice B

Multiply.

7. $3\frac{1}{8} \times 2$

8. $5\frac{3}{5} \times 2\frac{1}{2}$

9. $1\frac{3}{4} \times 1\frac{3}{5}$

10. $\frac{3}{4} \times \frac{3}{10}$

11. $\frac{6}{7} \times \frac{5}{12}$

12. $20 \times \frac{4}{5}$

13. $10 \times 2\frac{1}{2}$

14. $12 \times \frac{5}{24}$

15. $\frac{2}{5} \times \frac{2}{5}$

16. $\frac{3}{4} \times 3\frac{5}{6}$

17. $\frac{5}{6} \times \frac{3}{15}$

18. $\frac{2}{3} \times 15$

19. $16 \times 2\frac{3}{4}$

20. $24 \times 3\frac{1}{2}$

21. $\frac{6}{7} \times \frac{1}{2}$

22. $2\frac{4}{9} \times 1\frac{1}{2}$

23. $2\frac{5}{6} \times \frac{2}{5}$

24. $1\frac{7}{8} \times 5\frac{1}{9}$

Everyday Problem Solving

Ms. Cruz went food shopping. At the meat department, she saw this sign.

1. How much will $2\frac{1}{2}$ pounds of prime steak cost? Multiply $2\frac{1}{2} \times \$10$.

2. How much will $3\frac{1}{2}$ pounds of hamburger cost?

3. Which costs more: $2\frac{1}{2}$ pounds of prime steak or $4\frac{1}{2}$ pounds of veal cutlet?

4. Ms. Cruz buys a package of hamburger that costs $3. How much does the package weigh?

☆**Today's Specials**☆

Prime Steak	$10 per pound
Veal Cutlet	$ 8 per pound
Hamburger	$ 2 per pound

8-5 ▶ Dividing by Fractions

You can use fraction strips to divide by a fraction. What is $1 \div \frac{1}{3}$? How many $\frac{1}{3}$s are in 1?

1 whole		
$\frac{1}{3}$	$\frac{1}{3}$	$\frac{1}{3}$

$$1 \div \frac{1}{3} = 3$$

There are three $\frac{1}{3}$s in 1.

You can link division by a fraction to multiplication.

$$1 \div \frac{1}{3} = 1 \times \frac{3}{1} = 3$$

invert

To divide by a fraction, first you **invert** the second number. Then, you multiply.

▶ **EXAMPLE**

Divide. $5 \div \frac{2}{3}$

STEP 1 Write the whole number as a fraction. $5 = \frac{5}{1}$ Change the division sign to a multiplication sign.

$5 \div \frac{2}{3}$

$\frac{5}{1} \times$

STEP 2 Invert the second fraction. Do NOT change the first fraction.

$\frac{5}{1} \times \frac{3}{2}$

STEP 3 Multiply. Simplify the product, if possible.

$\frac{5}{1} \times \frac{3}{2} = \frac{15}{2} = 7\frac{1}{2}$

The quotient of 5 and $\frac{2}{3}$ is $7\frac{1}{2}$.

Follow the same steps to divide a fraction by a fraction.

$$\frac{1}{2} \div \frac{2}{3} = \frac{1}{2} \times \frac{3}{2} = \frac{3}{4}$$

Practice A

Divide. Remember to invert the second number. Then, multiply.

1. $3 \div \frac{1}{4}$ **2.** $4 \div \frac{1}{8}$ **3.** $5 \div \frac{1}{2}$ **4.** $9 \div \frac{1}{3}$

5. $6 \div \frac{3}{4}$ **6.** $8 \div \frac{2}{3}$ **7.** $10 \div \frac{5}{6}$ **8.** $9 \div \frac{3}{5}$

Practice B

Divide. Be sure that each answer is in lowest terms.

9. $\frac{2}{3} \div \frac{1}{3}$ **10.** $\frac{7}{12} \div \frac{1}{5}$ **11.** $\frac{12}{13} \div \frac{4}{5}$ **12.** $\frac{9}{24} \div \frac{2}{3}$

13. $\frac{4}{5} \div \frac{2}{5}$ **14.** $\frac{9}{10} \cdot \frac{6}{7}$ **15.** $\frac{4}{10} \div \frac{1}{5}$ **16.** $\frac{12}{20} \div \frac{1}{2}$

17. $\frac{3}{4} \div \frac{2}{3}$ **18.** $\frac{2}{5} \div \frac{3}{5}$ **19.** $\frac{4}{5} \div \frac{4}{5}$ **20.** $\frac{2}{3} \div \frac{8}{15}$

21. $\frac{3}{7} \div \frac{9}{10}$ **22.** $\frac{2}{7} \div \frac{3}{14}$ **23.** $\frac{1}{2} \div \frac{1}{7}$ **24.** $\frac{9}{10} \div \frac{1}{2}$

Everyday Problem Solving

In music, there are whole notes, half notes, quarter notes, and eighth notes. These notes tell you how long you need to hold a note.

1. How many half notes are in a whole note? Divide. $1 \div \frac{1}{2}$

2. How many quarter notes are in a whole note?

3. How many quarter notes are in a half note?

4. How many eighth notes are in a half note? Divide. $\frac{1}{2} \div \frac{1}{8}$

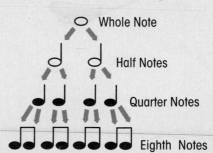

Dividing Fractions by Whole Numbers

You can divide a fraction by a whole number. First, change the whole number to an improper fraction.

▶ **EXAMPLE**

Divide. $\frac{7}{8} \div 5$

STEP 1 Change the whole number to an improper fraction. $5 = \frac{5}{1}$ Do NOT change the first fraction.

$\frac{7}{8} \div 5$

$\frac{7}{8} \div \frac{5}{1}$

STEP 2 Change the sign to multiplication.

$\frac{7}{8} \times$

STEP 3 Invert the second fraction.

$\frac{7}{8} \times \frac{1}{5}$

STEP 4 Multiply. Cancel, if possible.

$\frac{7}{8} \times \frac{1}{5} = \frac{7}{40}$

The quotient of $\frac{7}{8}$ divided by 5 is $\frac{7}{40}$.

Practice

Divide. Remember to invert the second number and multiply.

1. $\frac{2}{3} \div 3$

2. $\frac{1}{2} \div 4$

3. $\frac{3}{4} \div 5$

4. $3 \div \frac{7}{8}$

5. $25 \div \frac{1}{5}$

6. $\frac{1}{2} \div 7$

7. $\frac{2}{3} \div 18$

8. $\frac{4}{5} \div 20$

9. $20 \div \frac{5}{12}$

10. $16 \div \frac{6}{7}$

11. $\frac{7}{9} \div 6$

12. $52 \div \frac{2}{3}$

13. $49 \div \frac{7}{10}$

14. $10 \div \frac{1}{8}$

15. $\frac{1}{3} \div 10$

16. $6 \div \frac{3}{4}$

17. $\frac{3}{4} \div 6$

18. $\frac{5}{7} \div 13$

19. $\frac{8}{9} \div 24$

20. $\frac{10}{11} \div 20$

21. $18 \div \frac{2}{3}$

22. $\frac{5}{6} \div 5$

23. $20 \div \frac{4}{5}$

24. $16 \div \frac{1}{2}$

ON-THE-JOB MATH
Car Rental Agent

Jason works at a car rental agency. He checks the cars when they are returned. The fuel tank should be full. If the fuel tank is not full, the customer must pay to fill the tank.

Jason needs to know how many gallons are needed to fill the tank. Here is how Jason finds out.

Car A: The tank holds 20 gallons.

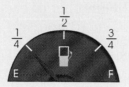

The gauge reads $\frac{1}{4}$ tank.

Jason multiplies to find how many gallons are in the tank.

$$20 \times \frac{1}{4} = 5 \text{ gallons}$$

Then he subtracts to find how many more gallons are needed to fill the tank.

$$20 - 5 = 15 \text{ gallons}$$

The customer pays for 15 gallons of gasoline to fill the tank.

Find out how many gallons are needed to fill each tank. The gauge shows the amount of gasoline in each tank.

Critical Thinking

How could Jason quickly figure the cost for a customer who just returned a car that is almost empty?

1.

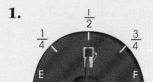

Holds 20 gallons

2.

Holds 24 gallons

3.

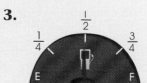

Holds 16 gallons

Problem Solving: Solve a Simpler Problem

Some word problems can seem confusing. Use simpler whole numbers to help you decide which operation to use. Then use the numbers in the problem to solve.

▶ **EXAMPLE**

At Mike's Auto Body Shop, it takes $\frac{5}{6}$ of an hour to polish one car. How many cars can be polished in 10 hours?

STEP 1 **READ** **What do you need to find out?**
You need to find the number of cars that can be polished in 10 hours.

STEP 2 **PLAN** **What do you need to do?**
Make the problem simpler. Use simple whole numbers.

Pretend it takes 2 hours to polish one car. How many cars can be polished in 10 hours?

Divide the total hours by the amount of hours to polish one car.
10 hours ÷ 2 hours for one car

Remember that when you divide, you invert the second fraction and mulitply.

STEP 3 **DO** **Follow the plan.**
Now, use the numbers from the original problem.

10 hours ÷ $\frac{5}{6}$ hour for one car
$\frac{10}{1} \times \frac{6}{5} = 12$ cars

STEP 4 **CHECK** **Does your answer make sense?**
Work backward. If one car takes $\frac{5}{6}$ hour, how long does it take 12 cars?

$$12 \times \frac{5}{6} = \frac{12}{1} \times \frac{5}{6} = 10 \text{ hours } ✓$$

In 10 hours, 12 cars can be polished.

Problem Solving

READ the problem. Replace the fraction with a whole number. Make a PLAN. Now use the original numbers to DO the plan to solve the problem.

1. Jon has a board that is $\frac{2}{3}$ yard long. He cuts the board into 6 equal pieces. How long is each piece?

   PLAN
   Pretend the board is 12 yards long. What would you divide?

2. Four people want to equally share $\frac{4}{5}$ pound of nuts. How much will each person have?

   PLAN
   Pretend there are 8 pounds of nuts. What would you divide?

3. At Ann's Auto Body Shop, it takes $\frac{3}{4}$ of an hour to paint one car. How long will it take to paint 8 cars?

   PLAN
   Pretend it takes 2 hours to paint one car. Would you multiply or divide?

Problem Solving Strategy

Sometimes, you can draw a picture to solve a problem.

> Diane found $\frac{1}{2}$ of a pie on the table. She ate $\frac{1}{4}$ of the $\frac{1}{2}$. How much of the pie did Diane eat?

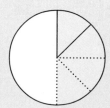

Draw a picture of $\frac{1}{2}$ pie. Then, split this piece into $\frac{1}{4}$s. How much of the whole pie is $\frac{1}{4}$ of $\frac{1}{2}$?

8·8   Dividing Mixed Numbers

Dividing a mixed number by a fraction is like dividing a fraction by another fraction.

▶ **EXAMPLE**

Remember:

$$4\frac{2}{3} = \frac{3 \times 4 + 2}{3} = \frac{14}{3}$$

Divide. $4\frac{2}{3} \div \frac{7}{9}$

STEP 1   Change the mixed number to an improper fraction.

$\frac{14}{3} \div \frac{7}{9}$

STEP 2   Change the sign to multiplication.

$\frac{14}{3} \times$

STEP 3   Invert the second fraction. Do NOT change the first fracton.

$\frac{14}{3} \times \frac{9}{7}$

STEP 4   Multiply. Simplify the quotient, if possible.

$\overset{2}{\underset{1}{\cancel{\frac{14}{3}}}} \times \overset{3}{\underset{1}{\cancel{\frac{9}{7}}}} = \frac{6}{1} = 6$

The quotient of $4\frac{2}{3}$ divided by $\frac{7}{9}$ is 6.

Practice A

Divide. Remember to change the mixed numbers to fractions.

1. $\frac{2}{3} \div 1\frac{2}{3}$ **2.** $4\frac{2}{5} \div \frac{2}{5}$ **3.** $2\frac{2}{7} \div \frac{4}{5}$ **4.** $\frac{3}{4} \div 1\frac{1}{3}$

5. $\frac{7}{8} \div 2\frac{3}{8}$ **6.** $2\frac{2}{3} \div \frac{1}{6}$ **7.** $\frac{7}{9} \div 3\frac{1}{2}$ **8.** $2\frac{1}{12} \div \frac{5}{6}$

9. $1\frac{1}{5} \div \frac{1}{5}$ **10.** $\frac{5}{6} \div 2\frac{1}{2}$ **11.** $2\frac{2}{7} \div \frac{6}{7}$ **12.** $\frac{5}{8} \div 1\frac{1}{2}$

13. $\frac{3}{5} \div 2\frac{1}{4}$ **14.** $1\frac{1}{9} \div \frac{5}{9}$ **15.** $\frac{2}{7} \div 1\frac{1}{3}$ **16.** $2\frac{1}{3} \div \frac{5}{6}$

Practice B

Divide. Remember to change the mixed numbers or whole numbers to fractions.

17. $8 \div \frac{4}{5}$

18. $\frac{3}{5} \div 2\frac{2}{3}$

19. $\frac{2}{7} \div \frac{3}{4}$

20. $\frac{3}{8} \div 4$

21. $\frac{3}{5} \div \frac{1}{5}$

22. $\frac{7}{8} \div 1\frac{1}{2}$

23. $9 \div \frac{2}{3}$

24. $\frac{1}{3} \div \frac{4}{5}$

25. $\frac{1}{3} \div \frac{8}{9}$

26. $\frac{4}{5} \div 2\frac{3}{5}$

27. $12 \div \frac{5}{6}$

28. $\frac{2}{3} \div 6$

29. $15 \div \frac{3}{5}$

30. $\frac{9}{10} \div 1\frac{2}{5}$

31. $\frac{7}{9} \div 21$

32. $\frac{3}{14} \div \frac{6}{7}$

Everyday Problem Solving

The gym displays a chart of daily running times. It shows the number of days each person runs in a month. It also shows the monthly total for each person. Some of the data are missing from the chart.

Running Times			
Name	Daily Time	Number of Days	Monthly Total
Bly	$\frac{3}{4}$ hour	?	$7\frac{1}{2}$ hours
Aki	$\frac{2}{3}$ hour	?	$10\frac{2}{3}$ hours
Tracy	$\frac{1}{2}$ hour	20 days	?
Lani	$\frac{7}{8}$ hour	24 days	?

1. How many days did Bly run on the track that month? Divide the monthly total by the daily time.

2. How many days did Aki run on the track that month?

3. Tracy ran $\frac{1}{2}$ hour each day for 20 days that month. What was her total running time for that month? Multiply 20 days by $\frac{1}{2}$ hour.

4. Lani ran $\frac{7}{8}$ hour each day for 24 days that month. What was his total running time for that month?

Dividing Mixed Numbers by Mixed Numbers

You can divide a mixed number by another mixed number.

EXAMPLE

Divide. $6\frac{1}{2} \div 5\frac{7}{9}$

STEP 1 Change the mixed numbers to improper fractions.

$\frac{13}{2} \div \frac{52}{9}$

STEP 2 Change the sign to multiplication.

$\frac{13}{2} \times$

STEP 3 Invert the second fraction. Do NOT change the first fraction.

$\frac{13}{2} \times \frac{9}{52}$

STEP 4 Multiply. Simplify the quotient, if possible.

$\frac{\overset{1}{\cancel{13}}}{2} \times \frac{9}{\underset{4}{\cancel{52}}} = \frac{9}{8} = 1\frac{1}{8}$

The quotient of $6\frac{1}{2}$ divided by $5\frac{7}{9}$ is $1\frac{1}{8}$.

Practice A

Divide. Remember to change the mixed numbers to improper fractions.

1. $6\frac{1}{8} \div 3\frac{1}{2}$ 2. $4\frac{2}{5} \div \frac{2}{5}$ 3. $3\frac{1}{8} \div \frac{7}{8}$ 4. $5\frac{1}{7} \div 1\frac{1}{3}$

5. $7\frac{1}{5} \div 2\frac{2}{5}$ 6. $2\frac{1}{9} \div 1\frac{2}{3}$ 7. $9\frac{3}{8} \div 4\frac{1}{2}$ 8. $4\frac{1}{3} \div 2\frac{1}{6}$

9. $8\frac{1}{8} \div 2\frac{1}{2}$ 10. $4\frac{2}{5} \div \frac{3}{10}$ 11. $8\frac{1}{2} \div 5\frac{2}{3}$ 12. $4\frac{3}{8} \div 3\frac{1}{8}$

13. $2\frac{1}{3} \div \frac{3}{5}$ 14. $3\frac{4}{7} \div 3\frac{4}{7}$ 15. $5\frac{4}{9} \div 3\frac{1}{2}$ 16. $4\frac{1}{6} \div \frac{7}{12}$

17. $2\frac{1}{4} \div \frac{3}{8}$ 18. $3\frac{7}{8} \div 1\frac{1}{2}$ 19. $5\frac{1}{10} \div \frac{7}{10}$ 20. $9\frac{4}{5} \div 3\frac{1}{2}$

Practice B

Divide or multiply.

21. $\frac{4}{5} \times 2\frac{3}{4}$ **22.** $10 \div \frac{2}{5}$ **23.** $\frac{1}{2} \div 1\frac{3}{4}$ **24.** $\frac{4}{5} \div 2$

25. $5\frac{1}{4} \times 8$ **26.** $3\frac{2}{3} \times \frac{5}{9}$ **27.** $3\frac{1}{4} \div \frac{3}{4}$ **28.** $\frac{3}{5} \times \frac{6}{7}$

29. $10 \div \frac{1}{7}$ **30.** $9 \times \frac{2}{3}$ **31.** $\frac{3}{5} \times 5\frac{1}{2}$ **32.** $\frac{5}{6} \div \frac{2}{3}$

33. $\frac{5}{6} \div 3$ **34.** $2\frac{2}{5} \times 1\frac{4}{5}$ **35.** $\frac{7}{9} \times 81$ **36.** $3\frac{3}{8} \div 1\frac{1}{4}$

Everyday Problem Solving

Jena's regular pay is $12 per hour at her job. She usually works 40 hours a week. Some weeks, she may work overtime. Overtime is any time more than 40 hours. For overtime, she is paid $1\frac{1}{2}$ times her regular pay. The time card shows her hours for three weeks.

1. How much is Jena paid for 1 hour of overtime? Multiply her regular pay by $1\frac{1}{2}$.

2. How many hours of overtime did Jena work during Week 1? Subtract 40 from the hours worked.

3. How much was she paid for overtime during Week 1? Multiply the overtime pay for1 hour by the overtime hours.

4. How much was Jena paid for the overtime in Week 2?

Name:	*Jena*
Week	Number of hours worked
1	45
2	48
3	40

8·10 Problem Solving: Does the Answer Make Sense?

It is important to check your answer to a word problem. You should be sure it makes sense.

EXAMPLE

Mr. Harris bought a large sub sandwich for a family picnic. He wants to cut the sandwich into slices $1\frac{4}{5}$ inches long. The sub is 72 inches long. How many slices will he have?

STEP 1 READ What do you need to find out?
You need to find how many slices Mr. Harris can cut.

STEP 2 PLAN What do you need to do?
Divide the length of the sub by the size of each slice.

Remember to change the mixed number to a fraction.
$$1\frac{4}{5} = \frac{9}{5}$$

STEP 3 DO Follow the plan.

72 inches $\div$ $\frac{9}{5}$ inches

↑ length of sub   ↑ size of each piece

$$\frac{72}{1} \times \frac{5}{9} = 40 \text{ slices}$$

↑ number of slices

STEP 4 CHECK Does your answer make sense?
Did you use the right operation in the right order? To check, reverse the order in the division problem.

$$1\frac{4}{5} \div 72 = \frac{1}{40} \text{ slice}$$

Does $\frac{1}{40}$ slice make sense? No.

So, 40 slices is correct. ✓

Mr. Harris can cut 40 slices.

Problem Solving

READ the problem. Determine if you will use multiplication or division for the PLAN. DO the plan to solve each problem. Answer the questions under CHECK.

1. It took Robert $6\frac{3}{4}$ hours to repair his car. Dave said that he could do it in $\frac{1}{2}$ the time. How long would it take Dave?

> **CHECK**
> Did you use the right numbers in the right order?
> Does the answer make sense?

2. Gloria made 96 cookies for the bake sale. She sold $\frac{2}{3}$ of them. How many cookies did she sell?

> **CHECK**
> Did you use the right numbers in the right order?
> Does the answer make sense?

3. The bookshelf is 40 inches long. Each book is $1\frac{1}{4}$ inches wide. How many books will fit on the shelf?

> **CHECK**
> Did you use the right numbers in the right order?
> Does the answer make sense?

Problem Solving Strategy

Sometimes, choosing the correct answer to a word problem is thinking about what makes sense.

David had to answer this problem on a test:

> About how many dogs could be groomed in one week?
>
> **(a)** $\frac{1}{50}$ dog   **(b)** 50 weeks   **(c)** 50 dogs   **(d)** $\frac{1}{50}$ week

Eliminate choices that don't make sense. Ask yourself:
Can you have $\frac{1}{50}$ of a dog?
Should your answer be about dogs or weeks?
What is the only answer that makes sense?

canceling
invert

Vocabulary Review

Answer each question.

1. Give an example of canceling when multiplying two fractions.

2. How do you invert a fraction? When is it necessary to invert a fraction? Give an example.

3. **Writing** Pretend you are tutoring someone. How would you show the student how to cancel?

Chapter Quiz

LESSONS 8·1 and 8·2

Test Tip
Use a common factor to cancel. Multiply numerators, then denominators.

Multiplying Fractions

Multiply. Cancel, if possible.

1. $\frac{1}{2} \times \frac{6}{7}$
2. $\frac{5}{6} \times \frac{12}{13}$
3. $\frac{3}{4} \times \frac{1}{8}$
4. $\frac{8}{9} \times \frac{1}{4}$
5. $\frac{3}{8} \times \frac{1}{8}$
6. $\frac{12}{17} \times \frac{17}{20}$

LESSONS 8·3 and 8·4

Test Tip
Change mixed numbers and whole numbers to improper fractions before multiplying.

Multiplying Whole Numbers, Mixed Numbers, and Fractions

Multiply. Cancel, if possible.

7. $45 \times \frac{5}{9}$
8. $\frac{3}{4} \times 36$
9. $\frac{2}{3} \times 3\frac{5}{6}$
10. $6\frac{3}{7} \times \frac{7}{8}$
11. $4\frac{3}{5} \times 2\frac{11}{23}$
12. $14 \times 3\frac{1}{2}$
13. $3\frac{7}{9} \times 2\frac{3}{17}$
14. $5\frac{3}{4} \times 5\frac{1}{3}$

Dividing with Fractions and Whole Numbers
Divide. Cancel, if possible.

15. $\frac{9}{10} \div 20$ **16.** $\frac{3}{4} \div \frac{3}{8}$

17. $\frac{4}{5} \div \frac{1}{5}$ **18.** $6 \div \frac{2}{3}$

19. $\frac{2}{5} \div \frac{9}{10}$ **20.** $36 \div \frac{3}{4}$

Dividing with Mixed Numbers
Divide. Cancel, if possible.

21. $2\frac{1}{2} \div \frac{3}{4}$ **22.** $\frac{5}{6} \div 3\frac{1}{12}$

23. $\frac{7}{9} \div 3\frac{5}{6}$ **24.** $4\frac{3}{7} \div \frac{3}{14}$

25. $3\frac{5}{8} \div 1\frac{1}{2}$ **26.** $5\frac{1}{9} \div 3\frac{2}{3}$

Solving Problems
Solve.

27. Jan bought $2\frac{5}{8}$ pounds of hamburger meat. Each pound is 16 ounces. How many ounces did she buy?

28. It took Jason $3\frac{3}{4}$ hours to cut the grass. Frank says he can cut the grass in $\frac{2}{3}$ the time. How long would it take Frank to cut the grass?

Group Activity
With your group, choose three favorite recipes. Double the first recipe. Find the new amount of each ingredient needed. Triple the second recipe. Find the new amounts of each ingredient. For the third recipe, find the ingredients for $2\frac{1}{2}$ times the recipe. Give the new number of servings for each recipe. What items or directions should not be changed?

This draftswoman is a skilled worker. She often needs to work with fractions on the job. She is looking at a blueprint. It tells her that she needs $50\frac{1}{2}$ feet of wood to build part of a wall. She has $25\frac{1}{2}$ feet of wood on order. How much more wood does she need to order?

9 ▶ Adding and Subtracting Fractions

Words to Know

like fractions	fractions that have the same denominator
unlike fractions	fractions that have different denominators

Activities Project

During the week, you have activities after school. You may have band practice, play basketball, or work. Make a list of the days that you have activities after school. For one week, write how long you do each activity. Use fractions of an hour, if you need to. Find the total hours for one week. Try this for one month.

Mon.	Band practice	$1\frac{1}{2}$ h
Tues.	Part-time job	$3\frac{1}{4}$ h
Wed.	Make dinner	$\frac{1}{2}$ h
Thurs.	Read book	$1\frac{1}{4}$ h
Fri.	Part-time job	$2\frac{3}{4}$ h
	TOTAL	$9\frac{1}{4}$ h

Learning Objectives

- Add and subtract like fractions.
- Add and subtract like mixed numbers.
- Subtract mixed numbers and fractions from whole numbers.
- Add and subtract unlike fractions.
- Add and subtract unlike mixed numbers.
- Solve multi-part fraction problems.
- Apply adding and subtracting fractions to find work hours.

9·1 Adding and Subtracting Like Fractions

Like fractions have the same denominators. The fraction strips below show how to add or subtract like fractions.

$$\frac{1}{5} + \frac{3}{5} = \frac{4}{5}$$

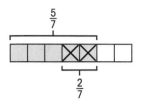

$$\frac{5}{7} - \frac{2}{7} = \frac{3}{7}$$

To add or subtract like fractions, add or subtract only the numerators. Use the common denominator as the denominator of your answer.

▶ **EXAMPLE 1**

If the answer is an improper fraction, change it to a mixed number. To change $\frac{15}{9}$, divide 15 by 9.

$$
\begin{array}{r}
1\frac{6}{9} \\
9\overline{)15} \\
-9 \\
\hline
6
\end{array}
$$

Add. $\frac{8}{9} + \frac{7}{9}$

STEP 1
Add the numerators. Keep the common denominator.

$$
\begin{array}{r}
\frac{8}{9} \\
+ \frac{7}{9} \\
\hline
\frac{15}{9}
\end{array}
$$

STEP 2
Write the answer in lowest terms.

$$
\begin{array}{r}
\frac{8}{9} \\
+ \frac{7}{9} \\
\hline
\frac{15}{9} = 1\frac{6}{9} \\
= 1\frac{2}{3}
\end{array}
$$

The sum of $\frac{8}{9}$ and $\frac{7}{9}$ is $1\frac{2}{3}$.

▶ **EXAMPLE 2**

Subtract. $\frac{7}{8} - \frac{3}{8}$

STEP 1
Subtract the numerators. Keep the common denominator.

$$
\begin{array}{r}
\frac{7}{8} \\
- \frac{3}{8} \\
\hline
\frac{4}{8}
\end{array}
$$

STEP 2
Write the answer in lowest terms.

$$
\begin{array}{r}
\frac{7}{8} \\
- \frac{3}{8} \\
\hline
\frac{4}{8} = \frac{1}{2}
\end{array}
$$

The difference between $\frac{7}{8}$ and $\frac{3}{8}$ is $\frac{1}{2}$.

Practice A

Add. Write the answer in lowest terms.

1. $\frac{1}{3}$
$+ \frac{1}{3}$

2. $\frac{2}{7}$
$+ \frac{4}{7}$

3. $\frac{7}{8}$
$+ \frac{1}{8}$

4. $\frac{4}{9}$
$+ \frac{2}{9}$

5. $\frac{2}{5}$
$+ \frac{4}{5}$

6. $\frac{5}{6}$
$+ \frac{3}{6}$

7. $\frac{7}{12}$
$+ \frac{5}{12}$

8. $\frac{5}{20}$
$+ \frac{7}{20}$

9. $\frac{3}{4}$
$+ \frac{3}{4}$

10. $\frac{7}{10}$
$+ \frac{9}{10}$

Practice B

Subtract. Write the answer in lowest terms.

11. $\frac{7}{9}$
$- \frac{2}{9}$

12. $\frac{13}{20}$
$- \frac{7}{20}$

13. $\frac{9}{10}$
$- \frac{5}{10}$

14. $\frac{11}{15}$
$- \frac{6}{15}$

15. $\frac{7}{15}$
$- \frac{2}{15}$

16. $\frac{11}{12}$
$- \frac{3}{12}$

17. $\frac{6}{7}$
$- \frac{1}{7}$

18. $\frac{4}{5}$
$- \frac{1}{5}$

19. $\frac{17}{18}$
$- \frac{9}{18}$

20. $\frac{13}{14}$
$- \frac{6}{14}$

Everyday Problem Solving

The bath shop sells perfumes in bottles of different sizes.

1. Tina bought a small bottle and a large bottle of perfume. How many ounces did she buy <u>in all</u>?

2. <u>How much more</u> perfume is contained in the large bottle than in the medium bottle?

🍃	Perfumes	🍃
	SIZE	FLUID OUNCES
🫗	Small	$\frac{1}{8}$
🫗	Medium	$\frac{3}{8}$
🫗	Large	$\frac{5}{8}$

9-2 Adding Like Mixed Numbers

Now that you know how to add like fractions, you can add like mixed numbers.

► EXAMPLE 1

Add. $2\frac{1}{5} + 3\frac{2}{5}$

STEP 1 Add the fractions.

$$2\frac{1}{5}$$
$$+\,3\frac{2}{5}$$
$$\overline{\quad\ \ \frac{3}{5}}$$

STEP 2 Add the whole numbers.

$$2\frac{1}{5}$$
$$+\,3\frac{2}{5}$$
$$\overline{5\frac{3}{5}}$$

The sum of $2\frac{1}{5}$ and $3\frac{2}{5}$ is $5\frac{3}{5}$.

Sometimes, the fraction part of the answer is not a proper fraction. You need to simplify the answer.

► EXAMPLE 2

If the numerator and denominator of a fraction are the same, the fraction is equal to 1.

$$\frac{2}{2} = 1 \quad \frac{5}{5} = 1 \quad \frac{12}{12} = 1$$

Add. $2\frac{1}{2} + 3\frac{1}{2}$

STEP 1 Add the fractions.

$$2\frac{1}{2}$$
$$+\,3\frac{1}{2}$$
$$\overline{\quad\ \ \frac{2}{2}}$$

STEP 2 Add the whole numbers.

$$2\frac{1}{2}$$
$$+\,3\frac{1}{2}$$
$$\overline{5\frac{2}{2}}$$

STEP 3 Change the fraction to a whole number. Add the whole numbers.

$$2\frac{1}{2}$$
$$+\,3\frac{1}{2}$$
$$\overline{5\frac{2}{2} = 5 + 1 = 6}$$

The sum of $2\frac{1}{2}$ and $3\frac{1}{2}$ is 6.

Practice A

Add. Write the answer in lowest terms.

1. $3\frac{2}{7}$
   $+ 1\frac{2}{7}$

2. $4\frac{2}{4}$
   $+ 2\frac{1}{4}$

3. $1\frac{6}{7}$
   $+ 2\frac{3}{7}$

4. $3\frac{1}{6}$
   $+ 1\frac{3}{6}$

5. $4\frac{5}{8}$
   $+ 1\frac{3}{8}$

6. $3\frac{1}{9}$
   $+ 2\frac{5}{9}$

7. $7\frac{3}{4}$
   $+ 1\frac{3}{4}$

8. $6\frac{5}{9}$
   $+ 2\frac{7}{9}$

Practice B

Add. Write the answer in lowest terms.

9. $3\frac{2}{5} + 7\frac{3}{5}$

10. $9\frac{2}{9} + 2\frac{1}{9}$

11. $3\frac{4}{11} + 5\frac{5}{11}$

12. $8\frac{5}{12} + 9\frac{5}{12}$

13. $3\frac{2}{7} + 7\frac{2}{7}$

14. $2\frac{19}{25} + 4\frac{3}{25}$

15. $6\frac{4}{5} + 1\frac{1}{5}$

16. $11\frac{2}{3} + 7$

17. $4\frac{5}{6} + 8\frac{4}{6}$

18. $5\frac{1}{8} + 4\frac{3}{8}$

19. $7\frac{2}{7} + 3\frac{4}{7}$

20. $1 + 4\frac{11}{13}$

Everyday Problem Solving

The local swim teams practice once a week. The practice schedule is on the wall at the pool.

1. Anita is a member of the Dolphins and Stingrays teams. How long does she practice each week? Add the hours.

2. Joe is on two teams. He practices $2\frac{1}{2}$ hours a week. Joe is on which two teams?

∼∼∼∼ POOL ∼∼∼∼		
Daily Practice Schedule		
SWIM TEAM	DAY	HOURS
Dolphins	Mon.	$2\frac{3}{4}$
Sharks	Tues.	2
Stingrays	Wed.	$1\frac{3}{4}$
Minnows	Thurs.	$1\frac{1}{4}$
Eels	Fri.	$1\frac{1}{4}$

Subtracting Like Mixed Numbers

Now that you know how to subtract like fractions, you can subtract like mixed numbers.

▶ **EXAMPLE 1**

Subtract. $7\frac{3}{4} - 2\frac{1}{4}$

STEP 1 Subtract the fractions.

$$\begin{array}{r} 7\frac{3}{4} \\ - 2\frac{1}{4} \\ \hline \frac{2}{4} \end{array}$$

STEP 2 Subtract the whole numbers. Write the answer in lowest terms.

$$\begin{array}{r} 7\frac{3}{4} \\ - 2\frac{1}{4} \\ \hline 5\frac{2}{4} = 5\frac{1}{2} \end{array}$$

The difference between $7\frac{3}{4}$ and $2\frac{1}{4}$ is $5\frac{1}{2}$.

Sometimes, you need to regroup a mixed number for more fraction parts.

$3\frac{1}{3}$ → $2\frac{4}{3}$

▶ **EXAMPLE 2**

Subtract. $3\frac{1}{3} - 1\frac{2}{3}$

STEP 1 Regroup so that you can subtract the fractions. Then, subtract the fractions.

$$\begin{array}{r} 3\frac{1}{3} = 2\frac{4}{3} \\ - 1\frac{2}{3} = - 1\frac{2}{3} \\ \hline \frac{2}{3} \end{array}$$

STEP 2 Subtract the whole numbers. Make sure the answer is in lowest terms.

$$\begin{array}{r} 3\frac{1}{3} = 2\frac{4}{3} \\ - 1\frac{2}{3} = - 1\frac{2}{3} \\ \hline 1\frac{2}{3} \end{array}$$

The difference between $3\frac{1}{3}$ and $1\frac{2}{3}$ is $1\frac{2}{3}$.

Subtract.

1. $4\frac{2}{3}$
   $- 1\frac{1}{3}$

2. $7\frac{7}{8}$
   $- 4\frac{3}{8}$

3. $9\frac{1}{2}$
   $- 3\frac{1}{2}$

4. $6\frac{5}{6}$
   $- 2\frac{2}{6}$

5. $9\frac{4}{5}$
   $- 1\frac{2}{5}$

6. $15\frac{6}{11}$
   $- 5\frac{3}{11}$

7. $9\frac{4}{5}$
   $- 5\frac{2}{5}$

8. $12\frac{5}{9}$
   $- 7\frac{2}{9}$

Practice B

Subtract. Be sure to regroup.

9. $6\frac{7}{11}$
   $- 2\frac{8}{11}$

10. $11\frac{7}{9}$
    $- 5\frac{8}{9}$

11. $24\frac{1}{10}$
    $- 10\frac{3}{10}$

12. $6\frac{1}{6}$
    $- 4\frac{5}{6}$

13. $7\frac{4}{9} - 1\frac{5}{9}$

14. $14\frac{3}{10} - 5\frac{9}{10}$

15. $8\frac{1}{4} - 4\frac{3}{4}$

16. $12\frac{2}{7} - 5\frac{6}{7}$

17. $9\frac{2}{6} - 7\frac{5}{6}$

18. $10\frac{7}{20} - 8\frac{9}{20}$

Everyday Problem Solving

Mountain climbing is Andrew's favorite sport. These are his favorite peaks.

1. How much higher is Borah than Washington?

2. How much higher is King than Grand Teton?

3. What is the difference in height between the highest peak and the lowest peak?

FAVORITE MOUNTAIN PEAKS

Peak	Location	Height (miles)
Grand Teton	WY	$2\frac{3}{5}$
King	Yukon	$3\frac{1}{5}$
Borah	ID	$2\frac{2}{5}$
Washington	NH	$1\frac{1}{5}$

9-4 Subtracting from a Whole Number

Sometimes, you need to regroup a whole number as a mixed number. Look at the subtraction below.

$$5$$
$$- 2\frac{2}{3}$$

There are no thirds from which to subtract $\frac{2}{3}$. Regroup 5 to make thirds.

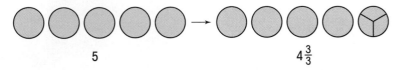

$$5 \qquad\qquad 4\frac{3}{3}$$

EXAMPLE 1

Subtract. $5 - 2\frac{2}{3}$

STEP 1 Regroup the whole number as a mixed number.

$$\begin{array}{rcl} 5 & = & 4\frac{3}{3} \\ -\ 2\frac{2}{3} & = & -\ 2\frac{2}{3} \\ \hline \end{array}$$

STEP 2 Subtract. Be sure the answer is in lowest terms.

$$\begin{array}{rcl} 5 & = & 4\frac{3}{3} \\ -\ 2\frac{2}{3} & = & -\ 2\frac{2}{3} \\ \hline & & 2\frac{1}{3} \end{array}$$

The difference between 5 and $2\frac{2}{3}$ is $2\frac{1}{3}$.

EXAMPLE 2

Subtract. $10 - \frac{1}{4}$

STEP 1 Regroup the whole number as a mixed number.

$$\begin{array}{rcl} 10 & = & 9\frac{4}{4} \\ -\ \frac{1}{4} & = & -\ \frac{1}{4} \\ \hline \end{array}$$

STEP 2 Subtract. Be sure the answer is in lowest terms.

$$\begin{array}{rcl} 10 & = & 9\frac{4}{4} \\ -\ \frac{1}{4} & = & -\ \frac{1}{4} \\ \hline & & 9\frac{3}{4} \end{array}$$

The difference between 10 and $\frac{1}{4}$ is $9\frac{3}{4}$.

Practice A

Subtract. Remember to regroup the whole number.

1. $\quad 4$
$\quad -2\frac{3}{4}$

2. $\quad 7$
$\quad -3\frac{1}{2}$

3. $\quad 6$
$\quad -\frac{5}{6}$

4. $\quad 8$
$\quad -\frac{7}{10}$

5. $\quad 6$
$\quad -\frac{3}{7}$

6. $\quad 10$
$\quad -4\frac{2}{9}$

7. $\quad 12$
$\quad -9\frac{3}{8}$

8. $\quad 20$
$\quad -3\frac{4}{5}$

Practice B

Subtract. Regroup, if necessary.

9. $\quad 9\frac{3}{4}$
$\quad -3\frac{1}{4}$

10. $\quad 7$
$\quad -5\frac{2}{5}$

11. $\quad 18\frac{1}{6}$
$\quad -10\frac{5}{6}$

12. $\quad 23$
$\quad -\frac{7}{8}$

13. $\quad 11$
$\quad -4\frac{1}{3}$

14. $\quad 19\frac{2}{7}$
$\quad -8\frac{5}{7}$

15. $\quad 8$
$\quad -3\frac{4}{7}$

16. $\quad 11\frac{3}{8}$
$\quad -7\frac{1}{8}$

Everyday Problem Solving

This is Ms. Rhode's grocery list for making fruit salad. Use the list to answer the questions. Look for clue words to decide when to add or subtract.

1. How <u>many more</u> pounds of apples <u>than</u> pears will she buy?

2. How <u>many more</u> pounds of apples <u>than</u> plums will she buy?

3. How many pounds of fruit will she buy <u>altogether</u>?

——— Grocery list ———

For Fruit Salad

3 pounds Apples

1$\frac{1}{4}$ pounds Plums

2$\frac{1}{4}$ pounds Pears

Adding Unlike Fractions

Unlike fractions have different denominators. You know how to add like fractions. To add unlike fractions, you first need to rename one or both fractions to make like fractions.

▶ **EXAMPLE**

Look for a common multiple of 3 and 5.
$M_3 = \{3, 6, 9, 12, 15, \ldots\}$
$M_5 = \{5, 10, 15, \ldots\}$

Add. $\frac{2}{3} + \frac{3}{5}$

STEP 1 Make like fractions. Use 15 as the denominator.

$$\frac{2}{3} = \frac{2 \times 5}{3 \times 5} = \frac{10}{15}$$
$$\frac{3}{5} = \frac{3 \times 3}{5 \times 3} = \frac{9}{15}$$

STEP 2 Add the like fractions. Write the answer in lowest terms.

$$\begin{array}{r} \frac{10}{15} \\ + \frac{9}{15} \\ \hline \frac{19}{15} = 1\frac{4}{15} \end{array}$$

The sum of $\frac{2}{3}$ and $\frac{3}{5}$ is $1\frac{4}{15}$.

Practice

Add. Remember to rename as like fractions.

1. $\begin{array}{r} \frac{3}{8} \\ + \frac{1}{4} \\ \hline \end{array}$

2. $\begin{array}{r} \frac{5}{12} \\ + \frac{3}{4} \\ \hline \end{array}$

3. $\begin{array}{r} \frac{7}{9} \\ + \frac{6}{27} \\ \hline \end{array}$

4. $\begin{array}{r} \frac{5}{7} \\ + \frac{11}{28} \\ \hline \end{array}$

5. $\begin{array}{r} \frac{1}{3} \\ + \frac{1}{5} \\ \hline \end{array}$

6. $\begin{array}{r} \frac{7}{8} \\ + \frac{2}{3} \\ \hline \end{array}$

7. $\begin{array}{r} \frac{5}{12} \\ + \frac{2}{3} \\ \hline \end{array}$

8. $\begin{array}{r} \frac{2}{3} \\ + \frac{2}{5} \\ \hline \end{array}$

9. $\frac{17}{20} + \frac{3}{10}$

10. $\frac{3}{4} + \frac{1}{3}$

11. $\frac{6}{15} + \frac{3}{5}$

12. $\frac{5}{8} + \frac{5}{6}$

13. $\frac{3}{5} + \frac{1}{2}$

14. $\frac{2}{5} + \frac{3}{4}$

15. $\frac{1}{4} + \frac{3}{16}$

16. $\frac{5}{6} + \frac{4}{9}$

MATH IN YOUR LIFE
Pay Day

Paul works part-time at a department store. He keeps a record of the hours he works each day. At the end of the week, he totals his hours. This helps him determine the amount of his paycheck.

HOURS WORKED

	Mon.	Tues.	Wed.	Thurs.	Fri.
May 5	4	$3\frac{1}{2}$	5	$5\frac{1}{2}$	$6\frac{1}{2}$
May 12	5	4	$3\frac{1}{2}$	4	$5\frac{1}{2}$
May 19	$3\frac{1}{2}$	0	$4\frac{1}{2}$	4	4
May 26	6	$3\frac{1}{2}$	5	$3\frac{1}{2}$	6

Use Paul's records to answer the following questions.

1. Find the total number of hours Paul worked the week of May 12.

2. Which week did Paul work the most hours? How many hours was that?

3. Which week did Paul work the least number of hours? How many hours was that?

4. How many more hours did Paul work during the week of May 5 than the week of May 12?

Critical Thinking

Paul gets paid $8 per hour. How much money did he make the week of May 26? Show your work.

Subtracting Unlike Fractions

To subtract unlike fractions, you need to rename one or both fractions to make like fractions. Then, subtract the like fractions.

► **EXAMPLE**

Subtract. $\frac{2}{3} - \frac{1}{4}$

Look for a common multiple of 3 and 4.

$M_3 = \{3, 6, 9, 12, \ldots\}$

$M_4 = \{4, 8, 12, \ldots\}$

STEP 1 Make like fractions. Use 12 as the denominator.

$\frac{2}{3} = \frac{2 \times 4}{3 \times 4} = \frac{8}{12}$

$\frac{1}{4} = \frac{1 \times 3}{4 \times 3} = \frac{3}{12}$

STEP 2 Subtract the like fractions. Make sure the answer is in lowest terms.

$$\begin{array}{r} \frac{8}{12} \\ - \frac{3}{12} \\ \hline \frac{5}{12} \end{array}$$

The difference between $\frac{2}{3}$ and $\frac{1}{4}$ is $\frac{5}{12}$.

Practice

Subtract. Remember to rename as like fractions.

1. $\begin{array}{r} \frac{7}{8} \\ - \frac{3}{4} \\ \hline \end{array}$ **2.** $\begin{array}{r} \frac{1}{2} \\ - \frac{1}{3} \\ \hline \end{array}$ **3.** $\begin{array}{r} \frac{2}{5} \\ - \frac{1}{10} \\ \hline \end{array}$ **4.** $\begin{array}{r} \frac{3}{4} \\ - \frac{1}{2} \\ \hline \end{array}$

5. $\begin{array}{r} \frac{7}{9} \\ - \frac{2}{3} \\ \hline \end{array}$ **6.** $\begin{array}{r} \frac{3}{5} \\ - \frac{4}{10} \\ \hline \end{array}$ **7.** $\begin{array}{r} \frac{5}{6} \\ - \frac{3}{4} \\ \hline \end{array}$ **8.** $\begin{array}{r} \frac{13}{20} \\ - \frac{2}{5} \\ \hline \end{array}$

9. $\begin{array}{r} \frac{7}{18} \\ - \frac{1}{3} \\ \hline \end{array}$ **10.** $\begin{array}{r} \frac{4}{5} \\ - \frac{3}{10} \\ \hline \end{array}$ **11.** $\begin{array}{r} \frac{6}{7} \\ - \frac{1}{5} \\ \hline \end{array}$ **12.** $\begin{array}{r} \frac{2}{5} \\ - \frac{2}{9} \\ \hline \end{array}$

13. $\frac{7}{10} - \frac{1}{4}$ **14.** $\frac{5}{6} - \frac{5}{8}$ **15.** $\frac{5}{6} - \frac{1}{5}$ **16.** $\frac{8}{9} - \frac{5}{6}$

USING YOUR CALCULATOR
Finding Common Denominators

To add or subtract unlike fractions, you need a common denominator. You can use your calculator to find a common denominator.

Add. $\frac{3}{4} + \frac{3}{10}$

First, find multiples for each denominator.

Begin by listing 4 as the first multiple of 4. $M_4 = \{4,$

Find the next multiple of 4.

PRESS $\boxed{4}$ $\boxed{+}$ $\boxed{4}$ $\boxed{=}$ $\boxed{\qquad 8.}$ $M_4 = \{4, 8,$

PRESS $\boxed{=}$ $\boxed{\qquad 12.}$ $M_4 = \{4, 8, 12,$

Continue to press $\boxed{=}$ for each new multiple of 4.
$M_4 = \{4, 8, 12, 16, 20, 24, 28, 32, 36, 40...\}$

List 10 as the first multiple of 10. $M_{10} = \{10,$
Then use your calculator to find multiples of 10.

PRESS $\boxed{1}$ $\boxed{0}$ $\boxed{+}$ $\boxed{1}$ $\boxed{0}$ $\boxed{=}$ $\boxed{\qquad 20.}$ $M_{10} = \{10, 20,$

PRESS $\boxed{=}$ $\boxed{\qquad 30.}$ $M_{10} = \{10, 20, 30,$

Continue to press $\boxed{=}$ for each new multiple of 10.
$M_{10} = \{10, 20, 30, 40, 50, ...\}$

Look at the two lists above. The least common multiple is 20.
The least common denominator of $\frac{3}{4}$ and $\frac{3}{10}$ is 20.

> **Calculator Tip**
> You can enter a problem.
> Press $\boxed{4}$ $\boxed{+}$ $\boxed{4}$ $\boxed{=}$
> $\boxed{\qquad 8.}$
> The calculator continues to add 4 each time you press $\boxed{=}$.

**Use your calculator to find the common denominator.
Then, add or subtract.**

1. $\frac{5}{18}$
$+ \frac{5}{12}$

2. $\frac{4}{9}$
$+ \frac{4}{7}$

3. $\frac{5}{21}$
$- \frac{3}{14}$

4. $\frac{3}{8}$
$- \frac{1}{6}$

5. $\frac{2}{15}$
$- \frac{3}{25}$

Unlike mixed numbers have unlike fractions. You can add unlike mixed numbers. First, rename to make like fractions. Then, add the like mixed numbers.

▶ **EXAMPLE**

Add. $7\frac{5}{6} + 3\frac{1}{4}$

STEP 1 Make like fractions. Use 12 as the denominator.

Think: $\frac{5}{6} = \frac{?}{12}$

$\frac{5}{6} = \frac{5 \times 2}{6 \times 2} = \frac{10}{12}$

Think: $\frac{1}{4} = \frac{?}{12}$

$\frac{1}{4} = \frac{1 \times 3}{4 \times 3} = \frac{3}{12}$

$$7\frac{5}{6} = 7\frac{10}{12}$$
$$+ 3\frac{1}{4} = 3\frac{3}{12}$$

STEP 2 Add the like mixed numbers. Write the answer in lowest terms.

$$7\frac{10}{12}$$
$$+ 3\frac{3}{12}$$
$$\overline{10\frac{13}{12} = 11\frac{1}{12}}$$

The sum of $7\frac{5}{6}$ and $3\frac{1}{4}$ is $11\frac{1}{12}$.

Practice A

Add. Remember to rename as like mixed numbers.

1. $\quad 2\frac{1}{3}$
$\quad + 3\frac{1}{2}$

2. $\quad 4\frac{2}{9}$
$\quad + 5\frac{1}{3}$

3. $\quad 7\frac{1}{2}$
$\quad + 5\frac{1}{4}$

4. $\quad 8\frac{2}{3}$
$\quad + 2\frac{1}{15}$

5. $\quad 3\frac{2}{7}$
$\quad + 4\frac{1}{3}$

6. $\quad 8\frac{3}{4}$
$\quad + 4\frac{2}{3}$

7. $\quad 9\frac{3}{8}$
$\quad + 4\frac{5}{6}$

8. $\quad 8\frac{1}{4}$
$\quad + 7\frac{5}{6}$

9. $\quad 7\frac{2}{3}$
$\quad + 2\frac{7}{9}$

10. $\quad 6\frac{3}{4}$
$\quad + 8\frac{5}{8}$

11. $\quad 9\frac{3}{5}$
$\quad + 5\frac{2}{3}$

12. $\quad 6\frac{7}{8}$
$\quad + 7\frac{5}{12}$

Practice B

Add. Remember to write each problem in vertical form.

13. $12\frac{11}{20} + 4\frac{3}{5}$

14. $5\frac{1}{3} + 6\frac{2}{5}$

15. $1\frac{4}{15} + 2\frac{2}{5}$

16. $4\frac{1}{2} + 5\frac{3}{4}$

17. $8\frac{3}{4} + \frac{7}{8}$

18. $4\frac{5}{12} + 1\frac{3}{4}$

19. $2\frac{5}{9} + 1\frac{2}{3}$

20. $5\frac{1}{6} + 2\frac{3}{4}$

21. $6\frac{7}{10} + 9\frac{1}{2}$

22. $19\frac{1}{3} + 5\frac{3}{4}$

23. $8\frac{1}{6} + 1\frac{5}{8}$

24. $7\frac{5}{9} + 2\frac{5}{6}$

Everyday Problem Solving

This neighborhood map helps people plan their routes. Use the map to answer the questions.

1. Brenda drove from Seattle to Summit and then to Stirling. How far did Brenda drive altogether?

2. A bus route goes from Swanson to Seattle and then to Summit. How long is the route?

3. Joe wants to jog 4 miles. What route should he jog?

4. Dena wants to drive from Stirling to Seattle. She can drive through Swanson or through Summit. Which is the shorter route? Explain.

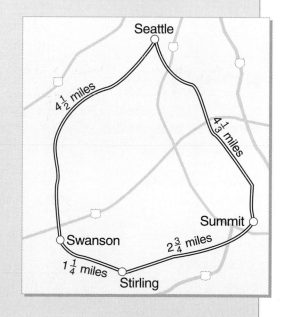

9·8 Subtracting Unlike Mixed Numbers

You can subtract unlike mixed numbers. First, rename the fractions to make like mixed numbers. Then, subtract the like mixed numbers.

▶ **EXAMPLE 1**

Subtract. $6\frac{3}{4} - 2\frac{1}{3}$

Think: $\frac{3}{4} = \frac{?}{12}$

$\frac{3}{4} = \frac{3 \times 3}{4 \times 3} = \frac{9}{12}$

Think: $\frac{1}{3} = \frac{?}{12}$

$\frac{1}{3} = \frac{1 \times 4}{3 \times 4} = \frac{4}{12}$

STEP 1 Make like fractions. Use 12 as the denominator.

$$6\frac{3}{4} = 6\frac{9}{12}$$
$$-\ 2\frac{1}{3} = 2\frac{4}{12}$$

STEP 2 Subtract the like mixed numbers. Make sure the answer is in lowest terms.

$$6\frac{9}{12}$$
$$-\ 2\frac{4}{12}$$
$$\overline{\quad 4\frac{5}{12}}$$

The difference between $6\frac{3}{4}$ and $2\frac{1}{3}$ is $4\frac{5}{12}$.

Sometimes, you need to regroup the first mixed number to subtract the fractions.

▶ **EXAMPLE 2**

Subtract. $15\frac{1}{2} - 3\frac{4}{5}$

Regroup $15\frac{5}{10}$ for more tenths. Take 1 from 15.

$15\frac{5}{10} = 14 + 1 + \frac{5}{10}$

Rename 1 as $\frac{10}{10}$.

$= 14 + \frac{10}{10} + \frac{5}{10} = 14\frac{15}{10}$

STEP 1 Make like fractions. Use 10 as the denominator.

$$15\frac{1}{2} = \quad 15\frac{5}{10}$$
$$-\ 3\frac{4}{5} = -\ 3\frac{8}{10}$$

STEP 2 Regroup so you can subtract. Make sure the answer is in lowest terms.

$$15\frac{5}{10} = \quad 14\frac{15}{10}$$
$$-\ 3\frac{8}{10} = -\ 3\frac{8}{10}$$
$$\overline{\qquad\qquad 11\frac{7}{10}}$$

The difference between $15\frac{1}{2}$ and $3\frac{4}{5}$ is $11\frac{7}{10}$.

Subtract. Write the answer in lowest terms.

1. $5\frac{6}{7}$
$-2\frac{1}{2}$

2. $8\frac{3}{5}$
$-1\frac{1}{3}$

3. $4\frac{3}{4}$
$-2\frac{3}{8}$

4. $9\frac{7}{10}$
$-3\frac{2}{5}$

5. $4\frac{7}{9}$
$-1\frac{1}{3}$

6. $5\frac{2}{3}$
$-2\frac{1}{5}$

7. $10\frac{5}{6}$
$-3\frac{2}{3}$

8. $5\frac{5}{9}$
$-2\frac{1}{6}$

9. $10\frac{7}{8} - 5\frac{5}{6}$

10. $5\frac{6}{7} - 2\frac{2}{3}$

Practice B

Subtract. Remember to regroup.

11. $6\frac{1}{4}$
$-2\frac{1}{3}$

12. $4\frac{1}{2}$
$-1\frac{9}{14}$

13. $8\frac{1}{3}$
$-\frac{1}{2}$

14. $9\frac{1}{2}$
$-4\frac{3}{4}$

15. $5\frac{1}{4}$
$-4\frac{5}{6}$

16. $6\frac{4}{9}$
$-1\frac{2}{3}$

17. $7\frac{3}{10}$
$-2\frac{3}{5}$

18. $12\frac{1}{3}$
$-5\frac{5}{6}$

Everyday Problem Solving

Tracy saw this chart in the Business section of the newspaper. The closing price of a stock is the price for the stock at the end of the day.

1. How much higher was the closing price of Kanga than that of Big Tees? Subtract.

2. How much higher was the closing price of Top Mart than that of Big Tees?

APRIL 10

STOCK QUOTES

STOCK	CLOSING PRICE
Top Mart	$38\frac{3}{8}$
Big Tees	$35\frac{1}{2}$
Kanga	$37\frac{3}{4}$

Problem Solving: Multi-Part Problems

Solving multi-part word problems is easier if you work on one part at a time.

EXAMPLE

Ms. Torres is making 3 costumes for a play. Each costume requires $\frac{3}{4}$ yard of green fabric and $1\frac{1}{2}$ yards of orange fabric. How much fabric does she need altogether?

STEP 1   READ   What do you need to find out?
You need to find how much fabric is needed for 3 costumes.

STEP 2   PLAN   What do you need to do?
How much fabric is needed for 1 costume? **Add** to find out.
How much fabric is needed for 3 costumes? **Multiply** to find out.

STEP 3   DO   Follow the plan.
Add.

$$\begin{array}{r} \frac{3}{4} = \quad \frac{3}{4} \\ + 1\frac{1}{2} = + 1\frac{2}{4} \\ \hline 1\frac{5}{4} = 2\frac{1}{4} \text{ yards} \end{array}$$

Multiply.

$$2\frac{1}{4} \times 3 = \frac{9}{4} \times \frac{3}{1} = \frac{27}{4} = 6\frac{3}{4} \text{ yards}$$

Remember:
$3 \times 2 = 6$
So $3 \times 2\frac{1}{4} > 6$.

STEP 4   CHECK   Does your answer make sense?
Notice that $2\frac{1}{4}$ is greater than 2.
This means that $3 \times 2\frac{1}{4}$ is greater than 6.
So, $6\frac{3}{4}$ yards makes sense. ✓

Ms. Torres needs $6\frac{3}{4}$ yards to make 3 costumes.

Problem Solving

READ the problem. Answer the questions under PLAN. DO the plan to solve the problem.

1. Ms. Torres bought $5\frac{1}{4}$ yards of white fabric and $6\frac{3}{4}$ yards of red fabric. Each yard cost $6. What is her total cost?

   PLAN
   How many yards of fabric did she buy?
   What is her total cost?

2. Ms. Torres had $5\frac{2}{3}$ yards of black fabric. She used $2\frac{1}{3}$ yards for one skirt and $1\frac{3}{4}$ yards for slacks. How much fabric does she have left?

   PLAN
   How much fabric was used?
   How much fabric is left?

3. It takes Ms. Torres $3\frac{3}{4}$ hours to sew one adult's costume and $2\frac{1}{2}$ hours to sew one child's costume. How long will it take to sew two of each costume?

   PLAN
   How long does it take to sew one of each costume?
   How long does it take to sew two of each costume?

Problem Solving Strategy

Sometimes, you can work backward to solve a problem.

Ms. Torres bought some fabric on sale. She used $1\frac{1}{2}$ yards for a costume. She has $\frac{1}{2}$ yard left. How much fabric did she buy?

Add to find how much fabric she bought.

$$\begin{array}{r} \rule{2em}{0.6em} \\ -\ 1\frac{1}{2}\ \text{yards} \\ \hline \frac{1}{2}\ \text{yard} \end{array} \qquad \begin{array}{r} 1\frac{1}{2}\ \text{yards} \\ +\ \frac{1}{2}\ \text{yard} \\ \hline \rule{2em}{0.6em} \end{array}$$

Vocabulary Review

like fractions
unlike fractions

Choose a phrase from the list that describes each pair of numbers.

1. $\frac{7}{8}$ and $\frac{5}{8}$

2. $\frac{1}{2}$ and $\frac{5}{7}$

3. $\frac{5}{6}$ and $\frac{3}{16}$

4. $\frac{2}{9}$ and $\frac{7}{9}$

5. **Writing** Explain why a common denominator is needed to add $\frac{3}{4}$ and $\frac{1}{3}$.

Chapter Quiz

LESSONS 9·1 to 9·3

Adding and Subtracting Like Fractions and Like Mixed Numbers

Test Tip
Add or subtract the numerators.
Keep the same denominator.

Add or subtract.

1. $\frac{5}{6} + \frac{4}{6}$

2. $\frac{7}{8} - \frac{5}{8}$

3. $\frac{5}{9} - \frac{3}{9}$

4. $\frac{5}{10} + \frac{7}{10}$

5. $1\frac{2}{6} + 1\frac{5}{6}$

6. $6\frac{7}{8} - 3\frac{2}{8}$

7. $3\frac{5}{7} + 9\frac{2}{7}$

8. $7\frac{2}{9} - 5\frac{8}{9}$

LESSON 9·4

Test Tip
Remember to regroup the whole number before you subtract the fraction or the mixed number.

Subtracting from a Whole Number

Subtract.

9. $7 - \frac{5}{6}$ **10.** $5 - 3\frac{2}{3}$

11. $8 - 5\frac{3}{4}$ **12.** $12 - \frac{9}{20}$

LESSONS 9·5 to 9·8

Test Tip
Be sure you find common denominators and rename the fractions before adding or subtracting.

Adding and Subtracting Unlike Fractions and Unlike Mixed Numbers

Add or subtract.

13. $\frac{4}{5} + \frac{9}{10}$ **14.** $\frac{5}{6} - \frac{2}{3}$

15. $\frac{2}{3} - \frac{2}{5}$ **16.** $3\frac{1}{6} + 1\frac{3}{4}$

17. $5\frac{1}{2} - 3\frac{1}{8}$ **18.** $7\frac{2}{9} - 1\frac{2}{3}$

LESSON 9·9

Test Tip
Make a plan before solving multi-part problems. Look for clue words.

Solving Multi-Part Problems

Solve.

19. Olga bought $3\frac{1}{2}$ yards of red ribbon, $3\frac{3}{4}$ yards of green ribbon, and $2\frac{7}{8}$ yards of fabric. How many more yards of ribbon than fabric did she buy?

20. Hank and his 3 brothers shared $5\frac{1}{3}$ pounds of pecans equally. Of his $\frac{1}{4}$ share, Hank ate $\frac{1}{3}$ pound. How many pounds does he have left?

Group Activity

With your group, choose 5 stocks to buy. Record the reasons that you would like to buy those stocks. Then, use the Business section of the newspaper to "buy" 100 shares of each stock at the closing prices. Follow the stocks for 5 business days and record the closing prices. Every day, find your profit or loss.

Unit 2 **Review**

Choose the letter for the correct answer.

Use the table to answer Questions 1 and 2.

Bagels Sold	
Type of Bagel	Number Sold
Cinnamon	13
Blueberry	15
Sesame	7
Raisin	5

1. What fraction of all the bagels sold were sesame bagels?

    A. $\frac{5}{7}$

    B. $\frac{5}{40}$

    C. $\frac{7}{40}$

    D. $\frac{7}{13}$

2. What fraction of all the bagels sold were raisin bagels?

    A. $\frac{1}{5}$

    B. $\frac{1}{8}$

    C. $\frac{3}{8}$

    D. None of the above

3. Which fraction is equivalent to $4\frac{5}{6}$?

    A. $\frac{15}{6}$

    B. $\frac{26}{6}$

    C. $\frac{29}{6}$

    D. $\frac{45}{6}$

4. Michelle bought $3\frac{1}{2}$ dozen bagels. One dozen is 12 bagels. How many bagels did she buy?

    A. 36

    B. 42

    C. 84

    D. None of the above

5. Find $4 \div \frac{4}{5}$.

    A. $\frac{1}{5}$

    B. $3\frac{1}{5}$

    C. 5

    D. None of the above

6. Which sum is greatest?

    A. $\frac{1}{2} + \frac{1}{3}$

    B. $\frac{2}{3} + \frac{1}{10}$

    C. $\frac{1}{2} + \frac{1}{10}$

    D. $\frac{1}{2} + \frac{2}{3}$

Critical Thinking

Use the table above. Yoko wants to buy 2 dozen bagels. She needs $\frac{2}{3}$ cinnamon and $\frac{1}{4}$ sesame. Will she have enough for 2 dozen bagels? Why or why not?

CHALLENGE How many more bagels does she need to buy 2 dozen? What could they be?

Unit 3 ▶ Other Types of Numbers

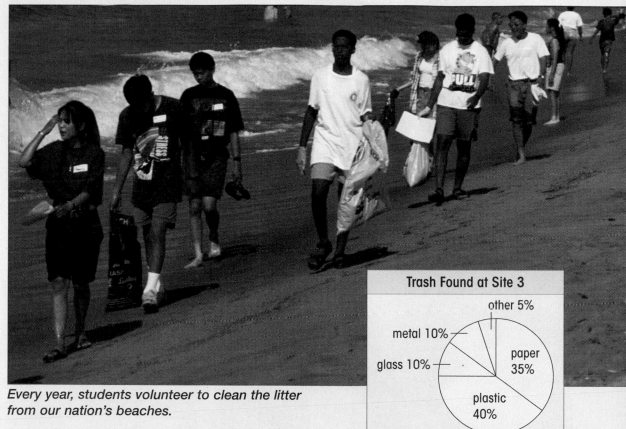

Every year, students volunteer to clean the litter from our nation's beaches.

Trash Found at Site 3

other 5%

metal 10%

glass 10%

paper 35%

plastic 40%

The graph and table on the right give information about a beach cleanup.

1. Which site had the most volunteers?

2. How many tons of trash were collected at Site 1?

3. What percent (%) of the trash at Site 3 was plastic?

Community Beach Cleanup			
Site	Number of Volunteers	Tons of Trash Collected	Pounds per Volunteer
1	6,893	161.4	46.83
2	12,722	199.6	30.89
3	9,789	155.6	31.79
4	8,824	197.3	44.72

These runners are at the end of a close race. Only .01 of a second may separate the winner from the runner in second place! How else are decimals used in sports?

Chapter 10 ▶ Decimals

Words to Know

decimal	a number that names part of a whole
decimal point	the dot in a decimal; a decimal has digits to the right of its decimal point
decimal places	the places to the right of a decimal point
mixed decimal	a number with a whole number and a decimal

Decimal Search Project

Look for decimals in different places. Try the newspaper, a magazine, or another textbook. For example, your science or social studies book might contain decimals. Tell the class what is described by the decimals you found. Write two problems using your decimals.

Learning Objectives

- Read and write decimals.
- Compare and order decimals.
- Add, subtract, multiply, and divide decimals.
- Change a decimal to a fraction.
- Change a fraction to a decimal.
- Round decimals.
- Solve problems using decimals.
- Apply knowledge of decimals to banking.

10-1 ▶ What Is a Decimal?

A **decimal** is a number that names part of a whole. A decimal has a **decimal point** with digits to its right.

▶ EXAMPLE 1

The number of digits to the right of the decimal point is the number of **decimal places**.

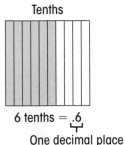

Tenths

6 tenths = .6
One decimal place

Hundredths

42 hundredths = .42
Two decimal places

▶ EXAMPLE 2

2 is a whole number.
.8 is a decimal.

A **mixed decimal** has a whole number part and a decimal part.

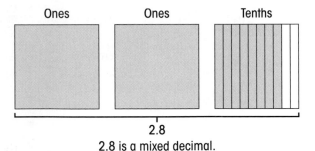

Ones   Ones   Tenths

2.8
2.8 is a mixed decimal.

Practice

Write the numbers on a separate sheet of paper. Draw a line under each decimal part. Then, tell the number of decimal places.

1. 9.7   **2.** 1.25   **3.** 4.33   **4.** 8.793   **5.** .004

6. 10.1   **7.** 18.2   **8.** 6.005   **9.** 28.555   **10.** 32.4

11. 32   **12.** 1.00   **13.** 100.1   **14.** 16.01   **15.** 700

Reading and Writing Decimals

You can show decimals on a place-value chart. From now on, we will use the word *decimal* for both decimals and mixed decimals.

thousands	hundreds	tens	ones	decimal point	tenths	hundredths	thousandths	ten thousandths
		1	5	.	0	6	4	
				.	2	0	3	9
		4	0	.	0	8		

The place-value chart can help you to read decimals.

▶ **EXAMPLE 1**

Read the decimal.   15.064

STEP 1   Read the whole number part.   fifteen

STEP 2   Read the decimal point as "and."   and

STEP 3   Read the decimal part.   sixty-four

STEP 4   Read the place value of the last digit.   thousandths

Read 15.064 as "fifteen and sixty-four thousandths."

You can write a decimal from words.

▶ **EXAMPLE 2**

Write forty and eight hundredths as a decimal.

STEP 1   Write the whole number part.   40

STEP 2   Write a decimal point for "and."   40.

STEP 3   Find the place name of the last digit.   hundredths

STEP 4   Write the decimal part.   40.08

Forty and eight hundredths is 40.08 as a decimal.

Practice A

Read aloud the numbers in the chart below. Remember to read the decimal point as "and" if it has a whole number part.

thousands	hundreds	tens	ones	decimal point	tenths	hundredths	thousandths	ten thousandths
1.				.	7	5	4	
2. 1	3	8	2	.	4	3	2	

1. seven hundred fifty-four thousandths

2. one thousand, three hundred eighty-two and four hundred thirty-two thousandths

Practice B

Write the place name of the last digit in each number below.

3. 32.7　　　　**4.** 239.13　　　　**5.** 62.472　　　　**6.** 136.02

7. 500.19　　　　**8.** 74.309　　　　**9.** 143.003　　　　**10.** 25.624

Practice C

Write each number as a decimal.

11. four tenths　　　　　　　　**12.** four hundredths

13. two hundred fifty-two thousandths　**14.** fifty and three thousandths

Everyday Problem Solving

A newspaper headline can have a decimal in it.

1. Write the number in Headline A as a decimal.

2. Write the number in Headline B in words.

3. Look in the newspaper for a decimal. If it is a number, write it in words. If it is in words, write it as a number.

Local News
(A) One and Four Tenths Inches Rain Breaks Record

Today's Sports
(B) Ripken's Batting Average Reaches .413

10-3 ▶ Comparing Decimals

Use the pictures to compare the decimals .4 and .04. Notice the different sizes of the shaded parts.

.4 > .04

You can also use what you know about whole numbers to compare decimals.

▶ **EXAMPLE 1**

> means greater than
< means less than
= means equal

Compare.   327.41 and 325.928

STEP Compare the whole number parts.   327.41 325.928
                                              327 > 325

The number 327.41 is greater than 325.928.

When the whole numbers are the same, compare the decimal parts.

▶ **EXAMPLE 2**

Compare.   89.147 and 89.235

STEP 1
Compare the whole number parts.   89.147   89.235
                                             89 = 89

STEP 2
Compare the decimal parts.   89.147   89.235
                                            .147 < .235

The number 89.147 is less than 89.235.

Sometimes decimals may look different, but they have the same value.

.2 = .20

You can write a zero to the right of the last decimal place without changing the value.

EXAMPLE 3

Compare. .147 and .23

STEP 1
Write zeros so that both decimals have the same number of decimal places.

.147   .230
3 places   3 places

STEP 2
Compare the numbers.

.147 < .230

The decimal .147 is less than the decimal .23.

Practice

Compare each pair of numbers. Use >, <, or =.

1. .3   .03

2. .12   1.2

3. .009   .09

4. .502   .52

5. .728   .71

6. .4   .45

7. 58.07   85.07

8. 36.5   360.5

9. 3.01   2.98

10. 21.339   21.39

11. .03   .005

12. 9.99   10

Everyday Problem Solving

In a library, books have call numbers on them. The books are put on shelves in order from the smallest to the largest call number. Each shelf is labeled with the call numbers that it holds.

1. If a book is numbered 827.5, which shelf would you find it on?

2. Will a book with the call number 926.16 be on the same shelf as a book with call number 953.16? Why or why not?

3. Which book will come first on Shelf 2: 946.17 or 946.62?

Library Bookshelves	
Shelf	Call Numbers
1	802.1 to 895.5
2	895.6 to 950
3	950.1 to 975.6

Ordering Decimals

Use what you know about comparing decimals to order decimals.

▶ **EXAMPLE**

Write these decimals in order from greatest to least.
5.091   5.6   5.19

STEP 1
Write zeros so that all the decimals have the same number of decimal places.

5.091 → 5.091
5.6   → 5.600
5.19 → 5.190

Same whole numbers
↓
5.091 ← Smallest
5.600 ← Largest
5.190

STEP 2
Compare the numbers.

The decimals in order are: 5.6   5.19   5.091.

Practice A

Write the decimals in order from largest to smallest.

1. 2.34
2.05
2.79

2. .27
.89
.56

3. 1.83
1.87
1.84

4. 7
7.32
7.086

Practice B

Write the decimals in order from largest to smallest.

5. .005   .5   .05

6. .72   .95   .53

7. .7   .2   .04

8. .025   .03   .3

9. .65   .32   .1

10. .5   .51   .49

11. 9.75   8.9   9.8

12. 3.82   3.4   3.078

13. 6.407   6.4   6.41

14. 2.5   3   .25

15. 9.99   10   10.01

16. 8.01   8.1   8.001

10·5 Adding Decimals

You can add decimals. Look at the grids below.

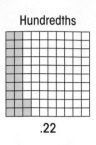

Hundredths	Hundredths	Hundredths
.22	.25	.47

.22   +   .25   =   .47

Add decimals the way you add whole numbers. Line up the decimal points one over the other before you add. Then, place the decimal point in the sum so that it lines up with the other decimal points.

▶ **EXAMPLE 1**

Add.   2.85 + 12.17

STEP 1		STEP 2	
Line up the decimal points.	2.85 + 12.17	Add. Place the decimal point in the sum.	¹ ¹ 2.85 + 12.17 15.02

Remember:
Vertical means up and down.

The sum of 2.85 and 12.17 is 15.02.

Sometimes you must write a decimal point and zeros so that you can line up the decimal points.

▶ **EXAMPLE 2**

Add.   6 + 14.85 + 2.5

STEP 1		STEP 2	
Line up the decimal points.	6.00 14.85 + 2.50	Add. Place the decimal point in the sum.	¹ ₁6.00 14.85 + 2.50 23.35

The sum of 6 and 14.85 and 2.5 is 23.35.

Practice A

Add. The decimal points have been lined up for you.

1.   8.4
     + 1.3

2.   2.37
     + 3.41

3.   5.232
     + .627

4.   5.1
     + 6.8

5. $1.05
     3.96
   + 2.15

6.   16.155
     4.073
   + 2.009

7. $3.28
     5.00
   + .50

8.   1.050
     4.000
   + 2.103

Practice B

Add. Remember to line up the decimal points. Write a decimal point and zeros if needed. Show your work in vertical form.

9. $3.4 + 5.1 + 8.2$

10. $.112 + .03$

11. $\$159 + \$.28$

12. $5.51 + .2 + 8.5$

13. $8 + 9.3 + .502$

14. $65 + 5.1 + .81$

15. $1.7 + .02 + 5.8$

16. $\$.03 + \$3 + \$87.50$

17. $.01 + .001 + .0001$

18. $5 + .05 + 5.005$

19. $4 + 42.2 + .08 + .03$

20. $\$25 + \$.15 + \$49$

Everyday Problem Solving

Jen went shopping. Look at the receipt on the right. Some of the information is missing.

1. How much will Jen spend before tax? Add the prices to find the subtotal.

2. What is the total she needs? Add the sales tax to the subtotal to find out.

3. Jen has $128.35. Does she have enough money to pay the total you found in question 2?

```
CLOTHES PLACE
ITEM          PRICE
SWEATSHIRT    $39.95
JEANS          45.99
DRESS SHIRT    29.79

SUBTOTAL

TAX            8.76
TOTAL
```

Subtracting Decimals

You can subtract decimals. Look at the grids below.

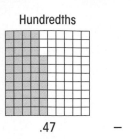

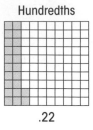

Hundredths		Hundredths		Hundredths
.47	−	.25	=	.22

Subtract decimals the way you subtract whole numbers. Line up the decimal points one over the other before you subtract. Then place the decimal point in the difference so that it lines up with the other decimal points.

▶ **EXAMPLE 1**

Subtract.   29.34 − 16.52

STEP 1
Line up the
decimal points.

$$\begin{array}{r} 29.34 \\ -\ 16.52 \end{array}$$

STEP 2
Subtract. Place the
decimal point
in the difference.

$$\begin{array}{r} \overset{8\ 13}{29.\cancel{3}4} \\ -\ 16.52 \\ \hline 12.82 \end{array}$$

The difference between 29.34 and 16.52 is 12.82.

Sometimes you must write a decimal point and zeros so that you can line up the decimal points.

▶ **EXAMPLE 2**

Subtract.   87 − 35.83

STEP 1
Line up the
decimal points.

$$\begin{array}{r} 87.00 \\ -\ 35.83 \end{array}$$

STEP 2
Subtract. Place the
decimal point
in the difference.

$$\begin{array}{r} \overset{6\ 9\,10}{8\cancel{7}.\cancel{0}\cancel{0}} \\ -\ 35.83 \\ \hline 51.17 \end{array}$$

The difference between 87 and 35.83 is 51.17.

Practice A

Subtract. The decimal points have been lined up for you.

1. 12.5
  − 8.3

2. 15.39
  − 7.62

3. 4.155
  − .706

4. 38.01
  − 19.43

5. 63.47
  − 45.28

6. 82.0
  − 46.2

7. 467.09
  − 18.50

8. 5.293
  − .750

Practice B

Subtract. Remember to line up the decimal points. Write a decimal point and zeros if needed. Show your work in vertical form.

9. 17.8 − 6.5

10. .321 − .09

11. $28.50 − $12.35

12. 37.005 − 8.3

13. 63.3 − .06

14. 65 − 5.1

15. $358.23 − $69.95

16. 91.2 − .125

17. $50 − $.79

18. $3.50 − $1.95

19. .3 − .003

20. 1 − .001

Everyday Problem Solving

Aaron found this chart in a magazine.

1. Who ran the fastest? The smallest number for time shows the fastest runner.

2. How much faster was Donovan Baily than Carl Lewis? Subtract to find out.

3. How much faster was Carl Lewis than Lindford Christies?

Olympic 100-Meter Run		
Year	Runner	Time
1988	Carl Lewis, United States	9.92 seconds
1992	Lindford Christies, United States	9.96 seconds
1992	Donovan Baily, Canada	9.84 seconds

10-7 Multiplying Decimals

Look at the grid. The green part shows .3 × .8.

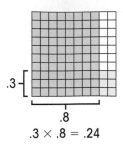

.3 {

.8

.3 × .8 = .24

Remember:
Factors are the numbers multiplied to get a product.

Multiply decimals the way you multiply whole numbers. The number of decimal places in the product is equal to the sum of the number of decimal places in the factors.

▶ **EXAMPLE 1**

Remember:
A product is the answer to a multiplication problem.

Multiply.   15.34 × 4.2

STEP 1
Multiply.

$$\begin{array}{r} 15.34 \\ \times\quad 4.2 \\ \hline 3068 \\ +\ 61360 \\ \hline 64428 \end{array}$$

STEP 2
Count the decimal places.

Place the decimal point.

$$\begin{array}{r} 15.34 \\ \times\quad 4.2 \\ \hline 3\ 068 \\ +\ 61\ 360 \\ \hline 64.428 \end{array}$$

← 2 decimal places
← 1 decimal place

← 3 decimal places

The product of 15.34 and 4.2 is 64.428.

Sometimes, you need to place zeros in the product.

▶ **EXAMPLE 2**

Multiply.   .09 × .07

STEP 1
Multiply.

$$\begin{array}{r} .09 \\ \times\ .07 \\ \hline 63 \end{array}$$

STEP 2
Count the decimal places.
Place the decimal point.
Write zeros if needed.

$$\begin{array}{r} .09 \\ \times\ .07 \\ \hline .0063 \end{array}$$

← 2 decimal places
← 2 decimal places
← 4 decimal places

The product of .09 and .07 is .0063.

Practice A

Copy the multiplication problem. Then, place the decimal point in the product. Write zeros if needed.

1.
$$\begin{array}{r} 5.82 \\ \times\ \ 2.3 \\ \hline 1\,3\,3\,8\,6 \end{array}$$

2.
$$\begin{array}{r} .08 \\ \times\,.06 \\ \hline 48 \end{array}$$

3.
$$\begin{array}{r} .04 \\ \times\ .5 \\ \hline 20 \end{array}$$

4.
$$\begin{array}{r} .2 \\ \times\,.2 \\ \hline 4 \end{array}$$

Practice B

Multiply.

5.
$$\begin{array}{r} 9.65 \\ \times\ .12 \\ \hline \end{array}$$

6.
$$\begin{array}{r} .18 \\ \times\,.06 \\ \hline \end{array}$$

7.
$$\begin{array}{r} .24 \\ \times\ .5 \\ \hline \end{array}$$

8.
$$\begin{array}{r} 4.23 \\ \times\ 1.2 \\ \hline \end{array}$$

9.
$$\begin{array}{r} 5.8 \\ \times\,.46 \\ \hline \end{array}$$

10.
$$\begin{array}{r} 5.77 \\ \times\ .26 \\ \hline \end{array}$$

11.
$$\begin{array}{r} 627.5 \\ \times\ 8.04 \\ \hline \end{array}$$

12.
$$\begin{array}{r} 5.04 \\ \times\ .67 \\ \hline \end{array}$$

13. $3.7 \times .05$

14. 7.003×68

15. $46.92 \times .01$

16. $\$65.49 \times 12$

17. $\$18.25 \times 30$

18. $\$5.99 \times 25$

19. $6.9 \times .4$

20. $36.4 \times .09$

21. $5.59 \times .6$

Everyday Problem Solving

Sam saw this advertisement in the newspaper.

1. How much do 4 CDs cost? Multiply to find out.

2. How much do 3 tapes cost? Multiply to find out.

3. How much money does Sam need to buy 4 CDs and 3 tapes?

POWER RECORDS
Best Price in Town

CDs $12⁹⁵

Tapes $7³⁵

Multiplying Decimals by 10, 100, 1,000

You can use what you know to learn a shortcut for multiplying decimals by 10, by 100, or by 1,000.

$$\begin{array}{r} .071 \\ \times\ \ 10 \\ \hline .710 \end{array} \qquad \begin{array}{r} .071 \\ \times\ \ 100 \\ \hline 7.100 \end{array} \qquad \begin{array}{r} .071 \\ \times\ 1,000 \\ \hline 71.000 \end{array}$$

Now look at this:

$.071 \times 10 = 0.71 = .71$

      1 zero   1 place to the right

$.071 \times 100 = 0\ 7.1 = 7.1$

      2 zeros   2 places to the right

$.071 \times 1,000 = 0\ 7\ 1. = 71$

      3 zeros   3 places to the right

To multiply by 10, by 100, or by 1,000, move the decimal point to the right. Write zeros if needed.

▶ **EXAMPLE**

Multiply. $32.5 \times 1,000$ 3 zeros

STEP 1   Count the zeros. $32.5 \times 1,000$

STEP 2   Move the decimal point. $3\ 2\ 5\ 0\ 0 = 32,500$
           Write zeros if needed.

The product of 32.5 and 1,000 is 32,500.

Practice

Multiply.

1. $.2 \times 10$ **2.** $.35 \times 10$ **3.** $.05 \times 10$ **4.** 2.97×100

5. $.539 \times 100$ **6.** 42.4×100 **7.** $22.8 \times 1,000$ **8.** $.457 \times 1,000$

9. $.9 \times 1,000$ **10.** 3.38×10 **11.** $.07 \times 1,000$ **12.** 463×100

ON-THE-JOB MATH
Bank Teller

Carmen Soleteri works for a bank. She is a bank teller. Carmen helps customers every day. They ask her to cash checks. They also ask her to make deposits and withdrawals. She also counts cash.

This is a good job for Carmen because she likes math and meeting people. She also stays calm under pressure.

To make a deposit, a customer must fill out a deposit slip. Carmen must make sure the total on the slip is correct.

Look at the deposit slips below. Tell whether or not the customer added correctly.

1.

DEPOSIT TICKET

J. J. SUMMERS
One Eastway Road
New Town, ST 00000

DATE _____

00022220   02

	1 3 8.4 3
	3 2.4 7
	2 4 5.6 3
Total $	,4 1 6.4 3

2.

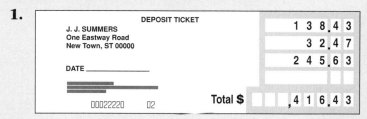

	2 3.6 4
	6.2 8
	5 4.7 6
Total $	,8 4.6 8

3.

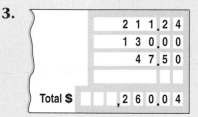

	2 1 1.2 4
	1 3 0.0 0
	4 7.5 0
Total $	,2 6 0.0 4

Critical Thinking

What do you think Carmen should say to a customer if the deposit slip is incorrect? Work with a partner to decide what she should say. Share your answer with the class.

10·9 Dividing Decimals by Whole Numbers

Remember:
A quotient is the answer to a division problem.

Divide decimals the way you divide whole numbers. Place the decimal point in the quotient above the decimal point in the dividend.

$$\begin{array}{r} .08 \leftarrow \text{Quotient} \\ \text{Divisor} \rightarrow 4)\overline{.32} \leftarrow \text{Dividend} \end{array}$$

▶ **EXAMPLE 1**

Multiply the quotient by the divisor to check.
$2.68 \times 35 = 93.8$

Divide. $93.8 \div 35$

STEP 1
Place the decimal in the quotient.

$$35)\overline{93.8}$$

STEP 2
Divide. You may need to write zeros on the end of the dividend.

$$\begin{array}{r} 2.68 \\ 35)\overline{93.80} \\ -\ 70 \\ \hline 238 \\ -\ 210 \\ \hline 280 \\ -\ 280 \\ \hline 0 \end{array}$$

The quotient of 93.8 divided by 35 is 2.68.

Sometimes, the decimal quotient will have a repeating pattern. When this happens, the division will never end. To end the division, draw a bar over the repeating pattern.

▶ **EXAMPLE 2**

Divide. $1.4 \div 33$

STEP 1
Divide until you see a repeating pattern.

$$\begin{array}{r} .04242 \\ 33)\overline{1.40000} \\ -\ 1\ 32 \\ \hline 80 \\ -\ 66 \\ \hline 140 \\ -\ 132 \\ \hline 80 \\ -\ 66 \\ \hline 14 \end{array}$$

STEP 2
Draw a bar over the repeating part of the answer.
$0.04242... \rightarrow .04\overline{2}$

The quotient of 1.4 divided by 33 is $.0\overline{42}$.

216   Chapter 10 • Decimals

Practice A

Copy each problem. Then, place the decimal point in the quotient.
Write zeros if needed. The first one is done for you.

1. $3\overline{).27}$ quotient $.09$ **2.** $5\overline{)6.25}$ quotient $1\ 25$ **3.** $12\overline{).048}$ quotient 4 **4.** $20\overline{)6.0}$ quotient 3

Practice B

Divide. Follow the directions from Practice A.

5. $4\overline{).24}$ **6.** $5\overline{).45}$ **7.** $8\overline{).56}$ **8.** $6\overline{).048}$

9. $58.56 \div 64$ **10.** $.150 \div 12$ **11.** $.526 \div 8$ **12.** $12.54 \div 76$

Practice C

Divide. Draw a bar over the repeating part of the quotient.

13. $6\overline{)45.8}$ **14.** $3\overline{)20}$ **15.** $9\overline{)60.4}$ **16.** $11\overline{)640}$

17. $9\overline{)4.1}$ **18.** $27\overline{)95.1}$ **19.** $22\overline{)53.4}$ **20.** $18\overline{)91.4}$

Everyday Problem Solving

The information on the right shows the cost of
Internet service. You can choose Plan A or Plan B.

1. Judy uses the Internet about 24 hours each
month. Which plan should she buy? To find
the cost of Plan B, you need to multiply
14 hours by $1.50 and then add $8.99.

2. Li uses the Internet 48 hours each month.
Which plan should he buy?

3. At how many hours of use will Plan A be
the better buy?

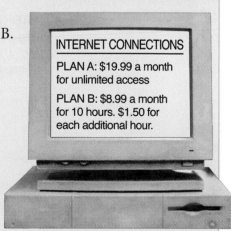

INTERNET CONNECTIONS

PLAN A: $19.99 a month
for unlimited access

PLAN B: $8.99 a month
for 10 hours. $1.50 for
each additional hour.

10·10 Dividing Decimals by Decimals

Multiplying the divisor and the dividend by 10, by 100, or by 1,000 will not change the quotient.

$$
3\overline{)\,.6}^{\,.2} \qquad 30\overline{)\,6.0}^{\,.2} \qquad 300\overline{)\,60.0}^{\,.2} \qquad 3{,}000\overline{)\,600.0}^{\,.2}
$$

When the divisor is a decimal, multiply the divisor and the dividend by 10, by 100, or by 1,000. This will make your divisor into a whole number.

▶ **EXAMPLE 1**

When you move the decimal point to the right, you are multiplying by 10, by 100, or by 1,000.

Divide. $2.24 \div 3.2$

STEP 1
Move the decimal point so that the divisor is a whole number. Place the decimal point in the quotient.

$$3.2\overline{)\,2.2.4}$$

STEP 2
Divide.

$$
\begin{array}{r}
.7 \\
32\overline{)22.4} \\
-\,22\,4 \\
\hline
0
\end{array}
$$

The quotient of 2.24 divided by 3.2 is .7.

Sometimes, you need to write end zeros for the dividend so that you can move the decimal point to the right.

▶ **EXAMPLE 2**

Divide. $18 \div .125$ Check your answer.

STEP 1
Move the decimal point. Add zeros if needed.

$$.125.\overline{)\,18.000.}$$

STEP 2
Divide.

$$
\begin{array}{r}
144 \\
125\overline{)18000} \\
-\,125 \\
\hline
550 \\
-\,500 \\
\hline
500 \\
-\,500 \\
\hline
0
\end{array}
$$

The quotient of 18 divided by .125 is 144.

To check, multiply the quotient by the original decimal divisor.

Check: $144 \times .125 = 18$ ✓

Practice A

Rewrite each problem to make the divisor a whole number.

1. $.4\overline{).8}$ **2.** $.15\overline{).45}$ **3.** $.012\overline{)1.56}$ **4.** $.007\overline{)4.921}$

Practice B

Divide. Multiply to check your answer.

5. $.4\overline{).8}$ **6.** $.15\overline{).45}$ **7.** $.012\overline{)1.56}$ **8.** $.007\overline{)4.921}$

9. $.6\overline{)72.18}$ **10.** $.08\overline{)170.4}$ **11.** $.12\overline{)1.56}$ **12.** $6.8\overline{)44.2}$

13. $62.7 \div 3.8$ **14.** $6.25 \div .25$ **15.** $30 \div .75$ **16.** $\$4.40 \div .55$

Practice C

Divide. The decimal part of some quotients will repeat. Remember to draw a bar over the repeating part.

17. $.06\overline{)5.6}$ **18.** $2.3\overline{).92}$ **19.** $.04\overline{)18.8}$ **20.** $.45\overline{)3.9}$

21. $55.04 \div 3.2$ **22.** $1.825 \div .25$ **23.** $3.596 \div 6.2$ **24.** $8.4 \div .012$

25. $2.75 \div .09$ **26.** $96 \div 4.8$ **27.** $91 \div .13$ **28.** $2.823 \div .45$

Everyday Problem Solving

Solve each word problem. Remember to divide.

1. Movie tickets cost $5.75 each on Saturday afternoons. On Saturday afternoon, the theater sold $690 worth of tickets. How many tickets were sold?

2. The theater club sold $679.50 worth of tickets for the school play. All tickets that were sold were the same price. If 151 people bought tickets, how much did each ticket cost?

Dividing Decimals by 10, 100, 1,000

You can use what you know to learn a shortcut for dividing decimals by 10, by 100, or by 1,000.

$$\frac{13.23}{10)\overline{132.30}} \qquad \frac{1.323}{100)\overline{132.300}} \qquad \frac{.1323}{1,000)\overline{132.3000}}$$

Now look at this:

$$132.3 \div 1\underbrace{0}_{\text{1 zero}} = 13.\underset{\text{1 place to the left}}{2\,3} = 13.23$$

$$132.3 \div 1\underbrace{00}_{\text{2 zeros}} = 1.\underset{\text{2 places to the left}}{3\,2\,3} = 1.323$$

$$132.3 \div 1,\underbrace{000}_{\text{3 zeros}} = .\underset{\text{3 places to the left}}{1\,3\,2\,3} = .1323$$

To divide by 10, by 100, or by 1,000, move the decimal point to the left. Write zeros if needed.

▶ **EXAMPLE**

Remember:
5 = 5.0

Divide. $5 \div 1,000$

$$\underbrace{}_{\text{3 zeros}}$$

STEP 1   Count the zeros. $5 \div 1,\!000$

STEP 2   Move the decimal point 3 places. $.0\,0\,5 = .005$
Write zeros if needed.

The quotient of 5 divided by 1,000 is .005.

Practice

Divide.

1. .62 ÷ 10

2. 9.3 ÷ 10

3. 8 ÷ 10

4. 5.74 ÷ 100

5. .834 ÷ 100

6. 2 ÷ 100

7. 38.6 ÷ 1,000

8. .5 ÷ 1,000

9. 7 ÷ 1,000

10. 12.09 ÷ 100

11. 38 ÷ 10

12. 74.5 ÷ 1,000

USING YOUR CALCULATOR
Number Patterns

You can use a calculator to find a pattern.

Find each sum.

$$29.5 + .5 = \blacksquare$$
$$299.5 + .5 = \blacksquare$$
$$2{,}999.5 + .5 = \blacksquare$$

DECIMAL POINT
Press to put a decimal point in a number.

PRESS [2] [9] [.] [5] [+] [.] [5] [=] [30.   ]

PRESS [C] [0.   ]

PRESS [2] [9] [9] [.] [5] [+] [.] [5] [=] [300.   ]

PRESS [C] [0.   ]

PRESS [2] [9] [9] [9] [.] [5] [+] [.] [5] [=] [3000.   ]

Now use the pattern to find $2{,}999{,}999.5 + .5 = \blacksquare$.

$$2{,}999{,}999.5 + .5 = 3{,}000{,}000$$

Guess each missing number. Use a calculator to check.

1. $29{,}999.5 + .5 = \blacksquare$ **2.** $29{,}999{,}999.5 + .5 = \blacksquare$ **3.** $299{,}999.5 + .5 = \blacksquare$

Use your calculator to find a pattern in the first row. Then guess each difference in the second row. Use a calculator to check.

4. $60 - .8 = \blacksquare$ **5.** $600 - .8 = \blacksquare$ **6.** $6{,}000 - .8 = \blacksquare$

7. $600{,}000 - .8 = \blacksquare$ **8.** $60{,}000 - .8 = \blacksquare$ **9.** $\blacksquare - .8 = 5{,}999{,}999.2$

Use your calculator to find a pattern in the first row. Then guess each quotient in the second row. Use a calculator to check.

10. $9 \div 2 = \blacksquare$ **11.** $9 \div 20 = \blacksquare$ **12.** $9 \div 200 = \blacksquare$

13. $9 \div 2{,}000 = \blacksquare$ **14.** $9 \div .2 = \blacksquare$ **15.** $9 \div .02 = \blacksquare$

Problem Solving: Multi-Part Decimal Problems

Some word problems can be solved if you work on one part at a time.

▶ **EXAMPLE**

Margaret bought 3 cans of corn. Corn costs $.43 a can. She also bought a bag of potatoes. The potatoes cost $1.99. How much change from $5 did she receive?

STEP 1 READ What do you need to find out?
You need to find the change from $5.
But first you need to find the total cost.

STEP 2 PLAN What do you need to do?
How much does the corn cost?
Multiply to find out.

What is the total cost?
Add to find out.

How much change did she receive?
Subtract to find out.

STEP 3 DO Follow the plan.

Multiply	Add	Subtract
$.43	$1.29 Corn	$5.00
× 3	+ 1.99 Potatoes	− 3.28
$1.29 Corn	$3.28 Total cost	$1.72 Change

STEP 4 CHECK Does your answer make sense?
Add $1.72 + $3.28. Does this equal $5?

$1.72 Change
+ 3.28 Total cost
$5.00 ✓

Margaret received $1.72 as change.

Problem Solving

READ the problem. Answer the questions under PLAN.
DO the plan to solve the problem.

1. Al bought 5 pounds of apples. The apples were $.39 a pound. He also bought a bag of grapes. The grapes were $2.58. How much change from $10 did he receive?

   PLAN
   How much did the apples cost? What was the total cost? How much change did he receive?

2. Helen bought 1 ear of corn and cabbage. Ten ears of corn cost $3.50. The cabbage was $.99. How much change from $2 did she receive?

   PLAN
   How much did 1 ear of corn cost? What was the total cost? How much change did she receive?

3. Bill bought 2 pounds of butter. Butter costs $1.78 a pound. He also bought 1 roll. Rolls cost $4.80 for 12 rolls. What was the total cost?

   PLAN
   How much did the butter cost? How much did the roll cost? What was the total cost?

Problem Solving Strategy

Often, problems can be solved by working backward.

Cathy bought tomatoes for $3.50. She also bought lettuce. Cathy gave the store clerk $5.00. Her change was $1.00. How much did the lettuce cost?

Fill in the blanks below to find the cost of the lettuce.

$1.00 Change $3.50 Tomatoes
+ ▓▓▓ Total cost   + ▓▓▓ Lettuce
  $5.00   ▓▓▓ Total cost

10·13 Renaming Decimals as Fractions

You can use place value to help you change decimals to fractions.

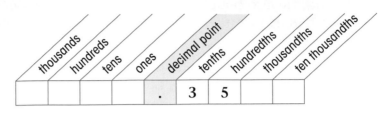

EXAMPLE

Rename the decimal .35 as a fraction.

STEP 1 Use the decimal digits as the numerator.

$$.35 = \frac{35}{}$$

STEP 2 Use the last place value as the denominator.

Hundredths
↓
$$.35 = \frac{35}{100}$$

STEP 3 Reduce the fraction to lowest terms.

$$\frac{35}{100} = \frac{35 \div 5}{100 \div 5} = \frac{7}{20}$$

.35 written as a fraction in lowest terms is $\frac{7}{20}$.

Practice

Rename each decimal as a fraction. Reduce to lowest terms.

1. .5   **2.** .05   **3.** .005   **4.** .076   **5.** .76

6. .845   **7.** .682   **8.** .98   **9.** .328   **10.** .455

11. .873   **12.** .605   **13.** .4   **14.** .40   **15.** .32

16. .8   **17.** .375   **18.** .75   **19.** .10   **20.** .28

You can change a fraction to a decimal. Divide the numerator by the denominator.

▶ **EXAMPLE**

Rename the fraction $\frac{7}{20}$ as a decimal.

STEP 1 Write the fraction as a division problem.

$$\frac{7}{20} \rightarrow 20\overline{)7}$$

STEP 2 Divide.

$$
\begin{array}{r}
.35 \\
20\overline{)7.00} \\
-\ 6\,0 \\
\hline
1\,00 \\
-\ 1\,00 \\
\hline
0
\end{array}
$$

$\frac{7}{20}$ written as a decimal is .35.

Practice A

Write each fraction as a division problem.

1. $\frac{3}{5}$ **2.** $\frac{1}{2}$ **3.** $\frac{11}{20}$ **4.** $\frac{3}{25}$ **5.** $\frac{27}{50}$

Practice B

Rename each fraction as a decimal by using division.

6. $\frac{3}{5}$ **7.** $\frac{1}{2}$ **8.** $\frac{11}{20}$ **9.** $\frac{3}{25}$ **10.** $\frac{1}{4}$

11. $\frac{11}{200}$ **12.** $\frac{19}{500}$ **13.** $\frac{31}{250}$ **14.** $\frac{101}{125}$ **15.** $\frac{39}{40}$

16. $\frac{4}{5}$ **17.** $\frac{3}{20}$ **18.** $\frac{53}{20}$ **19.** $\frac{39}{50}$ **20.** $\frac{47}{50}$

21. $\frac{9}{20}$ **22.** $\frac{87}{125}$ **23.** $\frac{7}{250}$ **24.** $\frac{23}{40}$ **25.** $\frac{27}{50}$

A number line can help you round decimals. Round the decimal 3.482 to the nearest hundredth.

3.482 is closer to 3.48 than to 3.49.
3.482 rounds to 3.48.

You can also follow steps to round decimals.

EXAMPLE 1

Round the decimal 3.482 to the nearest hundredth.

STEP 1 Underline the rounding place. Look at the digit to its right.   3.48<u>2</u>

STEP 2 Compare the digit to 5. 2 is smaller than 5.

STEP 3 Round as you would whole numbers.   Leave 8 alone.

STEP 4 Drop all digits to the right of the rounding place.   3.48

3.482 rounded to the nearest hundredth is 3.48.

Sometimes, you have to change the numbers in two places.

EXAMPLE 2

Round the decimal 2.963 to the nearest tenth.

STEP 1 Underline the rounding place. Look at the digit to its right.   2.<u>9</u>63

STEP 2 Compare the digit to 5.   6 is larger than 5.

STEP 3 Round as you would whole numbers.   Add 1 to 9 tenths.
$2.9 + .1 = 3.0$

STEP 4 Drop all digits to the right of the rounding place.   2.963 becomes 3.0.

Practice A

Write the name of the underlined place value.

1. 3.2<u>9</u>8   **2.** .<u>3</u>52   **3.** 1.0<u>1</u>5   **4.** 78.09<u>9</u>

5. .2<u>9</u>1   **6.** 2.1<u>5</u>2   **7.** 4.<u>6</u>21   **8.** 15.2<u>2</u>8

Practice B

Round each decimal to the nearest hundredth or cent.

9. .375   **10.** $1.496   **11.** 2.8724   **12.** 23.059

13. .913   **14.** 67.305   **15.** $105.995   **16.** 48.994

17. 3.534   **18.** 2.299   **19.** .864   **20.** 10.775

Practice C

Round each decimal to the nearest tenth.

21. 3.298   **22.** 54.351   **23.** 32.446   **24.** 99.321

25. .15   **26.** 26.547   **27.** 8.95   **28.** 5.09

29. 30.736   **30.** 15.792   **31.** 9.56   **32.** 1.309

Everyday Problem Solving

1. Jannie has $25. Does she have enough money to buy the items on the receipt on the right? Round up the prices to the nearest dollar. Then, find the total.

2. Why is it better to round prices up when you want to see if you have enough money?

AL'S TAKE-OUT
CHEESEBURGER $4.58
FOOT-LONG SUB $8.02
CHEF'S SALAD $6.84

| decimal |
| decimal places |
| decimal point |
| mixed decimal |

Vocabulary Review

Complete each sentence with a word from the list.

1. A __?__ is the dot in a decimal.

2. A number that names part of a whole number is a __?__.

3. A __?__ contains a whole number and a decimal.

4. __?__ are to the right of the decimal point.

5. **Writing** Show that you understand these words. Write a sentence for each word. Do not use the sentences above.

Chapter Quiz

LESSONS 10·1 to 10·4

Test Tip
When comparing decimals, first compare the whole number parts.

Writing, Comparing, and Ordering Decimals

Write each number as a decimal.

1. three hundredths

2. seven and five tenths

3. twenty-two thousandths

4. fifty and five hundredths

Compare each pair of numbers. Use >, <, or =.

5. 15.03   9.03

6. 1.52   1.63

7. 8.6   8.61

8. 7.23   7.203

9. 6.3   6.25

10. 45.03   45.03

LESSONS 10·5 and 10·6

Test Tip
Line up the decimal points when adding or subtracting decimals.

Adding and Subtracting Decimals

Add or subtract.

11. $8.65 + 9.37$

12. $5.8 + 26.98$

13. $16.25 - 9.7$

14. $6 + 4.59 + .729$

15. $14.05 - 8.59$

16. $7 - 3.075$

Multiplying and Dividing Decimals

Multiply. Show your work in vertical form.

17. 1.2×4

18. $.7 \times .06$

19. $2.5 \times .5$

20. 8.09×1.7

21. $38.5 \times .29$

22. 478×6.05

Divide.

23. $36.4 \div 24$

24. $448.7 \div 35$

25. $6 \div 12$

26. $37.95 \div 4.6$

27. $5 \div .09$

28. $.453 \div .15$

Solving Problems with Decimals

Solve each problem.

29. Greg buys 3 pounds of cheese at $1.29 a pound and bread for $2.29. How much change from $10 does he receive?

30. Janine has $20. Does she have enough money to buy socks for $2.99 and a T-shirt for $12.95?

Changing Decimals and Fractions

Rename each decimal as a fraction.

31. .2

32. .25

33. .03

Rename each fraction as a decimal.

34. $\frac{3}{5}$

35. $\frac{5}{8}$

36. $\frac{3}{4}$

Group Activity

With your group, use a grocery store flyer to shop for a family of three for a week. You have $125 to spend. Make a list of the items you want to buy and the cost. Decide on the items to purchase and explain your choices.

From the water's surface, you only see the tip of an iceberg. This is only 11% of the entire iceberg. The rest is hidden underwater. If an iceberg weighs 1,550,000 tons, what percent of its weight is above the surface? Multiply 11% times the weight. Subtract to find how much is hidden below the water.

Chapter 11 ▷ Percents

Words to Know

percent	a part of a whole divided into 100 parts
sales tax	a tax that is a percentage of the price of an item
discount	amount that a price is reduced
sale price	price of an item after the discount is subtracted
commission	payment based on a percent of sales
base salary	salary before adding commission
gross salary	commission plus the base salary
percent increase	percent more than an original number
percent decrease	percent less than an original number

Nutrition Facts Project

Nutrition facts are listed on all foods. They are given as a percentage of the "recommended daily allowance" (RDA). Collect several nutrition facts labels and record in your journal the name of the product and the %RDA of total fat, sodium, carbohydrates, and protein. Find out how many servings you would need to eat to get 100% of any nutrient.

Learning Objectives

- Write percents.
- Change among percents, decimals, and fractions.
- Find the part, the percent, and the whole in a problem.
- Find sales tax, discount, and commission.
- Find the percent increase or decrease and the original number.
- Solve problems about percents.
- Apply percents to find a tip.

11-1   What Is a Percent?

A **percent** is a part of a whole that is divided into 100 equal parts. The sign for percent is %.

EXAMPLE

What part of the whole is shaded?

STEP 1   Count the number of shaded squares.   48 out of 100

STEP 2   Write the number and percent sign.   48%

48% of the whole is shaded.

A percent more than 100% is more than one whole.

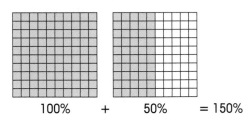

100%   +   50%   = 150%

Practice

Write the percent for the part shaded in each model.

1.

2.

3.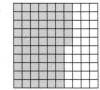

Changing Percents to Decimals

Percent means per hundred. You can write a percent as a decimal. The hundredths place is two places to the right of the decimal point.

▶ **EXAMPLE 1**

Change 36% to a decimal.

STEP 1 Drop the percent sign. Place a decimal point to the right of the last digit.

36% becomes 36.

STEP 2 Move the decimal point two places to the left.

.36

36% written as a decimal is .36.

Sometimes a percent is a mixed number.

▶ **EXAMPLE 2**

Change $4\frac{1}{2}$% to a decimal.

STEP 1 Change the mixed number to a decimal.

$4\frac{1}{2}$% = 4.5%

STEP 2 Drop the percent sign. Move the decimal point two places to the left. Fill any extra places with zeros.

4.5% = .045

$4\frac{1}{2}$% written as a decimal is .045.

Practice

Change each percent to a decimal.

1. 15%   **2.** 12%   **3.** 85%   **4.** 27%   **5.** 8%

6. 80%   **7.** 5%   **8.** $5\frac{1}{2}$%   **9.** $3\frac{1}{2}$%   **10.** 3.5%

11. 3%   **12.** 1%   **13.** 10%   **14.** 138%   **15.** 250%

Finding the Part

A percent problem consists of three numbers: the percent, the whole, and the part.

25% of 100 is 25

Percent · Whole · Part

You can find the part if you are given the percent and the whole. This problem can be asked in two ways.

Find 25% of 100.
What is 25% of 100?

▶ **EXAMPLE 1**

Find 35% of 80.

Remember that the clue word *of* means to multiply.

STEP 1 Change the percent to a decimal.

$35\% = .35$

STEP 2 Multiply the decimal by the number that comes after the word *of*. Write the decimal point in the correct place in the product.

```
        80  ← Whole
    ×  .35  ← Percent
      4 00
     24 00
     28.00  ← Part
```

35% of 80 is 28.

▶ **EXAMPLE 2**

What is 125% of 40?

STEP 1 Change the percent to a decimal.

$125\% = 1.25$

STEP 2 Multiply the decimal by the number that comes after the word *of*. Write the decimal point in the correct place in the product.

```
     1.25  ← Percent
    ×   40  ← Whole
    50.00  ← Part
```

50 is 125% of 40.

Practice A

Find the part.

1. 10% of 60 is ▨

2. 12% of 100 is ▨

3. 15% of 40 is ▨

4. 25% of 80 is ▨

5. 10% of 85 is ▨

6. 50% of 75 is ▨

7. 55% of 60 is ▨

8. 75% of 96 is ▨

9. 34% of 100 is ▨

10. 27% of 800 is ▨

11. 7% of 650 is ▨

12. 49% of 1,000 is ▨

Practice B

Answer each question.

13. What is 15% of 36?

14. What is 40% of 80?

15. What is 75% of 90?

16. What is 23% of 200?

17. What is 2% of 500?

18. What is 68% of 50?

19. What is 10% of 505?

20. What is 99% of 200?

21. What is 150% of 350?

22. What is 254% of 100?

Everyday Problem Solving

The student counselor made a chart of after-school jobs.

1. How many girls work at supermarkets? Find 65% of 60.

2. How many boys work at supermarkets?

3. How many girls work at video stores?

4. How many boys work at video stores? Explain.

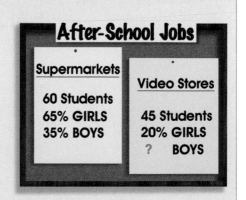

After-School Jobs

Supermarkets
60 Students
65% GIRLS
35% BOYS

Video Stores
45 Students
20% GIRLS
? BOYS

Many states charge **sales tax** on items you buy. The sales tax is a percent of the cost of the item. Finding the sales tax is a percent problem. It has the same three parts.

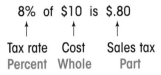

8% of $10 is $.80

Tax rate Cost Sales tax
Percent   Whole Part

EXAMPLE 1

A book costs $7.00. The sales tax is 6%. How much sales tax is charged?

Remember:
Part = Percent × Whole

STEP 1 Change the percent to a decimal.   6% = .06

STEP 2 Multiply the decimal by the cost of the item. This is the amount of sales tax.   .06 × $7 = $.42

The sales tax on the book is $.42.

To find the total cost, add the cost of the item to the sales tax.

EXAMPLE 2

A book costs $8.50. The rate of the sales tax is 8%. What is the total cost of the book, including the sales tax?

STEP 1 Change the percent to a decimal.   8% = .08

STEP 2 Multiply the decimal by the cost of the item. This is the amount of sales tax.   .08 × $8.50 = $.68

STEP 3 Add the sales tax to the cost of the book. $8.50 + $.68 = $9.18

The total cost of the book with sales tax is $9.18.

Practice A

Copy the chart below. Find the sales tax for each item. Then find the total cost.

	Sales Tax	Cost of Item	Amount of Sales Tax	Total Cost
1.	5%	$65	?	?
2.	7%	$35	?	?
3.	9%	$120	?	?
4.	12%	$555	?	?

Practice B

Solve.

5. The sales tax is 4%. The cost of lunch is $6.50. What is the amount of the sales tax?

6. The sales tax is 5%. The cost of a camera is $40. What is the amount of the sales tax?

7. A small television costs $150. If the sales tax is 6%, what is the total cost of the television?

8. The sales tax is 8%. A VCR costs $205. What is the amount of the sales tax?

9. A bike light costs $15. If the sales tax is 6%, what is the total cost of the light?

10. Computer software costs $36. The sales tax is $7\frac{1}{2}$%. What is the total cost of the software?

11·5   Discounts

Stores often put items on sale. During a sale, the regular price of an item is reduced. The amount the price is reduced is the **discount**. Finding a discount is a percent problem. It has the same three parts.

15% of $50 is $7.50

Discount rate   Price   Discount
Percent   Whole   Part

EXAMPLE 1

A shirt costs $35. It is on sale at 20% off. What is the discount?

Remember:
Part = Percent × Whole

STEP 1   Change the percent to a decimal.   20% = .20

STEP 2   Multiply the decimal by the price. This is the discount.   .20 × $35 = $7

The discount is $7.

To find the **sale price** of an item, you need to subtract the discount from the regular price.

EXAMPLE 2

A pair of sneakers costs $55. They are on sale at 20% off. What is the sale price?

STEP 1   Change the percent to a decimal.   20% = .20

STEP 2   Multiply the decimal by the price. This is the discount.   .20 × $55 = $11

STEP 3   Subtract the discount from the regular price. This is the sale price. $55 − $11 = $44

The sale price of the sneakers is $44.

Practice A

Copy the chart below. Find the discount for each item. Then find the sale price.

	Discount Rate	Price of Item	Discount	Sale Price
1.	5%	$35	?	?
2.	8%	$150	?	?
3.	15%	$62	?	?
4.	25%	$250	?	?

Practice B

Solve.

5. A pair of pants cost $40. They are on sale at 30% off. What is the discount?

6. What is the sale price of the pants in Question 5?

7. A shirt costs $18. It is on sale at 15% off. What is the sale price?

8. A key chain costs $7.50. It is on sale at 20% off. What is the discount?

9. Kevin gets an 8% discount on all videos. What does he pay for a $23 video?

10. A suit costs $350. It is on sale at 23% off. What is the sale price of the suit?

Commissions

A **commission** is payment based on a percent of sales. Finding a commission is a percent problem.

10% of $2,500 is $250

Commission rate   Sales Commission
Percent   Whole   Part

▶ **EXAMPLE 1**

Remember:
Part = Percent × Whole

Mr. Barnes sold $3,500 of pet food. As a salesperson, his commission is 9% of his sales. What is the amount of his commission?

STEP 1 Change the percent to a decimal.   9% = .09

STEP 2 Multiply the decimal by the total sales. This is the commission.   .09 × $3,500 = $315

Mr. Barnes's commission is $315.

The **base salary** is how much you get paid before adding in the commission. To find the **gross salary**, you add the commission to the base salary.

▶ **EXAMPLE 2**

Robin's base salary is $200 per week. Last week, her sales totaled $26,000. If her commission is 4%, what was her gross salary for the week?

STEP 1 Change the percent to a decimal.   4% = .04

STEP 2 Multiply the decimal by the total sales. This is the commission.   .04 × $26,000 = $1,040

STEP 3 Add the commission to the base salary. This is the gross salary.

    $1,040 ← Commission
 +   200 ← Base salary
    $1,240 ← Gross salary

Robin's gross salary for the week was $1,240.

Practice A

Copy the chart below. Find the commission and gross salary for each salesperson.

	Name	Base Salary	Total Sales	Commission Rate	Commission	Gross Salary
1.	Manny	$158	$7,800	6%	?	?
2.	Charles	$215	$4,200	5%	?	?
3.	Anne	$225	$3,000	4%	?	?
4.	Katerina	$175	$5,500	7%	?	?

Practice B

Solve.

5. Harry's sales are $480. His commission is 6% of sales. What is the amount of his commission?

6. Mr. Lee earns a 5% commission on sales. Last month, his sales were $7,100. What was the amount of his commission?

7. Margo's total sales were $38,920 last month. She is paid 7% commission. What was the amount of her commission?

8. Amy's base salary is $150 per week. Her sales this week total $3,500. If her commission is 20%, what is her gross salary for the week?

9. Ray's base salary is $300 per month. His commission is 5% of sales. If he sells $28,000 this month, what is his gross salary?

10. Sol's base salary is $950 per month. His commission is $8\frac{1}{2}$% of sales. If he sells $10,500 this month, what is his gross salary?

MATH IN YOUR LIFE
Tipping

Mario's special birthday dinner at Fiesta Restaurant costs $39.54. He plans to leave a 15% tip. Here is an easy way to find the dollar amount of a 15% tip.

Round up the cost to the nearest dollar.

$39.54 rounds to $40.

Find **10%** of the cost. Move the decimal point one place to the left.

10% × $40 = $4.0

Find half that amount to get **5%**.

$4 ÷ 2 = $2

Add the 10% and 5% amounts.

$4 + $2 = $6

Another time, Mario spent $25.70 on lunch. He left $3.90 as a tip. Did he leave enough?

The tip is about $6. Mario adds the tip to his bill. His total cost is $39.54 + $6 = $45.54.

Solve.

1. The tip for a banquet is 15%. The banquet total is $597. About how much will the tip be?

2. The cost of a family dinner was $58.25. Wesley tipped the waitress 15%. About how much was the tip? About what was the total cost?

Critical Thinking

At a different restaurant the service was extra special. Mario wanted to leave a 20% tip. How could he change his quick method to find 20%?

11·7 Changing Decimals to Percents

Percent means per hundred or hundredth. You can write a decimal as a percent.

EXAMPLE 1

Change .36 to a percent.

STEP 1 Move the decimal point two places to the right.

.36 becomes 36.

STEP 2 Since 36. is equal to 36, drop the decimal point. Write the percent sign.

36%

.36 written as a percent is 36%.

Sometimes, the decimal has more than two places to the right of the decimal point.

EXAMPLE 2

Change .045 to a percent.

STEP 1 Move the decimal point two places to the right.

.045 becomes 04.5

STEP 2 Drop the zero to the left of the number. Write the percent sign.

4.5%

.045 written as a percent is 4.5%.

Practice

Change each decimal to a percent.

1. .89   **2.** .07   **3.** 1.5

4. .173   **5.** 2   **6.** .5

7. .25   **8.** .13   **9.** .7

10. .225   **11.** .305   **12.** 62.3

Changing Fractions to Percents

A fraction can be written as a division problem.

$$\frac{\text{numerator}}{\text{denominator}} \rightarrow \text{denominator}\overline{)\text{numerator}}$$

Use this idea to change a fraction to a percent.

▶ **EXAMPLE**

Change $\frac{3}{4}$ to a percent.

Remember:
Write a decimal point and zeros in the dividend. Stop writing zeros when the quotient stops or repeats.

STEP 1 Write the fraction as a division problem in which the numerator is divided by the denominator.

$\frac{3}{4} \rightarrow 4\overline{)3}$

STEP 2 Divide. The quotient will be a decimal.

```
    .75
4)3.00
 -2 8
    20
  - 20
     0
```

STEP 3 Write the decimal as a percent. Move the decimal point two spaces to the right. Write the percent sign.

$75. = 75\%$

Practice

Change each fraction to a percent.

1. $\frac{1}{4}$ 2. $\frac{3}{5}$ 3. $\frac{3}{10}$ 4. $\frac{1}{2}$ 5. $\frac{1}{5}$

6. $\frac{5}{8}$ 7. $\frac{4}{5}$ 8. $\frac{7}{10}$ 9. $\frac{1}{8}$ 10. $\frac{1}{100}$

11. $\frac{1}{20}$ 12. $\frac{3}{8}$ 13. $\frac{2}{5}$ 14. $\frac{1}{25}$ 15. $\frac{1}{200}$

USING YOUR CALCULATOR
The Percent Key

You can use a calculator to do percent problems. Most calculators have a special percent (%) key that helps solve percent problems.

Find 30% of 60.

Of is a clue word for multiplication. Multiply 30% by 60.

PRESS `3` `0` `%` `0.3`

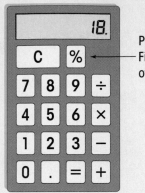

PERCENT KEY
Finds percent of a number.

The percent (%) key changed 30% into a decimal automatically.

PRESS `×` `6` `0` `=` `18.`

The display shows that 30% of 60 is 18.

Solve each problem using a calculator. Use the percent (%) key.

1. 25% of 88   **2.** 20% of 590

3. 75% of 240   **4.** 19% of 100

5. 50% of 98   **6.** 60% of 150

7. 150% of 400   **8.** 240% of 60

9. 175% of 360   **10.** 23% of 90

Solve each problem using a calculator. Compare the answers. What do you notice?

11. 20% of 35 and 35% of 20   **12.** 10% of 90 and 90% of 10

> **Calculator Tip**
> The % key may not work the same on all calculators. Sometimes, 30% of 60 must be entered as 60 × 30%. Here you do not need to press = to get the answer.

11·9 Finding the Percent

You can find the percent if you are given the whole and the part.

$$\underset{\text{Percent}}{25\%} \ \text{of} \ \underset{\text{Whole}}{100} \ \text{is} \ \underset{\text{Part}}{25}$$

EXAMPLE 1

What percent of 50 is 10?

STEP 1 Write a fraction. The denominator is the whole. It is the number after the word *of*. The numerator is the part.

$$\frac{10}{50} \quad \begin{array}{l} \leftarrow \text{Part} \\ \leftarrow \text{Whole} \end{array}$$

STEP 2 Divide the numerator by the denominator.

$$\begin{array}{r} .2 \\ 50\overline{)10.0} \\ -10\,0 \\ \hline 0 \end{array}$$

Remember:
To change a decimal to a percent, move the decimal two places to the right.

STEP 3 Change the decimal to a percent.

$$.2 = 20. = 20\%$$

10 is 20% of 50.

Be careful. Sometimes the percent is greater than 100%. Then the part will be greater than the whole. You will start with an improper fraction.

EXAMPLE 2

42 is what percent of 35?

STEP 1 Write a fraction. The denominator is the whole. It is the number after the word *of*. The numerator is the part.

$$\frac{42}{35} \quad \begin{array}{l} \leftarrow \text{Part} \\ \leftarrow \text{Whole} \end{array}$$

STEP 2 Divide the numerator by the denominator.

$$\begin{array}{r} 1.2 \\ 35\overline{)42.0} \\ -35 \\ \hline 7\,0 \\ -7\,0 \\ \hline 0 \end{array}$$

STEP 3 Change the decimal to a percent.

$$1.2 = 120. = 120\%$$

42 is 120% of 35.

Practice

Find the percent in each problem.

1. What percent of 24 is 12?

2. What percent of 100 is 5?

3. 24 is what percent of 96?

4. 6 is what percent of 60?

5. 36 is what percent of 300?

6. 36 is what percent of 100?

7. What percent of 4 is 12?

8. What percent of 125 is 9?

9. 20 is what percent of 200?

10. 19 is what percent of 38?

11. What percent of 75 is 25?

12. What percent of 40 is 5?

13. 12 is what percent of 6?

14. 105 is what percent of 60?

Everyday Problem Solving

Soccer is a popular sport all year. Use the chart to answer the questions.

1. How many games did the Tornadoes play?

2. What percent of their games did the Tornadoes win? What percent of their games did they lose?

3. How many games did the Blue Sox play? What percent of their games did they win?

4. What percent of their games did the Red Birds win?

5. A prize is given to the team with the highest percent of wins. Which team gets the prize?

THE WEEK IN SPORTS

TEAM	GAMES WON	GAMES LOST	GAMES TIED	TOTAL GAMES PLAYED
RED BIRDS	10	5	0	?
BLUE SOX	8	2	0	?
TORNADOES	9	3	0	?

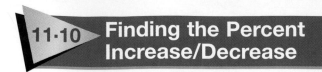

11·10 Finding the Percent Increase/Decrease

If an original number is made larger, you can find the **percent increase**. If an original number is made smaller, you can find the **percent decrease**.

EXAMPLE 1

The number 20 has been increased to 22. What is the percent increase?

STEP 1 Find the amount of increase. Subtract the original number from the new number.

$$\begin{array}{r} 22 \\ -\,20 \\ \hline 2 \end{array} \leftarrow \text{Increase}$$

STEP 2 Write a fraction that compares the increase with the original number.

$\frac{2}{20}$

STEP 3 Change the fraction to a percent.

$20\overline{)2} = .1 = 10\%$

The percent increase is 10%.

Notice that the fraction compares 2 with the original number, 20.

EXAMPLE 2

The number 48 has been decreased to 12. What is the percent decrease?

STEP 1 Find the amount of decrease. Subtract the new number from the original number.

$$\begin{array}{r} 48 \\ -\,12 \\ \hline 36 \end{array} \leftarrow \text{Decrease}$$

STEP 2 Write a fraction that compares this decrease with the original number.

$\frac{36}{48}$

STEP 3 Change the fraction to a percent.

$48\overline{)36} = .75 = 75\%$

The percent decrease is 75%.

Practice A

Copy the chart below. Find the percent increase or decrease for each stereo model.

Model Name	Price in June	Price in July	Percent Increase or Decrease
1. Hi Sound	$120	$126	?
2. Boomer	$80	$72	?
3. XKE	$90	$180	?
4. 10Z	$75	$60	?

Practice B

Solve to find the percent increase or decrease.

5. Lia's total sales were $1,200 last month. This month her sales are $1,500. What is the percent increase?

6. A baseball card is worth $55 now. Last year it was worth $50. What is the percent increase?

7. Your $200 printer now costs $140. What is the percent decrease?

8. A used skateboard sells for $66. Originally, it cost $100. What is the percent increase or decrease?

9. Your $150 CD player now sells for $210. What is the percent increase?

10. Last year, Ms. Cahill had 35 students in her class. This year she has 28 students. What is the percent decrease?

11·11　Finding the Whole

You know the three numbers in a percent problem.

25% of 100 is 25.

Percent　Whole　Part

You can find the whole if you are given the percent and the part.

EXAMPLE 1

20% of ■ is 5.

Remember:
Whole = Part ÷ Percent

STEP 1　Change the percent to a decimal.

$20\% = .20$

STEP 2　Divide the part by the percent. The quotient is the whole.

Percent → 20.$\overline{)500.}$ ← Part　25 ← Whole

$$-40$$
$$100$$
$$-100$$
$$0$$

20% of 25 is 5.

When the percent is greater than 100%, the part will be greater than the whole.

EXAMPLE 2

80 is 160% of what number?

STEP 1　Change the percent to a decimal.

$160\% = 1.60$

STEP 2　Divide the part by the percent. The quotient is the whole.

Percent → 160.$\overline{)8000.}$ ← Part　50 ← Whole

$$-800$$
$$0$$

80 is 160% of 50.

Notice that the part is 80. The whole is 50. The part is greater than the whole.

Practice A

Find the whole in each problem.

1. 10% of ▪ is 8
2. 50% of ▪ is 250
3. 5% of ▪ is 50
4. 9% of ▪ is 18
5. 12% of ▪ is 78
6. 20% of ▪ is 32
7. 74% of ▪ is 407
8. 66% of ▪ is 165
9. 24% of ▪ is 18
10. 60% of ▪ is 84
11. 15% of ▪ is 45
12. 49% of ▪ is 196

Practice B

Solve to find the whole in each problem.

13. 35 is 50% of what number?
14. 63 is 18% of what number?
15. 60% of what number is 72?
16. 75% of what number is 12?
17. 36 is 30% of what number?
18. 60 is 15% of what number?
19. 225% of what number is 54?
20. 110% of what number is 121?

Everyday Problem Solving

A bank pays money (called interest) to each person with a savings account. The interest rate times the savings (called the principal) equals the interest.

1. How much interest does Will get?
2. How much interest does Angela get?
3. Find Mr. Smythe's interest.
4. What is Mrs. Smythe's principal? (Hint: 5% of what number is $300?)

Annual Interest

Name	Interest Rate	Interest	Principal
Mr. Smythe	4%	?	$5,000
Mrs. Smythe	5%	$300	?
Will	6%	?	$1,000
Angela	8%	?	$750

11·12 Finding the Original Price

Suppose a price is changed by a percent. If you are given the percent and the new price, you can find the original price.

80% of $75 is $60

Percent Original New
price   price

Percent Whole Part

EXAMPLE 1

Remember:
Make the decimal divisor a whole number. Move the decimal point to the right.

80.)6000.

The original price of a pair of hiking boots was decreased by 20%. The boots now cost $60. What was the original price?

STEP 1 Find what percent the new price is of the original price. Subtract the percent decrease from 100.

$100\% - 20\% = 80\%$

STEP 2 Solve the percent problem. Find the whole. Divide the part by the percent.

80% of ? is 60.
$60 \div .80$ is $75.

The original price was $75. Notice that it was the original price that had a 20% decrease.

EXAMPLE 2

Remember:
Whole = Part ÷ Percent

A ski trip now costs $260. This is a 30% increase from the original price. What was the original price?

STEP 1 Find what percent the new price is of the original price. Add the percent increase to 100.

$100\% + 30\% = 130\%$

STEP 2 Solve the percent problem. Find the whole. Divide the part by the percent.

130% of ? is 260.
$260 \div 1.30$ is $200.

The original price was $200. The original price had a 30% increase.

Practice A

Copy the chart below. Find the original price for each item.

Item	Percent Increase or Decrease	New Price	Original Price
1. Printer	50% decrease	$125	?
2. Magazine subscription	30% decrease	$42	?
3. Club membership	10% increase	$88	?
4. Season tickets	20% increase	$75	?

Practice B

Solve to find the original cost in each problem.

5. A shirt is on sale for $10. This is 50% off the original price. What was thc original price?

6. Rosa's new bracelet costs $12. All bracelets are 60% off the original price. What was the original price?

7. Kevin's skateboard is 20% off the original price. If he pays $80, what was the original price?

8. A stamp album has increased in value 25%. It is now worth $4,500. What was its original value?

Problem Solving: Finding the Part, Percent, or Whole

To solve a percent word problem, you need to know what you are given and what you need to find. Look for the three parts of the percent problem.

EXAMPLE

At the Global Tire Factory, 25% of the employees ride to work by bus. There are 215 employees who ride the bus. How many employees work at the factory?

STEP 1 **READ** What do you need to find out?
You need to find the total number of employees at the factory.

STEP 2 **PLAN** What do you need to do?
Identify the percent problem you need to solve. Look at what you are given. What do you need to find?

25% of ? is 215
↑   ↑   ↑
Percent Whole Part

You need to find the whole.

Remember:
Whole = Part ÷ Percent
Part = Percent × Whole
Percent = Part ÷ Whole × 100

STEP 3 **DO** Follow the plan.
25% of what number is 215?
Divide the part by the percent.
$215 ÷ .25 = 860$ employees

STEP 4 **CHECK** Does your answer make sense?
25% of 860 employees should be 215.
$.25 × 860 = 215$ ✓

There are 860 employees at Global Tire Factory.

Problem Solving

READ each problem. Answer the questions under PLAN. DO the plan to solve each problem.

1. At a tire store yesterday, 20% of the day's customers bought premium tires. The salesman sold premium tires to 60 customers. How many total customers bought tires yesterday?

    PLAN
    What are you given?
    What do you need to find?

2. There are 900 tires manufactured at the Global Tire Factory every day. Today, 62% of them are shipped to stores out of state. How many tires were shipped out of state?

    PLAN
    What are you given?
    What do you need to find?

3. There were 500 people at the company picnic. Of the total, 125 people work in the shipping department. What percent of the people at the picnic work in the shipping department?

    PLAN
    What are you given?
    What do you need to find?

Problem-Solving Strategy

Sometimes a sentence diagram can help you plan. Write ✓ next to what you know. Write ? to show what to find.

Eric earns $2,000 each month at Global Tire. His rent is 28% of his salary. How much is his rent?

Sentence Diagram

▇% of $▇ is $▇

↑   ↑   ↑

Percent   Whole   Part

| base salary |
| commission |
| discount |
| gross salary |
| percent |
| percent decrease |
| percent increase |
| sale price |
| sales tax |

Vocabulary Review

Choose a words or words from the list to complete each sentence.

1. The __?__ will make an original number larger.

2. A store will add __?__ to the price of an item.

3. Payment based on the percent of sales is called __?__.

4. A __?__ tells how many of 100 parts are in a whole.

5. A price can be reduced by a __?__.

6. You get the __?__ of an item after subtracting the discount.

7. The sum of the __?__ and the commission is the __?__.

8. The __?__ will make an original number smaller.

9. **Writing** Write a paragraph entitled "Percents in Everyday Life." Use at least five words from the list above. Underline the words as you use them.

Chapter Quiz

LESSONS 11·1, 11·2, 11·7, and 11·8

Changing Fractions, Decimals, and Percents
Copy the chart. Fill in the missing numbers.

Test Tip
Change between percents and decimals by moving the decimal point 2 places left or right. Remember that percent is out of 100 parts.

	Percent	Fraction	Decimal
1.	7%	?	?
2.	?	$\frac{3}{4}$	?
3.	?	?	1.2
4.	16%	?	?
5.	?	$\frac{4}{5}$	?

LESSONS 11·3 to 11·6, 11·9, and 11·11

Finding the Part, Percent, or Whole

Test Tip
Change percents to decimals.
Whole = Part ÷ Percent
Part = Percent × Whole
Percent = Part ÷ Whole

Solve.

6. What number is 36% of 58?

7. What percent of 96 is 24?

8. 16 is 40% of what number?

9. Candy costs $3.75. The sales tax is 4%. What is the total cost of the candy?

10. A CD costs $15. It's on sale for 10% off. What is the discount?

11. Ed sold $2,400 in computer parts. His commission is 8%. How much did he make in commission?

LESSONS 11·10, 11·12, and 11·13

Solving Three Kinds of Percent Problems

Test Tip
Read carefully for clues. Decide which of the three kinds of percent problems needs to be solved. Be sure your answer makes sense.

Solve.

12. Dinner for two totaled $56.00. A 15% tip is required. What is the amount of the tip?

13. A briefcase was originally priced at $95. It now sells for $76. What is the percent decrease?

14. A shirt is on sale for $18. This is 25% off the original price. What is the original price?

15. Dana sold 45 tickets to the dance. This is 18% of all the tickets that were sold. How many tickets were sold?

Group Activity

Work with your group to find an advertisement that uses percents. Pretend to purchase three items from the ad. For each item, find and record the percent of discount, its original price, and the sale price. Decide which store has the fairest advertisement. Explain your reasoning.

Builders use models to show what a building should look like. Every model has a scale. You can use the scale to find the actual size of something in the model. Suppose a wall in a model is 6 inches long. The scale for the model is 1 inch = 2 feet. How long is the actual wall? Multiply the scale by the measurement of the wall in the model.

Words to Know

ratio	a comparison of one amount with another
proportion	a statement that two ratios are equal
cross products	the results of cross multiplying
rate	a comparison of two amounts with different units of measure
multiple unit pricing	the cost of a set of items
scale drawing	a picture that shows the proportional size of actual objects
scale	a ratio that compares the size of a drawing with the size of the original object

Scale Drawing Project

Make a scale drawing of your bedroom. Measure the length and width of the room. Measure the length and width of each piece of furniture. Choose a scale so that your drawing will fit on a sheet of graph paper. An example of a scale is 1 inch in your drawing = 2 feet in your room. Label the actual measurements on your drawing.

Learning Objectives

- Write ratios.
- Solve proportions.
- Find multiple unit prices.
- Use scale drawings to find actual sizes.
- Solve problems using proportions.
- Apply using map scales to find distances.

A **ratio** is a comparison of one amount with another. You can write a ratio to compare the number of blue squares with all squares in the picture.

The ratio of blue squares to all squares is three to five. There are three ways to write this ratio.

In words	With a ratio sign	As a fraction
3 to 5	3:5	$\frac{3}{5}$

If the ratio is an improper fraction, do not change it to a whole or mixed number.

▶ **EXAMPLE 1**

Write the ratio of yellow squares to blue squares.

STEP 1 Count the yellow squares.   3 Yellow
Count the blue squares.   4 Blue

STEP 2 Write the ratio as a fraction.
The order of the numbers is $\frac{3}{4}$ ← Yellow
important.   ← Blue

The ratio of yellow squares to blue squares is 3 to 4, 3:4, or $\frac{3}{4}$.

Ratios are written in lowest terms.

▶ **EXAMPLE 2**

Write the ratio of vowels to the total number of letters in the word GRAPES.

Remember:
$$\frac{2}{6} = \frac{2 \div 2}{6 \div 2} = \frac{1}{3}$$

STEP 1 Count the number of vowels in the word.

GRAPES ←2 vowels

Count the total number of letters in the word.

GRAPES ←6 letters

STEP 2 Write the ratio. Be sure it is in lowest tems.

$$\frac{2}{6} = \frac{1}{3}$$

The ratio of vowels to the total number of letters in GRAPES is 1 to 3, 1:3, or $\frac{1}{3}$.

Practice

Write each ratio with a ratio sign or as a fraction.

1. blue circles to all circles

2. blue circles to yellow circles

3. total number of letters to vowels in the word HOUSE

4. vowels to total number of letters in the word FLAVOR

Everyday Problem Solving

Eric uses the recipe shown to make punch.

1. What is the ratio of pineapple juice to orange juice?

2. What is the ratio of lemon juice to ginger ale?

3. What is the ratio of orange juice to lemon juice?

Party Punch

Mix the following ingredients:

12 cups pineapple juice

1 cup lemon juice

3 cups orange juice

18 cups ginger ale

What Is a Proportion?

A **proportion** shows two equal ratios. Look at the squares below. Each ratio compares the blue parts to all parts. The ratios are equal and form a proportion.

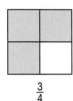

$$\frac{3}{4} \quad = \quad \frac{6}{8}$$

This proportion above is read:
Three **is to** four **as** six **is to** eight.

EXAMPLE 1

Write a ratio of the blue parts to all parts for each rectangle. Do the ratios form a proportion?

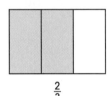

$$\frac{2}{3} \quad = \quad \frac{4}{6} \qquad \text{Yes } \checkmark$$

Thus, $\frac{2}{3}$ and $\frac{4}{6}$ do form a proportion.

You can tell if two ratios form a proportion by cross multiplying. The results are the **cross products**. If the cross products are equal, the ratios do form a proportion.

EXAMPLE 2

Do $\frac{3}{4}$ and $\frac{12}{16}$ form a proportion?

STEP 1 Find the cross products.

$$\frac{3}{4} \times \frac{12}{16}$$

Cross products:
$3 \times 16 = 48$
$4 \times 12 = 48$

STEP 2 Compare the cross products. If the cross products are equal, the ratios form a proportion.

$48 = 48 \checkmark$

The ratios $\frac{3}{4}$ and $\frac{12}{16}$ do form a proportion.

Practice A

Write a ratio of the blue parts to all parts for each figure.
Do the ratios form a proportion? Write *Yes* or *No*.

1.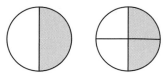

2.

3.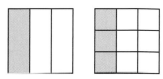

4.

5.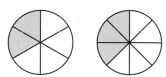

6.

Practice B

Decide if each pair of ratios forms a proportion. Write *Yes* or *No*.

7. $\frac{3}{4}$ $\frac{18}{24}$ **8.** $\frac{2}{7}$ $\frac{9}{10}$ **9.** $\frac{5}{9}$ $\frac{15}{27}$

10. $\frac{10}{15}$ $\frac{12}{18}$ **11.** $\frac{5}{8}$ $\frac{4}{5}$ **12.** $\frac{4}{5}$ $\frac{5}{7}$

13. $\frac{2}{9}$ $\frac{4}{18}$ **14.** $\frac{5}{8}$ $\frac{6}{7}$ **15.** $\frac{9}{24}$ $\frac{6}{16}$

16. $\frac{1}{7}$ $\frac{3}{20}$ **17.** $\frac{4}{10}$ $\frac{12}{30}$ **18.** $\frac{14}{16}$ $\frac{18}{24}$

Solving Proportions

You can find a missing number in a proportion.

EXAMPLE

Find the missing number in the proportion.

$$\frac{2}{3} = \frac{?}{21}$$

STEP 1 Find the cross product.

$$\frac{2}{3} \searrow \frac{?}{21}$$
$$2 \times 21 = 42$$

STEP 2 Divide the cross product by the remaining number in the proportion. The quotient is the missing number.

$$42 \div 3 = 14$$
$$? = 14$$

STEP 3 Check the cross products to be sure that they are equal.

$$\frac{2}{3} \times \frac{14}{21}$$
$$2 \times 21 = 3 \times 14$$
$$42 = 42 \checkmark$$

The missing number is 14.

Practice

Find the missing number in each proportion.

1. $\dfrac{?}{12} = \dfrac{5}{10}$

2. $\dfrac{3}{?} = \dfrac{7}{21}$

3. $\dfrac{8}{32} = \dfrac{?}{16}$

4. $\dfrac{3}{18} = \dfrac{4}{?}$

5. $\dfrac{4}{8} = \dfrac{?}{2}$

6. $\dfrac{11}{?} = \dfrac{2}{4}$

7. $\dfrac{4}{7} = \dfrac{?}{14}$

8. $\dfrac{9}{12} = \dfrac{3}{?}$

9. $\dfrac{5}{?} = \dfrac{50}{70}$

10. $\dfrac{8}{9} = \dfrac{16}{?}$

11. $\dfrac{?}{35} = \dfrac{3}{5}$

12. $\dfrac{15}{60} = \dfrac{1}{?}$

USING YOUR CALCULATOR
Solving Proportions

You can solve proportions with your calculator.
Find the missing number in the proportion.

$$\frac{3}{4} = \frac{?}{28}$$

Multiply to find the cross product.

    PRESS   3 × 2 8 *Do not press the equal sign.*

Divide by the remaining number.

    PRESS   ÷ 4 =   21.

The missing number is 21.

$$\frac{3}{4} = \frac{21}{28}$$

> **Calculator Tip**
>
> Some calculators display the product of the numbers after pressing the division key. This will not affect the answer.

Now, check the proportion. First, find the cross products. Write them down on your paper. Check to see if the cross products are equal.

    PRESS   3 × 2 8 =   84.

    PRESS   4 × 2 1 =   84.

84 = 84 ✓

The ratios form a proportion. The missing number is 21.

Find the missing number in each proportion. Then, check each proportion.

1. $\dfrac{50}{120} = \dfrac{5}{?}$

2. $\dfrac{?}{500} = \dfrac{9}{10}$

3. $\dfrac{11}{?} = \dfrac{55}{775}$

4. $\dfrac{36}{250} = \dfrac{144}{?}$

5. $\dfrac{160}{200} = \dfrac{?}{340}$

6. $\dfrac{50}{?} = \dfrac{400}{640}$

7. $\dfrac{?}{375} = \dfrac{96}{2250}$

8. $\dfrac{24}{360} = \dfrac{3}{?}$

9. $\dfrac{2}{38} = \dfrac{?}{475}$

12·4 Multiple Unit Pricing

A **rate** is a comparison of two amounts with different units of measure. An example of a rate is **multiple unit pricing.** Multiple unit pricing is the cost of a set of items. For example, suppose that 4 cans of cat food sell for $2. This can be written as

$$\frac{4 \text{ cans}}{\$2} \quad \text{or} \quad \frac{\$2}{4 \text{ cans}}$$

If you know the rate, you can use a proportion to find the price of any number of the same item.

> **EXAMPLE 1**

The price of workout shorts is $24.50 for 5 pairs. What is the price of 3 pairs of shorts?

STEP 1 Set up a proportion with a missing number.

$$\frac{\$24.50}{5 \text{ shorts}} \quad \frac{\$?}{3 \text{ shorts}}$$

STEP 2 Find the cross product.

$$\$24.50 \times 3 = \$73.50$$

STEP 3 Divide the cross product by the remaining number.

$$\$73.50 \div 5 = \$14.70$$

STEP 4 Check the ratios to see if they form a proportion.

$$\frac{\$24.50}{5 \text{ shorts}} \quad \frac{\$14.70}{3 \text{ shorts}}$$

The cross products are equal.
The ratios form a proportion.
The answer is correct.

$$\$24.50 \times 3 = \$14.70 \times 5$$
$$\$73.50 = \$73.50 \checkmark$$

The price of 3 pairs of workout shorts is $14.70.

You can use a proportion to find how many items you can buy for a certain amount of money.

► **EXAMPLE 2**   The price of workout shorts is $24.50 for 5 pairs. How many shorts can you buy for $9.80?

STEP 1 Set up a proportion with a missing number.

$$\frac{\$24.50}{5 \text{ shorts}} \nearrow \frac{\$9.80}{? \text{ shorts}}$$

STEP 2 Find the cross product.

$5 \times \$9.80 = \$49$

STEP 3 Divide the cross product by the remaining number.

$\$49 \div \$24.50 = 2$

STEP 4 Check the ratios to see if they form a proportion.

$$\frac{\$24.50}{5 \text{ shorts}} \diagdown\!\!\!\!\diagup \frac{\$9.80}{2 \text{ shorts}}$$

The cross products are equal.
The ratios form a proportion. $\$24.50 \times 2 = \$9.80 \times 5$
The answer is correct. $\$49 = \$49 \checkmark$

You can buy 2 pairs of shorts for $9.80.

Practice

Solve each problem using a proportion.

1. If 4 cans of soup cost $3.00, how much do 6 cans cost?

2. If 20 golf balls sell for $25.00, how much do 3 golf balls cost?

3. The Grand Prix Raceway charges $6.75 to make 5 laps around the track. How much would it cost to make 15 laps?

4. A bead store sells 200 crystal beads for $8.00. How many beads could you buy with $10.00?

5. Goetz Landscape charges $18.50 for 25 pounds of sand. How much would 80 pounds of sand cost?

6. A long-distance phone call to Ling's grandmother costs $4.35 for 3 minutes. How much would a 20-minute phone call cost?

12-5 ▸ Scale Drawings

A **scale drawing** shows an object that is either larger or smaller than actual size. The **scale** is the ratio of the size of the picture to the size of the original object.

Length = Larger wall
Width = Shorter wall

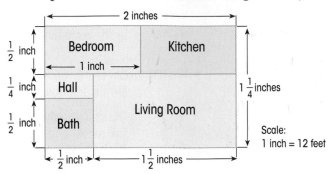

▸ EXAMPLE

Remember:
To multiply by a mixed number, change it to an improper fraction.

$12 \times 1\frac{1}{2}$

$= \frac{12}{1} \times \frac{3}{2} = \frac{36}{2} = 18$

Find the actual length of the living room.

STEP 1 Set up a proportion with a missing number.

Scale $\dfrac{1 \text{ in.}}{12 \text{ ft}} \nearrow\!\!\!\!/ \dfrac{1\frac{1}{2}}{? \text{ ft}}$

STEP 2 Find the cross product.

$12 \times 1\frac{1}{2} = 18$

STEP 3 Divide the cross product by the remaining number in the proportion.

$18 \div 1 = 18$

STEP 4 Check your answer.

$\dfrac{1 \text{ in.}}{12 \text{ ft}} \diagdown\!\!\!\!\diagup \dfrac{1\frac{1}{2} \text{ in.}}{18 \text{ ft}}$

$1 \times 18 = 12 \times 1\frac{1}{2}$

$18 = 18 \checkmark$

The length of the living room is 18 feet.

Practice

Use the scale drawing from the top of the page to find the actual size.

1. the width of the living room

2. the length of the kitchen

3. the length of the bedroom

4. the width of the bedroom

ON-THE-JOB MATH
Courier

Chris is a courier. He delivers packages to homes and businesses.

He uses the map scale to find distances from one location to another.

Use the scale from the map to find the distances Chris needs to ride to deliver packages.

1. Chris delivers the first package to Power Records. How far will he ride from the Courier's Office?

2. The next package is delivered to Hair Art. How far will Chris ride from Power Records?

3. From Hair Art, Chris rides to Eagle Carpet for a delivery. How far will he ride?

4. From Eagle Carpet, Chris rides to the Sub Zone for lunch. Then, he rides to Colony Cleaners. How far will he ride?

Critical Thinking

Chris uses the map to find distances between deliveries. How else does the map help him in his job?

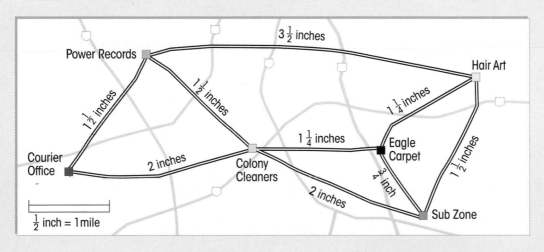

Problem Solving: Using Proportions

Proportions can be used to solve word problems. You can use ratios or rates to compare amounts.

EXAMPLE

Josh can mow 4 lawns in 3 hours. How long will it take him to mow 12 lawns?

STEP 1   READ   What do you need to find out?
You need to find out how long it will take Josh to mow 12 lawns.

STEP 2   PLAN   What do you need to do?
Set up a proportion and solve.

$$\frac{4 \text{ lawns}}{3 \text{ hours}} = \frac{12 \text{ lawns}}{? \text{ hours}}$$

STEP 3   DO   Follow the plan.
Solve the proportion.

$$\frac{4}{3} \quad \frac{12}{?}$$

Multiply the cross product.
$$3 \times 12 = 36$$

Divide by the remaining number.
$$36 \div 4 = 9$$

STEP 4   CHECK   Does your answer make sense?
Do the ratios form a proportion?
Check the cross products.

$$\frac{4}{3} \quad \frac{12}{9}$$

$$4 \times 9 = 36$$

$$3 \times 12 = 36$$

$$36 = 36 \checkmark$$

It will take Josh 9 hours to mow 12 lawns.

Problem Solving

READ the problem. Answer the question under PLAN. DO the plan to solve the problem.

1. Ali can deliver 12 pizzas in 30 minutes. How many pizzas can she deliver in 45 minutes?

   PLAN
   What proportion should you write?

2. Mary can deliver 8 pizzas in 20 minutes. How long will it take her to deliver 10 pizzas?

   PLAN
   What proportion should you write?

3. Sam can read 3 pages in 10 minutes. How long will it take him to read 15 pages?

   PLAN
   What proportion should you write?

Problem Solving Strategy

Drawing a picture can help you solve a problem.

Ann uses 2 bales of hay to feed 6 horses. How many horses can she feed with 3 bales of hay?

Draw a picture of 2 bales of hay and 6 horses. Each bale of hay feeds 3 horses. Now draw 1 more bale of hay with another 3 horses. Count all the horses.

cross products
multiple unit pricing
proportion
rate
ratio
scale
scale drawing

Vocabulary Review

Complete each sentence with a word from the list.

1. A __?__ is a comparison of two quantities.

2. A __?__ is made up of two equal ratios.

3. To check if two ratios are equal, compare the __?__ .

4. A __?__ is a comparison of two amounts with different units of measure.

5. Four cans of soup for $5 is an example of __?__ .

6. A drawing that shows an object and is either larger or smaller than its actual size is called a __?__ .

7. The ratio of the size of the picture to the size of the original object is called the __?__ .

8. **Writing** Give examples of a ratio, a proportion, and a cross product. Explain the relationship among the three terms.

Chapter Quiz

LESSON 12·1

Test Tip
To write a ratio, remember that the first amount named is written as the top number in a fraction.

Writing Ratios

Write each ratio using a ratio sign and a fraction.

1. all letters to vowels in ELEPHANT

2. vowels to all letters in SOCCER

LESSON 12·2

Test Tip
If cross products are equal, then the ratios form a proportion.

Identifying Proportions

Decide if each pair of ratios forms a proportion. Write *Yes* or *No*.

3. $\frac{4}{5}$ $\frac{8}{12}$

4. $\frac{14}{16}$ $\frac{28}{32}$

5. $\frac{5}{10}$ $\frac{6}{12}$

6. $\frac{3}{4}$ $\frac{6}{7}$

Solving Proportions

Find the missing number in each proportion.

7. $\dfrac{12}{8} = \dfrac{30}{?}$

8. $\dfrac{60}{80} = \dfrac{?}{36}$

9. $\dfrac{63}{3} = \dfrac{?}{2}$

10. $\dfrac{25}{75} = \dfrac{4}{?}$

Finding Multiple Unit Prices

Find the price or the number of items.

11. If 3 bars of soap cost $2, how much will 12 bars of soap cost?

12. Tennis balls cost 3 for $5. How many tennis balls can be bought with $20?

Using Scale Drawings

Use a proportion to solve each problem.

13. The scale on a map is 1 inch = 15 miles. A line on the map is 2 inches. How many miles does the line represent?

Solving Problems with Proportions

Solve each problem. Use a proportion.

14. If 18 trees are needed to cover 3 acres, how many trees are needed to cover 60 acres?

Group Activity

Work in a small group. Visit a supermarket or use newspaper ads to find items and their multiple unit prices. Record the item, the number of items, and the price. First, find the cost of five items. Second, find the number of items you could buy for $10. Write and solve a proportion for each part of this activity.

Unit 3 **Review**

Choose the letter for the correct answer.

Use the table to answer Questions 1–3.

Jo's Grocery	
Item	**Cost**
Beans	$.79 can
Tomatoes	$1.19 pound
Apples	5 for $1.20

1. Bruce wants to buy 5 cans of beans. He has $5. What can you conclude?
   A. He has exactly the money he needs.
   B. He does not have enough money.
   C. He will receive change.
   D. The beans are too expensive.

2. Sally bought 5 apples and 1 pound of tomatoes. Sales tax is 6%. What is her total cost?
   A. $2.39
   B. $2.54
   C. $6.36
   D. $7.63

3. How much do 8 apples cost?
   A. $1.92
   B. $2.00
   C. $3.60
   D. $9.60

4. Sue buys 3 pears and 9 apples. What percent of the fruit are apples?
   A. 9%
   B. 25%
   C. 75%
   D. $133\frac{1}{3}$%

5. 25% of Doug's order is for vegetables. His total cost is $12. How much does he spend on vegetables?
   A. $3
   B. $6
   C. $9
   D. $15

6. 30% of Lori's order is for meat. She spends $12 on meat. What is the total cost of her order?
   A. $3.60
   B. $15.60
   C. $20.40
   D. $40.00

Critical Thinking

What can you buy for $10? Choose items from the table above. List the number of items, the cost, and the total cost.

CHALLENGE When you choose the items to buy, come as close to $10 as you can.

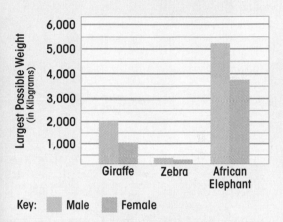

Key: ▮ Male ▮ Female

Animal	Height in Feet	Height in Meters
Giraffe	18	5.50
Zebra	4	1.22
African Elephant	10	3.05

On the African plains, there are many kinds of animals living together. Each type of animal has a different shape and color to protect it from its predators. The sizes of these animals are also very different. Giraffes can grow to be 18 feet tall. A typical zebra is 4 feet tall at the shoulders. The African Elephant is about 10 feet tall at the shoulders.

The graph and table above give information about the heights and weights of three different animals that live in Africa.

1. Which animal weighs more: the male giraffe or the female giraffe?

2. A zebra is about 4 feet tall. What is this height in meters?

3. Is the heaviest male animal also the tallest animal?

275

The scrap tires in this picture can no longer be used on cars. Each year about 250 million tires are scrapped. These tires are being recycled in different ways. For example, one tire can be recycled into about 2.5 gallons of oil. If every scrap tire from last year was recycled into oil, about how many gallons would be produced?

Chapter 13

Graphs and Statistics

Words to Know	
data	information gathered from surveys or experiments
graph	a visual display that shows data in different ways; includes bar, line, and circle graphs
pictograph	a graph that uses pictures to represent data
mean	sum of the data divided by the number of data; also called *average*
median	middle number when data are ordered from least to greatest
mode	number or numbers that appear most often in a set of data
histogram	a graph that shows how many times an event occurred
probability	the chance that an event will occur

Survey Graph Project

Write a survey question that can be answered by your classmates. For example, "What is your favorite flavor of ice cream?" List five possible answer choices. Post your question in the classoom. Have each student initial a choice. Then, use the data to make a graph. Display your results.

Learning Objectives

- Read and make pictographs, bar graphs, and line graphs.
- Read circle graphs and histograms.
- Find the mean, median, and mode of a set of data.
- Find simple probability.
- Solve problems about choosing a scale.
- Apply circle graphs to budgets.

Data is information gathered from surveys. A **graph** is a visual display of data. A **pictograph** uses pictures to show the data in the graph.

▸ EXAMPLE

Make a pictograph of the data in the table.

Corporate Contributions	
Name	Contribution
Maco, Inc.	$467,565
SpaceLab	$630,241
Tobias Co.	$342,882
LMB Industries	$486,037

STEP 1 Choose a picture to represent the information. Assign a number to the picture. This is the key.

Key   = $100,000

STEP 2 Round data to match the key. Round to the nearest $100,000.

STEP 3 Draw the graph. Be sure to give your graph a title.

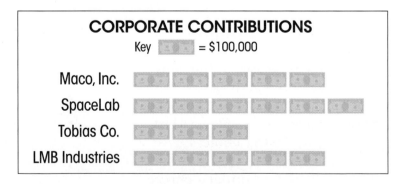

CORPORATE CONTRIBUTIONS
Key = $100,000

Maco, Inc.	
SpaceLab	
Tobias Co.	
LMB Industries	

Practice

Make a pictograph of the data in each table.

1. Round to the nearest hundred.

Summer Camp Attendance	
Name of Camp	Attendance
Voyagers	454
Camp White Water	638
Riding Camp	594
Safari Camp	719
Computer Camp	276

2. Round to the nearest thousand.

Automobile Sales	
Automobile	Number Sold
Subcompacts	5,014
Compacts	7,832
Midsized automobiles	4,910
Luxury automobiles	2,071

Everyday Problem Solving

Michael found this pictograph in the entertainment section of the newspaper.

1. Which type of movie do most people go to see?

2. Which type of movie do the fewest number of people go to see? How do you know?

3. About how many more people go to see comedies than dramas?

Attendance at Movies

Key 👤 = 100 people

Action	👤 👤 👤 👤
Comedy	👤 👤 👤 👤 👤 👤
Horror	👤 👤 👤
Drama	👤 👤 👤

Single Bar Graphs

A bar graph is a graph that uses bars to display data. The bars can be horizontal or vertical. Each bar stands for an item. The length of the bar shows the number of items you have.

EXAMPLE

Make a horizontal bar graph of the data in the table.

Cars in the Parking Lot	
Type of Car	Number
Honda	115
Chevrolet	90
Toyota	100
GM	65
Ford	80

STEP 1 Choose a scale. You need to show numbers from 65 to 115. Use intervals of **20**.

STEP 2 Write the names of the cars along the side. Write the intervals along the bottom.

STEP 3 Draw the bars to show the number of cars for each type.

STEP 4 Write a title for the graph and labels.

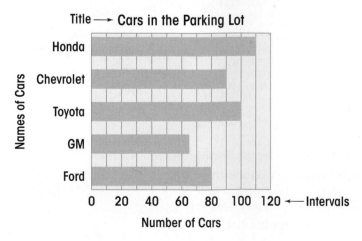

Practice

Make horizontal bar graphs of the data in each table.

1.

Speed of Pitches (miles per hour)	
Pitcher	Speed of Pitch
Oakley	75
Garcia	88
Wu	92
Vanderhoot	69
Turner	97

2.

School Enrollment	
School	Students
Franklin	150
Washington	250
Lincoln	375
Kennedy	225
Lee	100
Roosevelt	75

Everyday Problem Solving

Members of the Columbia School Science Club tested model rockets. They recorded the height of each rocket. This vertical bar graph displays their results.

1. How high did Rob's rocket go?

2. How high did Deb's rocket go?

3. Whose rocket reached a height of 325 feet?

4. Whose rocket went the highest?

5. How much higher did Rob's rocket go than Tom's rocket?

6. How much higher did Deb's rocket go than Ann's rocket?

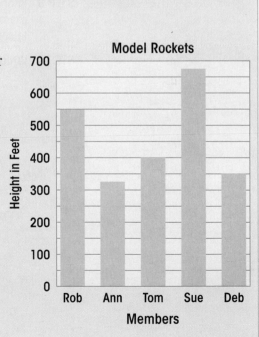

Double Bar Graphs

You can use a double bar graph to compare two different sets of data about the same thing.

> **EXAMPLE**

Make a horizontal double bar graph of the data below.

Heart Rate (beats per minute)		
Name	Before Exercise	After Exercise
Jacob	60	120
Paco	55	130
Lonnie	70	125
Elise	65	135

STEP 1 Choose a scale. You need to show numbers from 55 to 135. Use intervals of 25.

STEP 2 Write the names of the people along the side. Write the intervals along the bottom.

STEP 3 In one color, draw bars to show the heart rate before exercise. In another color, draw bars next to the first ones to show the heart rate after exercise.

STEP 4 Write a title for the graph and a key for the bars.

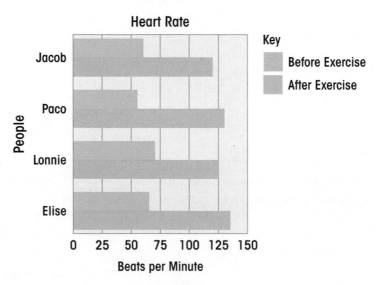

Practice

Make horizontal double bar graphs to display the data in each table.

1.

Baseball Games Won		
Team	1998	1999
Tigers	8	12
Sharks	10	14
Bulls	7	5
Volcanoes	9	9
Green Sox	15	11

2.

National Park Visitors		
Location	Fall to Spring	Summer
Arches Park	23,000	31,000
Ellis Island	13,000	16,000
Blue Ridge	20,000	23,000
Round Valley	10,000	11,000

Everyday Problem Solving

The cinema shows three different movies.

1. How many tickets were sold for the 7:00 show of movie 1?

2. How many tickets were sold for the 5:00 show of movie 2?

3. For which movie were the most tickets sold?

13-4 ▶ Single Line Graphs

Line graphs are used to show change, usually over a period of time. Data are plotted on the graph with dots. The dots are then connected by line segments.

▶ **EXAMPLE**

Make a line graph of the data in the table.

Rainfall	
Month	**Inches of Rain**
January	4.5
March	5.5
May	2.5
July	2.0
September	3.5
December	4.0

STEP 1 Choose a scale. You need to show numbers from 2.0 to 5.5. Start at 0. Use intervals of 1.

STEP 2 Write the months along the bottom. Write the intervals along the side.

STEP 3 Put a dot above each month to show the inches of rain that fell that month.

STEP 4 Connect the dots from left to right with a line.

STEP 5 Label the intervals. Write a title for the graph.

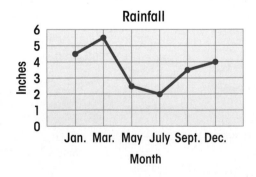

Practice

Make line graphs of the data in each table.

1.

Number of Songs Recorded	
Month	Number
January–February	175
March–April	250
May–June	200
July–August	150
September–October	300
November–December	100

2.

Corn Prices	
Year	Price (per Bushel)
1983	$2.75
1986	$4.50
1989	$1.90
1992	$2.25
1995	$3.00
1998	$4.90

Everyday Problem Solving

The town of Centerville displayed this graph at its last parade.

1. When was the population greatest?

2. What was the population in 1992?

3. Between which years did the population decrease? How do you know?

4. Between which years did the town have the greatest increase in population?

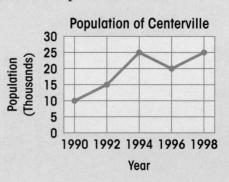

Double Line Graphs

A double line graph can be used to compare sets of related data.

EXAMPLE

Make a double line graph of the data in the table.

Population of the Twin Cities (Rounded Numbers)		
Year	St. Paul	Minneapolis
1960	75,000	125,000
1970	100,000	180,000
1980	110,000	240,000
1990	150,000	310,000

STEP 1 Choose a scale. You need to show numbers from 75,000 to 310,000. Use intervals of 50,000.

STEP 2 Write the years along the bottom. Write the intervals along the side.

STEP 3 In one color, put a dot above each year to show the population in St. Paul. In another color, put a dot to show the population in Minneapolis.

STEP 4 Connect the dots for each set of data. Be sure that there is a different color line for each city.

STEP 5 Write a title for the graph. Write a key for the lines.

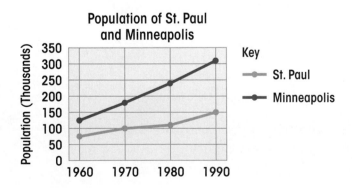

Practice

Make double line graphs of the data in each table.

1.

Communication Requests		
Month	Phone	Fax
January	175	75
February	150	125
March	125	125
April	150	175
May	100	250

2.

Temperature		
Time of Day	Indoors	Outdoors
7:00 A.M.	55°	30°
10:00 A.M.	70°	35°
1:00 P.M.	70°	45°
4:00 P.M.	65°	40°

Everyday Problem Solving

Ray's Sport Shop sells snowboards and surfboards. This is a graph of the store's sales.

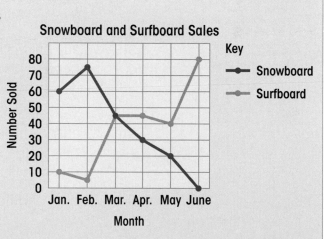

1. In which month are the most surfboards sold?

2. In which month are the fewest snowboards sold?

3. When are snowboard sales and surfboard sales about the same?

4. How could a retail store that sells both items use this information?

Problem Solving: Choosing a Scale

Graphs can be drawn to present different messages.

EXAMPLE

Sports Palace wants to show that it sells more skates than the competition. Which graph should it use and why?

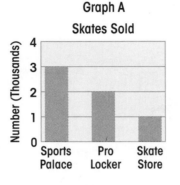

Graph A

Skates Sold

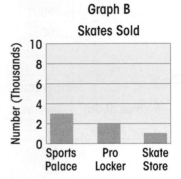

Graph B

Skates Sold

STEP 1   READ   What do you need to find out?
Which graph is better for Sports Palace?

STEP 2   PLAN   What do you need to do?
Look at each graph. Compare the lengh of the bars in each graph.

STEP 3   DO   Follow the plan.
Look at Graph A. The number of skates Sports Palace sold looks greater because the difference between the lengths of the bars is greater.

STEP 4   CHECK   Does your answer make sense?
The scale in Graph A makes it appear as if the sales are better.✓

Sports Palace should use Graph A.

Practice

READ the problems about the graphs shown. Make a PLAN.
DO the plan to solve the problems.

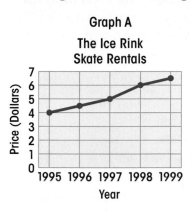

1. The Ice Rink wants to show customers that prices have not increased very much over five years. Which graph should it use and why?

2. The Ice Rink wants to show the owners that prices have increased a lot over 5 years. Which graph should it use and why?

Problem Solving Strategy

Graphs may be used to solve multipart problems.

What is the greatest difference between high and low temperatures shown in the graph?

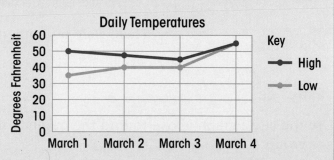

Find the date with the greatest temperature change.
Subtract the low from the high temperature.

13-7   Circle Graphs

Circle graphs are used to show how the total amount
(100%) of something is divided into parts. You can
compare amounts by comparing the sizes of the parts
of the graph.

▶ **EXAMPLE**

How many runners were 9 to 12 years old?

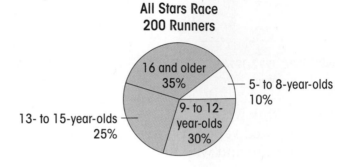

**All Stars Race
200 Runners**

STEP 1 Find out how much the
whole circle represents.

200 runners

STEP 2 Find the percent of
runners who were
9- to 12-year-olds.

30%

STEP 3 Multiply the percent of
9- to 12-year-olds by the
total number of runners.

30% × 200 = .30 × 200
= 60

There were 60 runners that were 9 to 12 years old.

Practice

Use the circle graph above to find the number of runners in each
age group.

1. 5- to 8-year-olds   **2.** 13- to 15-year-olds   **3.** 16 and older

4. A total of how many people are 13 and older?

MATH IN YOUR LIFE
Making a Budget

The Browns' total monthly income is $2,000. The Browns made a monthly budget of what they spend.

They want to make a circle graph to show their budget. They need to find what percent each cost is of the total monthly income.

Part ÷ Whole × 100 = Percent

$240 ÷ $2,000 × 100 = 12%
   ↑   ↑

Utilities   Income

The yellow part of the circle graph is marked to show Utilities 12%.

Find the percents for each cost in the Browns' budget. Copy the circle graph. Label the circle graph with the costs and percents.

1. Housing

2. Food

3. Transportation

4. Savings

5. Recreation

6. Other

BROWNS' MONTHLY BUDGET OF $2,000

Housing	$500
Food	$400
Transportation	$300
Utilities	$240
Recreation	$200
Other	$260
Savings	$100

Browns' Monthly Budget

Utilities 12%

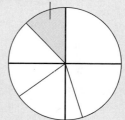

Critical Thinking
Next year, the Browns want to take a family vacation. They want to put more money in savings each month. How might they change their budget to save for vacation? Make a new graph that shows the new budget.

13-8 ▶ Mean (Average)

The **mean** is an average. The average is one way to describe the middle of a set.

To find the mean of a set of numbers, first add the numbers. Then, divide the sum by the number of numbers in the set.

$$\text{Mean} = \frac{\text{Sum of the numbers}}{\text{Number of numbers}}$$

The mean does not have to be a number in the set.

▶ **EXAMPLE 1**

Cindy's test grades in mathematics are 72, 85, 78, and 90. What is her mean test grade?

STEP 1 Find the sum of the numbers.

$72 + 85 + 78 + 90 = \textbf{325}$

STEP 2 Count the number of numbers.

4 tests

STEP 3 Divide the sum by the number of numbers.

$\frac{325}{4} = 325 \div 4$
$= 81.25 \leftarrow \text{Mean}$

Cindy's mean test grade is 81.25.

▶ **EXAMPLE 2**

Prices of CDs at Music Land are $8.50, $10.25, and $15. What is the mean price of the CDs?

STEP 1 Find the sum of the numbers.

$\$8.50 + \$10.25 + \$15.00 = \textbf{\$33.75}$

STEP 2 Count the number of numbers.

3 prices

STEP 3 Divide the sum by the number of numbers.

$\frac{33.75}{3} = 33.75 \div 3$
$= \$11.25 \leftarrow \text{Mean}$

Music Land's mean CD price is $11.25.

Practice

Find the mean of each set of numbers.

1. 4, 11, 23, 40

2. 54, 67, 110, 124, 145

3. 110, 110, 114, 130

4. 1, 3, 4, 5, 7, 8, 11, 12, 12

5. 54, 782, 1003

6. 78, 3, 47, 102, 78, 34

7. 12, 10, 8.5, 17.5

8. 60, 20, 24, 38, 56

9. 34, 40, 21, 52, 47

10. $1\frac{1}{2}$, 2, $3\frac{1}{2}$, 5

11. 125, 350, 275, 300, 225

12. $18.50, $25, $48.30, $42

Everyday Problem Solving

Usef is shopping for a stereo set. He recorded these prices from his favorite stores.

1. What is the mean price?

2. Usef finds a new store where the stereo is $130. Will this new price increase or decrease the mean?

3. Next month, each store will have a sale. All the stereos will be half price. Will the mean price be half price?

4. Usef decides to buy the stereo at Wayne's Electronics. How much money is he saving by not buying at Stereo City?

STORE	PRICE
Sounds and More	$90
Wayne's Electronics	$87
Stereo City	$105
The Right Music	$96

13-9 ▶ Median and Mode

The **median** is the middle number when a set of numbers is ordered from least to greatest.

| 3 | 5 | 8 | 10 | 14 | 16 | 19 |

↑
Median

If there is an even number of numbers, the median is the *average* of the two middle numbers.

EXAMPLE 1

Find the median.   12   11   16   9   13   11

Remember

$$\frac{23}{2} = 23 \div 2$$

STEP 1 Arrange the numbers from least to greatest. Find the two middle numbers.

9   11   <u>11   12</u>   13   16
middle numbers

STEP 2 Find the average of the two middle numbers.

$$\frac{11 + 12}{2} = \frac{23}{2} = 11.5$$

The median is 11.5.

The **mode** is the number that occurs most often.

EXAMPLE 2

Find the mode.   4   3   1   7   7   1   7

STEP Find the number that occurs most often.

4   3   1   7   7   1   7

The mode is 7.

Sometimes, there is no mode.

12, 18, 25, 36, 48 ← There is no mode.

Sometimes, there is more than one mode.

2, 5, 5, 8, 9, 9, 10 ← There are two modes.

Practice A

Find the median of each set of numbers. Remember to put the numbers in order first.

1. 55, 43, 17, 73, 29

2. 171, 89, 138, 211, 146

3. 30, 20, 26, 24

4. 674, 592, 460, 630, 525

5. 106, 95, 100, 86

6. 4, 8, 9, 3, 2, 10, 7, 8, 5

7. 1.7, 6.5, 7.4, 9.9, 1.2

8. 11.6, 17.5, 18.9, 12.5

Practice B

Find the mode of each set of numbers. If there is not a mode, write *none*.

9. 19, 32, 7, 12, 19, 11

10. 24, 23, 23, 22, 24, 25, 21

11. 450, 402, 452, 405

12. 1.5, 2.5, 1.4, 3.7, 1.6, 3.7

Everyday Problem Solving

Mr. Jones saw this graph on the weather channel.

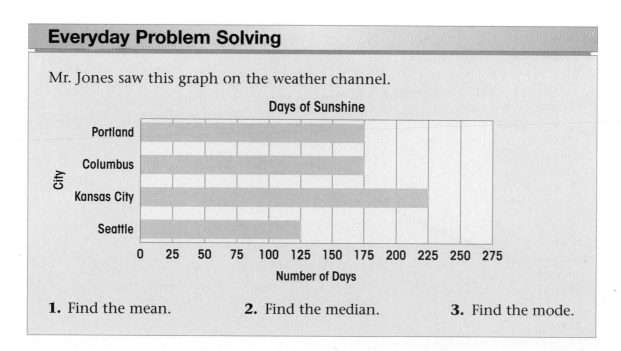

Days of Sunshine

1. Find the mean.

2. Find the median.

3. Find the mode.

13·10 Histograms

A **histogram** is a graph that shows how many items occur between two numbers.

EXAMPLE

A teacher asked 60 students how much time was spent doing homework last week. The histogram below is a graph of the data. How many students spent between 10 and 12 hours doing homework last week?

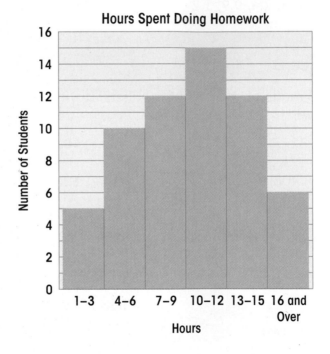

STEP 1 Find "10–12 hours" at the bottom of the graph.

STEP 2 The top of the bar shows the number of students who spent 10–12 hours doing homework.

STEP 3 Read the scale on the left.

Of the 60 students, 15 students spent between 10 and 12 hours doing homework last week.

Practice

Use the histogram below to answer Questions 1–5.

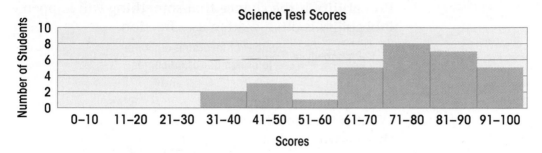

1. What does the histogram show?

2. How many students received a score between 81 and 90?

3. How many students received a score of 50 or below?

4. What scores were received most frequently?

Use the histogram below to answer Questions 6–10.

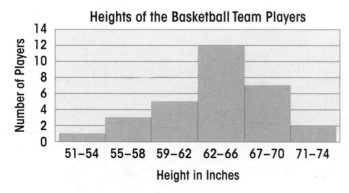

5. What does the histogram show?

6. How many players are between 55 and 58 inches tall?

7. How many players are over 62 inches tall?

8. What is the total number of players on the basketball team?

Probability is the chance that something will happen. Probability is often written as a fraction.

$$\text{Probability} = \frac{\text{Number of favorable outcomes}}{\text{Total number of outcomes}}$$

▶ **EXAMPLE**

Dave spins a spinner. What is the probability that he will land on yellow?

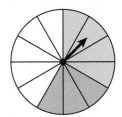

STEP 1	Count the number of yellow sections.	4 yellow sections
STEP 2	Count all the sections.	12 sections
STEP 3	Write the probability as a fraction. Reduce to lowest terms.	$\frac{4}{12} = \frac{1}{3}$

The probability that Dave will spin yellow is $\frac{1}{3}$.

Practice

Find the probability of each outcome.
Be sure fractions are in lowest terms.

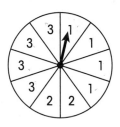

1. the probability of spinning a 1

2. the probability of spinning a 2

3. the probability of spinning a 3

4. the probability of spinning an odd number

5. the probability of spinning an even number

USING YOUR CALCULATOR
Showing Probability as a Decimal and a Percent

You can use a calculator to show the probability of an event as a decimal or a percent.

Max's school is selling raffle tickets for two CD players. Only 2 people can win. Exactly 80 tickets were sold. What is the probability of winning a CD player if someone buys one ticket?

$$\text{Probability} = \frac{\text{Number of winning tickets}}{\text{Total number of tickets sold}} = \frac{2}{80}$$

Calculator Tip
Remember not to clear the display after you find the decimal.

Show the probability of winning as a decimal.

PRESS $\boxed{2}$ $\boxed{\div}$ $\boxed{8}$ $\boxed{0}$ $\boxed{=}$ $\boxed{\quad 0.025}$

DO NOT clear the display.

A person who bought one raffle ticket has a .025 chance of winning a CD player.

Show the probability of winning as a percent.

PRESS $\boxed{\times}$ $\boxed{1}$ $\boxed{0}$ $\boxed{0}$ $\boxed{=}$ $\boxed{\quad 2.5}$

A person who bought one raffle ticket has a 2.5% chance of winning a CD player.

Show the probability of each event as a decimal and as a percent.

1. choosing a red marble

2. choosing a green marble

3. choosing a blue marble

4. choosing a white marble

5. choosing a yellow marble

data
graphs
histogram
mean
median
mode
pictograph
probability

Vocabulary Review

Complete each sentence with a word from the list.

1. __?__ can be information from a survey.

2. The __?__ is the middle number in a set of numbers.

3. The __?__ is found by adding the numbers and dividing by the number of numbers in the set.

4. __?__ is the chance that an event will occur.

5. The __?__ is the number or numbers that occur most often in a set of numbers.

6. A __?__ and a __?__ are two types of __?__.

7. **Writing** What kind of graph will best display data showing the 10 longest rivers in the world? Explain.

Chapter Quiz

LESSONS 13·1 to 13·5

Test Tip
To find the number of symbols in a pictograph row, divide the amount by the number represented by one symbol.

Reading and Making Pictographs, Bar Graphs, and Line Graphs

1. In a pictograph,

    = 1,000 tourists.

   How many symbols are needed to show each amount in the table?

City	Tourists
Paris	4,000
Rome	6,000
London	9,000
Miami	10,000

2. Make a bar graph using data from the table above.

3. Make a line graph using the following data about weekly museum tourists:

Monday	400	Friday	600
Tuesday	300	Saturday	1,000
Wednesday	0	Sunday	0
Thursday	550		

LESSON 13·7

Test Tip
For circle graphs, change the percents to decimals and multiply by the total number.

Reading Circle Graphs
Use the graph to answer each question.

4. How many members are in the Football Club?

5. How many total members are in the Hockey and Baseball Clubs?

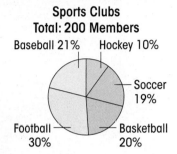

Sports Clubs
Total: 200 Members
Baseball 21%   Hockey 10%
Soccer 19%
Football 30%   Basketball 20%

LESSONS 13·8 and 13·9

Test Tip
Put a set of numbers in order before finding mean, median, or mode.

Finding Mean, Median, and Mode
Find the mean, median, and mode of each set of numbers.

6. 2, 6, 4, 5, 3, 7, 2, 6, 6, 8, 10, 12, 7

7. 12, 23, 33, 41, 12, 22, 22, 38, 40

LESSON 13·11

Test Tip
Always reduce probability answers to lowest terms.

Finding Probability
Find the probability of each event.

8. choosing a yellow golf ball

9. choosing a white golf ball

10. choosing a pink golf ball

11. choosing a green golf ball

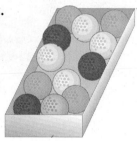

Group Activity

With your group, conduct a survey on a school issue. Interview friends, teachers, neighbors, and family. After the data have been recorded, organize them into one chart. Find the mean, median, and mode of the data. Then, display the data in a graph.

The Great Wall of China is the longest man-made object on Earth. Tourists can walk along the top of the wall. In some places, it is 25 feet high and 12 feet wide on top. The towers are 40 feet high. How much taller are the towers than the wall?

Chapter 14

Customary Measurement

Words to Know

length	how long an object is
Customary System of Measurement	measurement units used in the United States
weight	how heavy an object is
capacity	how much space is in a container
elapsed time	the amount of time that has passed between two given times
degrees (°)	units used to measure temperature

Million Project

Work with a partner. Choose one of the questions below. Explain how you will find the answer.

- How long (in days) would it take to count to a million if you say one number each second?

- How much water (in gallons) is in a million drops?

- How much would a million pennies weigh (in pounds)?

Learning Objectives

- Change units of length, weight, capacity, and time.
- Find elapsed time.
- Find changes in temperature.
- Solve problems using customary measurements.
- Apply measurement to framing.

14·1 Length

The **length** of an object is how long it is. In the United States, objects are measured in the **Customary System of Measurement**. The customary units for length from smallest to largest are inch, foot, yard, and mile.

Useful Facts		
1 foot (ft)	=	12 inches (in.)
1 yard (yd)	=	36 inches
1 yard	=	3 feet
1 mile (mi)	=	5,280 feet

Smallest ↓ in.
ft
yd
Largest mi

You may need to change from one unit of measure to another in your daily life. To change a larger unit to a smaller unit, multiply.

EXAMPLE 1

Change $2\frac{1}{2}$ feet to inches.

Remember:
$2\frac{1}{2} = \frac{5}{2}$

STEP 1 Choose the fact you need. — 1 foot = 12 inches

STEP 2 Decide whether to multiply or divide. — $2\frac{1}{2}$ feet to ■ inches; larger to smaller: multiply

STEP 3 Multiply. — $2\frac{1}{2} \times 12 = \frac{5}{2} \times 12 = 30$

There are 30 inches in $2\frac{1}{2}$ feet.

To change a smaller unit to a larger unit, divide.

EXAMPLE 2

Change 5 feet to yards.

STEP 1 Choose the fact you need. — 1 yard = 3 feet

STEP 2 Decide whether to multiply or divide. — 5 feet to ■ yards; smaller to larger: divide

STEP 3 Divide. — $5 \div 3 = 1\frac{2}{3}$

There are $1\frac{2}{3}$ yards in 5 feet.

Practice A

Multiply to change each measurement.

1. 2 feet = ■ inches

2. 5 yards = ■ feet

3. 2 yards = ■ inches

4. $2\frac{1}{2}$ miles = ■ feet

5. 8 feet = ■ inches

6. $9\frac{2}{3}$ yards = ■ feet

Divide to change each measurement.

7. 6 feet = ■ yards

8. 108 inches = ■ yards

9. 144 inches = ■ feet

10. 10,560 feet = ■ miles

11. 180 inches = ■ yards

12. 17 feet = ■ yards

Practice B

Change each measurement. First, decide whether to multiply or divide.

13. 12 yards = ■ feet

14. 100 inches = ■ feet

15. 1,760 feet = ■ mile

16. 10 feet = ■ inches

17. 32 feet = ■ yards

18. $3\frac{1}{2}$ yards = ■ inches

Everyday Problem Solving

Choose the best unit from the box to measure each object.

Unit Choices
inches
yards
feet
miles

1. a pencil

2. a soccer field

3. a car

4. a highway

14·2 Weight

The **weight** of an object tells how heavy it is. The customary units of weight from smallest to largest are ounce, pound, and ton.

Useful Facts
1 pound (lb) = 16 ounces (oz)
1 ton (tn) = 2,000 pounds

Smallest ↓ oz
lb
Largest ↓ tn

To change a larger unit to a smaller unit, multiply.

EXAMPLE 1

Change 2.5 pounds to ounces.

STEP 1 Choose the fact you need.　　　1 pound = 16 ounces

STEP 2 Decide whether to multiply　　2.5 pounds to ■ ounces
or divide.　　　　　　　　　　larger to smaller: multiply

STEP 3 Multiply.　　　　　　　　　2.5 × 16 = 40

There are 40 ounces in 2.5 pounds.

To change a smaller unit to a larger unit, divide.

EXAMPLE 2

Change 3,000 pounds to tons.

STEP 1 Choose the fact you need.　　　1 ton = 2,000 pounds

STEP 2 Decide whether to multiply　　3,000 pounds to ■ tons
or divide.　　　　　　　　　　smaller to larger: divide

STEP 3 Divide.　　　　　　　　　　3,000 ÷ 2,000 = 1.5

There are 1.5, or $1\frac{1}{2}$, tons in 3,000 pounds.

Practice A

Multiply to change each measurement.

1. 2 pounds = ■ ounces

2. 2 tons = ■ pounds

3. $4\frac{1}{2}$ pounds = ■ ounces

4. $3\frac{1}{2}$ tons = ■ pounds

5. 5.3 pounds = ■ ounces

6. 6.8 tons = ■ pounds

Divide to change each measurement.

7. 48 ounces = ■ pounds

8. 8,000 pounds = ■ tons

9. 104 ounces = ■ pounds

10. 6,400 pounds = ■ tons

11. 328 ounces = ■ pounds

12. 19,600 pounds = ■ tons

Practice B

Change each measurement. First, decide whether to multiply or divide.

13. 64 ounces = ■ pounds

14. 3 tons = ■ pounds

15. 9 pounds = ■ ounces

16. 12,000 pounds = ■ tons

17. 160 ounces = ■ pounds

18. 7.5 tons = ■ pounds

19. $\frac{5}{8}$ pound = ■ ounces

20. 1,000 pounds = ■ ton

Everyday Problem Solving

Choose the best unit from the box to measure each object.

1. small truck

2. bunch of strawberries

3. chair

4. raccoon

Unit Choices
ounces
tons
pounds

14·3 Capacity (Liquid Measure)

Capacity is the amount of space inside a container. Often, it is a measure for liquids. The customary units of liquid measure from smallest to largest are fluid ounce, pint, quart, and gallon.

Useful Facts	
1 pint (pt)	= 16 fluid ounces (fl oz)
1 quart (qt)	= 32 fluid ounces
1 quart	= 2 pints (pt)
1 gallon (gal)	= 4 quarts

Smallest   fl oz
  pt
  qt
Largest   gal

To change a larger unit to a smaller unit, multiply.

▶ **EXAMPLE 1**

Change $1\frac{1}{2}$ gallons to quarts.

STEP 1 Choose the fact you need.   1 **gallon** = 4 quarts

STEP 2 Decide whether to multiply $1\frac{1}{2}$ gallons to ■ quarts
or divide.   larger to smaller: multiply

STEP 3 Multiply. $1\frac{1}{2} \times 4 = \frac{3}{2} = \frac{4}{1} = 6$

There are 6 quarts in $1\frac{1}{2}$ gallons.

To change a smaller unit to a larger unit, divide.

▶ **EXAMPLE 2**

Change 6 pints to quarts.

STEP 1 Choose the fact you need.   1 **quart** = 2 pints

STEP 2 Decide whether to multiply   6 pints to ■ quarts
or divide.   smaller to larger: divide

STEP 3 Divide. $6 \div 2 = 3$

There are 3 quarts in 6 pints.

Practice A

Multiply to change each measurement.

1. 4 quarts = ▇ pints

2. 2 quarts = ▇ fluid ounces

3. 3 pints = ▇ fluid ounces

4. 5 gallons = ▇ quarts

5. $4\frac{1}{2}$ quarts = ▇ pints

6. $2\frac{1}{2}$ pints = ▇ fluid ounces

Divide to change each measurement.

7. 12 quarts = ▇ gallons

8. 10 pints = ▇ quarts

9. 96 fluid ounces = ▇ quarts

10. 11 pints = ▇ quarts

11. 2 quarts = ▇ gallon

12. 12 fluid ounces = ▇ pint

Practice B

Change each measurement. First, decide whether to multiply or divide.

13. 4 pints = ▇ quarts

14. 16 quarts = ▇ gallons

15. 7 pints = ▇ fluid ounces

16. 9 quarts = ▇ pints

17. 80 fluid ounces = ▇ quarts

18. 24 fluid ounces = ▇ pints

Everyday Problem Solving

Choose the best unit from the box to measure each object.

1. bathtub water

2. large carton of milk

3. juice glass

4. carton of cream

Unit Choices
fluid ounces
pints
quarts
gallons

14-4 Time

Time is how long it takes for something to happen. You can measure time with a clock, a stopwatch, or a calendar. The units of time from smallest to largest are shown below.

Remember:
To change a larger unit to a smaller unit, multiply. To change a smaller unit to a larger unit, divide.

Useful Facts

60 seconds (sec) = 1 minute (min)
60 minutes = 1 hour (hr)
24 hours = 1 day
7 days (d) = 1 week (wk)
52 weeks = 1 year (yr)
12 months (mo) = 1 year

Smallest → sec, min, hr, d, wk, mo
Largest → yr

EXAMPLE

Change $1\frac{1}{4}$ hours to minutes.

STEP 1 Choose the fact you need.   1 hour = 60 minutes

STEP 2 Decide whether to multiply or divide. $1\frac{1}{4}$ hours to ■ minutes larger to smaller: multiply

STEP 3 Multiply. $1\frac{1}{4} \times 60 = \frac{5}{4} \times \frac{60}{1} = 75$

There are 75 minutes in $1\frac{1}{4}$ hours.

Practice

Change each measurement. First, decide whether to multiply or divide.

1. 3 days = ■ hours

2. 4 years = ■ months

3. 104 weeks = ■ years

4. 360 minutes = ■ hours

5. 49 days = ■ weeks

6. 78 weeks = ■ years

7. 90 seconds = ■ minutes

8. 36 months = ■ years

USING YOUR CALCULATOR
How Old Are You?

The question above can be answered in several ways. A newborn baby might be 300 minutes old. A toddler can be 380 days old.

Suppose that Rachel is 15 years, 3 months, and 12 days old. About how old is she in days?

Remember that to change a larger unit to smaller units, multiply.

Change 15 years to days.

PRESS | 1 | 5 | × | 3 | 6 | 5 | = | 5,475 |

Change 3 months to days. Use 30 days = 1 month to find about how many days.

PRESS | 3 | × | 3 | 0 | = | 90 |

Add the extra 12 days.

PRESS | 5 | 4 | 7 | 5 | + | 9 | 0 | + | 1 | 2 | = | 5,577 |

Rachel is 5,577 days old.

Use a calculator to solve each problem.

1. Jenna is 10 years, 2 months, and 5 days old. How old is she in days?

2. Preston is 20 years, 7 months, and 10 days old. How old is he in days?

3. How old are you in days?

> **Calculator Tip**
> After pressing equals, remember to write down the total and then clear the display.

Problem Solving: Working with Units of Measure

Sometimes you need to regroup units of measure when you add or subtract quantities.

► EXAMPLE

Vince is using the recipe on the right to make punch for a party. Can he use a punch bowl that holds 2 gallons for his punch?

Party Punch
3 quarts apple juice
3 quarts cherry juice
2 quarts white grape juice
1 quart club soda

STEP 1   READ   What do you need to find out?
You need to find out how much punch Vince is making.

STEP 2   PLAN   What do you need to do?
Add to find the total number of quarts. Change the quarts to gallons. To do this, divide by 4. Will the punch fit in the bowl? Compare the total to 2 gallons.

Remember:
4 quarts = 1 gallon

STEP 3   DO   Follow the plan.

Add.

$$\begin{array}{r} 3 \text{ quarts} \\ 3 \text{ quarts} \\ 2 \text{ quarts} \\ + \ 1 \text{ quart} \\ \hline 9 \text{ quarts} \end{array}$$

Divide.

$9 \text{ quarts} \div 4 = 2\frac{1}{4} \text{ gallons}$

Compare.

$2\frac{1}{4} > 2$

STEP 4   CHECK   Does your answer make sense?
No, 8 quarts is the same as 2 gallons, so 9 quarts is more than 2 gallons. ✓

Vince needs a punch bowl that holds more than 2 gallons of punch.

Problem Solving

READ the problem. Answer the questions under PLAN. DO the plan to solve the problem.

1. Leroy made 2 gallons of chili on Saturday. He made 2 more gallons on Sunday, and 1 gallon on Monday. He wants to can the chili. He has 24 one-quart jars. Does he have enough jars to can all the chili?

   PLAN
   How many gallons of chili did Leroy make?
   How many quarts of chili did he make?

2. A group of climbers were climbing 2 miles to the top of a mountain. On the first day, they climbed 1,650 feet. On the second day, they climbed 2,725 feet. On the third day, they climbed 5,750 feet. Did they reach the top of the mountain on the third day?

   PLAN
   How many feet did they climb in 3 days?
   How many feet to the top of the mountain?

Problem Solving Strategy

Sometimes, a picture helps you find the information you need.

Jane wants to frame a picture that is $1\frac{1}{2}$ feet wide and 2 feet long. Framing costs $3 per foot. How much will the framing cost? Fill in the blanks.

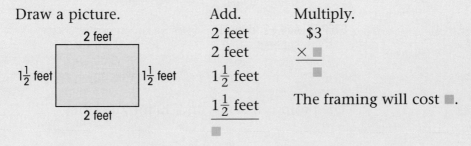

Draw a picture.

Add.
2 feet
2 feet
$1\frac{1}{2}$ feet
$1\frac{1}{2}$ feet
■

Multiply.
$3
× ■
■

The framing will cost ■.

Elapsed time is the amount of time that has passed from one given time to another. To solve problems involving elapsed time, you subtract.

Sometimes, you will need to rename 1 hour (hr) to 60 minutes (min) in order to subtract.

► **EXAMPLE 1**

Jamal's math class starts at 9:40 A.M. and ends at 11:10 A.M. How long is he in math class?

STEP 1 Set up a subtraction problem with hours and minutes. Write the later time first.

$$\begin{array}{r} 11 \text{ hr } 10 \text{ min} \\ - \ 9 \text{ hr } 40 \text{ min} \\ \hline \end{array}$$

STEP 2 Rename for more minutes. Subtract.

$$\begin{array}{r} {}^{10} \quad {}^{70} \\ \not{11} \text{ hr } \not{10} \text{ min} \\ - \ 9 \text{ hr } 40 \text{ min} \\ \hline 1 \text{ hr } 30 \text{ min} \end{array}$$

Jamal is in math class for 1 hour and 30 minutes.

Sometimes, the later time is after 12 noon or after 12 midnight. You will need to add 12 to the later time so that you can subtract.

► **EXAMPLE 2**

The Senior Prom begins at 8:00 P.M. and ends at 1:30 A.M. How long is the prom?

STEP 1 Set up a subtraction problem. Write the later time first.

$$\begin{array}{r} 1:30 \text{ A.M.} \\ - \ 8:00 \text{ P.M.} \\ \hline \end{array}$$

STEP 2 Add 12 to the 1. Subtract.

$$\begin{array}{r} {}^{13} \\ \not{1}:30 \text{ A.M.} \\ - \ 8:00 \text{ P.M.} \\ \hline 5:30 \end{array}$$

The prom is 5 hours and 30 minutes long.

Practice

Find the elapsed time.

1. 2:40 A.M. to 5:50 A.M.

2. 7:20 A.M. to 8:35 A.M.

3. 2:20 P.M. to 6:05 P.M.

4. 3:48 P.M. to 7:12 P.M.

5. 9:15 A.M. to 11:09 A.M.

6. 5:29 P.M. to 8:03 P.M.

7. 7:15 P.M. to 1:40 A.M.

8. 9:18 P.M. to 3:45 A.M.

9. 11:17 A.M. to 4:50 P.M.

10. 1:11 A.M. to 6:30 A.M.

11. 5:17 A.M. to 2:34 P.M.

12. 11:25 P.M. to 3:05 A.M.

Everyday Problem Solving

We use elapsed time every day.

1. How much time has elapsed from the time shown on Clock A to the time shown on Clock B?

2. Paul put a roast in the oven at the time shown. The roast needs to be in the oven for 2 hours 20 minutes. When should Paul take the roast out of the oven?

3. The plane departed from Denver. It arrived in Chicago at the time shown. The flight lasted 3 hours and 10 minutes. What time was it in Chicago when the plane departed?

4. Luke went to sleep at the time shown. He awoke at 6:30 A.M. How long did he sleep?

Temperature

Temperature is measured on a thermometer in degrees. A temperature of 43 degrees is written as 43°. The symbol for degree is °. A **rise** in temperature means an increase. You need to **add**. A **fall** in temperature means a decrease. You need to **subtract**.

EXAMPLE

The temperature was 59° in the morning. It rose 15° by afternoon. What was the temperature in the afternoon?

STEP 1 Decide whether to add or subtract.

It rose 15° means to add.

STEP 2 Add.

$$\begin{array}{r} 59° \\ + 15° \\ \hline 74° \end{array}$$

The temperature in the afternoon was 74°.

Practice

Add or subtract to find the new temperature. To decide, look for the clue words *rise* and *fall*.

1. By noon, the temperature was 98°. By late afternoon, the temperature had <u>risen</u> 6°. What was the temperature in the late afternoon?

2. The temperature was 22°. It <u>fell</u> 17° during the night. What was the temperature at the end of the night?

3. In the morning, the temperature was 57°. It <u>rose</u> 10° four hours later. What was the temperature four hours later?

4. In the morning, the temperature was 23°. In the afternoon, the temperature rose to 38°. How many degrees did it change?

ON-THE-JOB MATH
Picture Framer

Pedro Lopez is a picture framer. He cuts, fits, and builds picture frames. Pedro enjoys his job, because he works with his hands to create something new from plain wood. He is always proud of his work.

First, he measures to find the length and width of the frame. Then, he adds to find how much wood he needs to buy altogether. Wood comes in feet, so he needs to change inches to feet.

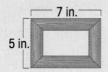

7 inches + 7 inches + 5 inches + 5 inches = 24 inches
24 inches ÷ 12 inches per feet = 2 feet

Pedro needs to buy 2 feet of wood.

Find the total amount of wood in feet for each frame.

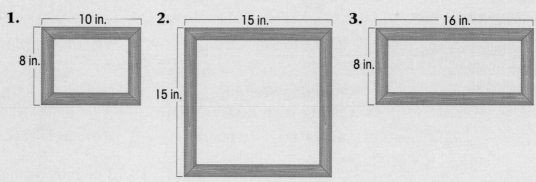

1. 10 in. 8 in.

2. 15 in. 15 in.

3. 16 in. 8 in.

Critical Thinking

Pedro has a frame that is 14 inches long and 8 inches wide. He can only buy wood in whole-foot measurements. How much wood should he buy? Why?

capacity

Customary System
of Measurement

degrees

elapsed time

length

weight

Vocabulary Review
Complete each sentence with a word from the list.

1. The temperature 14° means 14 __?__.

2. The __?__ of an object is a measure of how heavy
   it is.

3. The __?__ of an object is a measure of how long it is.

4. In the United States, we use the __?__.

5. The amount that a cup can hold is called its __?__.

6. The __?__ from 7:00 A.M. to 9:00 A.M. is 2 hours.

7. **Writing** Write a paragraph using all of the
   vocabulary words.

Chapter Quiz

LESSONS 14-1 to 14-3

Test Tip
To change a larger unit to a
smaller unit, multiply. To change
a smaller unit to a larger unit,
divide.

Changing Lengths
Change each measurement.

1. 6 yards = ▨ feet

2. 60 inches = ▨ feet

3. 2,640 feet = ▨ mile

4. 3 feet = ▨ inches

Changing Weights
Change each measurement.

5. 1.6 tons = ▨ pounds

6. 40 ounces = ▨ pounds

7. 6,000 pounds = ▨ tons

8. 3 pounds = ▨ ounces

Changing Capacity
Change each measurment.

9. 3 pints = ▨ fluid ounces

10. 6 pints = ▨ quarts

11. 12 quarts = ▨ gallons

12. 6 gallons = ▨ quarts

Changing Time
Change each measurement.

13. 360 seconds = ■ minutes   **14.** 12 hours = ■ day

15. 7 weeks = ■ days   **16.** 3 years = ■ months

Solving Problems with Measurements
Solve.

17. Sharon left the house early to run some errands on her way to work. She spent $\frac{1}{2}$ hour in the bakery, 20 minutes at the dry cleaners, and 50 minutes driving to work. How long did it take her to get to work?

Finding Elapsed Time
Find the elapsed time.

18. 2:38 P.M. to 3:55 P.M.   **19.** 6:38 A.M. to 10:19 A.M.

Finding Temperature
Find the change in temperature.

20. The temperature this morning was 65°. It rose 16° by the end of the day. What was the temperature at the end of the day?

Group Activity

Plan a class picnic with your group. Use a grocery store ad from a newspaper to decide what foods to serve. Decide how much of each item you need. List the items and amounts using weight or capacity. Find the total weight or capacity of the picnic food.

THINK METRIC

SPEED
LIMIT
45 MPH
70 KM/HR

NEW JERSEY   NEW

951

Measurements can be found all around you.
This sign is showing the speed limit on a
bridge in both customary and metric units.
Speed limits are measured in miles per hour
or in kilometers per hour. Which measurement
on the sign is the metric measurement?

Words to Know

metric system	the system of measurement based on the number 10 that is used in most countries
meter	the basic unit used to measure length
gram	the basic unit used to measure weight
liter	the basic unit used to measure liquid capacity
unit price	the cost of one item or one unit measure of an item

Metric Search Project

Look for metric measurements in different places. Try magazine and newspaper ads. Collect food labels that have both customary and metric units on them. Tell the class what types of items have metric units for measurements. Describe how the customary measurements compare with the metric. Write the items and measurements you find in your journal.

Learning Objectives

- Identify prefixes used in the metric system.
- Change metric units of length, mass, and liquid capacity.
- Compare metric and customary units of measurement.
- Solve problems using metric measurements.
- Apply metric measurements to finding the better buy.

What Is the Metric System?

The **metric system** is the system of measurement used by most countries. It is an easy system to use, because it is based on the number 10. There are three basic units. A **meter** is used to measure length. A **gram** is used to measure weight. A **liter** is used to measure capacity. Prefixes in front of a base tell you how many units there are.

Prefix	Value	Example
kilo-	1,000	1 kilometer = 1,000 meters
hecto-	100	1 hectometer = 100 meters
deka-	10	1 dekameter = 10 meters
deci-	.1	1 decimeter = .1 meter
centi-	.01	1 centimeter = .01 meter
milli-	.001	1 millimeter = .001 meter

You can use the same prefixes for liters and grams.

▶ **EXAMPLE**

How many liters are in a kiloliter?

STEP 1 Find the prefix.   kiloliter

STEP 2 Determine the value of the prefix.   *Kilo* means 1,000.

There are 1,000 liters in a kiloliter.

Practice

Answer each question. Use the chart above to help you.

1. How many grams in a kilogram?

2. How many meters in a hectometer?

3. How much of a meter is a centimeter?

4. How much of a liter is a milliliter?

MATH IN YOUR LIFE
Better Buy

Erica sees her favorite shampoo on sale. There are two different sizes. She wants to choose the size that will cost less per unit.

Erica needs to find the **unit price** of each bottle. The unit price is the price for 1 gram of shampoo. To find the price of 1 gram, she divides the price of the bottle by the number of units in the bottle.

SHAMPOO 400 g   SHAMPOO 600 g

$4.00 $7.20

Unit Price for Medium-size Bottle
$4.00 ÷ 400 grams = $.01 per gram
$.01 × 100 = 1¢ per gram

Unit Price for Large Bottle
$7.20 ÷ 600 grams = $.012 per gram
$.012 × 100 = 1.2¢ per gram

Erica chooses the medium-size bottle, because 1¢ per gram is less than 1.2¢ per gram.

Tell which item is the better buy.

1.

MILK 4 liters   MILK 3 liters

4 L for $2.90   3 L for $2.15

2.

SPAGHETTI 200 GRAMS   SPAGHETTI 100 GRAMS

200 g for $1.00   100 g for $.55

3.

EASTERN POTATOES 5 KILOGRAMS   EASTERN POTATOES 12 KILOGRAMS

5 kg for $3.80   12 kg for $9.00

Critical Thinking

Many supermarkets display the unit price of each item on the shelf label. How would this help Erica choose her purchases?

15·2 Length

In the metric system, the meter is used to measure length. All other measures of length are based on the meter.

Useful Facts	
1 kilometer (km)	= 1,000 meters (m)
1 hectometer (hm)	= 100 meters
1 dekameter (dam)	= 10 meters
1 meter	= 1 meter
10 decimeters (dm)	= 1 meter
100 centimeters (cm)	= 1 meter
1,000 millimeters (mm)	= 1 meter
10 millimeters	= 1 centimeter

Largest → km, hm, dam, m, dm, cm, mm ← Smallest

To change a larger unit to a smaller unit, multiply.

EXAMPLE 1

Change 1.2 kilometers to meters.

STEP 1 Choose the fact you need.   1 kilometer = 1,000 meters

STEP 2 Decide whether to multiply or divide.   1.2 kilometers to ■ meters
larger to smaller: multiply

STEP 3 Multiply. $1.2 \times 1,000 = 1,200$

There are 1,200 meters in 1.2 kilometers.

To change a smaller unit to a larger unit, divide.

EXAMPLE 2

Change 30 millimeters to centimeters.

STEP 1 Choose the fact you need.   10 millimeters = 1 centimeter

STEP 2 Decide whether to multiply or divide.   30 millimeters to ■ centimeters
smaller to larger: divide

STEP 3 Divide. $30 \div 10 = 3$

There are 3 centimeters in 30 millimeters.

Practice

Multiply to change each measurement.

1. 3 kilometers = ▨ meters

2. 5 meters = ▨ centimeters

3. 4 hectometers = ▨ meters

4. 2 meters = ▨ millimeters

5. 4 centimeters = ▨ millimeters

6. 2.1 meters = ▨ centimeters

Divide to change each measurement.

7. 50 centimeters = ▨ meter

8. 3,400 meters = ▨ kilometers

9. 6,000 millimeters = ▨ meters

10. 10 centimeters = ▨ meter

11. 1,700 meters = ▨ kilometers

12. 5 millimeters = ▨ centimeter

Everyday Problem Solving

Give the length of each item below in centimeters and meters.

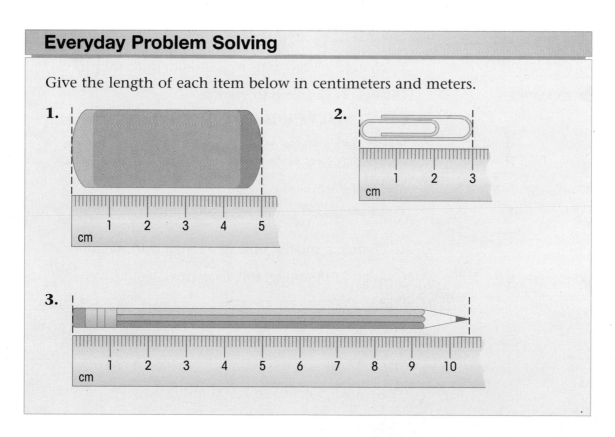

The gram is used to measure mass. At the earth's surface, the mass and the weight of an object are considered to be the same.

Useful Facts		
1 kilogram (kg)	= 1,000 grams (g)	
1 hectogram (hg)	= 100 grams	
1 dekagram (dag)	= 10 grams	
1 gram	= 1 gram	
10 decigrams (dg)	= 1 gram	
100 centigrams (cg)	= 1 gram	
1,000 milligrams (mg)	= 1 gram	
10 milligrams	= 1 centigram	

Largest kg
hg
dag
g
dg
cg
Smallest mg

To change a larger unit to a smaller unit, multiply.

EXAMPLE 1

Change 3 kilograms to grams.

STEP 1 Choose the fact you need.   1 kilogram = 1,000 grams

STEP 2 Decide whether to   3 kilograms to ▪ grams
multiply or divide.   larger to smaller: multiply

STEP 3 Multiply.   3 × 1,000 = 3,000

There are 3,000 grams in 3 kilograms.

To change a smaller unit to a larger unit, divide.

EXAMPLE 2

Change 2,500 milligrams to grams.

STEP 1 Choose the fact you need.   1,000 milligrams = 1 gram

STEP 2 Decide whether to   2,500 milligrams to ▪ grams
multiply or divide.   smaller to larger: divide

STEP 3 Divide.   2,500 ÷ 1,000 = 2.5

There are 2.5 grams in 2,500 milligrams.

Multiply to change each measurement.

1. 11 grams = ■ milligrams

2. 4.9 kilograms = ■ grams

3. 2.8 grams = ■ centigrams

4. 3.8 grams = ■ decigrams

5. .5 gram = ■ milligrams

6. 2.3 kilograms = ■ grams

Divide to change each measurement.

7. 900 milligrams = ■ gram

8. 7,700 grams = ■ kilograms

9. 400 centigrams = ■ grams

10. 4,500 grams = ■ kilograms

11. 50 grams = ■ dekagrams

12. 200 grams = ■ hectograms

Everyday Problem Solving

Use the nutrition fact label to answer the questions below. Grams are abbreviated as g, and milligrams are abbreviated as mg.

1. How many <u>milligrams</u> of total fat are in one serving of crackers? Multiply.

2. How many <u>grams</u> of sodium are in one serving of crackers? Divide.

3. How many <u>milligrams</u> of protein are contained in one serving of crackers?

4. Is there more sodium than protein in one serving of crackers? Explain your answer.

Nutrition Facts	
1 Serving = 1 Cracker	
Total fat	4.5g
Sodium	290m
Total carbohydrates	21g
Protein	2g

Capacity (Liquid Measure)

The liter is used to measure liquid capacity. All other measures of liquid capacity are based on the liter.

Useful Facts	
1 kiloliter (kL)	= 1,000 liters (L)
1 hectoliter (hL)	= 100 liters
1 dekaliter (daL)	= 10 liters
1 liter	= 1 liter
10 deciliters (dL)	= 1 liter
100 centiliters (cL)	= 1 liter
1,000 milliliters (mL)	= 1 liter
10 milliliters	= 1 centiliter

Largest → kL, hL, daL, L, dL, cL, mL ← Smallest

To change a larger unit to a smaller unit, multiply.

EXAMPLE 1

Change $1\frac{1}{2}$ kiloliters to liters.

STEP 1 Choose the fact you need. 1 kiloliter = 1,000 liters

STEP 2 Decide whether to multiply or divide. $1\frac{1}{2}$ kiloliters to ▓ liters larger to smaller: multiply

STEP 3 Multiply. $1\frac{1}{2} \times 1,000 = 1.5 \times 1,000 = 1,500$

There are 1,500 liters in $1\frac{1}{2}$ kiloliters.

To change a smaller unit to a larger unit, divide.

EXAMPLE 2

Change 3,200 milliliters to liters.

STEP 1 Choose the fact you need. 1,000 milliliters = 1 liter

STEP 2 Decide whether to multiply or divide. 3,200 milliliters to ▓ liters smaller to larger: divide

STEP 3 Divide. $3,200 \div 1,000 = 3.2$

There are 3.2 liters in 3,200 milliliters.

Practice

Multiply to change each measurement.

1. 3 kiloliters = ▇ liters

2. 3.4 liters = ▇ milliliters

3. 4 liters = ▇ milliliters

4. 55 liters = ▇ milliliters

5. 6 liters = ▇ milliliters

6. 4.7 liters = ▇ dekaliters

Divide to change each measurement.

7. 60 deciliters = ▇ liters

8. 9,300 liters = ▇ kiloliters

9. 2,900 milliliters = ▇ liters

10. 5,800 liters = ▇ kiloliters

11. 800 liters = ▇ hectoliters

12. 15,000 milliliters = ▇ liters

Everyday Problem Solving

Beverage containers always show their capacity.

1. How many milliliters of juice are in the apple juice bottle?

2. How many liters of cola are in the soda can?

3. Is the amount of the sports drink greater than or less than a half liter? Explain.

4. How many more milliliters of beverage are in the apple juice bottle than in the water bottle?

340 milliliters

473 milliliters

1.5 liter

1.89 liter

Comparing Metric and Customary Measurements

You can use either customary or metric units to describe the length, weight, or capacity of an item.

► **EXAMPLE**

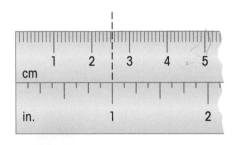

2.5 centimeters is about 1 inch.

1 liter is about 1 quart.

1.6 kilometers is about 1 mile.

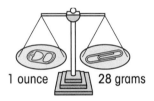

28 grams is about 1 ounce.

Practice

Complete each sentence.

1. 5 centimeters is about 2 ___?___.

2. 2 liters is about 2 ___?___.

3. 8 kilometers is about 5 ___?___.

4. 56 grams is about 2 ___?___.

5. 10 centimeters is about 4 ___?___.

6. 4 liters is about 4 ___?___ or 1 ___?___.

7. 16 kilometers is about 10 ___?___.

8. 14 grams is about $\frac{1}{2}$ ___?___.

USING YOUR CALCULATOR
Changing Measurements

You can use a calculator to change between metric and customary measurements.

Use the chart to the right to find the fact you need. Then, follow the instructions.

Change 14 inches to centimeters.

PRESS [1] [4] [×] [2] [.] [5] [4] [=] [35.56]

There are 35.56 centimeters in 14 inches.

Change each measure. Use a calculator and a fact from the chart.

inches x 2.54 → centimeters

feet x 30.48 → centimeters

yards x .9144 → meters

miles x 1.609 → kilometers

pints x .4732 → liters

quarts x .9464 → liters

gallons x 3.785 → liters

pounds x .4536 → kilograms

1. Change 4 feet to centimeters.

2. Change 22 pounds to kilograms.

3. Change 26 pints to liters.

4. Change 20 gallons to liters.

5. Change 12 inches to centimeters.

6. Change 17 yards to meters.

7. Change 16 quarts to liters.

8. Change 32 miles to kilometers.

Which is greater? Use a calculator and a fact from the chart.

9. 25 miles or 25 kilometers?

10. 6 yards or 6 meters?

11. 10 quarts or 10 liters?

12. 15 pounds or 15 kilograms?

Calculator Tip
When you enter numbers to multiply, always check to be sure they are correct. Incorrect numbers will give you the wrong product!

Problem Solving: Two-Part Problems

Some word problems are solved by working on one part at a time.

EXAMPLE

Marlene bought 2 kilograms of flour. She used 250 grams of flour on Saturday. On Sunday, she used 50 grams, and on Tuesday, she used 300 grams. How many kilograms of flour are left?

STEP 1 **READ** **What do you need to find out?**
You need to find out how many kilograms of flour were left. But first, you need to find how much flour Marlene used.

STEP 2 **PLAN** **What do you need to do?**
Add to find out how much flour Marlene used.
Subtract to find out how many grams were left.

STEP 3 **DO** **Follow the plan.**

Add	Subtract
250 grams	Change 2 kilograms to 2,000 grams
50 grams	2,000 grams
+ 300 grams	− 600 grams
600 grams	1,400 grams or 1.4 kilograms

STEP 4 **CHECK** **Does your answer make sense?**
Is your answer less than what Marlene started with? 1,400 grams is less than 2,000 grams. ✓

Marlene has 1.4 kilograms of flour left.

Problem Solving

READ the problem. Answer the questions under PLAN. DO the plan to solve the problem.

1. The vocational school is building a new 400-meter running track. The first day, 130 meters of track were laid. The second day, 110 meters were laid. On the third day, 90 meters of track were laid. How many meters of track are left to lay?

   PLAN
   How many meters of track were laid in 3 days?
   How many meters of track are left to lay?

2. Marlene made 1 liter of lemonade for herself and her friends. She drank 200 milliliters. One friend drank 350 milliliters. Another friend drank 175 milliliters. How much lemonade is left?

   PLAN
   How many milliliters in 1 liter?
   How many milliliters did the 3 friends drink altogether?
   How many milliliters were left after they all drank their lemonade?

Problem Solving Strategy

Sometimes, making a table can help you solve a problem.

Al's fruit drink has .5 liter of seltzer for every 2.5 liters of grape juice. How many liters of seltzer are needed to make 12 liters of fruit drink?

Copy the table. Fill in the blanks.

Seltzer	.5	?	1.5	?
Grape juice	2.5	5	7.5	?
Fruit drink	3	?	9	?

Chapter

15 ▷ Review

gram
liter
meter
metric system
unit price

Vocabulary Review

Match a word from the list to its description.

1. A system of measurement based on the number 10.

2. A basic unit of length.

3. The price of one unit of an item.

4. A basic unit of mass.

5. A basic unit of liquid capacity.

6. **Writing** Make a sentence with each vocabulary word. Each sentence should give an example of something that is measured with the given unit.

Chapter Quiz

Identifying Prefixes

LESSON 15·1

Test Tip
The prefix tells how many of a unit. The suffix tells the type of unit.

Answer each question.

1. How many liters in a kiloliter?

2. How many grams in a dekagram?

3. How much of a meter is a millimeter?

4. How much of a liter is a centiliter?

5. How many meters in a kilometer?

Changing Metric Units

LESSONS 15·2 to 15·4

Test Tip
To change a larger unit to a smaller unit, multiply. The prefix tells how many of a unit. The suffix tells the type of unit.

Change each measurement.

6. 4 liters = ■ milliliters

7. 45 meters = ■ kilometer

8. 10 kilometers = ■ meters

9. 7,600 milligrams = ■ grams

10. 19.2 meters = ■ centimeters

11. .008 kilogram = ▪ milligrams

12. 250 grams = ▪ kilogram

13. .012 kilometer = ▪ centimeters

14. 15,000 liters = ▪ kiloliters

15. 7,100 milliliters = ▪ liters

LESSON 15·5

Test Tip
2.5 centimeters → 1 inch
1 liter → 1 quart
1.6 kilometers → 1 mile
28 grams → 1 ounce

Comparing Metric and Customary Units
Complete each sentence.

16. 5 ounces is about __?__ grams.

17. 3 miles is about __?__ kilometers.

18. 8 inches is about __?__ centimeters.

19. 8 liters is about __?__ quarts.

LESSON 15·6

Test Tip
Solve by working on one part of the problem at a time.

Problem Solving
Solve.

20. Scott bought 2.5 kilograms of peanuts, pecans, and walnuts. There were 470 grams of peanuts and 780 grams of pecans. How many grams were walnuts?

Group Activity
With your group, make a Tourist's Guide on using the metric system while traveling. The guide should help travelers understand the different metric units they might see. Assume that they know nothing at all about the metric system. The guide should provide diagrams. It should be clearly written and easy to understand.

Many artists use geometry in their work. This sculpture is a solid shape called a cube. What flat shapes do you see?

Words to Know

angle	figure formed by two rays with the same endpoint
protractor	a tool used to measure angles
polygons	plane figures with three or more sides; examples are *triangles*, *quadrilaterals*, *pentagons*, *hexagons*, and *octagons*
perimeter	the distance around a figure
area	the amount of space inside a figure
parallelogram	a quadrilateral whose opposite sides are parallel; examples are *rectangles* and *squares*
circumference	the distance around a circle
radius	the distance from the center of a circle to its edge
space figure	a three-dimensional figure that has length, width, and height
volume	the amount of space inside a three-dimensional figure

Box Project

Find a box of any size, and number its sides 1 to 6. Keep a record of the lengths of each side, the perimeter and area of each side, and the volume of your box.

Learning Objectives

- Recognize points and lines.
- Use a protractor and calculate angles in a triangle.
- Identify polygons.
- Find perimeter, circumference, area, and volume.
- Solve area word problems.
- Apply angle measurement to physical therapy.

The table below shows the basic figures in geometry.

Figure	Picture	Name
A **point** is a location in space.	A ●	point *A*
A **line** is made up of many points. It extends endlessly in both directions.	◄●————●► A B	line *AB*
A **line segment** is a part of a line. It has two endpoints.	●————● A B	line segment *AB*
A **ray** is part of a line. It has one endpoint. When you name a ray, name the endpoint first.	◄●————● A B	ray *BA*

You can use the chart to identify the basic figures.

▶ **EXAMPLE**

Name the figure on the right.

STEP 1   Match the given figure to a figure in the chart above.

One endpoint
ray –

STEP 2   Name the figure.

Ray *CD*

The figure is ray *CD*.

When you name a ray, you name the endpoint first.

Practice A

Name each figure. Write *point, line, line segment,* or *ray.*

1.

2. • A

3.

4.

5.

6.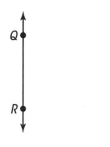

7. • M

8.

9.

Practice B

Draw and label a picture for each name.

10. line *EF*

11. ray *LM*

12. point *X*

13. line segment *YZ*

14. ray *YZ*

15. ray *ZY*

16. point *Q*

17. line *AB*

18. line segment *GH*

Everyday Problem Solving

Trace the drawing. Find points, lines, line segments, and rays.

16·2 Measuring Angles

An **angle** is formed by two rays with the same endpoint. The endpoint is called the vertex of the angle.

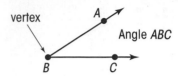

vertex

Angle *ABC*

You measure the space between the two rays with a **protractor**. An angle is measured in degrees. The symbol for degrees is °.

▶ **EXAMPLE 1**

Measure angle *ABC*.

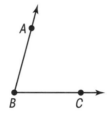

STEP 1   Place the center of the protractor's straight edge on the vertex. One ray must pass through 0° on the protractor.

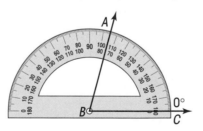

STEP 2   Read the number of degrees where the second ray crosses the protractor. Use the scale that reads 0° on the first ray.

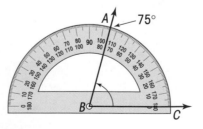

Angle *ABC* measures 75°.

Use the other scale on the protractor to measure angles that open to the left.

Measure angle *DEF*.

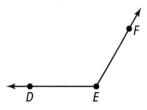

STEP 1   Place the center of the protractor's straight edge on the vertex. One ray must pass through 0° on the protractor.

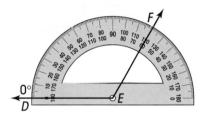

STEP 2   Read the number of degrees where the second ray crosses the protractor. Use the scale that reads 0° on the first ray.

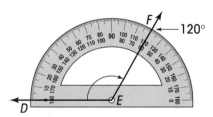

Angle *DEF* measures 120°.

Practice

Use a protractor to measure each angle.

1.

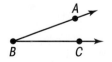

2.

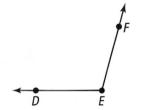

3.

16·3 Drawing Angles

You can use a protractor to draw angles.

> ► **EXAMPLE**

Draw a 115° angle.

STEP 1 Draw a ray.

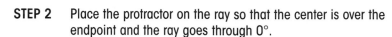

STEP 2 Place the protractor on the ray so that the center is over the endpoint and the ray goes through 0°.

Then find the number of degrees for the angle to be drawn. Use the scale that starts with 0° on your ray. Draw a point next to the number 115°.

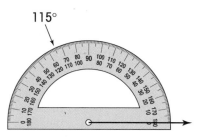

STEP 3 Draw a ray from the endpoint of the first ray to the point marked for 115°.

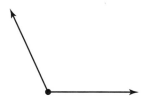

Practice

Use a protractor to draw an angle with each measure.

1. 30° **2.** 60° **3.** 90° **4.** 120°

5. 150° **6.** 180° **7.** 25° **8.** 75°

ON-THE-JOB MATH
Physical Therapist

Stephanie is a physical therapist. She shows injured people how to improve the use of their joints and muscles.

This is a good job for Stephanie because she likes to help people and she knows how the body works.

Stephanie uses a tool that looks like a protractor to measure how far a person can bend his or her arm or leg. She takes a measurement before and after a person exercises to see how well they are doing.

The measurement on the right is 90°.

Write the degree measure for each measurement below.

1. shoulder

2. knee

3. entire leg

Critical Thinking

Donna could only bend her wrist 40°. After she exercised, she could bend her wrist 110°, what is the percent increase in the movement of her wrist?

Angles in a Triangle

A triangle is a plane figure with three sides.
The sum of the angles in a triangle is always 180°.

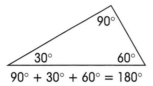

$$90° + 30° + 60° = 180°$$

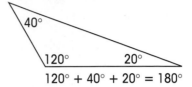

$$120° + 40° + 20° = 180°$$

If you know the size of two angles, you can find the size of the third angle without measuring.

▶ **EXAMPLE**

Find the measure of the third angle in triangle *ABC*.

STEP 1 Find the sum of the known angles.

$$\begin{array}{r} 40° \\ +\ 25° \\ \hline 65° \end{array}$$

STEP 2 Subtract the sum from 180°.

$$\begin{array}{r} 180° \\ -\ 65° \\ \hline 115° \end{array}$$

The measure of the third angle is 115°.

Practice

Find the measure of the third angle in each triangle.

1.

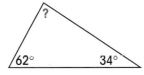

62°   34°

2.

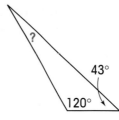

?

43°

120°

3.

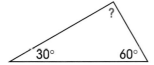

?

30°   60°

4.

?

27°   48°

5.

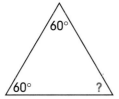

60°

60°   ?

6.

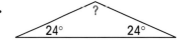

?

24°   24°

Everyday Problem Solving

Abdul is helping his father build a shed. He knows that the roof supports meet the rafters at an angle of 35°, as shown in the diagram.

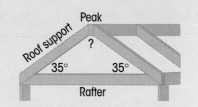

1. What is the sum of the two known angles?

2. What is the measure of the angle at the peak of the roof?

3. Abdul built another shed. The angle at the peak of the roof is 90°. What is the measure of each angle at the bottom of the triangle, where the roof supports meet the rafters?

Polygons are plane figures with three or more sides. Polygons are named by the number of sides they have.

EXAMPLE 1

Count the number of sides. Name each polygon.

A triangle
has three sides.

A quadrilateral
has four sides.

A pentagon
has five sides.

A hexagon
has six sides.

An octagon
has eight sides.

Triangles have special names. The names are based on their sides.

EXAMPLE 2

Look at the sides. Then name each triangle.

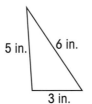

5 in. 6 in.
3 in.
Scalene triangle
No sides are equal.

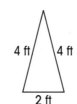

4 ft 4 ft
2 ft
Isosceles triangle
At least two sides are equal.

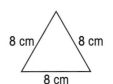

8 cm 8 cm
8 cm
Equilateral triangle
Three sides are equal.

Quadrilaterals also have special names.

Look at the sides and angles. Name the figure.

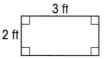

Parallelogram
A quadrilateral with the opposite sides parallel and equal in length.

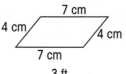

Rectangle
A parallelogram with all four angles equal to 90°.

Square
A rectangle with sides equal.

Practice A

Name each polygon.

1.

2.

3.

Practice B

Name each triangle or quadrilateral.

4.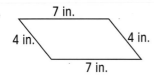

5.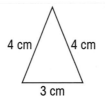

6.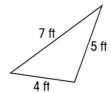

7.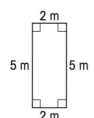

8.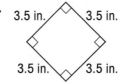

9.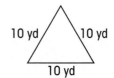

16·6 ▶ Perimeter

The **perimeter** is the total distance around a figure.

▶ **EXAMPLE 1**

Find the perimeter of this pentagon.

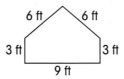

STEP	Add the lengths of the sides.	3 ft
		6 ft
		6 ft
		3 ft
		+ 9 ft
		27 ft

The perimeter of the pentagon is 27 ft.

In an equilateral triangle, three sides are equal. You can find the perimeter if you know the length of one side.

▶ **EXAMPLE 2**

Find the perimeter of an equilateral triangle whose sides measure 5 inches.

STEP 1 Draw the triangle. Label every side. All of the sides of an equilateral triangle are equal.

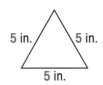

STEP 2 Add the lengths of the sides.   5 in. + 5 in. + 5 in. = 15 in.

The perimeter of the triangle is 15 inches.

In a rectangle, the opposite sides are equal. You can find the perimeter if you know the length and the width.

▶ **EXAMPLE 3**

Find the perimeter of a rectangle with width 6 feet and length 10 feet.

STEP 1 Draw the rectangle. Label each side.

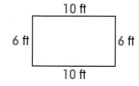

STEP 2 Add the lengths of the sides.

6 ft + 10 ft + 6 ft + 10 ft = 32 ft

The perimeter of the rectangle is 32 feet.

Practice

Find the perimeter of each figure.

1.

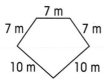
8 cm   8 cm
9 cm

2.

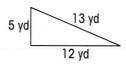
2 in.   11 in.   2 in.
11 in.

3.

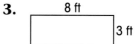
8 ft
3 ft

4.

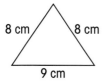
7 m
7 m   7 m
10 m   10 m

5.

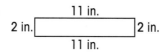
5 yd   13 yd
12 yd

6.

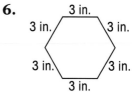
3 in.
3 in.   3 in.
3 in.   3 in.
3 in.

7. 3.5 cm   3.5 cm

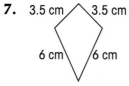
6 cm   6 cm

8.

9 mm
9 mm

9.

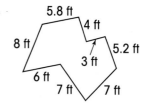
5.8 ft
4 ft
8 ft
5.2 ft
3 ft
6 ft
7 ft   7 ft

The **area** of a figure is the amount of space inside the shape. Area is measured in square units.

To find the area of a square or rectangle, multiply the length times the width. You can write a formula to help you to remember what to do.

Area = length × width

EXAMPLE 1

Find the area of this rectangle.

8 ft

3 ft

STEP 1   Write the formula.
Substitute 8 ft for the
length and 3 ft for the
width.

Area = length x width
Area = 8 ft × 3 ft

STEP 2   Multiply the length
times the width.

Area = 24 sq ft

The area of the rectangle is 24 sq ft. You read 24 sq ft as 24 square feet.

EXAMPLE 2

Find the area of this square.

4 in.

Remember:
The length and width of
a square have the same
measure.

STEP 1   Write the formula.
Substitute 4 in. for
the length and 4 in.
for the width.

Area = length × width
Area = 4 in. × 4 in.

STEP 2   Multiply the length
times the width.

Area = 16 sq in.

The area of the square is 16 sq in. You read 16 sq in. as 16 square inches.

Practice

Find the area of each figure.

1.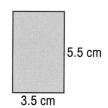

7 in.

3 in.

2.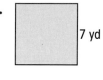

5.5 cm

3.5 cm

3.

7 yd

4.

1 ft 13.8 ft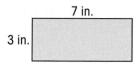

5.

8 in.

6.

6.5 m

8.2 m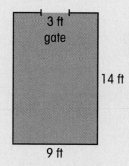

Everyday Problem Solving

Mr. Torres wants to plant a garden. A picture of the garden is shown below.

1. Mr. Torres needs to build a fence around the garden. How much fencing does he need? Do <u>not</u> include the gate.

2. Fencing costs $8 a foot. The gate costs $35. How much will it cost to fence the garden? Include the cost of the gate.

3. What is the area of the garden?

4. One-half of the garden will have corn. How much of the garden will have corn? Multiply the area by $\frac{1}{2}$.

5. Three-eighths of the garden will have tomatoes. How much of the garden will have tomatoes?

3 ft
gate

14 ft

9 ft

16·8 ▶ Area of Parallelograms

To find the area of a **parallelogram**, multiply the base times the height. The height of the parallelogram may *not* be one of the sides.

Area = base × height

▶ **EXAMPLE**

Find the area of this parallelogram.

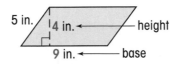

STEP 1 Write the formula. Substitute 9 in. for the base and 4 in. for the height.	Area = base × height Area = 9 in. × 4 in.
STEP 2 Multiply the length times the width.	Area = 36 sq in.

The area of the parallelogram is 36 square inches.

Practice

Find the area of each parallelogram.

1.
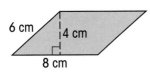

2.
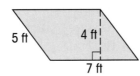

3.
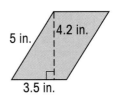

4.
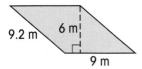

5.
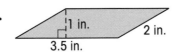

6.
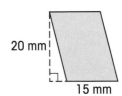

USING YOUR CALCULATOR
Finding Perimeter and Area

You can use a calculator to find the perimeter and area of figures. Play this game with a classmate.

The Rules: Player 1 will use a calculator to find perimeter.

Player 2 will use a calculator to find area.

Find the perimeter and area of this rectangle.

9 in.

4 in.

Player 1: PRESS [9] [+] [4] [+] [9] [+] [4] [=] _____ 26.

Player 2: PRESS [9] [×] [4] [=] _____ 36.

Take turns being Player 1 and Player 2.
Find the perimeter and area.

1. 6 in.

2.
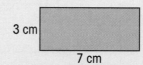
3 cm

7 cm

3.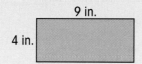
4 in. 3 in.

8 in.

4.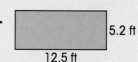
5.2 ft

12.5 ft

5.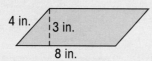
8.5 m 10 m

16.7 m

6.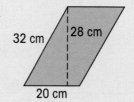
32 cm 28 cm

20 cm

16·9 Area of Triangles

When you cut a parallelogram in half, you get two triangles. The area of a triangle is one-half the area of the parallelogram.

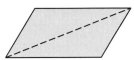

To find the area of a triangle, use this formula:

$$\text{Area} = \tfrac{1}{2} \times \text{base} \times \text{height}$$

► **EXAMPLE 1**

Find the area of this triangle.

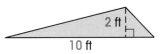

STEP 1 Write the formula. Substitute 10 ft for the base and 2 ft for the height.

$\text{Area} = \tfrac{1}{2} \times \text{base} \times \text{height}$

$\text{Area} = \tfrac{1}{2} \times 10 \text{ ft} \times 2 \text{ ft}$

STEP 2 Multiply.

$\text{Area} = 10 \text{ sq ft}$

The area of the triangle is 10 square feet.

Sometimes, the height will be outside the triangle.

► **EXAMPLE 2**

Find the area of this triangle.

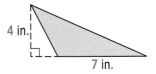

STEP 1 Write the formula. Substitute 7 in. for the base and 4 in. for the height.

$\text{Area} = \tfrac{1}{2} \times \text{base} \times \text{height}$

$\text{Area} = \tfrac{1}{2} \times 7 \text{ in.} \times 4 \text{ in.}$

STEP 2 Multiply.

$\text{Area} = 14 \text{ sq in.}$

The area of the triangle is 14 square inches.

Practice

Find the area of each triangle.

1.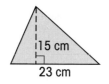
15 cm
23 cm

2.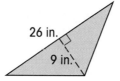
26 in.
9 in.

3.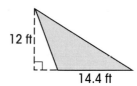
12 ft
14.4 ft

4.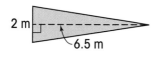
2 m
6.5 m

5.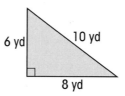
6 yd   10 yd
8 yd

6.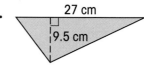
27 cm
9.5 cm

7.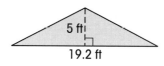
5 ft
19.2 ft

8.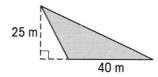
25 m
40 m

9.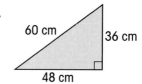
60 cm   36 cm
48 cm

Everyday Problem Solving

Which takes more felt to make: the rectangular pennant or the triangular pennant?

1. What is the area of the rectangular pennant?

2. What is the area of the triangular pennant?

3. Which pennant takes more felt to make? How much more felt?

4. **CHALLENGE** What would the height of the triangular pennant have to be for both pennants to have the same area? Keep the base of the triangle at 8 inches.

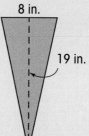
6 in.
12 in.
8 in.
19 in.

The **circumference** of a
circle is the distance
around the circle. To find
circumference, you need
to know the length of the
diameter or **radius**. You
also need to know pi.

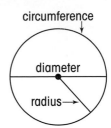

Pi is a special number you use with circles. The symbol
for pi is π. The value of π is about 3.14 or $\frac{22}{7}$.

To find the circumference, use either formula below.

$$\text{Circumference} = \pi \times \text{diameter}$$
$$\text{or} \quad \text{Circumference} = \pi \times 2 \times \text{radius}$$

EXAMPLE 1

The symbol $\approx$ means *about*.

Find the circumference of this circle.

STEP 1 Write the formula. Use 3.14 for π
and substitute 6 in. for the diameter.
Circumference $= \pi \times$ diameter
Circumference $\approx 3.14 \times 6$ in.

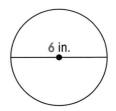

STEP 2 Multiply.
Circumference ≈ 18.84 in.

The circumference of the circle is about 18.84 inches.

EXAMPLE 2

Find the circumference of this circle.

STEP 1 Write the formula. Use $\frac{22}{7}$ for
π and substitute 7 ft for the radius.
Circumference $= \pi \times 2 \times$ radius
Circumference $\approx \frac{22}{7} \times 2 \times 7$ ft

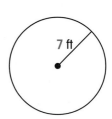

STEP 2 Multiply.
Circumference ≈ 44 ft

The circumference is about 44 feet.

Practice A

Find the circumference of each circle. Use $\frac{22}{7}$ for π.

1.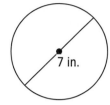
7 in.

2.
35 cm

3.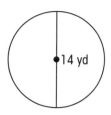
14 yd

Practice B

Find the circumference of each circle. Use 3.14 for π.

4. radius = 4 in.

5. diameter = 9 yd

6. diameter = 7 m

7. radius = 6.5 cm

8. radius = 10 ft

9. diameter = 3.75 in.

10. radius = 5.25 ft

11. diameter = 21 m

12. radius = 9 mm

Everyday Problem Solving

The members of the Hornets Marching Band want to decorate their drums with a strip of green tape. The tape will wrap around a drum with no overlap.

1. One drum has a diameter of 18 inches. About how long will the tape be? The length of the tape is the circumference of the drum.

2. The diameter of a snare drum is 9 inches. Will you need half as much tape as in Question 1? Explain.

Area of Circles

To find the area of a circle, you need to square the radius. Remember that to square the radius, you multiply the radius by itself.

To find the area of a circle, use this formula:

$$\text{Area} = \pi \times (\text{radius})^2$$

▶ **EXAMPLE 1**

Find the area of this circle.

STEP 1 Write the formula. Use 3.14 for π and substitute 4 in. for the radius.
Area $= \pi \times (\text{radius})^2$
Area $\approx 3.14 \times 4$ in. $\times 4$ in.

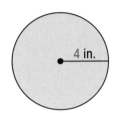

STEP 2 Multiply.
Area ≈ 50.24 sq in.

The area of the circle is about 50.24 square inches.

You can find the area of a circle if you know the diameter. Just divide the diameter by 2 to get the radius. Then use the formula above.

▶ **EXAMPLE 2**

Find the area of this circle.

STEP 1 Write the formula. Use 3.14 for π. Divide the diameter of 10 ft by 2. Use 5 ft for the radius.
Area $= \pi \times (\text{radius})^2$
Area $\approx 3.14 \times 5$ ft $\times 5$ ft

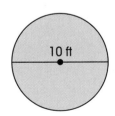

STEP 2 Multiply.
Area ≈ 78.5 sq ft

The area of the circle is about 78.5 square feet.

Practice A

Find the area of each circle. Use 3.14 for π.

1.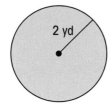
2 yd

2.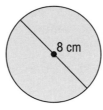
8 cm

3.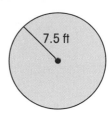
7.5 ft

Practice B

Find the area of each circle. Use 3.14 for π. Round your answers to one decimal place.

4. radius = 7 ft

5. diameter = 10 yd

6. diameter = 6.5 in.

7. radius = 9 cm

8. radius = 7.2 m

9. diameter = 23 in.

10. diameter = 8.5 mm

11. radius = 6.25 ft

12. diameter = 10.5 yd

Everyday Problem Solving

Every winter, City Center Park has a circular skating rink with a flagpole at its exact center.

1. The distance from the flagpole to the edge of the rink is 50 feet. What is the radius of the rink?

2. What is the area of the skating rink?

3. The rink is surrounded by a wall. How long is this wall? Find the circumference of the circle.

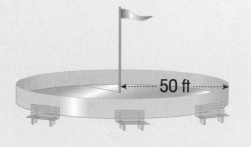
50 ft

Problem Solving: Subtracting to Find Area

16-12

Some word problems can be solved by breaking them down into smaller problems.

▶ **EXAMPLE**

Mary bought a frame for an 8 in. × 10 in. picture. If the outside of the frame is 9 in. × 11 in., what is the area of the frame?

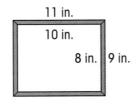

STEP 1   READ   What do you need to find out?
You need to find the area of the frame.

STEP 2   PLAN   What do you need to do?
What is the area of the large rectangle?
Multiply to find out.
What is the area of the small rectangle?
Multiply to find out.
What is the area of the frame?
Subtract to find out.

STEP 3   DO   Follow the plan.

Multiply	Multiply
Area = length × width	Area = length × width
Area = 9 × 11	Area = 8 × 10
Area = 99 sq in.	Area = 80 sq in.

Subtract
99 sq in. − 80 sq in. = 19 sq in.

STEP 4   CHECK   Does your answer make sense?
Does 19 sq in. + 80 sq in. = 99 sq in.?
99 sq in. = 99 sq in. ✓

The area of the frame is 19 square inches.

Problem Solving

Draw a diagram. Then answer the questions under PLAN
to solve each problem.

1. Brenda has a square picture frame with a square picture
   in it. The picture measures 4 inches on each side, and
   the outer edge of the frame is 7 inches on each side.
   What is the area of the frame?

   PLAN
   What is the area of the large rectangle?
   What is the area of the small rectangle?
   What is the area of the frame?

2. A fenced-in yard is 35 ft × 70 ft. A rectangular
   pool measures 25 ft × 60 ft. What is the area
   between the fence and the pool?

   PLAN
   What is the area of the large rectangle?
   What is the area of the small rectangle?
   What is the area of the walkway?

3. Amina put a blue border around the edge of a quilt.
   The quilt is 100 in. × 60 in. With the border it is
   120 in × 80 in. What is the area of the blue border?

   PLAN
   What is the area of the large rectangle?
   What is the area of the small rectangle?
   What is the area of the border?

Problem Solving Strategy

Sometimes, you can draw the diagram on
graph paper and count the square units.

   What is the area of the frame in
   square units?

16·13 Volume of Prisms

A **space figure** is a three-dimensional figure that has length, width, and height. A rectangular prism and a cube are space figures.

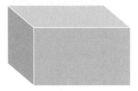

Rectangular Prism   Cube

Volume is the amount of space inside a space figure. Volume is measured in cubic units. To find the volume of a rectangular prism, use this formula:

Volume = length × width × height

▶ **EXAMPLE 1**

Find the volume of this prism.

7 in.
6 in.
10 in.

STEP 1 Write the formula.
Place the values you
know into the formula.
Volume = length × width × height
Volume = 10 in. × 6 in. × 7 in.

STEP 2 Multiply.
Volume = 420 cu in.

The volume of the prism is 420 cubic inches.

▶ **EXAMPLE 2**

Find the volume of this cube.

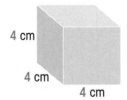
4 cm
4 cm
4 cm

STEP 1 Write the formula.
Place the values you
know in the formula.
Volume = length × width × height
Volume = 4 cm × 4 cm × 4 cm

STEP 2 Multiply.
Volume = 64 cu cm

The volume of the cube is 64 cubic centimeters.

Practice

Find the volume of each prism.

1. 2 in. 12 in. 15 in.

2. 7 cm 3 cm 3 cm

3. 8 ft 13 ft 9 ft

4. 11 m 17 m 9 m

5. 8 mm 8 mm 8 mm

6. 3 in. 11 in. 8.5 in.

Everyday Problem Solving

Allen has a fish tank that is 24 inches long, 14 inches wide, and 18 inches tall.

1. What is the capacity (volume) of the fish tank?

2. Allen fills the tank with water. He leaves 1 inch of space between the waterline and the top of the tank. What is the capacity of the water?

3. A gallon is 231 cubic inches of water. How many gallons of water are needed to fill this tank? Divide the answer you found to question 2 by 231. Round your answer to the nearest whole number.

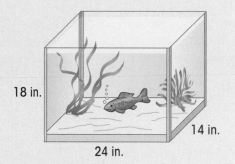

18 in. 14 in. 24 in.

Volume of Cylinders

A cylinder is a space figure
that has circles for the bases.
These two circles are the same
size. To find the volume of a
cylinder, use this formula:

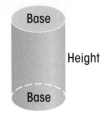

$$\text{Volume} = \pi \times (\text{radius})^2 \times \text{height}$$

▶ **EXAMPLE 1**

Find the volume of this cylinder.

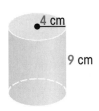

STEP 1 Write the formula. Place the values
you know into the formula.
Use 3.14 for π.
Volume = $\pi \times (\text{radius})^2 \times \text{height}$
Volume $\approx 3.14 \times (4 \text{ cm})^2 \times 9 \text{ cm}$
Volume $\approx 3.14 \times 4 \text{ cm} \times 4 \text{ cm} \times 9 \text{ cm}$

STEP 2 Multiply.
Volume ≈ 452.16 cu cm

The volume is 452.16 cubic centimeters.

▶ **EXAMPLE 2**

Find the volume of this cylinder.

STEP 1 Find the radius.
Divide the diameter by 2.
radius = 12 in. ÷ 2
radius = 6 in.

STEP 2 Use the formula. Use 3.14 for π.
Volume = $\pi \times (\text{radius})^2 \times \text{height}$
Volume $\approx 3.14 \times (6 \text{ in.})^2 \times 15 \text{ in.}$

STEP 3 Multiply.
Volume $\approx 1,695.6$ cu in.

The volume of this cylinder is 1,695.6 cubic inches.

Practice

Find the volume of each cylinder. Use 3.14 for π.

1. 1 in. 2.5 in.

2. 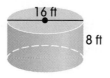 16 ft 8 ft

3. 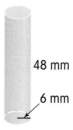 48 mm 6 mm

4. 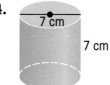 7 cm 7 cm

5. 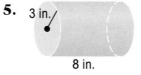 3 in. 8 in.

6. 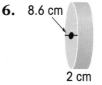 8.6 cm 2 cm

Everyday Problem Solving

A water tank is shaped like a cylinder. The diameter of the tank is 12 feet. The tank is 20 feet high.

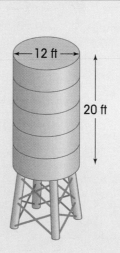
12 ft
20 ft

1. What is the radius of the base of the tank?

2. What is the area of the base of the tank?

3. What is the volume of the tank?

4. The tank is $\frac{2}{3}$ full. What is $\frac{2}{3}$ of the volume?

angles
area
circumference
parallelogram
perimeter
polygons
protractor
radius
space figure
volume

LESSONS 16·1 to 16·4

Test Tip
Be sure to use the correct scale
on the protractor.

Vocabulary Review

Answer *true* **or** *false* **for statements 1–5. If the
statement is false, rewrite it so that it becomes true.**

1. A *protractor* is used to measure *angles*.

2. The *circumference* is $\pi \times 2 \times$ radius.

3. The *area* of a figure measures the distance around
the outside of the figure.

4. A *parallelogram* is a three-dimensional figure.

5. The *volume* of a prism is length × width × height.

6. Writing Compare *prisms* and *cylinders*.
How are they alike? How are they different?

Chapter Quiz

Points, Lines, and Angles
Name each figure.

1. • *B*

2.

3. <img W X on line>

Draw an angle with each measure.

4. 12° **5.** 145° **6.** 80°

Find the measure of the third angle in the triangle.

7.

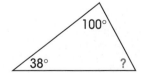

LESSONS 16·5 to 16·9

Test Tip
When finding perimeter, add
the lengths of each side.

Perimeter and Area of Polygons
Name each figure. Then find its perimeter.

8.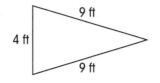

9.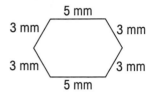

Find the area of each figure.

10. parallelogram with base = 11 in. and height = 3 in.

11. triangle with base = 7 yd and height = 6 yd

LESSONS 16·10 and 16·11

Test Tip
Be sure not to confuse radius
and diameter in the formulas.

Circles
Find the circumference and area of each circle.

12. radius = 3 in.   13. diameter = 8 cm

LESSON 16·12

Test Tip
Draw and label a diagram for
each problem.

Problem Solving

14. A window measures 30 inches by 60 inches.
There is a wood frame around the window that is
6 inches wide. What is the area of the wood frame?

LESSONS 16·13 and 16·14

Test Tip
Write out the formula you need.
Then place values you know
into the formula.

Prisms and Cylinders
Find the volume of each space figure.

15. prism with length = 9 m, width = 7 m, and
height = 6 m

16. cylinder with diameter = 10 m and height = 3 m

Group Activity

Each member of the group should bring in three different-sized cans or boxes
from food products. Have them guess the volume of the containers. Then
measure and calculate the actual volumes. Were your predictions accurate?
Did any of the results surprise you? Write a summary of your results.

Unit 4 **Review**

Choose the letter for the correct answer.

Use the graph to answer Questions 1 and 2.

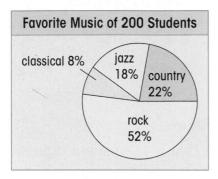

Favorite Music of 200 Students

classical 8%
jazz 18%
country 22%
rock 52%

1. Which statement is true?

   A. More students like jazz than country music. F
   B. More students like classical than country music. F
   C. Most students like rock music.
   D. Fewer students like country than classical music.

2. How many students like jazz music?

   A. 182
   B. 44
   C. 36
   D. 3,600

3. Gen went to work at 7:55 A.M. He left work at 4:45 P.M. Find the elapsed time.

   A. 3 hours 10 minutes
   B. 8 hours 50 minutes
   C. 12 hours
   D. None of the above

4. Suki made 5 liters of punch. She used 1,200 milliliters of ginger ale. Then she added fruit juice. How many milliliters of juice did she add to the punch?

   A. 1,700 ml
   B. 700 ml
   C. 6,000 ml
   D. None of the above

5. Find the area of the parallelogram below.

   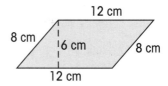

   12 cm
   8 cm
   6 cm
   8 cm
   12 cm

   A. 36 sq cm
   B. 40 sq cm
   C. 96 sq cm
   D. 72 sq cm

Critical Thinking

The area of a rectangle is 36 sq cm. What are some of the possible widths and lengths of this rectangle?

CHALLENGE The area of the rectangle is 36 sq cm. What is the largest possible perimeter of this rectangle?

New York City, 1995	
Month	Snowfall in Inches
January	7.5
February	8.6
March	5.0
April	.9
May	0
June	0
July	0
August	0
September	0
October	0
November	.9
December	5.4

The total snowfall in New York City for 1995 was only 28.3 inches. In January 1996, a blizzard dropped about 20 inches of snow on the city.

The graph and table give information on the snowfall in New York City in 1995.

1. Using the line graph, which month in 1995 had the most snowfall? How do you know?

2. Which 6 months have zero inches of snowfall? Why was there no snowfall during these months?

3. How much more snow fell in March than in April.

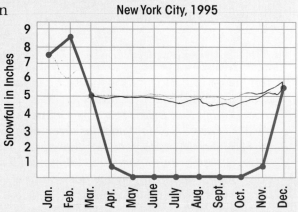

New York City, 1995

The height of a mountain is measured in feet above sea level. Depths under the ocean are measured in feet below sea level. Suppose a hiker is at +8,500 feet and this diver is at − 200 feet. Why do you think there are a + and − before the numbers? What number do you think would signify the position of a person in a kayak on the ocean?

Chapter 17 ▷ Integers

Words to Know

integers	numbers in the set {..., $^-3$, $^-2$, $^-1$, 0, $^+1$, $^+2$, $^+3$, ...}
positive integers	integers to the right of zero on the number line
negative integers	integers to the left of zero on the number line
opposites	two numbers that are the same distance from zero on the number line but are on opposite sides of zero

Integer Search Project

Search for five different integers. Find one example of each topic listed below.

- Temperature
- Stock market
- Money
- Height/depth
- Sports

Be sure to copy each topic. Look in magazines, newspapers, and an atlas. Next to the topic, write the example you found. Then, write what the example is about.

Temperature	*$^+32$*	*degrees*
Stock	*$^-1$*	*stock points*

Learning Objectives

- Identify and write integers.
- Add integers with like signs.
- Add integers with unlike signs.
- Subtract integers.
- Multiply integers.
- Divide integers.
- Solve problems using integers.
- Apply integers to wind chill temperatures.

What Is an Integer?

Integers are numbers that describe direction and quantity. **Positive integers** are greater than zero. **Negative integers** are less than zero. Zero is neither positive nor negative.

The integer $^+4$ is read: positive four or four.
The integer $^-4$ is read: negative four.

Decimals and fractions are **not** integers. For example, 3.5 and $^-3.5$ are not integers.

You can write a positive integer without the positive sign. The integers $^+4$ and 4 are the same number.

The numbers $^+4$ and $^-4$ are called **opposites.** Opposites are the same distance from zero on the number line but are on opposite sides of zero.

► **EXAMPLE 1**

What integer describes point A? Write its opposite.

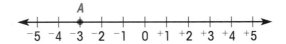

STEP 1 Find point A on the number line.

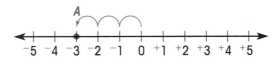

Point A is 3 units to the **left** of 0. Point A is at $^-$**3**.

STEP 2 Find the opposite of $^-$3.

Count 3 units to the **right** of 0. The opposite of $^-$**3** is $^+$**3**.

STEP 3 Write the integers that describe these points. $^-$**3** and $^+$**3**

$^-$3 describes point A. The opposite of $^-$3 is $^+$3.

Integers often describe real-life situations.

▶ **EXAMPLE 2**

Use an integer to describe 10 degrees below 0.

STEP 1 Should the integer be positive or   −
negative? Use a **negative** integer
to describe **below** zero.

STEP 2 Write the integer.   ⁻10

The integer ⁻10 describes 10 degrees below 0.

Practice A

Copy the number line. Then, on the line, mark a point for
each integer below.

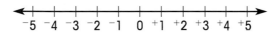

1. ⁺2   **2.** ⁻5   **3.** ⁺3   **4.** ⁺1   **5.** ⁻2

6. ⁻1   **7.** 0   **8.** ⁺5   **9.** ⁻4   **10.** ⁻3

Practice B

Write the integer that describes each point. Then write its opposite.

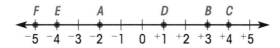

11. point *A*   **12.** point *B*   **13.** point *C*

14. point *D*   **15.** point *E*   **16.** point *F*

Practice C

Write an integer to describe each situation.

17. a $5 profit   **18.** a $7 loss   **19.** 12° above zero

20. 9 ft below sea level   **21.** a 6-point gain   **22.** a 5-point loss

You can use a number line to add integers. Start at 0. Move to the right to add a positive integer. Move to the left to add a negative integer. You can make the number line any size you need.

▶ **EXAMPLE 1**

Add. $^+3 + {}^+6$

STEP 1 Start at 0. Move right 3 spaces to $^+3$.

STEP 2 Then, to add $^+6$, move to the right 6 spaces.

STEP 3 The number you end at is the sum. Write the sum.

$$^+3 + {}^+6 = {}^+9$$

The sum of $^+3$ and $^+6$ is $^+9$.

▶ **EXAMPLE 2**

Add. $^-4 + {}^-2$

STEP 1 Start at 0. Move left 4 spaces to $^-4$.

STEP 2 Then, to add $^-2$, move to the left 2 spaces.

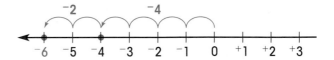

STEP 3 The number you end at is the sum. Write the sum.

$$^-4 + {}^-2 = {}^-6$$

The sum of $^-4$ and $^-2$ is $^-6$.

Practice

Add.

1. $^{+}2 + {}^{+}8$

2. $^{-}5 + {}^{-}3$

3. $^{+}9 + {}^{+}7$

4. $^{-}10 + {}^{-}11$

5. $^{-}5 + {}^{-}8$

6. $^{+}6 + {}^{+}8$

7. $^{-}3 + {}^{-}9$

8. $^{+}5 + {}^{+}14$

9. $^{-}3 + {}^{-}16$

10. $^{+}4 + {}^{+}6$

11. $^{-}5 + {}^{-}5$

12. $^{-}6 + {}^{-}2$

13. $^{-}7 + {}^{-}8$

14. $^{+}8 + {}^{+}4$

15. $^{-}9 + {}^{-}5$

16. $^{-}9 + {}^{-}9$

17. $^{+}7 + {}^{+}6$

18. $^{-}8 + {}^{-}3$

Everyday Problem Solving

Dana hiked down a mountain from the peak. She went down 500 feet, and then she rested. Then she went down 400 feet more to her camp site.

1. What are the two integers described in this problem?

2. How far did Dana hike from the peak to the camp site? Use an integer to describe the distance and direction.

3. Dana's car is parked 600 feet below the camp site. How far did Dana hike from the peak to the car?

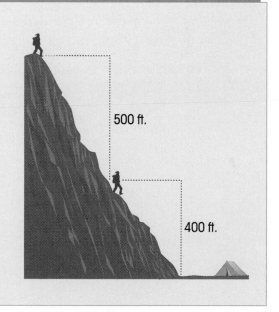

500 ft.

400 ft.

You can use a number line to add integers with unlike signs. Start at 0. Move to the right to add a positive integer. Move to the left to add a negative integer.

► **EXAMPLE 1**

Add. $^-2 + {}^+5$

STEP 1 Start at 0. Move left 2 spaces to $^-2$.

STEP 2 Then, to add 5, move to the right 5 spaces.

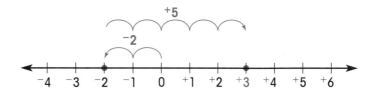

STEP 3 The number you end at is the sum. Write the sum.

$$^-2 + {}^+5 = {}^+3$$

The sum of $^-2$ and $^+5$ is $^+3$.

► **EXAMPLE 2**

Add. $^+6 + {}^-8$

STEP 1 Start at 0. Move right 6 spaces to $^+6$.

STEP 2 Then, to add $^-8$, move to the left 8 spaces.

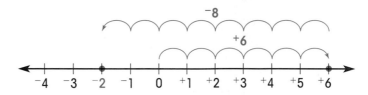

STEP 3 The number you end at is the sum. Write the sum.

$$^+6 + {}^-8 = {}^-2$$

The sum of $^+6$ and $^-8$ is $^-2$.

Practice

Add.

1. $^-2 + {}^+7$
2. $^+9 + {}^-6$
3. $^-8 + {}^+6$

4. $^-7 + {}^+1$
5. $^-4 + {}^+8$
6. $^+3 + {}^-3$

7. $^+9 + {}^-10$
8. $^-1 + {}^+6$
9. $^+8 + {}^-6$

10. $^-11 + {}^+8$
11. $^+10 + {}^-4$
12. $^-6 + {}^+4$

13. $^+5 + {}^-11$
14. $^+5 + {}^-9$
15. $^-12 + {}^+2$

16. $^-2 + {}^+12$
17. $^+9 + {}^-12$
18. $^-8 + {}^+17$

19. $^-15 + {}^+1$
20. $^+1 + {}^-9$
21. $^+13 + {}^-4$

22. $^-8 + {}^+8$
23. $^+100 + {}^-100$
24. $^-15 + {}^+9$

25. $^+7 + {}^-5$
26. $^-7 + {}^+5$
27. $^-8 + {}^+9$

28. $^-9 + {}^+6$
29. $^+10 + {}^-2$
30. $^-12 + {}^+8$

Everyday Problem Solving

In a football game, Jeff started on the 40 yard line. He lost 4 yards on one play. Then he gained 7 yards on the next play.

1. Use an integer to describe a 4-yard loss.

2. Use an integer to describe a 7-yard gain.

3. In all, how many yards did Jeff gain or lose on the two plays?

Subtracting Integers

You can use a number line to see how subtracting integers is like adding the opposite integers.

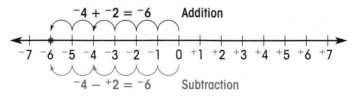

This shows the addition: $^-4 + {^-2} = {^-6}$
This shows the subtraction: $^-4 - {^+2} = {^-6}$
Notice that **subtracting $^+2$** is just like **adding $^-2$**.

To subtract an integer, add its opposite.

► EXAMPLE 1

Subtract. $^-4 - {^-3}$

STEP 1 Write the problem as given. $^-4 - {^-3}$

STEP 2 $^+3$ is the opposite of $^-3$. $^-4 + {^+3}$
Change the problem to adding $^+3$.

STEP 3 Use the number line to add.
$^-4 + {^+3} = {^-1}$

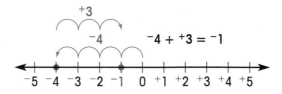

STEP 4 The number you end at is the answer to the
problem as given. Write the answer.
$^-4 - {^-3} = {^-1}$

The difference between $^-4$ and $^-3$ is $^-1$.

▶ **EXAMPLE 2**

Subtract. $^-2 - {}^+7$

STEP 1 Write the problem as given. $^-2 - {}^+7$

STEP 2 $^-7$ is the opposite of $^+7$. $^-2 + {}^-7$
Change the problem to adding $^-7$.

STEP 3 Use the number line to add. $^-2 + {}^-7 = {}^-9$

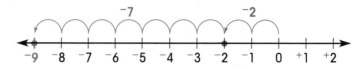

STEP 4 The number you end at is the $^-2 - {}^+7 = {}^-9$
answer to the problem as given.
Write the answer.

The difference between $^-2$ and $^+7$ is $^-9$.

Practice A

Rewrite each subtraction as an addition.

1. $^-2 - {}^-1$ **2.** $^-5 - {}^+2$

3. $^+4 - {}^-3$ **4.** $^+6 - {}^-2$

5. $^+6 - {}^+2$ **6.** $^+1 - {}^-4$

7. $^-10 - {}^-1$ **8.** $^-8 - {}^+7$

9. $^-5 - {}^-5$ **10.** $^-12 - {}^-12$

Practice B

Subtract. Remember to rewrite each subtraction as an addition first.

11. ⁻2 − ⁻4

12. ⁺4 − ⁺2

13. ⁺3 − ⁺8

14. ⁻8 − ⁻4

15. ⁻2 − ⁺4

16. ⁺5 − ⁻11

17. ⁺6 − ⁻3

18. ⁻3 − ⁺2

19. ⁺10 − ⁻7

20. ⁻5 − ⁻1

21. ⁻1 − ⁻9

22. ⁺9 − ⁺5

23. ⁻5 − ⁺6

24. ⁻7 − ⁺2

25. ⁺4 − ⁻9

26. ⁺2 − ⁻7

27. ⁻12 − ⁻10

28. ⁺3 − ⁻4

29. ⁺7 − ⁺5

30. ⁺8 − ⁻7

31. ⁻9 − ⁻6

Everyday Problem Solving

Sam went scuba diving. He dove 12 feet below the surface of the water. Sam went down another 5 feet.

1. Write a subtraction problem to describe the situation.

2. Write an addition problem to describe the situation.

3. In all, how far below the surface of the water did Sam dive?

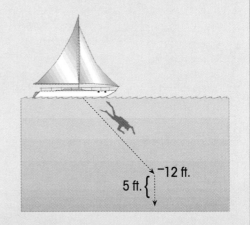

Then, Sam rose 9 feet toward the surface of the water.

4. How far below the surface of the water is he now?

USING YOUR CALCULATOR
Keying In Integers

You can use your calculator to add and subtract integers. Most calculators have a button that looks like this: +/-

This button will change the sign of the number shown on the calculator. For example, if you press 3 +/-, the result will be ⁻3. Practice entering negative integers in your calculator. Be sure you press the +/- button <u>after</u> entering the number, not before. For a positive number, just enter the number itself.

Now you are ready to learn how to add and subtract integers on your calculator. Here are some examples.

To add ⁻3 + 5:

   PRESS 3 +/- + 5 = [2.]

To subtract ⁻6 − ⁻4:

   PRESS 6 +/- − 4 +/- = [⁻2.]

Use a calculator to add or subtract.

1. ⁻2 + ⁺7   2. ⁺5 + ⁻8   3. ⁻3 − ⁺2

4. ⁺4 + ⁻3   5. ⁻8 − ⁻2   6. ⁻6 + ⁻8

7. ⁻5 + ⁻7   8. ⁺6 − ⁺10   9. ⁺12 − ⁻3

10. ⁺9 + ⁻10   11. ⁻1 − ⁻5   12. ⁺8 − ⁺12

Calculator Tip

To make a number negative, be sure you do not use the − button by mistake. It will just subtract the next integer you enter.

17·5 Multiplying Integers

When you multiply integers, you need to decide if the product is positive or negative.

Multiplication is the process of adding the same number one or more times. Adding $^-2 + {}^-2 + {}^-2$ is the same as multiplying $3 \times {}^-2$. You can use the number line to find the product.

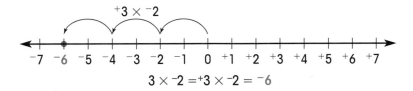

$$3 \times {}^-2 = {}^+3 \times {}^-2 = {}^-6$$

Remember:
A positive number can be written without the + sign.

Notice that a positive integer times a negative integer is a negative integer.

Remember this rule:
    If the signs are **different**, the product is **negative**.

▶ **EXAMPLE 1**

Multiply. $^-7 \times {}^+8$

STEP 1 Look at the signs. Are the signs the same or different?
$^-7 \times {}^+8$
The signs are different.

STEP 2 Multiply the numbers without the signs.
$7 \times 8 = 56$

STEP 3 Decide on the sign of the product. The signs are different. The product is negative.
$^-7 \times {}^+8 = {}^-56$

The product of $^-7$ and $^+8$ is $^-56$.

The product of two positive integers is positive.

$$^+2 \times {}^+3 = {}^+6$$

Is the product of two negative integers positive? To find out, look at the pattern below. Begin with what you know: $^+3 \times {}^-2 = {}^-6$.

$^+3 \times {}^-2 = {}^-6$	Each product is 2 more.
$^+2 \times {}^-2 = {}^-4$	
$^+1 \times {}^-2 = {}^-2$	
$0 \times {}^-2 = 0$	
$^-1 \times {}^-2 = {}^+2$	
$^-2 \times {}^-2 = {}^+4$	
$^-3 \times {}^-2 = {}^+6$	

Notice that $^-3 \times {}^-2 = {}^+6$. A negative integer times a negative integer is a positive integer.

Remember this rule:

If the signs are the same, the product is positive.

▶ **EXAMPLE 2**

Multiply. $^-7 \times {}^-8$

STEP 1 Look at the signs. Are the signs the same or different?

$^-7 \times {}^-8$
The signs are the same.

STEP 2 Multiply the numbers without the signs.

$7 \times 8 = 56$

STEP 3 Decide on the sign of the product. The signs are the same. The product is positive.

$^-7 \times {}^-8 = {}^+56$

The product of $^-7$ and $^-8$ is $^+56$.

Practice A

Multiply. If the signs are different, the product is negative.

1. $^-4 \times {}^+3$

2. $^-5 \times {}^+8$

3. $^+7 \times {}^-9$

4. $^+6 \times {}^-5$

5. $^-1 \times {}^+9$

6. $^+8 \times {}^-3$

7. $^+2 \times {}^-2$

8. $^-6 \times {}^+3$

9. $^-5 \times {}^+7$

10. $^-100 \times {}^+1$

11. $^+100 \times {}^-1$

12. $^+1 \times {}^-1$

Practice B

Multiply. If the signs are the same, the product is positive.

13. $^-5 \times {}^-4$

14. $^+6 \times {}^+9$

15. $^-8 \times {}^-7$

16. $^+8 \times {}^+2$

17. $^+6 \times {}^+7$

18. $^-3 \times {}^-9$

19. $^-7 \times {}^-4$

20. $^+8 \times {}^+8$

21. $^-8 \times {}^-6$

22. $^+9 \times {}^+6$

23. $^-9 \times {}^-6$

24. $^-50 \times {}^-2$

Practice C

Multiply. Decide if the product is positive or negative.

25. $^-7 \times {}^-3$

26. $^-8 \times {}^+9$

27. $^+4 \times {}^+6$

28. $^-8 \times {}^+4$

29. $^+5 \times {}^-5$

30. $^-9 \times {}^-4$

31. $^+5 \times {}^+9$

32. $^+9 \times {}^-9$

33. $^-7 \times {}^+7$

34. $^-6 \times {}^+9$

35. $^-8 \times {}^-5$

36. $^+9 \times {}^+7$

MATH IN YOUR LIFE
Wind Chill Temperature

The wind can make you feel colder than the temperature that is on a thermometer. Suppose the thermometer reads 10°F. A wind blowing at 10 mph makes the air feel as if it were ⁻9°F. This is called the *wind chill temperature*.

Louise heard on the five day weather report that the temperatures and wind speeds would vary.

Wind Chill					
Wind Speed	Temperature				
0 mph	0°F	10°F	20°F	30°F	40°F
5 mph	⁻5	6	16	27	37
10 mph	⁻22	⁻9	3	16	28
15 mph	⁻31	⁻18	⁻5	9	23
20 mph	⁻39	⁻24	⁻10	4	19
25 mph	⁻44	⁻29	⁻15	1	16

Use the table to answer the questions.

1. On Monday, the temperature was 10°F. The wind speed was 15 mph. What was the wind chill temperature?

2. On Tuesday, the temperature was 20°F. The wind blew at 25 mph. What was the wind chill temperature?

3. On Wednesday, the temperature was 30°F. The wind speed was 5 mph. What was the wind chill temperature?

4. On Thursday, the temperature was 0°F. The wind blew at 20 mph. What was the wind chill temperature?

5. On Friday, the temperature was still 0°F. But wind speed was only 5 mph. What was the wind chill temperature?

6. What was the difference in wind chill temperatures between Thursday and Friday?

Critical Thinking
Why is wind chill important to consider?

Dividing Integers

When you divide integers, you need to decide if the quotient is positive or negative. The rules for dividing integers are the same as the rules for multiplying integers.

Follow these rules:

If the signs are different, the quotient is negative.
If the signs are the same, the quotient is positive.

▶ **EXAMPLE 1**

Divide. $^-32 \div {}^+4$

STEP 1   Look at the signs. Are the signs the same or different?

$^-32 \div {}^+4$
The signs are different.

STEP 2   Divide the numbers without the signs.

$32 \div 4 = 8$

STEP 3   Decide on the sign of the quotient. The signs are different. The quotient is negative.

$^-32 \div {}^+4 = {}^-8$

The quotient of $^-32$ and $^+4$ is $^-8$.

▶ **EXAMPLE 2**

Divide. $^-10 \div {}^-2$

STEP 1   Look at the signs. Are the signs the same or different?

$^-10 \div {}^-2$
The signs are the same.

STEP 2   Divide the numbers without the signs.

$10 \div 2 = 5$

STEP 3   Decide on the sign of the quotient. The signs are the same. The quotient is positive.

$^-10 \div {}^-2 = {}^+5$

The quotient of $^-10$ and $^-2$ is $^+5$.

Practice A

Divide. If the signs are different, the quotient is negative.

1. $^-4 \div {}^+2$ **2.** $^+21 \div {}^-3$ **3.** $^-32 \div {}^+8$

4. $^-45 \div {}^+9$ **5.** $^+42 \div {}^-7$ **6.** $^+81 \div {}^-9$

7. $^+54 \div {}^-9$ **8.** $^-40 \div {}^+5$ **9.** $^-9 \div {}^+9$

10. $^-15 \div {}^+5$ **11.** $^-81 \div {}^+9$ **12.** $^+24 \div {}^-3$

Practice B

Divide. If the signs are the same, the quotient is positive.

13. $^+16 \div {}^+2$ **14.** $35 \div {}^-5$ **15.** $^+24 \div {}^+8$

16 $^-49 \div {}^-7$ **17.** $^+20 \div {}^+5$ **18.** $^-72 \div {}^-9$

19. $^-28 \div {}^-4$ **20.** $^+12 \div {}^+4$ **21.** $^-30 \div {}^-6$

22. $^+16 \div {}^+4$ **23.** $^-40 \div {}^-5$ **24.** $^-2 \div {}^-2$

Practice C

Divide. Decide if the sign of the quotient is positive or negative.

25. $^-18 \div {}^+3$ **26.** $^-56 \div {}^-7$ **27.** $^-64 \div {}^-8$

28. $^+36 \div {}^-6$ **29.** $^+27 \div {}^-3$ **30.** $^+48 \div {}^+6$

31. $^+63 \div {}^+7$ **32.** $^-24 \div {}^+6$ **33.** $^+36 \div {}^-9$

34. $^-20 \div {}^-4$ **35.** $^+49 \div {}^-7$ **36.** $^+72 \div {}^-8$

17·7 Problem Solving: Using Integers

Sometimes you can use integers to solve word problems.

EXAMPLE

The Evergreen football team lost 5 yards on its first play and gained 12 yards on the second play. What was the team's total gain?

STEP 1 **READ** What do you need to find out?
You need to find the total gain in yards.

STEP 2 **PLAN** What do you need to do?
Add the yards lost (a negative integer) and the yards gained (a positive integer).

STEP 3 **DO** Follow the plan.
Add. $^-5 + {^+}12$

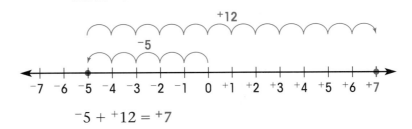

$^-5 + {^+}12 = {^+}7$

STEP 4 **CHECK** Does your answer make sense?
Yes. Look at the numbers.

The yards gained are greater than the yards lost. The total should be positive.
The sum is $^+7$.

One number is positive. The other number is negative. The total should be less than the yards gained.
7 is less than 12. ✓

The Evergreen team gained 7 yards for the two plays.

Practice

READ the problem. Answer the questions under PLAN.
DO the plan to solve the problem.

1. The Clarksville Hornets football team lost 5 yards on its
    first play, and it lost 6 yards on the second play. What
    was the team's total for the two plays?

    PLAN
    What operation will you use?
    What integers will you use?

2. The Hawks football team gained 7 yards on its first play
    and lost 9 yards on the second play. What was the
    team's total for the two plays?

    PLAN
    What operation will you use?
    What integers will you use?

3. The Eagles football team lost 2 yards on each of 3 plays.
    What was the team's total loss for the 3 plays?

    PLAN
    What operation will you use?
    What integers will you use?

Problem-Solving Strategy

Often, problems can be solved by drawing a diagram.

> Rick lost 4 yards on each of the last two plays.
> Draw a diagram to find the total number of
> yards he gained or lost.

Draw a number line. Use a negative integer to
describe yards lost.

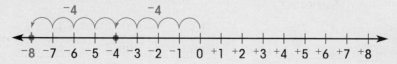

integers
negative integers
opposites
positive integers

Vocabulary Review
Fill in each blank with a word from the list.

1. The integers to the left of zero on the number line are called ___?___.

2. The numbers $^+6$ and $^-6$ are called ___?___ because they are the same distance from zero but on different sides of zero.

3. ___?___ are any numbers in the set $\{...,^-3, ^-2, ^-1, 0, ^+1, ^+2, ^+3,...\}$.

4. The integers to the right of zero on the number line are called ___?___.

5. **Writing** Explain two situations where negative numbers are used in "real life."

Chapter Quiz

LESSON 17·1

Writing Integers
Write an integer to describe each situation.

1. a $3 loss

2. a 9 point gain

LESSONS 17·2 and 17·3

Adding Integers
Add.

Test Tip
The sum of positive integers is positive. The sum of negative integers is negative. If the signs are different, use the number line.

3. $^-5 + ^-3$ **4.** $^+4 + ^+6$ **5.** $^+7 + ^-3$

6. $^-8 + ^-2$ **7.** $^+6 + ^+6$ **8.** $^-9 + ^+7$

9. $^-3 + ^-3$ **10.** $^+12 + ^-13$ **11.** $^+4 + ^-4$

LESSON 17·4

Subtracting Integers
Subtract.

Test Tip
To subtract, add the opposite of the second integer.

12. $^+8 - ^+7$ **13.** $^+7 - ^+9$ **14.** $^-3 - ^+2$

15. $^-10 - ^-4$ **16.** $^+6 - ^-8$ **17.** $^-4 - ^-5$

18. $^+9 - ^+15$ **19.** $^-3 - ^-6$ **20.** $^+4 - ^-4$

Multiplying and Dividing Integers

Multiply.

Test Tip
If the signs are the same,
the answer is positive.
If the signs are different,
the answer is negative.

21. $^-2 \times {}^-8$ **22.** $^+9 \times {}^-6$ **23.** $^-8 \times {}^+3$

24. $^+7 \times {}^+7$ **25.** $^-8 \times {}^-9$ **26.** $^+4 \times {}^-7$

27. $^+3 \times {}^+11$ **28.** $^-5 \times {}^-2$ **29.** $^-1 \times {}^+15$

Divide.

30. $^+24 \div {}^+3$ **31.** $^+18 \div {}^-3$ **32.** $^-5\overline{)\,{}^-25}$

33. $^-80 \div {}^+10$ **34.** $^-32 \div {}^-8$ **35.** $^-7\overline{)\,{}^+21}$

36. $^-24 \div {}^-4$ **37.** $^+54 \div {}^-6$ **38.** $^-81 \div {}^+9$

Solving Problems Using Integers

Solve.

Test Tip
Use a positive number for an
increase. Use a negative
number for a decrease.

39. A stock in the stock market was worth 1 point when it first came on the market. It then rose 4 points, dropped 3 points, and then dropped 2 more points by the end of the day. Where did the stock end?

40. This morning, the temperature was $^-4°$. By noon, the temperature had risen by $^+21°$. What was the temperature at noon?

Group Activity

Make sure that each member on the team has an atlas. Each student should look through the atlas and try to find the highest place above sea level and the lowest place below sea level. Compare these places and choose the highest and lowest from the group. Next, draw a picture of the places and label their heights or depths. Then find the difference between the two.

This acrobat is balancing himself on the tightrope. He does this by using his arms. He likes to keep an equal number of circles on each arm. This is much like an algebra equation. The two sides need to balance, or be the same. If he puts six rings on his right arm, how many will he want to put on his left arm?

Chapter 18 ▷ Algebra

Words to Know

equation	a mathematical sentence stating that two quantities are equal
variable	a letter that stands for a number
number expression	a number or numbers together with operation symbols
solution	the value of a variable that makes an equation true
simplify	to write a shorter or easier form of an expression; or to find its value
parentheses ( )	marks around an operation that should be done first
order of operations	the specific order to do the four basic operations when more than one operation is in an equation

Equation Project

In this chapter, you will learn about the equation $d = r \times t$. In the equation, d stands for distance, r stands for rate, and t stands for time. Research to find five more equations with letters. Look in your math book, your science book, or a reference book. Write each equation. Describe what each letter represents. Then explain one important use of the equation.

Learning Objectives

- Identify solutions to equations.
- Simplify expressions with parentheses and using the order of operations.
- Solve equations with one operation.
- Solve equations with more than one operation.
- Solve problems using one-step equations and two-step equations.
- Apply algebra to computer programming.

Look at the scale below. This scale is balanced when x is 5.

$x = 5$ ← equation

An **equation** is like a balanced scale. An equation states that two quantities are equal. The equation above contains the **variable** x. A variable is a letter that stands for a number.

An equation may contain one or more operations.

$$y + 8 = 10 \qquad 3m = 6 \qquad 2x + 1 = 7$$

To solve an equation, you find the value of the variable that makes the equation true. This value is called the **solution**.

▶ **EXAMPLE 1**

Is $y = 2$ the solution to the equation $y + 8 = 10$?

STEP 1   Replace y with 2 in the equation. Is this a true statement? $y + 8 = 10$
Does $2 + 8$ equal 10?

STEP 2   Do the calculation. If the new statement is true, you have found the solution to the given equation. $2 + 8 ? 10$
$10 = 10$ ✓

Yes, $y = 2$ is the solution to the equation $y + 8 = 10$.

A number next to a variable means multiply. For example, the expression $3m$ means 3 times m.

Is $m = 7$ the solution to the equation $3m = 24$?

STEP 1	Replace m with 7 in the equation. Is this a true statement?	$3m = 24$ Does 3×7 equal 24?
STEP 2	Do the calculation. If the new statement is false, you have not found the solution to the given equation.	$3 \times 7 ? 24$ $21 \neq 24$

No, $m = 7$ is <u>not</u> a solution to the equation $3m = 24$.

Practice

Tell whether the number is a solution to the equation. Write *Yes* or *No*.

1. $x + 2 = 5; x = 3$

2. $m - 5 = 4; m = 9$

3. $f - 7 = 1; f = 5$

4. $a + 4 = 9; a = 4$

5. $p + 1 = 10; p = 11$

6. $m - 6 = 3; m = 9$

7. $h - 11 = 0; h = 12$

8. $k \div 3 = 8; k = 24$

9. $g - 4 = 5; g = 9$

10. $y + 3 = 32; y = 20$

11. $4c = 25; c = 3$

12. $17 - v = 9; v = 8$

13. $5e = 20; e = 4$

14. $10 - x = 5; x = 6$

15. $2w = 12; w = 6$

16. $15 \div n = 10; n = 3$

17. $a \div 3 = 6; a = 9$

18. $8q = 45; q = 5$

A **number expression** is a number or numbers together with operation symbols. When you find the value of an expression, you **simplify** the expression. Some expressions contain **parentheses**. Parentheses around an operation tell you to do this operation first.

▶ **EXAMPLE 1**

The four operations are: addition, subtraction, multiplication, and division.

Simplify. $(7 + 4) - 6$

STEP 1 Do the addition inside the parentheses first.

$(7 + 4) - 6$
$11 - 6$

STEP 2 Then subtract.

5

The value of $(7 + 4) - 6$ is 5.

Parentheses can also mean to multiply.

▶ **EXAMPLE 2**

Simplify. $3(7 - 3)$

STEP 1 Do the subtraction inside the parentheses first.

$3(7 - 3)$
$3(4)$

STEP 2 Then multiply.

12

The value of $3(7 - 3)$ is 12.

Practice

Simplify each expression.

1. $(3 + 9) - 7$

2. $38 - (9 \times 2)$

3. $(3 \times 8) + 1$

4. $(7 \times 8) - 26$

5. $2 (8 + 1)$

6. $27 + (5 \times 12)$

7. $4(15 - 8)$

8. $(5 + 7) - (6 + 3)$

9. $(24 + 8) \times 9$

10. $93 - (63 - 9)$

11. $(12 \times 8) - (4 \times 7)$

12. $5(6 + 9) + (2 \times 8)$

ON-THE-JOB MATH
Computer Programmer

Andrea is a computer programmer. She writes programs in special languages for computers. Other people use these programs to make their jobs easier.

Andrea uses algebra in almost every program she writes. One computer language that Andrea uses is called Basic. Here is an example of a Basic program.

```
10 PRINT:"Type a number from 1 to 10" for x
20 LET    y=2*x
30 LET    z=5+y
40 LET    a=-z
50 PRINT:"We changed your number to:"
60 PRINT a
```

Line 10 identifies your number as *x*. Suppose you choose 3 for *x* .

Line 20 multiplies 3 by 2 and calls the answer *y*. Now *y* = 6.

Line 30 adds 5 to 6 and calls the answer *z*. Now *z* = 11.

Line 40 takes the opposite of this number and calls the answer *a*. Now *a* = ⁻11.

The computer then prints: "We changed your number to: ⁻11."

Work with a partner. Use the number given for *x*. Find the number the computer will print.

  1. 1   **2.** 6   **3.** 5   **4.** 10   **5.** 7

Critical Thinking

Andrea has a printout of her friend's results. Her friend entered a number into the program. How can Andrea find out what number her friend entered?

Some expressions do not contain parentheses that tell you what to do first. Then you need to follow the **order of operations**. This means that you do the operations in this order:

1. Multiply and divide from left to right.
2. Add and subtract from left to right.

▶ **EXAMPLE 1**

Simplify. $8 - 2 \times 3$

STEP 1 Do all multiplication and division first. $8 - \underbrace{2 \times 3}$

STEP 2 Then do all addition and subtraction. $\underbrace{8 - 6}$

$$2$$

The value of $8 - 2 \times 3$ is 2.

Sometimes a problem contains just multiplication and division or just addition and subtraction. Do the operations in order from left to right.

▶ **EXAMPLE 2**

Simplify. $22 \div 2 \times 3$

STEP Do all multiplication and division in order from left to right.

$\underbrace{22 \div 2} \times 3$

$\underbrace{11 \times 3}$

$$33$$

The value of $22 \div 2 \times 3$ is 33.

Practice A

Simplify each expression. Remember to multiply or divide first.

1. $7 + 6 \div 2$ **2.** $33 - 3 \times 4$ **3.** $6 + 6 \times 15$

4. $9 - 2 \times 3$ **5.** $19 - 1 \times 8$ **6.** $64 - 8 \div 8$

7. $40 + 6 \times 8$ **8.** $18 - 4 \times 4$ **9.** $37 - 7 \times 3$

Practice B

Simplify each expression. Remember to follow the order of operations.

10. $10 + 7 \times 6$ **11.** $52 \div 2 \times 2$ **12.** $14 - 2 \times 6$

13. $99 + 11 - 8$ **14.** $56 \div 7 + 3$ **15.** $25 - 2 \times 7$

16. $24 + 4 \times 9$ **17.** $8 \times 5 - 6$ **18.** $6 \div 6 \times 13$

19. $32 - 8 \times 3$ **20.** $70 + 25 \div 5$ **21.** $49 - 7 + 1$

22. $45 - 12 \div 4$ **23.** $18 + 2 \times 9$ **24.** $3 \times 8 \div 6$

Everyday Problem Solving

Jackson is shopping for clothes for a new job. The store is having a sale.

1. If Jackson buys 3 T-shirts, how much does each T-shirt cost? Use the expression $36 \div 3$ to find the cost of one T-shirt.

2. How much would only 2 T-shirts cost? The expression 12×2 tells you what to do.

3. If he buys 4 dress shirts, how much does each one cost? Write an expression that tells you what to do.

4. How much would 5 ties cost altogether? Write an expression that tells you what to do.

5. Is the expression $45 \div 3 \times 5$ the same as $45 \div (3 \times 5)$? why or why not?

STORE WIDE SALE

T-Shirt Sale	3 for $36
Tie Sale	3 for $45
Dress Shirt Sale	4 for $76

18·4 Solving Equations with Addition and Subtraction

To solve equations, you will need to *undo* operations. Look at the examples below.

$$5 - 2 + 2 \qquad\qquad 5 + 2 - 2$$
$$3 + 2 \qquad\qquad\qquad 7 - 2$$
$$5 \qquad\qquad\qquad\qquad 5$$

To solve an equation that has addition, undo the addition with subtraction.

► EXAMPLE 1

Remember:
Whatever you do to one side of an equation, you must do to the other side to keep the equation balanced.

Solve. $x + 8 = 15$

STEP 1 Undo addition with subtraction. Subtract 8 from both sides of the equation.

$$x + 8 = 15$$
$$x + 8 - 8 = 15 - 8$$

STEP 2 Simplify each side.

$$x + 0 = 7$$
$$x \quad = 7$$

STEP 3 Check your work. Replace the variable in the equation with your solution.

$$x + 8 = 15$$
$$7 + 8 \,?\, 15$$
$$15 = 15 \checkmark$$

The solution to the equation $x + 8 = 15$ is $x = 7$.

To solve an equation that has subtraction, undo the subtraction with addition.

► EXAMPLE 2

Solve. $y - 3 = 10$

STEP 1 Undo subtraction with addition. Add 3 to both sides of the equation.

$$y - 3 = 10$$
$$y - 3 + 3 = 10 + 3$$

STEP 2 Simplify each side.

$$y + 0 = 13$$
$$y \quad = 13$$

STEP 3 Check your work. Replace the variable in the equation with your solution.

$$y - 3 = 10$$
$$13 - 3 \,?\, 10$$
$$10 = 10 \checkmark$$

The solution to the equation $y - 3 = 10$ is $y = 13$.

Practice

Solve each equation.

1. $x + 6 = 13$

2. $y + 5 = 14$

3. $p - 7 = 8$

4. $2 = h - 8$

5. $c + 3 = 9$

6. $f \quad 2 = 4$

7. $m - 4 = 10$

8. $15 = r - 7$

9. $9 = w + 2$

10. $12 = k - 7$

11. $n - 11 = 3$

12. $x - 8 = 5$

13. $20 = j - 9$

14. $m + 15 = 23$

15. $e - 13 = 19$

16. $50 + k = 75$

17. $h + 8 = 26$

18. $30 = x - 45$

19. $27 = r - 8$

20. $s + 7 = 22$

21. $g - 19 = 40$

Everyday Problem Solving

Algebra can be used to represent everyday situations.

1. Mary is 8 years older than Tom. Tom is t years old. Which expression shows how old Mary is?

    (a) $t + 8$ **(b)** $t - 8$ **(c)** $8t$ **(d)** $t \div 8$

2. Mary is 8 years older than Tom. Tom is t years old. Mary is 12 years old. Which equation shows this relationship?

    (a) $t + 8 = 12$ **(b)** $t - 8 = 12$ **(c)** $8t = 12$ **(d)** $t \div 8 = 12$

3. How old is Tom? To find out, solve the equation $t + 8 = 12$.

4. Eileen is 5 years younger than Peter. She is 23 years old. How old is Peter? Write an equation and solve.

5. Nora is 15 years old. She is 6 years older than her brother Abel. How old is Abel? Write an equation and solve.

18·5 Solving Equations with Multiplication and Division

To solve equations with multiplication or division, you will need to *undo* each operation. Look at the examples below.

$$6 \times 3 \div 3 \qquad\qquad 6 \div 3 \times 3$$
$$18 \div 3 \qquad\qquad 2 \times 3$$
$$6 \qquad\qquad\qquad 6$$

To solve an equation that has multiplication, divide.

▶ **EXAMPLE 1**

Remember:
2*m* means 2 × *m*.

Solve. $2m = 10$

STEP 1 Undo multiplication with division. Divide both sides of the equation by 2.

$2m = 10$
$2m \div 2 = 10 \div 2$

STEP 2 Simplify each side.

$m = 5$

STEP 3 Check your work. Replace the variable in the equation with your solution.

$2m = 10$
$2 \times 5 ? 10$
$10 = 10 ✓$

The solution to the equation $2m = 10$ is $m = 5$.

To solve an equation that has division, multiply.

▶ **EXAMPLE 2**

Remember:
$\frac{y}{3}$ means $y \div 3$

Solve. $\frac{y}{3} = 7$

STEP 1 Undo division with multiplication. Multiply each side of the equation by 3.

$y \div 3 = 7$
$y \div 3 \times 3 = 7 \times 3$

STEP 2 Simplify each side.

$y = 21$

STEP 3 Check your work. Replace the variable in the equation with your solution.

$\frac{y}{3} = 7$
$\frac{21}{3} ? 7$
$7 = 7 ✓$

The solution to the equation $\frac{y}{3} = 7$ is $y = 21$.

Practice

Solve each equation.

1. $24 = 4c$

2. $\dfrac{m}{5} = 4$

3. $4n = 20$

4. $\dfrac{k}{8} = 18$

5. $36 = 9f$

6. $9s = 144$

7. $9 = \dfrac{x}{5}$

8. $24 = 3m$

9. $\dfrac{s}{17} = 2$

10. $16v = 80$

11. $\dfrac{g}{12} = 9$

12. $52 = 13k$

13. $7 = \dfrac{y}{8}$

14. $12x = 72$

15. $4 = \dfrac{w}{12}$

16. $8a = 808$

17. $\dfrac{c}{3} = 70$

18. $75 = 25x$

Everyday Problem Solving

Algebra can be used to represent everyday situations.

1. Tasha is twice as old as Barbara. Barbara is b years old. Which expression shows how old Tasha is?

    (a) $b + 2$ **(b)** $b - 2$ **(c)** $2b$ **(d)** $b \div 2$

2. Tasha is twice as old as Barbara. Barbara is b years old. Tasha is 20 years old. Which equation shows this relationship?

    (a) $b + 2 = 20$ **(b)** $b - 2 = 20$ **(c)** $2b = 20$ **(d)** $b \div 2 = 20$

3. How old is Barbara? To find out, solve the equation $2b = 20$.

4. Sam is three times as old as Carol. He is 48. How old is Carol? Write an equation and solve.

5. Vince is half as old as Gail. Vince is 14 years old. How old is Gail? Write an equation and solve.

Problem Solving: Using a One-Step Equation

18·6

Suppose that a car travels 55 miles per hour for 3 hours. How far does the car travel? You can solve an equation to find out.

$$\text{Distance} = \text{rate} \times \text{time}$$
$$d = r \times t$$
$$d = 55 \times 3 = 165 \text{ miles}$$

If you know two of the three values in the equation, you can find the third value.

▶ **EXAMPLE**

Michael drove 78 miles in 2 hours. At what rate (in miles per hour) did he drive?

STEP 1 READ What do you need to find out?
You need to find how fast Michael drove.

STEP 2 PLAN What do you need to do?
Write the equation.
Replace d with 78 miles.
Replace t with 2 hours.
Solve for r.

STEP 3 DO Follow the plan.
Write the equation. Replace.

$$d = r \times t \qquad\qquad 78 = r \times 2$$
$$78 \div 2 = r \times 2 \div 2$$
$$39 = r$$

STEP 4 CHECK Does your answer make sense?
Replace the variable with the solution.

$$r \times t = d$$
$$39 \times 2 = 78 \text{ miles } \checkmark$$

Michael drove at a rate of 39 miles per hour.

Problem Solving

READ the problem. Follow the instructions under PLAN.
DO the plan to solve the problem.

1. Lucia drove for 6 hours at an average speed of
   47 mph. How far did she travel?

   PLAN
   What is the equation?
   What given values can be replaced in the equation?
   Substitute given values in the equation and solve.

2. A plane went 945 miles in 3 hours. What was the plane's
   average rate, in miles per hour?

   PLAN
   What is the equation?
   What given values can be replaced in the equation?
   Substitute given values in the equation and solve.

3. A train went 375 miles at 75 mph. How long did the trip take?

   PLAN
   What is the equation?
   What given values can be replaced in the equation?
   Substitute given values in the equation and solve.

Problem Solving Strategy

Sometimes, distance problems can be solved by making a table.

A train went 248 miles at 62 mph.
How long did the trip take?

Complete the table to find the time.

Time	62 mph × t	Distance
1	62 × 1	62
2	62 × 2	? 124
? 3	?	? 186
? 4	?	? 248

Solving Equations with More Than One Operation

To solve equations involving more than one operation, do the following steps:

1. First undo any addition and subtraction.
2. Then undo any multiplication or division.

▶ **EXAMPLE 1**

Solve for x. $2x + 5 = 15$

STEP 1 First undo the addition with subtraction. Subtract 5 from both sides.

$$2x + 5 - 5 = 15 - 5$$
$$2x = 10$$

STEP 2 Then undo the multiplication with division. Divide both sides by 2.

$$2x \div 2 = 10 \div 2$$
$$x = 5$$

STEP 3 To check, replace the variable in the equation with your answer.

$$2x + 5 = 15$$
$$2 \times 5 + 5 \; ? \; 15$$
$$10 + 5 \; ? \; 15$$
$$15 = 15 \checkmark$$

The solution to the equation $2x + 5 = 15$ is $x = 5$.

▶ **EXAMPLE 2**

Remember:
$$\frac{y}{3} = y \div 3$$

Solve for y. $\frac{y}{3} - 7 = 5$

STEP 1 First undo the subtraction with addition. Add 7 to both sides.

$$\frac{y}{3} - 7 + 7 = 5 + 7$$
$$\frac{y}{3} = 12$$

STEP 2 Then undo the division with multiplication. Multiply both sides by 3.

$$y \div 3 \times 3 = 12 \times 3$$
$$y = 36$$

STEP 3 To check, replace the variable in the equation with your answer.

$$\frac{y}{3} - 7 = 5$$
$$\frac{36}{3} - 7 \; ? \; 5$$
$$12 - 7 \; ? \; 5$$
$$5 = 5 \checkmark$$

The solution to the equation $\frac{y}{3} - 7 = 5$ is $y = 36$.

Practice A

Solve each equation. First undo the addition or the subtraction. Then undo the multiplication.

1. $2a + 8 = 28$

2. $3w - 5 = 16$

3. $3x + 2 = 8$

4. $4m - 6 = 10$

5. $11v + 8 = 19$

6. $4a + 7 = 19$

7. $4n - 1 = 11$

8. $9f + 5 = 32$

9. $5k + 8 = 28$

10. $2r + 6 = 10$

11. $7y + 13 = 48$

12. $8c - 30 = 2$

13. $6x - 15 = 15$

14. $12n + 10 = 58$

Practice B

Solve each equation. First undo the addition or the subtraction. Then undo the division.

15. $\frac{z}{7} - 1 = 3$

16. $\frac{u}{3} + 9 = 18$

17. $\frac{e}{4} + 14 = 16$

18. $\frac{y}{5} - 3 = 2$

19. $\frac{n}{9} - 6 = 0$

20. $\frac{s}{3} - 5 = 3$

21. $\frac{w}{8} + 4 = 8$

22. $\frac{a}{9} + 7 = 16$

23. $\frac{f}{5} - 7 = 2$

24. $\frac{h}{6} + 8 = 11$

25. $\frac{m}{6} + 13 = 19$

26. $\frac{r}{7} - 5 = 1$

27. $\frac{x}{2} - 6 = 9$

28. $\frac{x}{12} + 6 = 10$

Practice C

Solve each equation

29. $\dfrac{x}{8} - 1 = 7$ **30.** $4u + 9 = 37$

31. $\dfrac{t}{2} - 14 = 36$ **32.** $9y - 30 = 150$

33. $\dfrac{p}{7} - 3 = 4$ **34.** $3s - 15 = 75$

35. $6w + 4 = 46$ **36.** $\dfrac{n}{5} + 7 = 18$

37. $8f - 7 = 65$ **38.** $\dfrac{y}{6} + 9 = 17$

Everyday Problem Solving

A Portland taxi had this sign about its fares.

1. How much will it cost to ride 1 mile?

2. How much will it cost to ride 2 miles? What did you do to find out?

3. How much will it cost to ride m miles? Choose an equation. Let c represent the cost.
   (a) $c = \$1.25m$ **(b)** $c = \$1.25m + \$1.75$

4. How much will it cost to ride 5 miles? Use the equation $c = \$1.25m + \$1.75$. Replace m with 5 in the equation and calculate the cost.

5. How many miles can you travel for $20.50? Replace c in your equation with $20.50 and solve the equation for m.

USING YOUR CALCULATOR
Checking Solutions to Equations

You can use your calculator to check the solution to an equation.

John solved the equation $3x + 5 = 20$. He found that the solution was $x = 5$. He now needs to check his answer.

John can check his answer on paper.

$$3x + 5 = 20$$
$$3 \times 5 + 5 \: ? \: 20$$
$$15 + 5 \: ? \: 20$$
$$20 = 20 \: \checkmark$$

> **Calculator Tip**
> On some calculators, the first product may be displayed before the final answer.

Or, John can use a calculator.

PRESS $\boxed{3}\;\boxed{\times}\;\boxed{5}\;\boxed{+}\;\boxed{5}\;\boxed{=}\;\boxed{\qquad\quad 20.}$ $\checkmark$

John's solution of $x = 5$ is correct.

Use your calculator to check each solution.

1. $2x + 7 = 19$; $x = 6$

2. $3y - 13 = 5$; $y = 10$

3. $5n + 6 = 20$; $n = 3$

4. $27 = 5m + 7$; $m = 4$

5. $19 = 4w - 9$; $w = 7$

6. $14x = 98$; $x = 7$

7. $f + 25 = 8$; $f = 17$

8. $26 = 8y - 6$; $y = 4$

9. $5t - 4 = 49$; $t = 9$

10. $29 = 7v + 8$; $v = 3$

11. $15 = 3r + 3$; $r = 6$

12. $26 = 7s - 2$; $s = 4$

Problem Solving: Using a Two-Step Equation

The equation below shows how to find the cost of renting an item by the day.

Cost = rate per day × number of days + renter's fee

$$c \ = \ r \ \times \ d \ + \ f$$

▶ EXAMPLE

Remember:
In a two-step equation, first undo addition or subtraction, then undo multiplication or division.

The cost to rent a tent is $4 per day plus a renter's fee of $10. Shawn paid $22 to rent a tent. For how many days will he rent the tent?

STEP 1   **READ**   **What do you need to find out?**
You need to find the number of days that Shawn will rent the tent.

STEP 2   **PLAN**   **What do you need to do?**
Write the equation.
Replace r with $4.
Replace f with $10.
Replace c with $22.
Solve for d.

STEP 3   **DO**   **Follow the plan.**

Write the equation.   Replace and solve.

$c = r \times d + f$ $22 = 4 \times d + 10$

$22 - 10 = 4 \times d + 10 - 10$

$12 = 4 \times d$

$12 \div 4 = 4 \times d \div 4$

$3 = d$

STEP 4   **CHECK**   **Does your answer make sense?**
Work backward. If Shawn rents the tent for 3 days, how much will it cost?

$3 \times 4 + 10 \ ? \ 22$

$12 + 10 \ ? \ 22$

$22 = 22$ ✓

Shawn will rent the tent for 3 days.

Practice

READ the problem. Follow the instructions under PLAN. DO the plan to solve the problem.

1. The cost to rent a car is $35 per day plus a fee of $20. Mr. Hillwig rented a car for $195. For how many days did he rent the car?

    PLAN
    Write the equation.
    Substitute the given values in the equation and solve.

2. The cost to rent a table is $5 per day plus a fee of $20. The drama club paid a total of $30 to rent a table. For how many days did they rent the table?

    PLAN
    Write the equation.
    Substitute the given values in the equation and solve.

3. The cost to rent a lawn tent is $16 per day plus a fee of $41. Ms. Fare rented a lawn tent for $89. For how many days did she rent the tent?

    PLAN
    Write the equation.
    Substitute given values in the equation and solve.

Problem Solving Strategy

Rental problems sometimes can be solved by making a table.

The cost to rent a tent is $15 per day plus a fee of $38. Al paid $113 to rent a tent. How many days did he rent it?

Number of Days	$15 × d + $38	Total Cost
1	$15 × 1 + $38	$53
2	$15 × 2 + $38	?
3	? a	?
? 4	? b	?
? 5	? c	?

Copy and complete the table to find the number of days.

equation
order of operations
parentheses
simplify
solution
variable

Vocabulary Review

Choose a word from the list to complete each sentence.

1. $6x + 1 = 13$ is an example of a(n) __?__.

2. The __?__ of $3y = 24$ is $y = 8$.

3. Following the __?__ means to do all multiplication and division before addition and subtraction.

4. The __?__ in $5y + 7 = 12$ is y.

5. You can __?__ to find the value of an expression.

6. You can write __?__ around an expression to show that it should be done first.

7. **Writing** Explain in words how to find the solution to $4r + 12 = 24$.

Chapter Quiz

LESSON 18·1

Test Tip
The solution to an equation makes the equation true.

Identifying Solutions
Is the number a solution? Write *Yes* or *No*.

1. $x + 5 = 9$; $x = 10$

2. $3y = 15$; $y = 5$

3. $a \div 6 = 3$; $a = 18$

LESSONS 18·2 and 18·3

Test Tip
Remember to do what is in the parentheses first. Then, follow the order of operations.

Simplifying Expressions
Solve.

4. $3(10 - 4)$

5. $9 - 2 + 4$

6. $24 - 16 \div 8$

7. $5 + 5 \times 2$

8. $(8 + 3) - (6 + 1)$

9. $(18 - 6) \div 2$

LESSONS 18·4 and 18·5

Test Tip
Whatever you do on one side of the equal sign must be done on the other side, too.

Solving Equations with One Operation
Solve.

10. $9 + c = 29$

11. $4m = 16$

12. $n - 5 = 34$

13. $\dfrac{y}{5} = 9$

LESSON 18·6

Test Tip
Read the problem carefully. Decide if the given numbers are the distance, rate, or time.

Problem Solving: Using a One-Step Equation
Solve. Use the formula $d = r \times t$.

14. Jenny drove for 5 hours at 55 mph. How far did she drive?

15. When Lee went on vacation, he flew 1,140 miles in 4 hours. What was the plane's average rate of speed?

LESSON 18·7

Test Tip
Undo the addition or subtraction first, then undo the multiplication or division.

Solving Equations with More Than One Operation
Solve.

16. $4a - 7 = 17$

17. $5n + 23 = 33$

18. $\dfrac{c}{3} - 6 = 3$

19. $\dfrac{x}{6} + 2 = 4$

LESSON 18·8

Test Tip
Look at each number given in the problem. Carefully decide which variable it will replace in the equation.

Problem Solving: Using a Two-Step Equation
Solve each problem. Use $c = r \times d + f$.

20. Van rented a pair of skates for $19. The rental cost $5 plus a daily rate of $2. For how many days did he rent the skates?

Group Activity
With your group, decide on an item to rent. Some examples might be a car, a television set, tools, or sports equipment. Contact local businesses to ask about rental fees. Record the fees. Then calculate the total cost of renting the item for 1 week, 12 days, and 1 month. Is it less expensive to rent on a daily, weekly, or monthly basis? Write a paragraph about your findings.

Unit 5 **Review**

Choose the letter for the correct answer.

Use the graph to answer Questions 1 and 2.

Day	°F
Monday	⁻4
Tuesday	3
Wednesday	18
Thursday	⁻7

1. How much warmer was Tuesday than Monday?

   A. $^+7°$

   B. $^-7°$

   C. $^+1°$

   D. $^+3°$

2. Find the coldest and warmest temperatures in the table. What is the difference between these temperatures?

   A. $^+11°$

   B. $^+15°$

   C. $^+25°$

   D. None of the above.

3. Which expression simplifies to 4?

   A. $(12 - 4) \div 2$

   B. $2 + 10 \div 3$

   C. $4 \div 2 - 2$

   D. $(4 + 8) \div 2$

4. Which equation has a solution of $x = -4$?

   A. $2x = 2$

   B. $4x - 6 = {^+22}$

   C. $4x - 5 = {^+11}$

   D. $x - 4 = 8$

5. Adam drove 165 miles at 55 mph. How long did it take?

   A. 220 minutes

   B. 110 hours

   C. 3 minutes

   D. 3 hours

6. Which is not true?

   A. $^-4 \times {^-5} = {^+20}$

   B. $^-4 + {^-5} = {^+9}$

   C. $^-20 \div {^-4} = {^+5}$

   D. $^+5 - {^-4} = {^+9}$

Critical Thinking

Look at the table above. It was colder on Friday than it was on Thursday. What could have been Friday's temperature? Explain.

CHALLENGE What was the average temperature for the four days. (Add the temperatures. Then divide by 4.)

Extra Practice Chapter 1

▶**Lessons 1·3 and 1·4**   *Pages 6–11*

Rename each number to show the place value of each digit.

1. 403   **2.** 2,067   **3.** 6,050

4. 12,090   **5.** 304,700   **6.** 70,007

Write each number using digits and in words.

7. 5 thousands + 7 tens

8. 7 ten thousands + 2 hundreds + 4 ones

9. 8 millions + 3 thousands + 9 hundreds

▶**Lesson 1·6**   *Pages 12–13*

Compare each pair of numbers from left to right.
Use the symbol >, <, or =.

1. 345   354   **2.** 2,760   990   **3.** 45,302   45,302

4. 72,909   72,911   **5.** 3,749   3,689   **6.** 1,000,843   1,000,782

▶**Lesson 1·8**   *Pages 16–18*

Round each number to the nearest hundred.

1. 567   **2.** 34,181   **3.** 70,338

4. 1,850   **5.** 56,987   **6.** 219,843

Round each number to the nearest ten thousand.

7. 34,931   **8.** 193,722   **9.** 49,604

10. 1,208,306   **11.** 371,672   **12.** 389,682

Extra Practice Chapter 2

Lessons 2·1 and 2·2   *Pages 26–27*

Add. Use the basic addition facts.

1.	4 + 8	**2.**	8 + 1	**3.**	9 + 7	**4.**	5 + 5
5.	6 + 2	**6.**	3 + 7	**7.**	0 + 4	**8.**	7 + 5

9. $4 + 6$ **10.** $5 + 7$ **11.** $6 + 5$

12. $8 + 9$ **13.** $3 + 6$ **14.** $8 + 7$

Lessons 2·3 and 2·4   *Pages 29–31*

Add. Remember to line up the digits by place value.

1. $3 + 8 + 6$ **2.** $7 + 7 + 5$ **3.** $3 + 8 + 4 + 6$

4. $4 + 5 + 1 + 9$ **5.** $9 + 3 + 1 + 4$ **6.** $3 + 8 + 2$

7. $34 + 11$ **8.** $67 + 10$ **9.** $23 + 44$

10. $231 + 600$ **11.** $171 + 515$ **12.** $249 + 440$

Lessons 2·6 and 2·7   *Pages 34–37*

Add. Regroup if needed.

1.	56 + 15	**2.**	345 + 444	**3.**	1,284 + 1,417	**4.**	623 + 455
5.	6,084 + 1,659	**6.**	591 + 2,777	**7.**	2,385 + 9,368	**8.**	2,655 + 8,329

Extra Practice Chapter 3

Lessons 3·1 and 3·2 *Pages 44–45*

Subtract. Use the basic subtraction facts.

1.   9
   − 3

2.   18
   − 9

3.   17
   − 8

4.   15
   − 7

5.   16
   − 9

6.   13
   − 7

7.   11
   − 7

8.   13
   − 5

Lesson 3·3 *Page 47*

Subtract. Remember to line up the digits by place value.

1. $45 - 22$

2. $284 - 251$

3. $598 - 316$

4. $656 - 431$

5. $7,415 - 305$

6. $5,493 - 1,272$

Lessons 3·5 and 3·6 *Pages 50–55*

Subtract. Regroup if needed.

1. $314 - 75$

2. $3,456 - 83$

3. $6,493 - 675$

4. $938 - 93$

5. $8,763 - 988$

6. $7,573 - 5,832$

Lesson 3·7 *Pages 56–57*

Subtract. Regroup if needed.

1.   3,000
  − 2,675

2.   5,005
  − 2,184

3.   7,000
   − 371

4.   10,000
    − 371

5.   80,090
  − 5,500

6.   35,000
  − 23,485

7.   79,000
  − 39,722

8.   70,070
  − 53,091

Extra Practice Chapter 4

Lessons 4·1 and 4·2 *Pages 64–65*

Multiply. Use the basic multiplication facts.

1. 4×6
2. 3×5
3. 8×7
4. 9×8

5. 7×6
6. 4×8
7. 3×8
8. 5×8

9. 9×7
10. 6×6
11. 3×7
12. 8×6

13.
$$\begin{array}{r} 7 \\ \times\ 4 \\ \hline \end{array}$$
14.
$$\begin{array}{r} 4 \\ \times\ 9 \\ \hline \end{array}$$
15.
$$\begin{array}{r} 7 \\ \times\ 5 \\ \hline \end{array}$$
16.
$$\begin{array}{r} 5 \\ \times\ 6 \\ \hline \end{array}$$
17.
$$\begin{array}{r} 9 \\ \times\ 9 \\ \hline \end{array}$$
18.
$$\begin{array}{r} 3 \\ \times\ 9 \\ \hline \end{array}$$

Lesson 4·3 *Pages 66–68*

Multiply. Add partial products, if needed.

1.
$$\begin{array}{r} 23 \\ \times\ 3 \\ \hline \end{array}$$
2.
$$\begin{array}{r} 11 \\ \times\ 8 \\ \hline \end{array}$$
3.
$$\begin{array}{r} 343 \\ \times\ 2 \\ \hline \end{array}$$
4.
$$\begin{array}{r} 73 \\ \times\ 21 \\ \hline \end{array}$$

5.
$$\begin{array}{r} 54 \\ \times\ 12 \\ \hline \end{array}$$
6.
$$\begin{array}{r} 23 \\ \times\ 33 \\ \hline \end{array}$$
7.
$$\begin{array}{r} 32 \\ \times\ 13 \\ \hline \end{array}$$
8.
$$\begin{array}{r} 84 \\ \times\ 21 \\ \hline \end{array}$$

Lesson 4·4 and 4·5 *Pages 70–73*

Multiply. Regroup if needed.

1.
$$\begin{array}{r} 47 \\ \times\ 34 \\ \hline \end{array}$$
2.
$$\begin{array}{r} 86 \\ \times\ 42 \\ \hline \end{array}$$
3.
$$\begin{array}{r} 192 \\ \times\ 75 \\ \hline \end{array}$$
4.
$$\begin{array}{r} 864 \\ \times\ 56 \\ \hline \end{array}$$

5.
$$\begin{array}{r} 712 \\ \times\ 87 \\ \hline \end{array}$$
6.
$$\begin{array}{r} 1,345 \\ \times\ 732 \\ \hline \end{array}$$
7.
$$\begin{array}{r} 40 \\ \times\ 67 \\ \hline \end{array}$$
8.
$$\begin{array}{r} 105 \\ \times\ 93 \\ \hline \end{array}$$

Extra Practice Chapter 5

Lessons 5·1 and 5·2 *Pages 86–87*

Divide. Use the basic division facts.

1. $45 \div 9$ **2.** $32 \div 8$ **3.** $16 \div 4$ **4.** $20 \div 5$

5. $36 \div 4$ **6.** $18 \div 2$ **7.** $56 \div 8$ **8.** $12 \div 3$

9. $5\overline{)15}$ **10.** $8\overline{)48}$ **11.** $3\overline{)24}$ **12.** $7\overline{)35}$

13. Forty-five divided by nine   **14.** Forty-two divided by seven

15. Forty divided by five   **16.** Eighty-one divided by nine

Lesson 5·3 *Pages 88–89*

Divide. If the reminder is 0, do not write it.

1. $25 \div 6$ **2.** $60 \div 7$ **3.** $33 \div 4$ **4.** $78 \div 8$

5. $11 \div 3$ **6.** $35 \div 5$ **7.** $45 \div 7$ **8.** $89 \div 9$

9. $6\overline{)56}$ **10.** $4\overline{)90}$ **11.** $8\overline{)90}$ **12.** $5\overline{)67}$

Lesson 5·4 *Pages 90–91*

1. $3\overline{)696}$ **2.** $5\overline{)340}$ **3.** $2\overline{)678}$ **4.** $4\overline{)548}$

5. $9\overline{)558}$ **6.** $6\overline{)870}$ **7.** $8\overline{)295}$ **8.** $2\overline{)976}$

9. $410 \div 7$ **10.** $492 \div 4$ **11.** $397 \div 3$ **12.** $709 \div 6$

13. $357 \div 8$ **14.** $381 \div 5$ **15.** $333 \div 9$ **16.** $537 \div 7$

Extra Practice Chapter 5

Lessons 5·1 to 5·8   *Pages 86–99*

Find each quotient.

1. $25 \overline{)325}$ **2.** $32 \overline{)897}$ **3.** $7 \overline{)1,473}$ **4.** $16 \overline{)1,127}$

5. $11 \overline{)957}$ **6.** $27 \overline{)2,270}$ **7.** $18 \overline{)414}$ **8.** $8 \overline{)777}$

9. $9 \overline{)972}$ **10.** $6 \overline{)4,845}$ **11.** $43 \overline{)2,455}$ **12.** $12 \overline{)1,089}$

13. $869 \div 20$ **14.** $732 \div 38$ **15.** $2,421 \div 3$ **16.** $502 \div 29$

17. $2,632 \div 56$ **18.** $1,795 \div 5$ **19.** $1,165 \div 36$ **20.** $7,932 \div 13$

Lessons 5·6 and 5·9   *Pages 94–95 and 100–101*

Solve each problem. Look for clue words whenever possible.

1. Exactly 210 students signed up for soccer. Each team has 14 players. How many teams can be formed?

2. The soccer coach ordered 4 pairs of socks, 2 jerseys, 1 sweatshirt, and 3 pairs of shorts for each team member. If each team has 14 players, how many pairs of socks are ordered for each team?

3. Last season, each soccer team practiced a total of 180 hours. If practice was held 2 hours each day, how many days did the team practice?

4. Each soccer team played 3 games in September, 6 games in October, and 5 games in November. Each game lasted 2 hours. How many total hours of game time did each team have?

Extra Practice Chapter 6

▶Lessons 6·1 to 6·3 *Pages 106–112*

Use a divisibility test to answer each question.

1. Is 5,632,380 divisible by 10?   **2.** Is 5,943 divisible by 6?

3. Is 7,236 divisible by 4?   **4.** Is 6,109 divisible by 9?

▶Lesson 6·4 *Pages 114–115*

Find the greatest common factor of each pair of numbers.

1. 8   28   **2.** 10   15   **3.** 18   24   **4.** 12   15

5. 18   45   **6.** 12   20   **7.** 21   28   **8.** 18   30

▶Lesson 6·5 *Pages 116–117*

Find the least common multiple of each pair of numbers.

1. 6   12   **2.** 3   4   **3.** 6   8   **4.** 25   50

5. 9   15   **6.** 8   12   **7.** 5   6   **8.** 15   20

▶Lesson 6·6 *Page 118*

Write the prime factorization of each number.

1. 12   **2.** 8   **3.** 10   **4.** 15   **5.** 20

▶Lessons 6·7 and 6·8 *Pages 119–120*

Find the value of each expression.

1. 6^2 **2.** 2^3 **3.** 1^9 **4.** $\sqrt{36}$ **5.** $\sqrt{25}$ **6.** $\sqrt{49}$

Extra Practice Chapter 7

▶ **Lesson 7·3** *Pages 132–133*

Write each fraction in lowest terms.

1. $\frac{16}{40}$ 2. $\frac{44}{88}$ 3. $\frac{45}{81}$ 4. $\frac{15}{20}$ 5. $\frac{8}{100}$

6. $\frac{75}{100}$ 7. $\frac{70}{90}$ 8. $\frac{24}{32}$ 9. $\frac{49}{70}$ 10. $\frac{27}{36}$

11. $\frac{9}{99}$ 12. $\frac{30}{35}$ 13. $\frac{28}{56}$ 14. $\frac{16}{40}$ 15. $\frac{35}{100}$

▶ **Lesson 7·4** *Pages 134–135*

Write each fraction in higher terms. Use the denominator shown.

1. $\frac{2}{3} = \frac{?}{6}$ 2. $\frac{13}{14} = \frac{?}{28}$ 3. $\frac{11}{20} = \frac{?}{40}$ 4. $\frac{1}{4} = \frac{?}{28}$

5. $\frac{4}{10} = \frac{?}{50}$ 6. $\frac{3}{5} = \frac{?}{20}$ 7. $\frac{7}{15} = \frac{?}{45}$ 8. $\frac{5}{6} = \frac{?}{18}$

▶ **Lesson 7·5** *Pages 136–137*

Change each pair of fractions to like fractions.

1. $\frac{3}{4}$ $\frac{2}{3}$ 2. $\frac{2}{3}$ $\frac{5}{12}$ 3. $\frac{1}{2}$ $\frac{3}{8}$ 4. $\frac{1}{3}$ $\frac{1}{6}$

5. $\frac{1}{2}$ $\frac{2}{5}$ 6. $\frac{3}{4}$ $\frac{1}{8}$ 7. $\frac{5}{6}$ $\frac{7}{12}$ 8. $\frac{1}{2}$ $\frac{2}{3}$

▶ **Lesson 7·9** *Page 144*

Change each mixed number to an improper fraction.

1. $3\frac{2}{3}$ 2. $2\frac{5}{6}$ 3. $5\frac{1}{2}$ 4. $8\frac{3}{4}$

Extra Practice Chapter 8

► **Lesson 8·1**   *Pages 154–155*

Multiply.

1. $\frac{1}{3} \times \frac{1}{4}$

2. $\frac{1}{2} \times \frac{1}{9}$

3. $\frac{2}{5} \times \frac{3}{7}$

4. $\frac{1}{6} \times \frac{7}{9}$

5. $\frac{4}{5} \times \frac{1}{5}$

6. $\frac{1}{8} \times \frac{5}{6}$

► **Lesson 8·2**   *Pages 156–157*

Multiply. Cancel, if possible.

1. $\frac{3}{8} \times \frac{8}{9}$

2. $\frac{4}{9} \times \frac{9}{16}$

3. $\frac{3}{5} \times \frac{10}{13}$

4. $\frac{11}{12} \times \frac{2}{3}$

5. $\frac{3}{4} \times \frac{8}{9}$

6. $\frac{5}{9} \times \frac{3}{10}$

► **Lessons 8·3 and 8·4**   *Pages 158 and 160–161*

Multiply. Remember to change whole and mixed numbers to improper fractions.

1. $\frac{3}{4} \times 16$

2. $20 \times \frac{4}{5}$

3. $\frac{5}{9} \times 27$

4. $9 \times 2\frac{2}{3}$

5. $1\frac{3}{7} \times 7$

6. $8 \times 3\frac{5}{8}$

7. $\frac{5}{6} \times 1\frac{1}{2}$

8. $2\frac{4}{9} \times 18$

9. $2\frac{2}{3} \times \frac{9}{10}$

10. $21 \times 2\frac{3}{7}$

11. $\frac{5}{6} \times 2\frac{3}{10}$

12. $15 \times 4\frac{2}{3}$

13. $4\frac{5}{6} \times 1\frac{1}{2}$

14. $2\frac{3}{8} \times 1\frac{2}{19}$

15. $3\frac{3}{4} \times 2\frac{4}{5}$

Extra Practice Chapter 8

▶**Lesson 8·5** *Pages 162–163*

Divide. Remember to invert the second fraction and then multiply.

1. $\frac{1}{2} \div \frac{2}{3}$

2. $\frac{3}{4} \div \frac{1}{5}$

3. $\frac{2}{3} \div \frac{1}{4}$

4. $\frac{8}{9} \div \frac{1}{4}$

5. $\frac{3}{7} \div \frac{1}{4}$

6. $\frac{2}{5} \div \frac{3}{7}$

7. $\frac{2}{9} \div \frac{3}{4}$

8. $\frac{3}{8} \div \frac{1}{9}$

9. $\frac{1}{6} \div \frac{1}{5}$

10. $\frac{4}{5} \div \frac{1}{5}$

11. $\frac{2}{3} \div \frac{1}{6}$

12. $\frac{5}{9} \div \frac{2}{3}$

13. $\frac{3}{4} \div \frac{3}{8}$

14. $\frac{11}{12} \div \frac{1}{6}$

15. $\frac{3}{14} \div \frac{2}{7}$

▶**Lessons 8·6, 8·8, and 8·9** *Pages 164 and 168–171*

Divide. Remember to cancel, if possible.

1. $\frac{3}{5} \div 5$

2. $\frac{4}{9} \div 8$

3. $\frac{2}{3} \div 4$

4. $27 \div \frac{3}{4}$

5. $36 \div \frac{4}{9}$

6. $42 \div \frac{6}{7}$

7. $\frac{1}{2} \div 2\frac{1}{2}$

8. $\frac{5}{6} \div 1\frac{1}{2}$

9. $\frac{9}{10} \div 2\frac{1}{4}$

10. $4\frac{3}{4} \div \frac{3}{8}$

11. $3\frac{6}{7} \div \frac{3}{5}$

12. $5\frac{1}{3} \div \frac{3}{4}$

13. $5\frac{1}{2} \div 1\frac{2}{3}$

14. $7\frac{1}{4} \div 2\frac{3}{4}$

15. $6\frac{3}{5} \div \frac{3}{10}$

16. $2\frac{5}{6} \div 1\frac{1}{2}$

17. $3\frac{1}{8} \div 1\frac{1}{4}$

18. $4\frac{3}{5} \div 1\frac{1}{10}$

Extra Practice Chapter 9

► **Lesson 9·1** *Pages 178–179*

Add or subtract. Remember to write each answer in lowest terms.

1. $\dfrac{1}{9}$
    $+\dfrac{7}{9}$

2. $\dfrac{5}{6}$
    $+\dfrac{5}{6}$

3. $\dfrac{9}{10}$
    $+\dfrac{7}{10}$

4. $\dfrac{7}{8}$
    $-\dfrac{3}{8}$

5. $\dfrac{4}{5}$
    $+\dfrac{3}{5}$

6. $\dfrac{9}{14} - \dfrac{3}{14}$

7. $\dfrac{7}{12} - \dfrac{5}{12}$

8. $\dfrac{8}{9} - \dfrac{5}{9}$

► **Lesson 9·2** *Pages 180–181*

Add. Remember to write each answer in lowest terms.

1. $2\dfrac{1}{5}$
    $+\ 1\dfrac{2}{5}$

2. $3\dfrac{3}{4}$
    $+\ 4\dfrac{1}{4}$

3. $5\dfrac{3}{7}$
    $+\ 2\dfrac{1}{7}$

4. $4\dfrac{5}{6}$
    $+\ 2\dfrac{3}{6}$

5. $8\dfrac{5}{8}$
    $+\ 1\dfrac{1}{8}$

6. $3\dfrac{2}{3} + 2\dfrac{2}{3}$

7. $7\dfrac{5}{7} + 3\dfrac{2}{7}$

8. $6\dfrac{1}{9} + 4\dfrac{5}{9}$

► **Lesson 9·3** *Pages 182–183*

Subtract. Remember to regroup, if needed.

1. $4\dfrac{4}{5}$
    $-\ 3\dfrac{1}{5}$

2. $7\dfrac{5}{8}$
    $-\ 3\dfrac{1}{8}$

3. $7\dfrac{8}{9}$
    $-\ 4\dfrac{5}{9}$

4. $11\dfrac{1}{3}$
    $-\ 5\dfrac{2}{3}$

5. $10\dfrac{2}{5}$
    $-\ 6\dfrac{4}{5}$

6. $5\dfrac{5}{6} - 1\dfrac{2}{6}$

7. $7\dfrac{3}{10} - 2\dfrac{7}{10}$

8. $3\dfrac{3}{8} - 2\dfrac{7}{8}$

Extra Practice Chapter 9

▶ **Lesson 9·4** *Pages 184–185*

Subtract. Remember to regroup the whole number.

1. $5 - \dfrac{3}{4}$

2. $7 - 3\dfrac{1}{4}$

3. $8 - 2\dfrac{4}{6}$

4. $9 - 3\dfrac{2}{3}$

5. $8 - 3\dfrac{3}{10}$

6. $6 - 2\dfrac{1}{7}$

7. $11 - 5\dfrac{4}{9}$

8. $12 - 10\dfrac{5}{7}$

▶ **Lesson 9·5** *Page 186*

Add. Remember to rename as like fractions.

1. $\dfrac{3}{14} + \dfrac{1}{2}$

2. $\dfrac{5}{8} + \dfrac{3}{4}$

3. $\dfrac{2}{3} + \dfrac{8}{9}$

4. $\dfrac{7}{10} + \dfrac{1}{5}$

5. $\dfrac{1}{2} + \dfrac{2}{3}$

6. $\dfrac{1}{3} + \dfrac{5}{12}$

7. $\dfrac{3}{4} + \dfrac{2}{3}$

8. $\dfrac{5}{6} + \dfrac{5}{12}$

▶ **Lesson 9·6** *Page 188*

Subtract. Remember to rename as like fractions.

1. $\dfrac{7}{8} - \dfrac{1}{4}$

2. $\dfrac{5}{6} - \dfrac{2}{3}$

3. $\dfrac{3}{4} - \dfrac{5}{12}$

4. $\dfrac{9}{14} - \dfrac{1}{2}$

5. $\dfrac{2}{3} - \dfrac{2}{9}$

6. $\dfrac{11}{12} - \dfrac{1}{4}$

7. $\dfrac{3}{5} - \dfrac{1}{10}$

8. $\dfrac{5}{8} - \dfrac{1}{3}$

Extra Practice Chapter 9

Lesson 9·7   *Pages 190–191*

Add. Remember to rename as like mixed numbers.

1. $3\frac{1}{2}$
    $+ 9\frac{2}{3}$

2. $7\frac{1}{3}$
    $+ 9\frac{2}{5}$

3. $6\frac{2}{5}$
    $+ 1\frac{3}{10}$

4. $5\frac{3}{4}$
    $+ 3\frac{5}{8}$

5. $6\frac{1}{6}$
    $+ 6\frac{3}{5}$

6. $8\frac{5}{6}$
    $+ 3\frac{2}{9}$

7. $8\frac{1}{10}$
    $+ \ 5\frac{2}{5}$

8. $2\frac{3}{8}$
    $+ 1\frac{1}{4}$

9. $2\frac{3}{7} + 3\frac{1}{3}$

10. $7\frac{3}{11} + 2\frac{1}{2}$

11. $1\frac{1}{4} + 8\frac{1}{3}$

12. $9\frac{2}{5} + 5\frac{3}{4}$

Lesson 9·8   *Pages 192–193*

**Subtract. Remember to rename as like mixed numbers.
Regroup if needed.**

1. $5\frac{3}{4}$
    $- 1\frac{1}{8}$

2. $7\frac{1}{2}$
    $- 4\frac{2}{5}$

3. $3\frac{4}{5}$
    $- 1\frac{3}{10}$

4. $6\frac{2}{3}$
    $- 2\frac{7}{8}$

5. $3\frac{8}{9}$
    $- 1\frac{2}{3}$

6. $\frac{19}{10}$
    $- \ \frac{2}{5}$

7. $6\frac{1}{3}$
    $- 2\frac{1}{10}$

8. $5\frac{7}{8}$
    $- 2\frac{1}{6}$

9. $3\frac{1}{7} - 1\frac{1}{4}$

10. $5\frac{3}{5} - 5\frac{1}{3}$

Extra Practice Chapter 9

Lessons 9·1 to 9·8   *Pages 178–193*

Add or subtract.

1.
$$\frac{4}{5}$$
$$+ 3\frac{1}{5}$$

2.
$$6\frac{3}{5}$$
$$- 1\frac{3}{20}$$

3.
$$8\frac{3}{4}$$
$$- 2\frac{2}{3}$$

4.
$$8$$
$$+ 5\frac{6}{7}$$

5. $9 - 5\frac{5}{9}$

6. $12\frac{2}{3} + 6\frac{5}{6}$

7. $5\frac{3}{8} - 1\frac{2}{3}$

8. $7\frac{4}{9} + 3\frac{5}{9}$

9. $\frac{3}{10} + \frac{6}{7}$

10. $5\frac{2}{3} - 2\frac{4}{6}$

Lesson 9·9   *Pages 194–195*

Solve. Work on one part at a time.

1. Jamie practiced piano for $3\frac{1}{2}$ hours on Monday and $2\frac{3}{4}$ hours on Tuesday. On Wednesday, she practiced the drums for 5 hours. How much longer did she practice piano than drums?

2. Reid decided to run 26 miles over three days. He ran $9\frac{7}{8}$ miles on Monday and $8\frac{1}{2}$ miles on Tuesday. How many miles should he run on Wednesday to complete the 26 miles?

3. Stock for a carpet company closed at $35 per share. The next day, it rose $1\frac{1}{2}$. The day after that, it dropped $2\frac{1}{4}$. What is the new closing price?

4. Marna, Sam, and Julie are weight training. Marna lost $5\frac{1}{2}$ pounds. Sam lost double Marna's amount. Julie lost $1\frac{3}{4}$ pounds more than Sam. How many pounds did Julie lose?

5. Mrs. Henderson had 12 pounds of peanuts. She divided them into three equal bags. Then she gave away two bags. From the bag that was left, she ate $\frac{1}{2}$ pound of peanuts. How many pounds of peanuts does she have left?

428   Extra Practice

Extra Practice Chapter 10

Lesson 10·2 *Pages 203–204*

Write each decimal in words.

1. 39.7   **2.** .046   **3.** 5.14   **4.** .799

5. 160.52   **6.** 800   **7.** .008   **8.** 4.9

Write each number as a decimal.

9. thirty-five thousandths   **10.** two hundred and seven tenths

11. eight and five hundredths   **12.** sixty-eight and seventeen thousandths

Lesson 10·3 *Pages 205–206*

Compare each pair of numbers. Use <, >, or =.

1. 4.2   4.02   **2.** 5.1   5.11   **3.** 2.35   2.36

4. 6.899   6.9   **5.** 136.8   13.68   **6.** .027   .127

7. .99   1   **8.** 1.1   1.059   **9.** 9.041   10.014

Lesson 10·4 *Page 207*

Write the decimals in order from largest to smallest.

1. 4.063   4.31   4.03   **2.** .148   .014   .483

3. .8   .081   .81   **4.** 3.144   3.15   3.158

5. 7.81   7.18   7.03   **6.** 41.28   41.6   40.31

Extra Practice Chapter 10

▶**Lesson 10·5** *Pages 208–209*

Add.

1.   1.3
     + 4.5

2.   5.7
     + 3.8

3. $12.45
     +   8.29

4.   2.067
     + .200

5. 34.9 + 2.8

6. 8 + .6

7. $23.08 + $3.90

8. 15.762 + 8.04

9. $24.99 + $18.49

10. 10.4 + .08 + 1.349

▶**Lesson 10·6** *Pages 210–211*

Subtract.

1.   4.8
     − 1.5

2.   14.1
     − 5.7

3. $10.00
     −   4.99

4.   80.60
     − 6.03

5. 13.78 − 10.45

6. 15 − 3.22

7. $23.75 − $23.58

8. 4.088 − .726

9. 2.9 − 1.045

10. .5 − .025

▶**Lesson 10·7** *Pages 212–213*

Multiply.

1.   .4
     × .7

2.   .2
     × .3

3.   4.5
     × 1.5

4.   13.25
     × .04

5. 3.5 × .8

6. $23.00 × 1.05

7. 23.05 × 2.9

8. 34.89 × .1

9. 3.024 × 28

10. .005 × 12.8

Extra Practice Chapter 10

Lesson 10·9   *Pages 216–217*

Divide.

1. $2\overline{).24}$ 2. $6\overline{).54}$ 3. $9\overline{).027}$ 4. $15\overline{)30.45}$

5. $.81 \div 6$ 6. $.75 \div 15$ 7. $12.96 \div 40$

8. $4.3 \div 8$ 9. $.008 \div 25$ 10. $18.32 \div 50$

Lesson 10·10   *Pages 218–219*

Divide.

1. $.06\overline{).48}$ 2. $3.8\overline{)2.128}$ 3. $.05\overline{)21}$ 4. $.3\overline{)91.44}$

5. $28.45 \div .15$ 6. $12.09 \div .06$ 7. $4.8 \div .16$

8. $6.75 \div .3$ 9. $15 \div .02$ 10. $34.3 \div 1.225$

Lesson 10·12   *Pages 222–223*

Use the chart to solve each problem.

1. Find the price of each item with tax.

2. What is the price with tax of 15 mechanical pencils?

3. A math club has 20 members. They need 10 rulers, 20 pencils, and 5 calculators. The club will split the total cost equally among themselves. How much will each member pay, including tax?

School Supplies		
Item	Price	Tax
ruler	$ 1.29	$.07
mechanical pencil	.99	.05
calculator	14.00	.70

Extra Practice Chapter 10

▶ Mixed Practice

Calculate.

1. $\begin{array}{r} 5.27 \\ + 1.19 \\ \hline \end{array}$

2. $\begin{array}{r} 4.96 \\ - 4.87 \\ \hline \end{array}$

3. $\begin{array}{r} 35.8 \\ \times\ .5 \\ \hline \end{array}$

4. $4.8\overline{)96}$

5. $\begin{array}{r} 7.92 \\ \times 1.06 \\ \hline \end{array}$

6. $\begin{array}{r} 32.97 \\ -\quad .055 \\ \hline \end{array}$

7. $1.9\overline{)15.58}$

8. $\begin{array}{r} 7.904 \\ + 3.176 \\ \hline \end{array}$

9. $21 - .409$

10. $.16 - .07$

11. $1.007 + .08 + 7$

12. $825 \div .25$

13. 8.63×4.9

14. $1.4 \div 6$

15. $\$39.58 + \$11.79$

16. $\$155.40 \div 12$

17. $\$18.98 \times 100$

▶ Lesson 10·13 *Page 224*

Rename each decimal as a fraction. Reduce if possible.

1. .25

2. .04

3. .8

4. .125

5. .4

6. .5

7. .75

8. .6

9. .625

10. .05

▶ Lesson 10·14 *Page 225*

Rename each fraction as a decimal.

1. $\frac{3}{4}$

2. $\frac{1}{2}$

3. $\frac{3}{10}$

4. $\frac{1}{8}$

5. $\frac{2}{3}$

6. $\frac{7}{8}$

7. $\frac{3}{5}$

8. $\frac{1}{4}$

9. $\frac{2}{5}$

10. $\frac{7}{10}$

Extra Practice Chapter 11

Lesson 11·1 *Page 232*

Write the percent for each description.

   1. 12 parts out of 100 are shaded. What percent is shaded?

   2. If 3 parts out of 100 are red, what percent is red?

   3. Each whole has 100 equal parts. 140 parts are shaded. What percent is shaded?

   4. What percent is shaded if 35 out of 100 parts are shaded?

Lesson 11·2 *Page 233*

Change each percent to a decimal.

   1. 43%   **2.** 28%   **3.** 2%   **4.** $2\frac{1}{2}\%$

   5. $8\frac{1}{2}\%$ **6.** 8.5%   **7.** $14\frac{1}{2}\%$ **8.** 2.5%

   9. 118%   **10.** 255%   **11.** 6%   **12.** 145%

Lesson 11·3 *Pages 234–235*

Find the part in each problem.

   1. 50% of 66 is ■   **2.** 25% of 36 is ■   **3.** 10% of 70 is ■

   4. 19% of 100 is ■   **5.** 20% of 450 is ■   **6.** 125% of 32 is ■

   7. What is 16% of 30?   **8.** What is 30% of 88?

   9. What is 150% of 40?   **10.** What is 200% of 85?

Extra Practice Chapter 11

Lesson 11·4 *Pages 236–237*

Solve each problem about sales tax.

1. The sales tax in New Jersey is 6%. Your purchases total $17.50. What is the amount of tax?

2. The sales tax in the city is 11%. Your purchase is $58. What is the amount of sales tax?

3. An ice cream cone costs $1.60. If the sales tax is 5%, what is the total cost of the ice cream cone?

4. The sales tax on home furnishings is 7%. How much tax will be paid on a purchase of $880?

5. A new kitchen table costs $148. The sales tax is 5%. What is the total cost of the table?

Lesson 11·5 *Pages 238–239*

Solve each problem about discounts.

1. The television costs $450. It is on sale at 30% off. What is the discount?

2. A new washing machine, originally $360, is on sale at 25% off. What is the discount?

3. All tools are on sale at 10% off. At the original prices, your tool purchase totals $48. What is your sale price?

4. The radio is on sale at 25% off. The original price was $20. What is the sale price?

5. The original cost of a cassette player is $235. The salesperson offers you a 15% discount. How much will you save?

Extra Practice Chapter 11

▶**Lesson 11·6** *Pages 240–241*

Solve each problem about commissions.

1. A new car costs $20,000. If the salesperson's commission is 3%, what is the amount of the commission?

2. Sally receives 7% commission on greeting card sales. If she sells $5,600 worth of cards, what is the amount of her commission?

3. At your new job, the base salary is $200 per week. In addition, the commission on sales is 4%. If you sell $4,000 in sales for the week, what is your gross salary?

4. The real estate commission on the property is 5%. If the property sells for $110,000, what is the amount of the commission?

▶**Lesson 11·7** *Page 243*

Change each decimal to a percent.

1. .23   2. .08   3. .17   4. .6

5. 1.12   6. 2.53   7. .234   8. 2.7

▶**Lesson 11·8** *Page 244*

Change each fraction to a percent.

1. $\frac{11}{100}$ 2. $\frac{2}{5}$ 3. $\frac{3}{20}$ 4. $\frac{4}{25}$

5. $\frac{7}{10}$ 6. $\frac{1}{8}$ 7. $\frac{3}{50}$ 8. $\frac{2}{5}$

Extra Practice Chapter 11

Lesson 11·9 *Pages 247–248*

Find the percent to solve each problem.

1. What percent of 60 is 30?

2. What percent of 104 is 26?

3. What percent of 100 is 450?

4. What percent of 560 is 280?

5. 16 is what percent of 80?

6. 196 is what percent of 560?

7. 200 is what percent of 50?

8. 90 is what percent of 30?

Lesson 11·10 *Pages 248–249*

Find the percent increase or decrease to solve each problem.

1. David's autographed baseball is worth $100 now. Last year, it was worth $80. What is the percent increase?

2. Jan's stocks are worth $2,160 now. Last month, they were worth $2,400. What is the percent decrease?

3. A car worth $10,000 last year is now worth $7,000. What is the percent decrease?

4. Your $2,000 art collection is now worth $5,000. What is the percent increase?

Lesson 11·11 *Pages 250–251*

Find the whole to solve each problem.

1. 20 is 10% of what number?

2. 23 is 50% of what number?

3. 11 is 25% of what number?

4. 60 is 75% of what number?

5. 80% of what number is 100?

6. 45% of what number is 90?

Extra Practice Chapter 11

▶ **Lesson 11·12**   *Pages 252–253*

Find the original price to solve each problem.

1. Leo's book costs $20. All books are on sale at 20% off. What was the original price of the book?

2. A media rack is on sale for $19. This is 50% off the original price. What was the original price?

3. An art collection has increased in value by 10%. It is now worth $2,200. What was its original value?

4. Dues this year are $30. This is a 25% increase from last year. What were last year's dues?

▶ **Lesson 11·13**   *Pages 254–255*

Solve each problem. Be careful: all three types of percent problems are used.

1. Nancy's workout is 90 minutes long. She spends 30% of her time swimming. How many minutes does she spend swimming?

2. Clark spends 25% of his workout time on the exercise bike. If he spends 30 minutes on the bike, how long is his workout?

3. Marianne spends 15 minutes of her 75-minute workout doing step aerobics. What percent of her workout is spent doing step aerobics?

4. Thomas plays tennis 3 hours every week. This is 50% of his weekly exercise. How long is his weekly exercise?

5. Caitlin jogs 25 miles each month. She jogs with a partner for 10 of those miles. What percent of her jogging is with a partner?

Extra Practice Chapter 12

▶ Lesson 12·1 *Pages 260–261*

Write a ratio for each problem using fractions or ratio signs.

1. blue squares to all squares ▢ ▢ ▢ ▢ ▢ ▢ ▢ ▢

2. In a class of 29 students, 13 students are male. What is the ratio of all students to male students?

3. Of the 32 total movies in John's collection, 13 are cartoons, 5 are action, and 14 are comedies. What is the ratio of action movies to the total number of movies?

▶ Lesson 12·3 *Page 264*

Find the missing number in each proportion.

1. $\frac{2}{?} = \frac{8}{12}$
2. $\frac{3}{7} = \frac{?}{28}$
3. $\frac{4}{?} = \frac{1}{4}$
4. $\frac{?}{10} = \frac{2}{5}$

5. $\frac{8}{56} = \frac{1}{?}$
6. $\frac{3}{?} = \frac{18}{24}$
7. $\frac{8}{?} = \frac{24}{36}$
8. $\frac{5}{7} = \frac{15}{?}$

▶ Lesson 12·4 to 12·6 *Pages 266–268 and 270–271*

Use a proportion to solve each problem.

1. Charlotte bought 3 pizzas for $12. How many pizzas can she buy for $36?

2. Suppose that 2 buses can carry 44 people. How many buses are needed if there are 132 people?

3. The scale on a map is 1 inch = 10 miles. The distance on the map is 5 inches. How many miles does this represent?

4. Zachary can buy 7 plates for $14. How much will he pay for 21 plates?

Extra Practice Chapter 13

► Lesson 13·1 *Pages 278–279*

Make a pictograph of the information in the table.

Ice Cream Bars Sold	
Day	Number Sold
Monday	45
Tuesday	35
Wednesday	30
Thursday	50
Friday	85
Saturday	100
Sunday	90

► Lessons 13·2 and 13·3 *Pages 280–283*

Make a bar graph of the information in each table.

1.

Area of Metro Counties	
County	Square Miles
Washington	3,000
Ramsey	6,500
Hennepin	9,000
Cooke	7,500
Beaver	2,000

2.

Carnival Rides		
Ride	Children	Adults
Roller Coaster	32	58
Ferris Wheel	45	63
Bumper Cars	68	25

Extra Practice Chapter 13

▶Lessons 13·4 and 13·5   *Pages 284–287*

Make a line graph of the information in each table.

1.

Number of Businesses in Springfield	
Year	Number
1994	250
1995	300
1996	375
1997	400
1998	475

2.

Rainfall in Scottsdale		
Season	Predicted Number of Inches	Actual Number of Inches
Spring	8	11
Summer	6	3
Fall	4	5
Winter	6	3

▶Lesson 13·6   *Pages 288–289*

Use the graphs to answer questions 1 and 2.

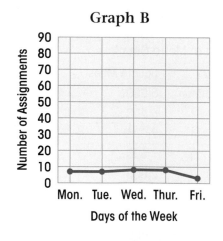

1. The teachers want to send home a graph showing the parents that they do not give too much homework in one week. Which graph should they use and why?

2. The students want to send home a graph showing the parents that the teachers do send home a lot of homework in one week. Which graph should they use and why?

Extra Practice Chapter 13

▶**Lesson 13·7** *Page 290*

Use the information in the circle graph to answer each question.

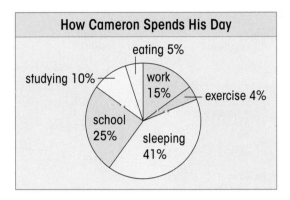

How Cameron Spends His Day

eating 5%
studying 10%
work 15%
exercise 4%
school 25%
sleeping 41%

1. How does Cameron spend most of his day?

2. What percent of his day is spent in school and studying?

3. How many hours a day does Cameron work?

4. How many hours does Cameron sleep each night?

▶**Lesson 13·8** *Pages 292–293*

Find the mean of each set of numbers.

1. 24, 15, 18, 27

2. 45, 93, 100, 38, 20, 88

3. 11, 13, 15, 17, 19

4. 8, 35, 40, 2, 16, 25

▶**Lesson 13·9** *Pages 294–295*

Find the median and the mode of each set of numbers.

1. 27, 89, 65, 101, 48, 89, 32

2. 7, 16, 3, 95, 21, 12

3. 5, 5, 4, 3, 1, 7, 7, 3, 2, 9, 5, 1

4. 31, 72, 89, 31, 38, 21, 89, 72

Extra Practice Chapter 13

▶Lesson 13·10 *Pages 296–297*

Use the histogram to answer each question.

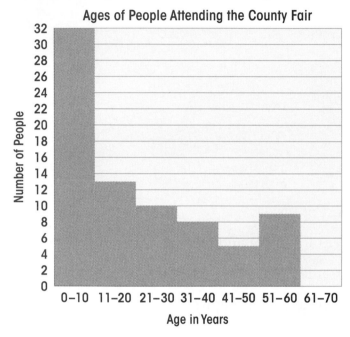

Ages of People Attending the County Fair

1. Most people attending the fair were in what age group?

2. How many people attending the fair were between 21 and 30 years old?

3. How many people attending the fair were 30 years old or less?

4. How many people attending the fair were 41 years old or older?

▶Lesson 13·11 *Page 298*

A bag contains 7 white marbles, 15 green marbles, 6 red
marbles, 2 yellow marbles, and 10 blue marbles. You choose
one marble without looking. Find the probability of each event.

1. choosing a red marble
2. choosing a white marble

3. choosing a green marble
4. choosing a blue or white marble

Extra Practice Chapter 14

▶ **Lesson 14·1** *Pages 304–305*

Change each measurement. First, decide whether to multiply or divide.

1. 36 inches = ■ feet

2. 3 miles = ■ feet

3. 9 yards = ■ feet

4. 16 feet = ■ yards

5. 5 yards = ■ inches

6. $\frac{1}{3}$ foot = ■ inches

7. 108 inches = ■ yards

8. 42 inches = ■ feet

9. 1.5 yards = ■ inches

10. $\frac{1}{3}$ yard = ■ inches

11. 1.1 miles = ■ feet

12. $\frac{7}{8}$ mile = ■ feet

▶ **Lesson 14·2** *Pages 306–307*

Change each measurement. First, decide whether to multiply or divide.

1. 3 pounds = ■ ounces

2. 3 tons = ■ pounds

3. 64 ounces = ■ pounds

4. 2.7 tons = ■ pounds

5. 2.5 pounds = ■ ounces

6. 8 ounces = ■ pound

7. 1,000 pounds = ■ ton

8. $\frac{1}{8}$ pound = ■ ounces

9. 200 ounces = ■ pounds

10. 5.2 pounds = ■ ounces

11. $1\frac{1}{8}$ pounds = ■ ounces

12. $\frac{1}{2}$ ton = ■ pounds

Extra Practice Chapter 14

▶ **Lesson 14·3**   *Pages 308–309*

Change each measurement. First, decide whether to multiply
or divide.

1. 6 quarts = ■ pints

2. 5 gallons = ■ quarts

3. 70 pints = ■ quarts

4. 128 fluid ounces = ■ quarts

5. 6 pints = ■ fluid ounces

6. 50 pints = ■ quarts

7. 44 quarts = ■ gallons

8. 80 fluid ounces = ■ pints

9. 2.5 gallons = ■ quarts

10. 1.5 quarts = ■ pints

11. 8 pints = ■ gallons

12. 10 quarts = ■ gallons

▶ **Lesson 14·4**   *Page 310*

Change each measurement. First, decide whether to multiply
or divide.

1. 5 hours = ■ minutes

2. 240 hours = ■ days

3. 540 minutes = ■ hours

4. 9 years = ■ months

5. 90 seconds = ■ minutes

6. 3 years = ■ weeks

7. 63 days = ■ weeks

8. 364 weeks = ■ years

9. 390 minutes = ■ hours

10. 12.5 years = ■ months

11. 9.5 days = ■ hours

12. 102 months = ■ years

Extra Practice Chapter 14

▶ Lesson 14·6   *Pages 314–315*

Find the elapsed time.

1. 5:15 P.M. to 7:40 P.M.

2. 9:36 A.M. to 11:10 A.M.

3. 3:23 A.M. to 9:45 A.M.

4. 4:52 P.M. to 1:13 A.M.

5. 7:32 P.M. to 12:00 midnight

6. 6:10 A.M. to 10:04 A.M.

7. 8:39 P.M. to 3:13 A.M.

8. 5:21 A.M. to 8:48 A.M

9. 4:29 P.M. to 11:11 P.M.

10. 3:15 A.M. to 2:19 P.M.

11. 1:46 A.M. to 7:29 A.M.

12. 2:13 P.M. to 9:00 P.M.

▶ Lesson 14·7   *Pages 316*

Add or subtract to find the new temperature.

1. The temperature was 55° in the morning. By noon, it rose 15°. What was the temperature at noon?

2. The temperature was 42° It fell 18° during the night. What was the temperature at the end of the night?

3. In the afternoon, the temperature was 85°. It fell 6° five hours later. What was the temperature five hours later?

4. In the morning, the temperature was 35°. By noon, the temperature fell 10°. What was the temperature by noon?

Extra Practice Chapter 15

Lesson 15·2 *Pages 324–325*

Change each measurement. First, decide whether to multiply or divide.

1. 4 kilometers = ▦ meters

2. 800 meters = ▦ hectometers

3. 950 centimeters = ▦ meters

4. 7,400 millimeters = ▦ meters

5. 60 millimeters = ▦ centimeters

6. 45 decimeters = ▦ meters

7. 4 dekameters = ▦ meters

8. 800 millimeters = ▦ meter

9. 3.4 kilometers = ▦ meters

10. 790 centimeters = ▦ meters

Lesson 15·3 *Pages 326–327*

Change each measurement. First, decide whether to multiply or divide.

1. 3.8 kilograms = ▦ grams

2. 400 grams = ▦ decigrams

3. 7.5 grams = ▦ milligrams

4. 5,000 grams = ▦ kilograms

5. 890 centigrams = ▦ grams

6. 4,600 milligrams = ▦ grams

7. 9,000 grams = ▦ kilograms

8. 6.2 grams = ▦ milligrams

Lesson 15·4 *Pages 328–329*

Change each measurement. First, decide whether to multiply or divide.

1. 6 liters = ▦ milliliters

2. 5,000 liters = ▦ kiloliters

3. 20,000 milliliters = ▦ liters

4. 9.6 kiloliters = ▦ liters

5. 3.5 kiloliters = ▦ liters

6. 3,400 milliliters = ▦ liters

7. 4.8 liters = ▦ milliliters

8. 100 liters = ▦ kiloliter

Extra Practice Chapter 16

Lesson 16·2 *Pages 340–341*

Use a protractor to measure each angle.

1.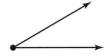

2.

3.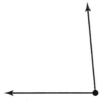

4.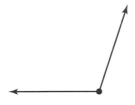

Lesson 16·4 *Pages 344–345*

Find the measure of the unknown angle in each triangle.

1.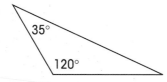

2.

3.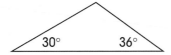

4.

5.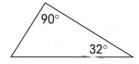

6.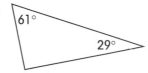

Extra Practice Chapter 16

▶ **Lesson 16·6**   *Pages 348–349*

Find the perimeter of each figure.

1.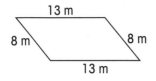
13 m
8 m
8 m
13 m

2.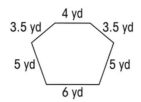
4 yd
3.5 yd
3.5 yd
5 yd
5 yd
6 yd

3.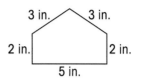
3 in.
3 in.
2 in.
2 in.
5 in.

▶ **Lessons 16·7 and 16·8**   *Pages 350–352*

Find the area of each figure.

1.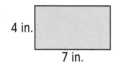
4 in.
7 in.

2.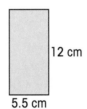
12 cm
5.5 cm

3.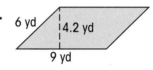
6 yd
4.2 yd
9 yd

4.
5.6 ft

5.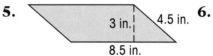
3 in.
4.5 in.
8.5 in.

6.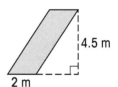
4.5 m
2 m

▶ **Lesson 16·9**   *Pages 354–355*

Find the area of each triangle.

1.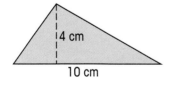
4 cm
10 cm

2.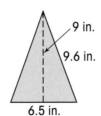
9 in.
9.6 in.
6.5 in.

3.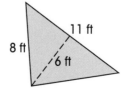
11 ft
8 ft
6 ft

Extra Practice Chapter 16

▶**Lessons 16·10 and 16·11** *Pages 356–359*

Find the circumference of each circle. Find the area of each circle.

1.

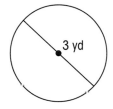

3 yd

2.

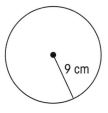

9 cm

3.

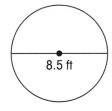

8.5 ft

4. radius = 5 ft

5. diameter = 13 in.

6. diameter = 8.2 yd

▶**Lesson 16·13** *Pages 362–363*

Find the volume of each prism.

1.

4 in.
6 in.
13 in.

2.

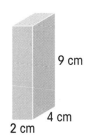

9 cm
4 cm
2 cm

3.

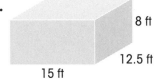

8 ft
12.5 ft
15 ft

▶**Lesson 16·14** *Pages 364–365*

Find the volume of each cylinder.

1.

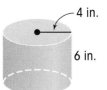

4 in.
6 in.

2.

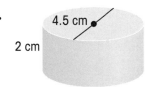

4.5 cm
2 cm

3.

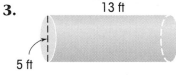

13 ft
5 ft

Extra Practice Chapter 17

Lesson 17·2   *Pages 374–375*

Add.

1. $^-6 + ^-2$ 2. $^+8 + ^+7$ 3. $^-5 + ^-1$

4. $^-4 + ^-7$ 5. $^-5 + ^-1$ 6. $^+6 + ^+9$

7. $^-9 + ^-4$ 8. $^-2 + ^-6$ 9. $^-1 + ^-3$

10. $^+8 + 0$ 11. $^-4 + ^-3$ 12. $^-12 + 0$

13. $^-7 + ^-3$ 14. $^+12 + ^+7$ 15. $0 + ^-13$

Lesson 17·3   *Pages 376–377*

Add.

1. $8 + ^-6$ 2. $^-7 + ^+9$ 3. $^-5 + ^+3$

4. $4 + ^-10$ 5. $^+6 + ^-3$ 6. $^-4 + ^+5$

7. $^-9 + 0$ 8. $^+2 + ^-8$ 9. $^-3 + ^+7$

10. $12 + ^-15$ 11. $^+11 + ^-7$ 12. $^-9 + ^+9$

13. $^-1 + ^+7$ 14. $^-12 + ^+8$ 15. $^+10 + ^-2$

Lesson 17·4   *Pages 378–380*

Subtract.

1. $^-7 - ^+3$ 2. $^+6 - ^+10$ 3. $^-2 - ^-9$

4. $^+3 - ^+5$ 5. $^+14 - ^+7$ 6. $^-4 - ^-4$

7. $^-1 - ^-6$ 8. $^+15 - ^-3$ 9. $^-5 - ^+6$

10. $^-12 - ^-12$ 11. $^-4 - ^+8$ 12. $^+20 - ^+9$

13. $^+2 - ^+12$ 14. $^+9 - ^-8$ 15. $^-3 - ^-10$

Extra Practice Chapter 17

Lesson 17·5 *Pages 382–384*

Multiply.

1. $^+2 \times {}^-5$
2. $^-4 \times {}^+3$
3. $^+9 \times {}^+6$

4. $^+9 \times {}^-7$
5. $^+8 \times {}^-6$
6. $^-8 \times {}^+3$

7. $^+4 \times {}^-9$
8. $^-3 \times {}^-9$
9. $^-6 \times {}^-4$

10. $^-5 \times {}^+8$
11. $^-5 \times {}^+9$
12. $^+12 \times {}^-1$

13. $^+7 \times {}^+4$
14. $8 \times {}^-4$
15. $^+11 \times {}^+5$

Lesson 17·6 *Pages 386–387*

Divide.

1. $^+16 \div {}^+4$
2. $^-12 \div {}^+6$
3. $^+27 \div {}^-3$

4. $^+49 \div {}^-7$
5. $^-24 \div {}^-8$
6. $^-20 \div {}^-2$

7. $^-18 \div {}^+3$
8. $^-15 \div {}^-1$
9. $^-35 \div 5$

10. $^-30 \div {}^-5$
11. $^+48 \div {}^+6$
12. $^-64 \div {}^-8$

13. $^-54 \div {}^+9$
14. $^+32 \div {}^-4$
15. $^+55 \div {}^+11$

Lesson 17·7 *Pages 388–389*

Solve.

1. The temperature was 5 degrees above zero at noon. It dropped 6 degrees. Then, it rose 3 degrees. What was the temperature after all the changes?

2. In the All-State football game, Terry gained 6 yards. Then, he lost 18 yards. What was Terry's total loss or gain?

3. The Blue Giants gained 6 yards, lost 2 yards, and then gained 9 yards. What was the team's total loss or gain?

Extra Practice Chapter 18

Lesson 18·2   *Page 396*

Simplify each expression.

1. $40 - (10 + 2)$
2. $6(8 - 2)$
3. $(5 \times 3) + 4$

4. $(8 + 6) - 3$
5. $(9 \times 4) - 16$
6. $12(7 - 5) + 1$

7. $74 - (42 - 5)$
8. $(11 \times 9) - (6 \times 11)$
9. $4(8 + 5) + 5$

Lesson 18·3   *Pages 398–399*

Simplfy each expression. Remember to multiply or divide first.

1. $18 + 2 - 12$
2. $41 - 7 \times 3$
3. $24 \div 6 \div 2$

4. $50 \div 2 \div 5$
5. $6 \times 8 \div 4$
6. $19 - 7 + 13$

7. $26 - 8 - 2$
8. $14 \times 3 + 1$
9. $9 + 6 \times 3$

Lesson 18·4   *Pages 400–401*

Solve each equation.

1. $x + 7 = 15$
2. $y - 8 = 2$
3. $15 = t + 3$

4. $w + 19 = 40$
5. $24 = c - 8$
6. $f + 4 = 10$

7. $29 = h + 9$
8. $j - 12 = 3$
9. $46 = p + 8$

Lesson 18·5   *Pages 402–403*

Solve each equation.

1. $\frac{m}{6} = 4$
2. $8s = 56$
3. $\frac{w}{3} = 5$

4. $48 = 6t$
5. $9 = \frac{x}{7}$
6. $7v = 49$

7. $17 = 2r$
8. $14e = 42$
9. $120 = 12d$

Extra Practice Chapter 18

Lesson 18·6 *Pages 404–405*

Solve. Use the formula $d = r \times t$.

1. Cara took a train to Boston. The train's rate was 56 mph. She rode the train for 5 hours. How far did she ride the train?

2. Chen drove 192 miles in 4 hours. What was his average rate of speed?

Lesson 18·7 *Pages 406–408*

Solve each equation.

1. $7a + 5 = 26$

2. $\frac{m}{4} - 2 = 6$

3. $32 = 3c + 8$

4. $\frac{w}{9} + 15 = 18$

5. $17 = \frac{x}{3} + 10$

6. $5h - 6 = 14$

7. $16 = 5r - 14$

8. $15y - 12 = 33$

9. $\frac{v}{4} + 12 = 19$

Lesson 18·8 *Pages 410–411*

Solve. Use the formula $c = r \times d + f$.

1. Leroy rented a lawn mower. The rental cost $8 per day plus a fee of $25. He paid a total of $49. For how many days did he rent the lawn mower?

2. Seung paid $100 to rent a ladder. It cost $12 per day plus $4 for the renter's fee. For how many days did she rent the ladder?

Reference Pages: Multiplication Table

Look at the multiplication chart below. It is easy to find the product of any two numbers on the chart. Find one number in the first column going down. Find the second number in the top row going across. Move across from the first column and down from the top row. The box in which the row and column meet contains the product of the two numbers.

x	0	1	2	3	4	5	6	7	8	9
0	0	0	0	0	0	0	0	0	0	0
1	0	1	2	3	4	5	6	7	8	9
2	0	2	4	6	8	10	12	14	16	18
3	0	3	6	9	12	15	18	21	24	27
4	0	4	8	12	16	20	24	28	32	36
5	0	5	10	15	20	25	30	35	40	45
6	0	6	12	18	24	30	36	42	48	54
7	0	7	14	21	28	35	42	49	56	63
8	0	8	16	24	32	40	48	56	64	72
9	0	9	18	27	36	45	54	63	72	81

Reference Pages: Formulas

▶ Percents Formulas

Percent = Part ÷ Whole
Part = Percent ÷ Whole
Whole = Part ÷ Percent

Sales tax = Tax rate × Cost
Total cost with tax = Cost + Sales tax

Discount = Discount rate × Price
Sale price = Original price − Discount

Commission = Commission rate × Sales
Gross salary = Base salary + Commission

Percent increase/decrease = Difference ÷ Original number

▶ Algebra Formulas

Order of Operations
   1. Multiply and divide from left to right.
   2. Add and subtract from left to right.

Distance = Rate × Time
Rate = Distance ÷ Time
Time = Distance ÷ Rate

Cost = Rate per day × Number of days + Renter's fee

Reference Pages: Tables of Measures

▶ Customary System

Length

1 foot (ft)	= 12 inches (in.)
1 yard (yd)	= 36 inches
1 yard	= 3 feet
1 mile (mi)	= 5,280 feet

Capacity

1 pint (pt)	= 16 fluid ounces (fl oz)
1 quart (qt)	= 32 fluid ounces
1 quart	= 2 pints (pt)
1 gallon (gal)	= 4 quarts

Weight

1 pound (lb)	= 16 ounces (oz)
1 ton (tn)	= 2,000 pounds

Time

See below.

▶ Metric System

Length

1 kilometer (km)	= 1,000 meters (m)
1 hectometer (hm)	= 100 meters
1 dekameter (dam)	= 10 meters
1 meter	= 1 meter
10 decimeters (dm)	= 1 meter
100 centimeters (cm)	= 1 meter
1,000 millimeters (mm)	= 1 meter

Capacity

1 kiloliter (kL)	= 1,000 liters (L)
1 hectoliter (hL)	= 100 liters
1 dekaliter (daL)	= 10 liters
1 liter	= 1 liter
10 deciliters (dL)	= 1 liter
100 centiliters (cL)	= 1 liter
1,000 milliliters (mL)	= 1 liter

Mass (weight)

1 kilogram (kg)	= 1,000 grams (g)
1 hectogram (hg)	= 100 grams
1 dekagram (dag)	= 10 grams
1 gram	= 1 gram
10 decigrams (dg)	= 1 gram
100 centigrams (cg)	= 1 gram
1,000 milligrams (mg)	= 1 gram

Time

60 seconds (sec)	= 1 minute (min)
60 minutes	= 1 hour (hr)
24 hours	= 1 day
7 days (d)	= 1 week (wk)
52 weeks	= 1 year (yr)
12 months (mo)	= 1 year

Reference Pages: Geometry

Perimeter of polygons = sum of the lengths of all sides

Rectangle

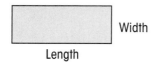

Area = length × width

Parallelogram

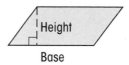

Area = base × height

Triangle

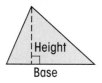

Area = $\frac{1}{2}$ × base × height

Circle

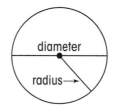

Diameter = radius × 2
Area = π × (radius)^2
Circumference = π × diameter
Circumference = π × 2 × radius
π ≈ 3.14

Rectangular Prism

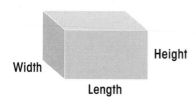

Volume = length × width × height

Cylinder

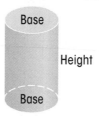

Volume = π × (radius)^2 × height

Reference Pages: Table of Squares

Number	Square	Number	Square	Number	Square	Number	Square
1	1	26	676	51	2,601	76	5,776
2	4	27	729	52	2,704	77	5,929
3	9	28	784	53	2,809	78	6,084
4	16	29	841	54	2,916	79	6,241
5	25	30	900	55	3,025	80	6,400
6	36	31	961	56	3,136	81	6,561
7	49	32	1,024	57	3,249	82	6,724
8	64	33	1,089	58	3,364	83	6,889
9	81	34	1,156	59	3,481	84	7,056
10	100	35	1,225	60	3,600	85	7,225
11	121	36	1,296	61	3,721	86	7,396
12	144	37	1,369	62	3,844	87	7,569
13	169	38	1,444	63	3,969	88	7,744
14	196	39	1,521	64	4,096	89	7,921
15	225	40	1,600	65	4,225	90	8,100
16	256	41	1,681	66	4,356	91	8,281
17	289	42	1,764	67	4,489	92	8,464
18	324	43	1,849	68	4,624	93	8,649
19	361	44	1,936	69	4,761	94	8,836
20	400	45	2,025	70	4,900	95	9,025
21	441	46	2,116	71	5,041	96	9,216
22	484	47	2,209	72	5,184	97	9,409
23	529	48	2,304	73	5,329	98	9,604
24	576	49	2,401	74	5,476	99	9,801
25	625	50	2,500	75	5,625	100	10,000

Reference Pages: Square Roots of Perfect Squares

The number that was squared is called the square root.

$$9^2 = 81 \qquad \sqrt{81} = 9$$

Perfect Square	Square Root
1	1
4	2
9	3
16	4
25	5
36	6
49	7
64	8
81	9
100	10
121	11
144	12
169	13
196	14
225	15

Perfect Square	Square Root
256	16
289	17
324	18
361	19
400	20
441	21
484	22
529	23
576	24
625	25
676	26
729	27
784	28
841	29
900	30

Glossary

add put numbers together; find the total amount

angle figure formed by two rays with the same endpoint

area the amount of space inside a figure

base salary salary before adding commission

canceling dividing a numerator and a denominator by the same number

capacity how much space is in a container

circumference the distance around a circle

column numbers placed one below the other

commission payment based on a percent of sales

composite number number with more than two factors

cross products the results of cross multiplying

Customary System of Measurement measurement units used in the United States

data information gathered from surveys or experiments

decimal a number that names part of a whole

decimal places the places to the right of a decimal point

decimal point the dot in a decimal; a decimal point has digits to its right

degrees (°) units used to measure temperature

denominator the bottom number in a fraction

diameter the distance across the middle of a circle

difference the amount obtained by subtracting; the amount by which one number is larger or smaller than another

digits the symbols used to write numbers: 0, 1, 2, 3, 4, 5, 6, 7, 8, and 9

discount amount that a price is reduced

dividend the number to be divided

divisible can be divided without a remainder

division the process of finding out how many times one number contains another

divisor the number to divide by

elapsed time the amount of time that has passed between two given times

equation a mathematical sentence stating that two quantities are equal

equivalent fractions   fractions with different numbers but equal values

estimate   to quickly find an answer that is close to an exact answer; to make a good guess

even numbers   numbers that end in 0, 2, 4, 6, or 8

exponent   tells how many times to use a number as a factor

factors   the numbers that are multiplied to obtain a product

fraction   a form of a number that shows part of a whole

gram   the basic metric unit used to measure mass (weight)

graph   a visual display that shows data in different ways; includes bar, line, and circle graphs

greatest common factor (GCF)   the largest factor that two or more numbers share

gross salary   commission plus the base salary

histogram   a graph that shows how many times an event occurred

horizontal   written across the page from left to right

integers   numbers in the set {..., –3, –2, –1, 0, 1, 2, 3, ...}

invert   to reverse the positions of the numerator and denominator of a fraction

least common multiple (LCM)   the smallest multiple that two or more numbers share

length   how long an object is

like fractions   fractions that have the same denominator

liter   the basic metric unit used to measure liquid capacity

lowest terms   when only 1 divides evenly into both the numerator and denominator of a fraction

mean   sum of the data divided by the number of data; also called average

median   middle number when data are ordered from least to greatest

meter   the basic metric unit used to measure length

metric system   the system of measurement based on the number 10 that is used in most countries

minus   the symbol or word that means to subtract

mixed decimal   a number with a whole number and a decimal

mixed number   a number made up of a whole number and a fraction

mode   number or numbers that appear most often in a set of data

multiples   possible products of a given number

multiple unit pricing   the cost of one item or one unit measure of an item

multiplication   a quick way to add; repeated addition

multiply   to add a number to itself one or more times; 2 + 2 + 2 + 2 = 8 or 4 x 2 = 8

negative integers   integers to the left of zero on the number line

number expressions   a number or numbers together with operation symbols

number line   numbers in order shown as points on a line

numerator   the top number in a fraction

odd numbers   numbers that end in 1, 3, 5, 7, or 9

opposites   two numbers that are the same distance from zero on the number line but are on opposite sides of zero

order of operations   the specific order to do the four basic operations when more than one operation is in an equation

parallelogram   a quadrilateral whose opposite sides are parallel; examples are rectangles and squares

parenthesis ( )   marks around an operation that should be done first

partial product   the number obtained by multiplying a number by only one digit of a two or more digit number

percent   a part of a whole divided into 100 parts

percent decrease   percent less than an original number

percent increase   percent more than an original number

perimeter   the distance around a figure

pictograph   a graph that uses pictures to represent data

plus   the symbol or word that means to add

polygons   plane figures with three or more sides; examples are triangles, quadrilaterals, pentagons, hexagons, and octagons

positive integers   integers to the right of zero on the number line

prime number   number with only itself and 1 as factors

probability   the chance that an event will occur

product   the final answer to a multiplication problem

proportion   a statement that two ratios are equal

protractor   a tool used to measure angles

quotient   the number obtained by dividing one number into another; the answer in a division problem

radius   the distance from the center of a circle to its edge

rate   a comparison of two amounts with different units of measure

ratio   a comparison of one amount with another

regroup (in addition) to rename and then carry a tens digit to the place on the left when adding; (in subtraction) to rename and then carry a tens digit to the place on the right when subtracting

remainder the number left over in a division problem

rename to show a number another way; to show place value, 28 can be renamed as 2 tens + 8 ones

rounding changing a number to the nearest ten, hundred, thousand, or so on

sale price price of an item after the discount is subtracted

sales tax a tax that is a percentage of the price of an item

scale a ratio that compares the size of a drawing with the size of the original object

scale drawing a picture that shows the proportional size of actual objects

simplify to write a shorter or easier form of an expression; or to find its value

solution the value of a variable that makes an equation true

solve to find the answer to a problem

space figure a three-dimensional figure that has length, width, and height

square product of multiplying a number by itself

square root number that was squared

subtract to take away one number from another; to find the amount that remains

sum the amount obtained by adding; the total

unit price the cost of one item or one unit measure of an item

unlike fractions fractions that have different denominators

variable a letter that stands for a number

vertical written as one thing under the other

volume the amount of space inside a three-dimensional figure

weight how heavy an object is

whole numbers 0, 1, 2, 3, 4, 5, 6, 7, and so on

Index

Length
    customary measurement, 303, 304–305
    metric measurement, 324–325
Line graphs
    double, 286–287
    single, 284–285
Lines, 338–339
Liquid measure
    customary measurement, 303, 308–309
    metric measurement, 328–329
Liter, 321, 322

M

Mass. See Weight (mass)
Math in Your Life, 21, 53, 102, 121, 145,
    187, 242, 269, 291, 323, 385
Mean, 277, 292–293
Measurement. See Customary system of;
    Metric system of
Median, 277, 294–295
Meter, 321, 322
Metric measurement, 321, 322
    capacity (liquid measure), 328–329
    compared with customary system of
        measurement, 330
    length, 324–325
    weight (mass), 326–327
    in word problems, 332–333
Mixed numbers, 29, 142
    adding, 180–181, 190–191
    changing fractions to, 142–143
    changing to fractions, 144
    dividing, 168–171
    multiplying, 160–161
    subtracting, 182–185, 192–193
    in word problems, 172–173
Mode, 277, 294–295
Multiples, 107, 116–117
Multiple unit pricing, 259, 266–267
Multiplication, 63, 64
    of decimals, 212–214
    of fractions, 154–158
    of integers, 382–384
    of mixed numbers, 160–161
    of whole numbers, 63–83, 158

    in word problems, 74–77, 80–81
    zeros in, 78–79

N

Number lines, 3, 4, 27, 45

O

Octagons, 346
One-step equations, 400–405
"On-the-Job" Math, 39, 77, 121, 165,
    215, 317, 343, 397
Opposites, 371, 372
Ordering
    decimals, 207
    fractions, 140, 146–147
    whole numbers, 14–15
Order of operations, 393, 398
Original price, 252–253

P

Parallelograms, 337, 347
    area of, 352
Parentheses
    in algebra, 393, 396
Pentagons, 346
Percent, 231, 232
    changing decimals to, 243
    changing fractions to, 244
    changing to decimals, 233
    finding the part, 234–235
    finding the percent, 246–247
    finding the whole, 250–251
    in word problems, 254–255
Percent increase/decrease, 231, 248
Perimeter, 337, 348–349
Pi, 356
Pictographs, 277, 278–279
Place value
    decimals, 203–204
    whole numbers, 6–7
Polygons, 337, 346–347
Prime factorization, 118
Prime numbers, 107, 118
Prisms, volume of, 362–363
Probability, 277, 298

W

Weight (mass)
    customary measurement, 303, 306–307
    metric measurement, 326–327
Whole numbers, 3, 4
    adding, 25–41
    comparing, 12–13
    dividing, 85–105
    multiplying, 63–83, 158
    even and odd numbers, 5
    ordering, 14–15

place value, 6–9
rounding, 18–20
subtracting, 43–61
in word problems, 16–17, 21, 166–167

Z

Zeros
    in multiplication, 78–79
    in quotient, 98–99
    in subtraction, 56–57

Photo Credits